I0094543

Lauri Karvonen, Heikki Paloheimo & Tapio Raunio (eds)

The Changing Balance
of Political Power in Finland

Santérus
Academic Press
Sweden

www.santerus.se

© 2016 The authors and Santérus Academic Press Sweden

ISBN 978-91-7335-051-8

Cover art: Spatial Force Construction (1921)

Painting by the Russian artist Lyobov Popova.

Cover profile: Sven Bylander

Santérus Academic Press is an imprint of
Santérus Förlag, Stockholm, Sweden

info@santerus.se

www.santerus.se

Printed by BOD, Germany 2016

Contents

5

Preface

The past three and a half decades have witnessed a major transformation of the political landscape in Finland. Like everywhere in the democratic West these changes have pertained to the economic and social underpinnings of the political process as well as to the concrete substance of government policy. Unlike most comparable countries, however, the transformation of Finnish politics has also been a matter of major institutional change. In fact, as this book argues at length, the basic regime type of the Finnish political system has changed.

Despite the magnitude of change, there is still little in the way of a comprehensive analysis of power relations in modern Finnish politics. The present volume attempts to fill part of that void. The book is the result of the research project 'Political Power in Finland: An Analysis of Central Government Institutions and Actors' financed by the Academy of Finland in 2011–2014. Ten scholars representing the University of Tampere, Åbo Akademi and University of Turku collaborated in this undertaking.

We are happy to acknowledge the importance of our steering committee of senior political scientists: professors Dag Anckar, Anne Kovalainen, Jaakko Nousiainen and Hannu Nurmi, and docent Seppo Tiihonen. Their advice has left a profound mark on our research, and their comments on our manuscripts have been invaluable.

Our sincere thanks are due to the Academy of Finland for its financial support. The Academy grant made it possible for several members of our group to devote a number of critical months to full time work in the project. We would also like to thank Santérus Academic Press for the publication of our final report, as well as Åbo Akademi University and the University of Tampere for financial support that made the publication of this book possible.

Tampere and Turku, Finland

May 2016

Lauri Karvonen   Heikki Paloheimo   Tapio Raunio

Introduction: Finland 1970–2015
– A Transformed Political Landscape

LAURI KARVONEN, HEIKKI PALOHEIMO & TAPIO RAUNIO

The political systems of democratic countries are remarkably stable. Even when societies experience significant structural change, the impact of such socio-economic transformation is mainly limited to the party system. Constitutional change regarding political institutions is much less frequent and is often linked to democratization or major domestic crisis as in Central and Eastern Europe. The more affluent 'Western' European countries, on the other hand, display considerable constitutional rigidity. Societies may change, but political systems do not. (Strøm *et al.* 2003)

Finland is a noteworthy exception to this rule. Indeed, Finland is a rare example of a democratic country that has experienced major constitutional reform peacefully without domestic conflict. International literature has traditionally categorized the Finnish political system as semi-presidential, with the executive functions divided between an elected president and a cabinet that is accountable to the parliament. However, recent constitutional reforms have radically transformed Finnish politics. The new constitution, which entered into force in 2000[1], completed a period of far-reaching constitutional change that curtailed presidential powers and brought the Finnish political system closer to a normal parliamentary democracy. The president is today almost completely excluded from the policy process in domestic matters; leadership by presidents has

---

1 The Constitution of Finland, 11 June, 1999 (731/1999). An English translation of the 2000 constitution can be accessed at http://www.finlex.fi/en/laki/kaan-nokset/1999/en19990731.pdf.

been replaced with leadership by strong majority governments. In contrast to most democratic countries, the Finnish political system has arguably also become less subject to external constraints. The end of the Cold War removed the shadow of the Soviet Union from Finnish policy-making, but particularly through European Union (EU) membership Finland has become much more involved in global and regional integration.

Drawing on unique and comprehensive longitudinal data, this book analyses the distribution of political power in Finland since the 1970s. The objective of the volume is not simply to extrapolate change within and between governing institutions and political parties, but also to understand the causal mechanisms explaining this significant period of constitutional and political reform. After outlining the constitutional reform itself, this introductory chapter contextualizes our period of analysis, providing a necessarily brief but important overview of the socio-economic and geopolitical changes that have impacted on the distribution of power subjected to more detailed investigation in the subsequent chapters.

Constitutional reform

Finland is frequently categorized as a semi-presidential regime, with the executive functions divided between an elected president and a government accountable to parliament (*the Eduskunta*). In fact, Finland was by a wide margin the oldest semi-presidential country in Europe, with the semi-presidential form of government adopted in 1919, two years after the country achieved independence. Until 1982, the president was elected by an electoral college of 300 members (301 in 1982), who were elected by the same proportional system as MPs. A new direct-election system for choosing the president was first used in 1994.[2] If a candidate receives more than half of the votes, he or she is elected president. If none of the candidates receives the majority of the votes, a new election is held

---

2   A one-time experiment was conducted in the 1988 election, involving a mixed two-ticket system of direct and indirect voting. To be elected by a direct vote, a candidate needed to receive 50 per cent of the votes. As no candidate reached this share, the election was passed on to a simultaneously elected electoral college.

on the third Sunday after the first election. In the second round, the two persons who received the most votes in the first round run against each other. The candidate who receives the majority of vote is then elected president.

Under the old constitution, the president was recognised as the supreme executive power. For example, Duverger (1980) ranked Finland highest among the West European semi-presidential systems in terms of the formal powers of the head of state and second only to France with respect to the actual exercise of presidential power. The peak of presidential powers was reached during the reign of President Kekkonen, who made full use of his powers and arguably even overstepped the constitutional prerogatives of the presidency. During the Cold War, the balance between cabinet and president was therefore strongly in favour of the president until the constitutional reforms of the 1990s, which were in part a response to the excesses of the Kekkonen era. A period of parliamentarization started in 1982, when President Mauno Koivisto took office after a quarter of a century of politics dominated by Kekkonen. President Koivisto and the political elite in general favoured strengthening parliamentarism and curtailing the powers of the president. Table 1 summarizes the development of presidential powers during Finland's independence, illustrating the fundamental changes that have taken place after the Kekkonen era and particularly in the post-Cold War context of European integration.

These constitutional and political changes are dealt with in considerable detail in the subsequent chapters of this volume, and hence it is sufficient to pay attention here to the comprehensive sweep of the reforms. In government formation the role of the president is now limited to formally appointing the prime minister and the cabinet chosen by parliament; moreover, the president cannot force the government to resign. Governments are thus now accountable to the Eduskunta and not to the president, as effectively was the case before. The president has only an ineffective delaying power in legislation, and even the appointment powers of the president have been drastically reduced. Overall, the president is almost completely excluded from the policy process in domestic matters. Turning to external relations, the government is responsible for EU affairs while foreign policy leadership is shared between the president and the government. Foreign and defence policy excluded, Finland

Table 1. Powers of parliament, government and president in the Finnish constitution in four time periods

Duty	Division of power according to the constitution	
	Old constitution 1919-1980	Old constituti● 1990s
General authority in executive decision-making	president	president
Government formation	president has autonomous power	president, after● ing parliament● party groups
Government resignation	parliament, or prime minister, or president indirectly by dissolving parliament	parliament, or ● minister
Dissolution of parliament and calling of new elections	president	president upon● tive by prime m●
Government bills	president may alter	president may ●
Legislation: power of veto	president may postpone bills beyond next election	president may ● postpone until ● legislative sessi●
Legislative decrees	president and government	president and g● ment
Leadership in foreign policy	president	president
Leadership in foreign policy: decisions to be made in the EU		government
Commander-in-chief of armed forces	president	president
Appointment of senior civil servants	president appoints a considerable portion of senior civil servants; other civil servants appointed by government or by ministries	number of seni● servants appoin● president reduc●

Source: The Constitution Act of Finland (Act 94/1919) with later amendments.

is now effectively a parliamentary regime. Presidential leadership has been replaced by leadership by strong majority cabinets, which have ruled without much effective opposition since the early 1980s. (Hallberg *et al.* 2009; Jyränki & Nousiainen 2006; Nousiainen 2001; Paloheimo 2001, 2003; Raunio 2011).

The transformation of the Finnish polity has also conceptual

constitution from 2000 on	New constitution from 2012 on
...rnment	government
...ament, president's role purely formal	parliament, president's role purely formal
...ament, or prime minister	parliament or prime minister
...dent upon initiative by prime minister	president upon initiative by prime minister
...dent's power basically eliminated	president's power basically eliminated
...ament may immediately override veto	president has no veto power, in case of disagreement parliament decides
...rnment	government
...dent in co-operation with government	president in co-operation with government; conflicts between president and government decided by parliament
...rnment; no clear norms on Finnish representation ...J summits	government; prime minister represents Finland at EU summits
...dent	president
...dent appoints only a very limited group of top civil ...ants	president's power to appoint top civil servants limited further

repercussions. We argue that it simply does not make sense to classify or treat Finland as a semi-presidential country. The concept of semi-presidentialism was first used by Maurice Duverger in the 1970s, who also formulated the 'classic' or 'original' definition of such regimes: 'A political regime is considered as semi-presidential if the constitution which established it combines three elements: (1) the president of the republic is elected by universal suffrage; (2)

he possesses quite considerable powers; (3) he has opposite him, however, a prime minister and ministers who possess executive and governmental power and can stay in office only if the parliament does not show its opposition to them.' (Duverger 1980: 166) Duverger's definition has not been universally endorsed by other scholars, with most of the criticism concerning his claim that the president should possess 'quite considerable powers'. After all, it can be inherently difficult to judge what constitutes such powers and where to draw the line between considerable and inconsiderable powers. The situation is made worse by the often blatant discrepancy between the text of the constitution and the actual real-world role of the presidents. It is evident that national political culture or established patterns impact on how constitutions work in practice. Different holders of the same office may also decide to make fuller use of their powers, depending for example on party-political constellations or on the state of societal affairs in the country – as indeed was the case in Finland for much of the 20st century.

According to Elgie (1999: 13), a 'semi-presidential regime may be defined as the situation where a popularly elected fixed-term president exists alongside a prime minister and cabinet who are responsible to parliament'. This has become the standard definition of semi-presidentialism, utilized by basically all recent studies (Schleiter & Morgan-Jones 2009: 875). When compared with the Duvergerian approach, it is easy to appreciate the simplicity of Elgie's constitution-based definition, for it makes the recognition of semi-presidential regimes a clearly more straightforward process. However, the definition at the same time runs the risk of conceptual stretching. Currently the universe of semi-presidential countries contains a very heterogeneous mix of countries, and even the European ones display considerable variation from the more president-led polity of France to cases where the role of the president is essentially symbolic or ceremonial (such as Ireland and Slovenia) (Elgie & Moestrup 2008; Elgie 2011). While scholars have responded to this heterogeneity by focussing on sub-categories of semi-presidentialism, we feel that it is both theoretically and empirically inaccurate to label Finland as a semi-presidential regime. Constitutionally and politically Finland is essentially a parliamentary democracy with a government that is accountable to the parliament and a directly-elected president. We shall return to this conceptual discussion in the concluding chapter of the volume.

Structural transformation

Political organization and the distribution of power reflect the character of the economic foundations on which a society rests. How the means of livelihood and the economic resources emanating from them are distributed among major population segments largely determines the nature of political conflict and party formation. In Finland, as in much of Western Europe, politics has long been marked by the important role of conflicts based on socio-economic structure (Mair 1997; Oskarson 2005).

What sets Finland apart in a West European comparison is the prolonged predominance of the primary sector (agriculture and forestry) in the economy. When Finland in 1939 entered the Second World War it was still and overwhelmingly rural society. After the war, however, the structure of the Finnish economy changed rapidly. Markets for pulp and paper industry boomed, and war reparations to the Soviet Union made it necessary to expand the share of the metal industry in Finland's industrial output. In 1930 only 15 per cent of the labour force was employed in the secondary (industrial) sector of the economy. In 1960 the figure was 30.5 per cent. However, the secondary sector of the economy never became as important in Finland as in Britain, Germany or many other West European states. From the 1970s on, Finland rapidly became a post-industrial society where the tertiary sector of the economy (private and public services) engaged more than half of the labour force. In 2011, about 74 per cent of the Finnish labour force was employed in the tertiary sector (Table 2).

A closer comparison between Finland and the rest of Western Europe[3] since 1920 indicates that Finland is an extreme case in several respects. The predominance of the primary sector during much

---

3   Ten countries culturally and politically closest to Finland were selected for this comparison: Austria, Belgium, Denmark, France, Germany (between 1950 and 1990: West Germany), the Netherlands, Norway, Sweden, Switzerland and United Kingdom.

Table 2. Economically active population in Finland 1920–2014 by sector

Year	Primary	Secondary	Tertiary
1920	68.8	12.8	18.3
1930	64.6	14.7	20.7
1950	45.9	27.7	26.3
1960	35.5	31.5	33.1
1970	20.3	34.3	45.5
1980	12.6	33.4	54.1
1990	8.5	28.3	63.2
2000	5.7	26.9	67.4
2014	4.5	22.4	73.1

Source: International Historical Statistics, Europe 1750–2005, 147–170, and Statistics Finland.

of the period, the lateness of socioeconomic transformation and the rapidity of the change once it got under way are striking features of the Finnish trajectory (Kangas & Saloniemi 2013: 29). Not a single one of the countries in the comparison group can match the Finnish development; in fact none of them comes anywhere near Finland in these respects. The share of the workforce employed in the primary sector fell by roughly 64 percentage points in Finland between 1920 and 2011. The corresponding figure for the comparison group was less than 30. Tertiary employment rose by more than 55 points in Finland during the same period, as compared to an average growth by less than 40 points in the ten other countries. In Finland, industry was never the largest sector in terms of employment, while this was the case in the comparison group in both the 1950s and 1960s. With a minor simplification, one may argue that Finland went from a preindustrial directly to a postindustrial social structure. The lion's share of this structural transformation took place between the Second World War and 1980. Elsewhere in Western Europe, the corresponding process had started much earlier and proceeded much more smoothly over an extended period of time.

From conflict to consensus

In the first four decades of its existence as an independent state, Finland experienced a civil war, a heated linguistic strife, a strong right-wing extremist movement, two periods of war against the

Soviet Union, and a painful settlement after World War II. It is no wonder that the level of conflict in domestic politics was high. Multiple and deep trenches separated the various political and organizational 'camps'. Not least, there was a deep division between social democratic and communist-controlled unions in the labour movement.

All of this is clearly visible in both parliamentary politics and labour market relations in the first postwar decades. Stable governments were extremely difficult to form; during a prolonged period, the average duration of a Finnish cabinet was less than a year. At the same time, numerous industrial disputes characterized the labour relations field.

The shift from conflict to consensus took place through three interrelated processes, partly parallel, partly consecutive. In each of these fields, the change was astonishingly rapid given the previous level of conflict. First, the pattern of labour market contracts changed as of 1968. That year, the first comprehensive Incomes Policy Agreement was concluded between the central organizations of labour and employers and the government. This was to be the first of a dozen such agreements in the 1970s and 1980s (Kyntäjä 1993: 128–129). The core of these agreements concerned industrial wages. However, thanks to the active role of the government, important legislative reforms supported the agreements: 'Employer and employee organizations bargained over wages while the government tried to promote agreements by using sticks and carrots' (Kangas & Saloniemi 2013: 17). Many social policy reforms came about thanks to incomes policy agreements. As a result of this development, Finland has for decades belonged to the Scandinavian model of highly coordinated wage bargaining. Although somewhat attenuated in recent years, important elements of this model still persist in Finland as well as among its Scandinavian neighbours (Calmfors 2014: 24).

Several factors help explain this change in wage agreement policies. Between 1969 and 1974, the labour union movement overcame its organizational split. Prior to this, separate organizations led by communists and social democrats operated in the labour relations field, thus complicating negotiations and maintaining a high level of unrest and conflict. For the employers, the incomes policy agreements were a way to enhance continuity and predictability in the labour market. Many of them also believed that comprehensive agreements would favour the reformist social democratic element among the unions.

A second area where Finland went from conflict to consensus was industrial relations. As long as the labour union movement remained organizationally split and parliamentary politics divisive and unstable, the Finnish labour market was characterized by frequent and often large work stoppages. With the establishment of a pattern of comprehensive incomes policy agreements and the growing political consensus, the high level of industrial disputes was also replaced with a more conciliatory style of conflict resolution. Some data may be used to illustrate this change. The average annual number of workdays lost due to industrial disputes was (in thousands of days) 1322 in the 1950s. In the 1970s the corresponding figure was still 1051, but in the 1980s as low as 316. During the first nine years of the 2000s it was down to 152 (International Historical Statistics, 186–7; http://laborsta.ilo.org/). These figures bear witness of a shift from a pattern of industrial relations where manifest conflict is the overarching principle to the consensual culture typical of most of Northern Europe.

Finally, a marked change in cabinet stability took place as of about 1980. Up until then, cabinets frequently resigned after about a year. Outright cabinet crises were common, and many cabinets did not represent a parliamentary majority. Caretaker cabinets were frequently resorted to due to problems of forming political coalitions. All of this changed after the 1970s. From there on, stable majority coalitions have been the norm (for details, see chapters by Isaksson, Paloheimo and Karvonen). Clearly, the changes in the labour market helped usher in a more general transition to consensual politics in Finland.

External change

For centuries, Finland has been a 'borderland' in between east and west, as a part of Sweden, as part of Russia, and then from 1917 on, as an independent state trying to find its position between east and west (Tiilikainen 1998; Alapuro 2004). Between 1939 and 1944, Finland fought two wars against the Soviet Union: the Winter War

(1939–40) and the Continuation War (1941–44), and in accordance with the armistice agreement with the Soviet Union, was engaged in battle against German forces in Lapland in 1944–45. As a result of the peace settlement, Finland was forced to concede a significant amount of its territory, mainly from the Karelia region, to her eastern neighbour. The war led also to close economic and political ties with the Soviet Union, consolidated in the Treaty of Friendship, Cooperation and Mutual Assistance (FCMA) signed in 1948. The FCMA treaty constituted limitations to Finnish armed forces, and prohibited military cooperation with any country hostile to the Soviet Union.

The Cold War entailed a delicate balancing act, with priority to good relations with the Soviet Union reconciled with democratic political institutions at home and integration into markets in the West. Finnish integration policy vis-à-vis the West was launched in the 1950s with the purpose to counterbalance the special relationship with Moscow and to give Finland more international room of manoeuvre while still maintaining good relations with the Soviet Union. While the direct interference of the Soviet leadership in Finnish politics has often been exaggerated, the Finnish political elite nevertheless was always forced to anticipate the reactions from Moscow, and this set firm limits to Finland's cooperation with Western European and Nordic countries. Due to these constraints Finland was a latecomer in joining several international organizations. Finland joined the Nordic Council in 1955 three years after the organisation was established and with the reservation that its membership would not include security policy matters or relations between the superpowers. Finland joined the United Nations in 1955, became in 1961 an associate member of the European Free Trade Association (EFTA) and signed a free trade agreement with the European Economic Community (EEC) in 1973. Finland became a full member of EFTA in 1986 and joined the Council of Europe as late as in 1989.

Another tenet that grew out of Finnish history was that of a small state, and by the early 1990s the Finns had become used to living in a world where state sovereignty and national security formed the uncontested starting points for political life. Finnish foreign policy was very much driven by the policy of neutrality, and this culminated in 1975 when Finland hosted the Conference on Security and Cooperation in Europe (CSCE). From the mid-

1960s at least until the mid-1980s, this foreign policy line enjoyed virtual unanimous political and public approval. During the long reign of President Urho Kekkonen (1956–1981) foreign policy was personally identified with the president, who was more or less visibly supported by political elites within the Soviet Union. Political debate and contestation on foreign policy were rare during this era of 'compulsory consensus' that placed a premium on maintaining amicable relations with the Soviet Union (Arter 1987).

When the Cold War had ended and the Soviet Union collapsed, Finland wasted no time in seizing the opportunity to become fully engaged in European integration. While joining the European Community (EC) was not on the political agenda during the Cold War, Finnish industry, especially the influential wood processing sector, had expressed its preferences by investing heavily in Western Europe (Väyrynen 1993). Finland applied for membership in the European Economic Area (EEA) in 1990 and joined it in 1994. Application for EC membership followed suit in March 1992. Finland joined the EU from the beginning of 1995, following a membership referendum held in October 1994 in which 57 per cent voted in favour of entering the Union. (Pesonen 1994; Arter 1995; Jenssen *et al.* 1998) While the pro-EU camp argued that by joining the Union Finland would merely be maintaining or consolidating its place among west European countries, there is little doubt that especially among foreign observers the 'western' identity of Finland had been far less clear. Indeed, the significance of EU membership for Finland should not be underestimated, for it clearly constituted a key element in the 'process of wholesale re-identification on the international stage.' (Arter 2000: 691)

Finland's integration policy can be characterized as flexible and constructive. Successive governments have constantly underlined the importance of being present where decisions that concern Finland are taken. According to the political elite, national interests can be best pursued through active and constructive participation in EU decision-making. Underlying this stance is a conviction that strong and efficient European institutions and common rules can best protect the rights and interests of smaller member states, as intergovernmental processes tend to favour the larger member states. Pragmatism and adaptability are the leading qualities of national EU policy, behavioural traits obviously influenced by the

Cold War experiences. Finnish integration policy stands thus in quite striking contrast to the EU policies of Denmark and Sweden (and of course Norway and Iceland), both of which have been far less supportive of further integration. Finland is also the only Nordic country that belongs to the Eurozone, with the single currency adopted without much political contestation. The policy of neutrality or military non-alignment has been compromised, or even abandoned altogether, as Finland has played an active part in the further development of the foreign and security policy of the EU. And even though foreign and security policy are now subject to broader domestic debate, largely the same logic continues to guide decision-making in foreign policy and EU issues, with emphasis on achieving national unity and avoiding public cleavages. (Raunio & Tiilikainen 2003)[4]

Patterns of party politics

In a West European comparison, the following features that are in many ways strongly intertwined appear characteristic of the Finnish party system:

1. *The high degree of party system fragmentation and the large number of parties that gain parliamentary representation.* The largest party normally wins a maximum of one-fourth of the seats in parliament.

2. *The absence of a party that is decisively larger than its main competitors.* No party has been able to establish itself even as *primus inter pares* among the largest parties. In recent decades, the social democrats, the conservatives (National Coalition)

---

4   However, in the run-up to the 2011 Eduskunta elections the problems affecting the Eurozone triggered heated debates, and the EU – or more precisely the role of Finland in the bailout measures – became the main topic of the campaign. The 2011 electoral triumph – repeated in the 2015 election – of the Eurosceptic and populist Finns Party has clearly impacted national EU policy. Since 2011, cabinets have taken a tougher stance in EU negotiations, for example demanding bilateral guarantees for bailout payments. Whether this signals a more long-term change to national integration policy remains to be seen, but at least the rise of The Finns Party and the euro crisis have brought about significant politicization and public contestation of European integration in Finland.

and the Centre Party have pursued a close contest for this position. Up until the mid-1970s, the communist-dominated Finnish People's Democratic Union (FPDU) also belonged to the category of the largest parties. The 2011 'earthquake election' created a new pattern whereby all the three largest parties were challenged by the landslide won by the populist The Finns Party. The 2015 election repeated this pattern. As a result, the Finnish party system is even more fragmented than previously, with four rather than three parties of a relatively equal size, along with another four minor parties represented in parliament.

3. *The increased weakness of the parties on the left.* A unique election in 1966 resulted in a parliamentary majority for the left. Since then, the electoral and parliamentary strength of the left has been in steady decline. In 2007, the combined strength of the two left parties (the Social Democrats and the Left Alliance) sank below one-third for the first time; the 2011 and 2015 elections continued this declining trend. As early as the 1980s, however, the left was down to around forty per cent of the seats in parliament. A left wing government has not been a numerically viable option for a very long time.

4. *The strength of the Centre Party that is historically an agrarian party.* The Finnish Centre Party, until 1965 the Agrarian Union, is a rare case of the survival of basically agrarian politics in a post-industrial society. Aided by the lateness of the urbanization process in Finland and supported by a strong organizational network, the Centre Party has displayed considerable strength despite the decline of similar parties in most of Western Europe (Kangas & Saloniemi 2013).

5. *Recurrent waves of populist protest.* In the 1970s and early 1980s, the populist Rural Party won a couple of spectacular victories. Its successor, The Finns Party, lifted the electoral support of populism to an all-time high in 2011. Populist electoral success has several times coincided with a poor showing for the Centre Party. In 2015, however, both these parties emerged victorious.

Table 3. *Proportion of votes cast for different parties in Parliamentary elections in 1945–2011 (per cent)*

	Soc dem	Cent	Cons	Left P	Green	Swe	Christ	Pop	Lib	Others
1945	25.1	21.3	15.0	23.5	–	7.9	–	–	5.2	2.0
1948	26.3	24.2	17.1	20.0	–	7.3	–	–	3.9	1.2
1951	26.5	23.2	14.6	21.6	–	7.3	–	–	5.7	1.1
1954	26.2	24.1	12.6	21.6	–	6.8	–	–	7.9	0.6
1958	23.2	23.1	15.3	23.2	–	6.5	–	–	5.9	2.8
1962	19.5	23.0	15.0	22.0	–	6.1	–	2.2	6.3	5.9
1966	27.2	21.2	13.8	21.1	–	5.7	0.5	1.0	6.5	2.9
1970	23.4	17.1	18.0	16.6	–	5.3	1.1	10.5	6.0	2.0
1972	25.8	16.4	17.6	17.0	–	5.1	2.5	9.2	5.2	1.2
1975	24.9	17.6	18.4	18.9	–	4.7	3.3	3.6	4.3	4.3
1979	23.9	17.3	21.7	17.9	–	4.3	4.8	4.6	3.7	1.8
1983	26.7	17.6	22.1	13.5	1.4	4.9	3.0	9.7	–	1.1
1987	24.1	17.6	23.1	13.6	4.0	5.6	2.6	6.3	1.0	2.1
1991	22.1	24.8	19.3	10.1	6.8	5.5	3.1	4.8	0.8	2.7
1995	28.3	19.8	17.9	11.2	6.5	5.1	3.0	1.3	0.6	6.3
1999	22.9	22.4	21.0	10.9	7.3	5.1	4.2	1.0	0.2	5.0
2003	24.5	24.7	18.6	9.9	8.0	4.6	5.3	1.6	0.3	2.5
2007	21.4	23.1	22.3	8.8	8.5	4.6	4.9	4.1	0.1	2.2
2011	19.1	15.8	20.4	8.1	7.3	4.3	4.0	19.1	–	1.9
2015	16.5	21.1	18.2	7.1	8.5	4.9	3.5	17.7	–	2.5
Average for 1991–2015	22.1	21.7	19.7	9.4	7.6	4.9	4.0	7.1	0.3	3.3

Party abbreviations

Soc dem	Social Democratic Party
Cent	From 1907 to 1965 Agrarian Union, thereafter the Center Party
Cons	National Coalition
Left P	From 1945 to 1990 Finnish People's Democratic Union (FPDU), from 1991 on Left Alliance (LA)
Green	Green League
Swe	Swedish People's Party in Finland
Christ	From 1966 to 2002 Finnish Christian League, thereafter Finnish Christian Democrats
Pop	From 1958 to 1966 Small farmers' Party, from 1966 to 1995 Finnish Rural Party, thereafter The Finns Party
Lib	From 1918 to 1950 National Progressive Party, from 1951 to 1965 Finnish People's Party, from 1965 to 1983 Liberal People's Party. In the parliamentary election of 1983 the Liberal People's Party was a member organization of the Center Party. From 1987 to 2002 Liberal People's Party, thereafter the Liberals

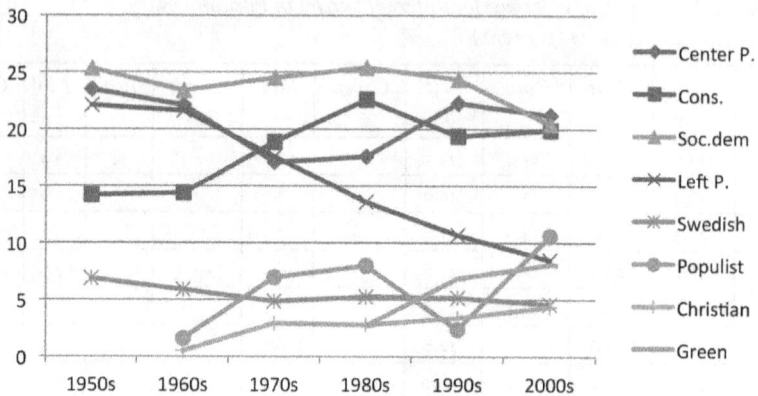

Figure 1. Support for eight party families 1950–2015; average vote shares (per cent) for each decade.

Source: Electoral statistics.

Important portions of the patterns of party politics are explicable in terms of structural change. The rapid economic transformation described above was connected with a marked decline in the number of rural population, and a drop in the number of small farms. This development had clear political consequences. Support for communism and left-wing socialism was strong among small farmers. From the 1940s to the 1960s, small farmers and their families formed a majority of the rural population. The 1960s was a decade of the 'great migration'. Along with the rapid economic transformation, small farms were merged into bigger ones, and the rural overpopulation, mainly younger generations, moved from rural to urban areas. As a result rural support for communism and left-wing socialism declined, while populism thrived on the rootlessness of those groups whose lives had been transformed by the decline of farming and the rapid process of urbanization. Along with urbanization and the expansion of the tertiary sector, support for conservative party increased. Remarkably, however, the Centre Party has been largely successful in the face of this social transformation. Although it has at times been challenged electorally by the populists, it has, over the long haul, retained its position to a much higher extent than might have been expected.

The decline of the extreme left must, of course, also be seen against the backdrop of the international collapse of communism.

The FPDU had in many ways depended on Soviet backing; with bankruptcy of Soviet communism, the electoral support of the extreme left in Finland dwindled rapidly.

About this book

The subsequent chapters of this book examine what the changes described above have meant from the point of view of political *power*. The scope of the analysis is broad, but the majority of the chapters deal with traditional core aspects of political analysis: government institutions, parties, political leaders and representatives. The project is guided by the notion that while not all power is political in nature and while all political power cannot be studied through institutions and actors immediately connected to these institutions, the structures of government remain a central arena for the use of political power. If and when institutions change, the conditions for political power are altered. One overarching objective is to track changes in Finnish government institutions that may have altered political power relations and the conditions for actors connected with these institutions.

While stressing the importance of institutional relations, however, the project has the ambition of looking beyond this perspective as well. Important aspects of political power defy institutional categorizations, and they must be studied from alternative perspectives. In order to present a more comprehensive analysis of political power in Finland the book therefore also examines phenomena such as political and social elites, citizen activism and gender relations. In all these respects, the case Finland offers interesting observations and developments without which the picture would remain incomplete.

The constitutional change described at the beginning of this introduction has placed the parliament at the center stage in the Finnish political system. It is therefore natural that the first substantive chapter of this book focuses on the position of the *Eduskunta*. *Guy-Erik Isaksson* shows that the changes have altered the parliament's position vis-à-vis the executive sphere. While the constitutional reform has underlined the central role of parliament, the predominance of stable surplus governments has strengthened the de facto influence of the cabinet sphere. Internally, parliament has changed relatively little, although the influx of EU matters has shifted the balance among parliamentary committees and tended to crowd the parliamentary agenda.

Heikki Paloheimo's chapter on the executive provides an account for the shift from semi-presidentialism to parliamentary rule. He analyses the division of power between government and president and government and parliament. On the behavioral side, he notes the paradox that presidential elections have continued to mobilize voters better than parliamentary elections, despite the much greater political importance of the latter. By the same token, there is a considerable amount of nostalgia among Finnish citizens for the earlier, president-centred system of government.

The next two chapters by *Lauri Karvonen* and *Vesa Koskimaa*, respectively, focus on political parties. Karvonen examines the influence of political parties over time concerning cabinet formation and central government budgets. Parties today have a much more influential role in government formation than in the 1970s. As for the budgetary process, the picture is less clear cut; on the whole, political parties have at least not lost power over time. Koskimaa looks at parties as organizations. In tune with comparative research on party organizations, he finds that the role of the 'party in public office' has been accentuated in terms of organizational resources as compared with the party organization at large. This, however, need not reflect a definite shift in power relations; rather, a combination of technological advances and a stronger focus on publicity and the electoral process has created shared interests throughout party organizations.

Among the institutional features that sets Finland apart from most comparable countries is the open-list proportional system used in elections. The system creates strong incentives for individual electioneering. Åsa von Schoultz examines the individual attributes that help candidates pass 'the needle's eye' to political positions. Besides incumbency and political experience, celebrity status and gender may be of importance in rather an intriguing manner.

In the Finnish debate, it is commonplace to underline the strong position of the central government bureaucracy vis-à-vis the political sphere. *Eero Murto* examines this notion both longitudinally and with the aid of a survey gauging the views of politicians and civil servants concerning power relations in Finnish central government. Overall, the bureaucracy has managed to retain its influential position, although increased government stability has improved the conditions of political oversight by ministers and cabinets.

More than in the case of neighboring Scandinavia, domestic politics in Finland has always reflected the state of the country's external relations. Small wonder, therefore, that *Tapio Raunio*'s chapter on the effects of Finland's EU membership and of internationalization more generally points to several changes that can best be understood against an international background. The constitutional reform process itself was influenced by external factors. The enhanced role of the prime minister and the finance minister similarly reflect Finland's involvement in the EU and in the global economy. The domestic legislative agenda is clearly restricted by the necessity of abiding by EU decisions and global commitments. Although Finland of course shares many of these features with other European nations, the Finnish case does display features that are interesting in an international comparison.

The study of political and societal elites offers a fruitful alternative perspective that complements institutionally oriented research on political power. Based on a unique data set compiled through three surveys in 1991–2011, *Ilkka Ruostetsaari* examines the composition of and interaction between seven elites in Finnish society. He finds that the political elite has become less open in terms of socioeconomic recruitment over time; moreover, the circulation between politics and other elite spheres has increased. Although the increased elitism of the political class can be deemed worrisome, the intensified horizontal circulation may be seen as a sign of lowered barriers between societal elites.

An important aspect of political power is how it is perceived by citizens, politicians and civil servants. In *Maija Mattila*'s study of such perceptions, the case of the Talvivaara mine is the focal point. This huge enterprise represents a combination of immense economic interests – both private and public – regional development as well as highly troublesome environmental effects. Overall, the impression conveyed by the interviews in her chapter is that power is highly elusive, making the quest of accountability hard for citizens as well as for elected politicians.

Women's involvement in politics has long historical roots in Finland, and Finland has always been among the countries in which the share of women holding elective office is highest. *Mari Niemi*'s analysis focuses on the ascendancy of women as party leaders. Although it is clear that a breakthrough of sorts has occurred in the 21st century, her study shows that there are several kinds of glass ceilings that continue to be operative.

The concluding chapter discusses the wider implications of the findings by reflecting on themes that run through most of the analyses in the book. Evidently, the Finnish case in several ways reflects the lateness and rapidity of social change described in this introduction. The pattern of societal, institutional and cultural change is a complex and intriguing one; one may argue that political culture among citizens has not always been abreast with institutional transformation. Overall, political power in Finland has evolved in a manner that offers interesting insights for broader comparative research.

References

Alapuro, R. (2004). What is Western and What is Eastern in Finland? *Thesis Eleven* Vol. 77, 1: 85–101.

Arter, D. (1987). *Politics and Policy-Making in Finland: A Study of a Small Democracy in a West European Outpost*. Basingstoke, Palgrave Macmillan.

— (1995). The EU Referendum in Finland on 16 October 1994: A Vote for the West, not for Maastricht. *Journal of Common Market Studies* Vol. 33, 3: 361–387.

— (2000). Small State Influence Within the EU: The Case of Finland's "Northern Dimension Initiative". *Journal of Common Market Studies* Vol. 38, 5: 677–697.

Calmfors, L. (2014). How Well is the Nordic Model Doing? Recent Performance and Future Challenges. In T. Valkonen & V. Vihriälä (eds.), *The Nordic Model – Challenged but Capable of Reform*. TemaNord 2014:531. Copenhagen, The Nordic Council of Ministers: 17–90.

Duverger, M. (1980). A New Political System Model: Semi-Presidential Government. *European Journal of Political Research* Vol. 8, 2: 165–187.

Elgie, R. (2011). *Semi-presidentialism: Sub-Types and Democratic Performance*. Oxford, Oxford Univ. Press.

Elgie, R. & Moestrup, S. (eds.) (2008). *Semi-presidentialism in Central and Eastern Europe*. Manchester, Manchester University Press.

Hallberg, P., Martikainen, T., Nousiainen, J. & Tiikkainen, P. (2009). *Presidentin valta: hal-*

litsijanvallan ja parlamentarismin välinen jännite Suomessa 1919–2009. Helsinki, WSOY.

Jenssen, A.T., Pesonen, P. & Gilljam, M. (eds.) (1998). *To Join or Not to Join: Three Nordic Referendums on Membership in the European Union.* Oslo, Scandinavian University Press.

International Historical Statistics. Europe 1750–2005. Edited by B.R. Mitchell. Basingstoke: Palgrave Macmillan.

Jyränki, A. & Nousiainen, J. (2006). *Eduskunnan muuttuva asema. Suomen eduskunta 100 vuotta, osa 2.* Helsinki, Edita.

Kangas, O. & Saloniemi, A. (2013). Historical Making, Present and Future Challenges for the Nordic Welfare State Model in Finland. *Fafo report 2013:40.* Oslo, Fafo.

Kyntäjä, T. (1993). *Tulopolitiikka Suomessa. Tulopoliittinen diskurssi ja instituutiot 1960-luvulta 1990-luvun kynnykselle.* Helsinki, Gaudeamus.

Mair, P. (1997). *Party System Change. Approaches and Interpretations.* Oxford, Oxford University Press.

Nousiainen, J. (2001). From Semi-presidentialism to Parliamentary Government: Political and Constitutional Developments in Finland. *Scandinavian Political Studies* Vol. 24, 2: 95–109.

Oskarson, M. (2005). Social Structure and Party Choice. In J. Thomassen (ed.), *The European Voter. A Comparative Study of Modern Democracies.* Oxford, Oxford University Press: 84–105.

Paloheimo, H. (2001). Divided Government in Finland: From a Semi-presidential to a Parliamentary Democracy. In R.

Elgie (ed.), *Divided Government in Comparative Perspective.* Oxford, Oxford University Press: 86–105.

— (2003). The Rising Power of the Prime Minister in Finland. *Scandinavian Political Studies* Vol. 26, 3: 219–243.

Pesonen, P. (ed.) (1994). *Suomen EU-kansanäänestys 1994: Raportti äänestäjien kannanotoista.* Helsinki, Ulkoasiainministeriö, Eurooppatiedotus.

Raunio, T. (2011): Finland: Moving in the Opposite Direction. In T. Bergman & K. Strøm (eds.), *The Madisonian Turn: Political Parties and Parliamentary Democracy in Nordic Europe.* Ann Arbor, The University of Michigan Press: 112–157.

Raunio, T. & Tiilikainen, T. (2003). *Finland in the European Union.* London, Frank Cass.

Schleiter, P. & Morgan-Jones, E. (2009). Review Article: Citizens, Presidents and Assemblies: The Study of Semi-Presidentialism beyond Duverger and Linz. *British Journal of Political Science* Vol. 39, 4: 871–892.

Strøm, K., Müller, W.C. & Bergman, T. (eds.) (2003). *Delegation and Accountability in Parliamentary Democracies.* Oxford, Oxford University Press.

Tiilikainen, T. (1998). *Europe and Finland: Defining the Political Identity of Finland in Western Europe.* Aldershot, Ashgate.

Väyrynen, R. (1993). Finland and the European Community: Changing Elite Bargains. *Cooperation and Conflict* Vol. 28, 1: 31–46.

Parliamentary Authority: Expansion and Adaptation

GUY-ERIK ISAKSSON

As noted in the introductory chapter, on a constitutional level the political system of Finland has changed radically during recent decades. The Finnish constitution of 1919 prescribed a dual executive and a semi-presidential form of government. As a consequence, the prime minister operated, more or less, in the shadow of the head of state. President Koivisto engineered a series of piecemeal reforms, which, collectively, strongly reduced the powers of the presidency and increased those of the prime minister. Most important, according to the new Finnish constitution of 2000, the president was excluded from the government formation process. The new constitution also limited the president's powers in the field of foreign policy. Today, the president directs foreign policy in co-operation with the government. Among other things, the prime minister represents Finland at European Council meetings (Arter 2006: 131–132).

One of the main goals of the constitutional reform process was to move Finland further in the direction of a parliamentary system of government. Consequently, Finland can no longer be described as a semi-presidential system, although the head of state is still by no means a purely ceremonial figure. Today, the Finnish political system can best be characterized as a parliamentary system.

In terms of power it is obvious that parliament and cabinet, and especially the prime minister, are the winners. Nowadays, the position of the Finnish prime minister is quite comparable to the other heads of government in the EU. By the same token, it is very apparent that president is the big looser in the power sharing reforms in

Finland. It is obvious that the reforms have shifted power from the president to the other political actors.

In this chapter the power of the Finnish parliament (*Eduskunta*) will be discussed. How and why has the power of the parliament increased? What consequences does this strengthening of parliamentary power have for the work of the parliament?

The discussion has two main aspects: firstly, there is an external perspective on changes in the parliament's relations to other central political actors and, secondly, the internal perspective on how the changes are reflected in the organization, working methods and workload of the parliament. Throughout the discussion a comparative, mainly Nordic perspective will be applied. The chapter is concluded by a few comprehensive conclusions.

The external dimension: parliament in relation to other central actors

Two important factors form focus of this section. Both of them have a major significance for the shaping of a political system. Taken altogether these factors to a large extent determine how parliamentary a political system is and thereby how much power the parliament has. The factors in question are government formation and dissolution of parliament.

In Finland the constitutional regulation regarding these factors has been radically reformed during the last decades. These reforms have, all in all, meant a major shift in power from the president to the parliament and government. The focus will be on how, and why, the power of the parliament has been strengthened as a result of the development during the past decades.

Government formation

The present analysis focuses on the *constitutional* division of power in the cabinet formation process. For an empirical analysis of cabinet formation, see chapter by Karvonen.

In a parliamentary system the government is appointed by the parliament, in a semi-presidential system it is the president who appoints the government. In Finland the power to appoint the government was transferred from the president to the parliament when the new constitution came into force in the year 2000. But already previously parliamentary practice had restricted the role of the president in the process of forming the government.

Up until the year 2000, the provisions concerning cabinet formation were found in section 36 of the 1919 Instrument of Government (Constitution):

> The President shall appoint native citizens of Finland known for their honesty and ability to serve as members of the Council of State[1].

Corresponding contemporary provisions are to be found in sections 61 and 62 of the Finnish Constitution that went into effect in 2000:

> The Parliament elects the Prime Minister, who is thereafter appointed to the office by the President of the Republic. The President appoints the other Ministers in accordance with a proposal made by the Prime Minister (section 61).

> The Government shall without delay submit its programme to the Parliament in the form of a statement. The same applies when the composition of the Government is essentially altered (section 62).[2]

The forms for negotiations and the voting procedures are also regulated in the 2000 constitution. The groups represented in the parliament shall negotiate on the political program and the composition of the government before the prime minister is elected. On the basis of the outcome of these negotiations, the President shall inform the parliament of the nominee for prime minister. Moreover, before this presidential information, the president shall hear the speaker of the parliament and the parliamentary groups.

The new role of the president in the government formation process is both interesting and surprising. As the last step in the formation process, the president *formally* appoints the prime minister elected by the parliament and the other ministers in accordance with the proposal made by the prime minister. It should be empha-

---

1   The formal designation of the cabinet.
2   The English version can be accessed at http://www.finlex.fi/en/laki/kaannok-set/1999/en19990731.pdf

sized that this presidential right to nominate is explicitly formal. In other words, the president cannot refuse to appoint the prime minister the parliament has elected or the ministers that have been proposed for the cabinet, neither can the president appoint some other persons as ministers than those proposed to him. The president's right to nominate is at this point purely and explicitly formal. This is clearly stated in the introductory argumentation contained in the proposal for the constitution. Consequently, the power of the president is basically eliminated when it comes to government formations.

Bearing this in mind it is rather surprising that the president is involved in the formal formation process at all. Once the government formation is in the hands of the political parties represented in the parliament, it may be argued that it is totally unnecessary for the president to be even formally involved in the process *before* the final formal appointment of the new government. Why must the president inform the parliament of a decision that the parliament itself just has taken? It should be taken for granted that the representatives of the parliament are aware of the decision they have just made, especially when this decision determines what kind of government Finland is going to have for the next four years.

Consequently, the government formation process could easily have been made less complex and less complicated. It seems quite controversial that in reality the political parties succeeded to deprive the president all political power when it comes to forming a new government. Apparently, there was not enough political courage to minimize the formal involvement of the president in the constitution. Therefore, the new stipulations about this decision making process may give the impression that the president, after all, still has real power in the government formation process. But that is not the case.

In fact, the early and formal involvement of the Finnish president in the process is quite similar to the corresponding processes in many monarchies. It is still quite common that the monarch formally appoints the person who is going to form the new government. However, this does not mean that the monarch has real political power regarding government formation. Rather, it is more a matter of symbolic deference to the formal head of state.

When the parliament, not the president, selects a government, this also strengthens the guarantees that the principle of representative democracy will be observed. This means that the composition of the government should reflect as directly as possible the results of the parliamentary elections. A president dominated government formation process might be a 'disturbing' element when parliamentary recommendations and principles are to be implemented.

For example, the president may have a strong preference as to which parties should be included in the new government, regardless of how these parties succeed in the elections. This may result in a government that foremost or even entirely, consists of parties that lost the elections, and at the same time the winning parties will be in opposition. Provided that the election result happens to be in line with the president's party preference there will, on the other hand, be no noticeable conflict. In the context of a presidential rule, the president can obviously also influence the life-span of the government. The president can, if he or she chooses to do so, essentially influence both the forming of the government and its downfall. In this case the president takes control of functions that in a parliamentary system should belong to the parliament.

When the head of state is fully integrated in the process, not just as the one who formally appoints the government, he is the one who chooses the person who explores the different possibilities for establishing a government. Furthermore, the head of state can express more or less definite demands as to the composition of the government. The head of state has the initiative and can steer the formation of government in a certain direction, toward a certain goal. The actions of the head of state restrict the potential options for forming the government and create an environment for negotiations that clearly differs from an environment where the formation of the government exclusively is handled by the parliament (Strøm *et al.* 1994).

The role of the head of state is usually regulated in the constitution. If the head of the state is given a formal role to appoint the government, his influence will be marginal or non-existent. It is, however, not quite uncommon that the head of state has a certain real influence on the formation of a new government. According to one study about half of the states in Western Europe have a head of state that has moderate or strong influence in this area (De Winter 1995: 118). According to another study about one third of the states in Western Europe have a system where the head of state plays an active role, *i.e.* the republics like France, Italy, Portugal and Finland (up to the year 2000), but also monarchies as Spain and the Netherlands (Laver & Schofield 1990: 64). Sweden is an extreme case, as the monarch has not even a ceremonial role in this regard.

It is obvious that the size of a party matters for the probability that it will be a government party. The position as the largest party greatly increases the prospects of being included in the government. Previous studies show rather clearly that the position as the largest party is an advantage in the negotiating a government. In many parliamentary systems there is a clear view that the largest party after an election shall be given the assignment of government formation. This party will first get the opportunity to form a government and if it succeeds, it will be the prime minister party. This priority position gives a major strategic advantage in relation to the other parties and may influence the outcome in forming the new government. However, in a formation process led by the president this fundamental priority position can easily be eliminated by the president, especially if the differences in size between the parties are not considerable (Mitchell & Nyblade 2008: 214; Gallagher *et al.* 2011: 416; Isaksson 2013).

It is obvious that the formation of government in Finland has changed in a fundamental way during the last fifty years. It is obvious that the most important individual factor that has changed is the president's role. As a matter of fact the formation of the government took on parliamentary features already in the 1980s. However, the constitutional stipulations regarding the formation of government in all essential matters were not reformed until the new constitution entered into force.

The radical change from a president-centred to a parliament-centred practice in Finland is very interesting. As a matter of fact one could conclude that a president-led government formation should be more rapid than a process that requires negotiations with parties without an 'external' leader (De Winter & Dumont 2008: 151). As regards Finland it seems undeniably that the president's active participation did not speed up the process, it rather complicated the formation process in a time consuming way. It should, however, be noted that the party political constellations were not as stable during the 1960s and 1970s as they have been during the last three decades. Nevertheless, the development seems to indicate that the president's participation in the government formation process was rather a more disturbing than a supportive element. For details, see chapter by Karvonen.

Correspondingly the length of governmental life-span has dramatically changed during the last fifty years. Finland has a profile of its own; it differs both from the Scandinavian and West European countries. This transformation in the political system of Finland is as dramatic as it is remarkable. Finland was once one of the countries in Western Europe with the most short-lived governments, but now the country is one of those with the most durable governments. Finland no longer, together with Italy, belongs to the group of the countries with short-lived governments (Müller & Strøm 2000: 584; Saalfeld 2008: 327–334; Gallagher *et al.* 2011: 445–454).

The Nordic countries form today a very uniform pattern regarding the role of the head of state in government formation. This pattern, furthermore, differs strikingly from the West European one. In none of the Nordic countries can one say that the head of state plays an active role in the formation of government. This general statement is, however, valid for the present rather than for the past. Before the year 2000 the Finnish president could play a major, even decisive, role in forming a new government. With the new constitutional law the government formation has become parliamentary and thereby it has also been adapted to the overall Nordic pattern as to government formation processes.

Dissolution of parliament

The right to dissolve the parliament can take on different forms, which have varying impact on the position of the parliament and the relations to other central political actors. The authority to dissolve the parliament can be connected to the government, to the head of state or to the parliament itself. In earlier studies different information is available regarding countries in which the government can dissolve the parliament. According to one study the governments in most of the West European countries have the possibility to dissolve the parliament (Gallagher *et al.* 2011: 415). Another study indicates the opposite (Davidsson 2004: 188–196).

In Finland the dissolution of parliament was for a long period a presidential preserve. According to the old constitution the president alone had the power to dissolve parliament and order new elections. However , a constitutional amendment in 1991 made dissolution conditional upon the prime minister's initiative (Pesonen & Riihinen 2002: 36). The new constitution states that:

> The President of the Republic, in response to a reasoned proposal by the Prime Minister, and after having heard the parliamentary groups, and while the Parliament is in session, may order that extraordinary parliamentary elections shall be held. Thereafter, the Parliament shall decide the time when it concludes its work before the elections (section 26).

The new rule means that the possibility of presidential action aimed at the dissolution of parliament has radically diminished. The president still retains a certain role, however. According to the dualistic logic in the old constitution it was seen as important that the president could decide to dissolve the parliament independently, even against the will of the political parties. Today, the dissolution instrument is part of normal parliamentarianism. The dualistic element in the Finnish constitution has hereby been greatly weakened as concerns the dissolution of the parliament (Nousiainen 1998: 207–209).

As the presidential authority regarding dissolution of the parliament is linked to the prime minister, the parliamentary connection is obvious. Hereby, the parliament also has an indirect link to the dissolution instrument. The essential point is that neither the prime minister nor the president alone can dissolve the parliament. The participation and agreement of both parts are needed. From a parliamentary point of view the main thing is that the road to a presidentially initiated dissolution is blocked.

The linking of the president to the government was also probably deemed as an effective way to avoid dissolutions on politically dubious grounds. Therefore, in the 1980s it was suggested that the president should have the authority to dissolve the parliament only once during his term in office (Anckar 1984: 102–107).

Historical experiences of dissolutions of the parliament in Finland also contributed to the reform. Some of the implemented dissolutions were not regarded as being in line with the intentions expressed in the old constitution. Dissolution of parliament has in Finland been applied six times (in 1924, 1929, 1930, 1962, 1972 and 1975) (Jansson 1992: 282–287). The last three dissolutions were enforced by president Kekkonen. Lindman stated already in 1974 that 'it is difficult to evade the impression that the dissolution instrument in Finland has been used in an excessive manner and sometimes without sufficient reason' (Lindman 1979: 49). Especially the dissolutions in 1972 and 1975 have been criticized. These two dissolutions also led to the resignation of the government, which should by no means be the case in dissolutions of the parliament.

The government's proposal for the present constitution emphasized that new elections shall be conducted only in exceptional cases. In connection with the reform of the dissolution instrument the parliament already in 1990 stated that a dissolution can be considered only in connection with a prolonged parliamentary crisis that makes it difficult to form a political cabinet. Dissolution of parliament could also be motivated if there are strong indications that the parliament's ability to function or its structure is somehow threatened. It was explicitly emphasized that the government's own internal or external difficulties must not result in the dissolution of the parliament. A government crisis or a conflict between the parliament and the government shall not be solved by dissolution of the parliament or by a threat of dissolution. If necessary a new government shall be established. Only if it is quite impossible to form a functioning government the dissolution of the parliament may be considered (HE 1/1998, 83–84).

In the Nordic context Norway is the deviant case regarding the dissolution of parliament. Norway is the only country where it is not possible at all to dissolve the parliament before the ordinary period ends. The Norwegian *Stortinget* is therefore uniquely strong; it never has to worry about dissolution. Denmark is at the other extreme, as the Danish government, or rather the prime minister, has the unconditional right to dissolve the *Folketinget*.

In the new democracies in Eastern Europe no country has chosen to give the government the right to dissolve the parliament. Hereby the parliament's supremacy in relation to the government is emphasized, and this also strengthens the feature of parliamentarianism in the constitution. However, if the right to dissolve the parliament is vested in the head of state, the feature of parliamentarianism will be considerably weakened. In most eastern European countries the head of state can, under certain circumstances, dissolve the parliament. This can occur if the negotiations to form a government fail or a new government cannot be appointed within a given time frame.

In Western Europe it is still common that the government in one way or another can influence the dissolution of parliament. In countries like Austria, France, Iceland, Italy and Luxembourg the head of state has relatively unlimited rights to make a decision on dissolving the parliament (Davidsson 2004: 188–196; Isaksson 2013: 23).

All in all, it is obvious that the power of the Finnish parliament has increased significantly. This change is a consequence of several constitutional reforms during the last decades. In fact, the political system of Finland has been transformed from a semi-presidential system to a parliamentary one.

The internal dimension: changes inside the parliament

General aspects

It is obvious that the power of the Finnish parliament has increased during recent decades. It is equally obvious that the political power of the president has radically decreased during the same period. The most important single reason for this development is the transfer of power concerning government formation from president to parliament. However, although the competence to select the government is crucial in a parliamentary system, it does not affect the daily work in parliament. Moreover, a new cabinet is usually appointed only every four years, which means that the task to select the government is very important, but does not occur very often.

Has the generally more powerful position of parliament also affected power relations inside the parliament? Parliament has three key arenas: the plenary session makes final decisions, the committees prepare matters and the parliamentary groups shape policy. Legislation is enacted according to the Constitutional Law and Parliament's Rules of Procedure (December 17th, 1999).

In Finland the new Parliament's Rules of Procedure that replaced the old rules from 1927 were introduced in 2000 parallel with the new constitution. Several changes were made related to parliamentary processes and organisation. For instance, the enactment process was truncated from three plenary readings to two, and the rules relating to the various forms of initiatives of MPs were systematically set out (Arter 2006: 210).

On the national level the Finnish Parliament plays a strong role in decision-making on EU-affairs compared to many other member states. It must be emphasised that the principle of accountability to parliament also applies to the activities of governments within the EU.

Organisation

The plenary session is the most visible aspect of the parliament's work. However, less visible but very important is the work done in committees. Almost all decisions made in parliament are based on committee reports.

The committee system was very stable for many decades after WW II. On the whole, the number of parliamentary committees remained stable for a long period of time. Not until the 1980s did a need to reform and to modernise the committee system appear. The structure of the parliamentary committees should be more in line with the department divides in the public sector. This would improve the co-operation and the communication between government and parliament. Through the committee reform of 1991 this kind of change was implemented. In addition, the reform created better opportunities for parliament to control the government. Two committees were abolished and three new committees were established. Nowadays, the committees meet more often than earlier and the meetings are longer than earlier (Raunio & Wiberg 2014: 16).

Today, there are 15 permanent special committees and the Grand Committee, which focuses mainly on EU affairs. The parliament may also establish temporary committees. The Grand Committee shall adopt its own rules of procedure (Parliament's Rules of Procedure, section 7).

The permanent committees are:

1. Constitutional Law Committee (1907)
2. Foreign Affairs Committee (1918)
3. Finance Committee (1863)

The position of these three committees is stipulated in constitutional law.

4. Legal Affairs Committee (1863)
5. Commerce Committee (1863)
6. Agriculture and Forestry Committee (1907)
7. Social Affairs and Health Committee (1907)
8. Education and Culture Committee (1908)
9. Transport and Communications Committee (1929)
10. Defence Committee (1937)
11. Administration Committee (1991)
12. Employment and Equality Committee (1991)
13. Environment Committee (1991)
14. Committee for the Future (1993)
15. Audit Committee (2007)

(Parliament's Rules of Procedure, section 7).

The profile of the two newest committees differs from the other committees. Neither the Committee for Future nor the Audit Committee is connected to a ministry. Unlike other committees, the primary task of these two committees is not law-drafting. Through the Audit Committee established in 2007 the parliamentary control of the government finances was improved (Mattila 2014: 122). The Committee for the Future deals with matters related to development models and alternatives, futures research and the social impact of technological development.

The Grand Committee serves as the EU committee of the parliament. It's most important task is to ensure that parliament has influence over EU decision-making. In the case of EU's common foreign and security policy, the views of parliament are expressed by the Foreign Affairs Committee. The special committees also play significant roles in EUaffairs. This is a distinctive feature of the Finnish system. The special committees issue statements to the Grand Committee on EU affairs in their respective fields. The Grand Committee generally concurs with the views of the special committees. (For more information about EU effects on the Finnish parliament, see the chapter by Raunio.)

However, in the 1970s and 1980s, criticism against the Grand Committee became quite strong. Again, there were many varying opinions in parliament regarding the way the Grand Committee should be reformed. According to one position, the committee should be entirely abolished; another opinion did not want any reforms at all of the committee. In practice, only minor reforms were made in the position of the Grand Committee (Helander & Pekonen 2007: 45–48). Even scholars suggested that the Grand Committee could be abolished or, at least, be given other and more specific tasks (Anckar 1990: 173). Only a few years later, Finland became an EU member and the Grand Committee was rapidly transformed into an EU committee dealing with totally different issues than earlier.

Traditionally, the parliamentary committees have had varying status. In the 1950s and the 1960s the Finance Committee and the Foreign Affairs Committee had a very high status among the MPs. Therefore, the seats in these committees were much coveted. As a consequence, the seats in these committees were mostly occupied by senior MPs. A seat in an important committee could even make it easier for the MP to be re-elected. In those days the Defence Committee was the least rated committee in which new MPs easily could get a seat (Noponen 1989: 181). During the post-war time the differences in prestige between parliamentary committees have grown over time. This development can be seen as a functional differentiation that has occurred over the years when the work load of the parliament has grown considerably (Wiberg & Mattila 1997: 236).

According to a study covering the post-war period until the middle of the 1990s, the Finance Committee, the Foreign Affairs Committee, the Agriculture and Forestry Committee, the Education and Culture Committee and the Social and Health Affairs Committee were the highest rated parliamentary committees (Mattila 2014: 124). In another study, the Constitutional Law Committee and the Grand Committee were highly rated as well. The prestige

of the Grand Committee has grown radically after Finland joined
the EU. The new function as an EU committee is the reason to this
change. In fact, before the EU membership the prestige of the Grand
Committee was very low among the MPs (Mattila 2014: 124).

Processes

The process of legislation is stated in chapter 6 in the constitutional
law. The basic statement is about legislative initiative.

> The proposal for the enactment of an Act is initiated in the Parliament
> through a government proposal submitted by the Government or
> through a legislative motion submitted by a Representative. Legislative
> motions can be submitted when the Parliament is in session (section 70).

In other words, legislative proposals are presented to parliament in
the form of government bills or initiatives of the MPs. In both cases
the process begins with a preliminary debate in plenary session.
After that the bill is sent to a special committee.

The committees prepare government bills, legislative initiatives,
government reports and other matters for handling in plenary session. Committees usually deal with the matters referred to them as
soon as possible in form of preliminary and final handling of the
matter. It usually takes one or two months for a committee to finish
handling a matter, but urgent matters can be dealt with in just a few
days. However, the handling of major legislative reforms can easily
take many months or even years. At the end of the electoral period,
bills are allowed to lapse, except for EU affairs.

Preliminary handling begins with hearings at which experts present their own views of the case. After hearings the committee con-
ducts a general debate and tentatively decides on details. In the case
of legislation this includes going over a bill section by section. After
a preliminary committee report is made, the final handling of the
matter begins. A matter must be put to a vote if a committee cannot
reach unanimity. If there are diverging opinions after a vote in the
committee, the minority can have its views appended to the report.

A committee can recommend that a bill be approved as it or
with minor or major changes. It can also recommend that a bill be
rejected. In its report a committee presents its views on a matter

together with supporting arguments and recommends what course of action parliament should take. Committee meetings are not open to the public. However, committee reports and statements are public documents.

After the committee handling, a bill returns to the plenary session where it is subjected to two readings. In the first reading the content of the bill is decided section by section. In the second reading the bill is either approved or rejected.

> Once the relevant report of the Committee preparing the matter has been issued, a legislative proposal is considered in two readings in a plenary session of the Parliament.
>
> In the first reading of the legislative proposal, the report of the Committee is presented and debated, and a decision on the contents of the legislative proposal is made. In the second reading, which at the earliest takes place on the third day after the conclusion of the first reading, the Parliament decides whether the legislative proposal is accepted or rejected (section 72).

Until 2000, bills went through three readings but as a part of the constitutional reform the first and the second reading was combined and the procedure was condensed to two readings only. Moreover, until 1992 a parliamentary minority with one third of the seats in Parliament was able, in fact, to retard or even to block the legislation proposed by the government. To avoid the postponement of a law proposal the government was obliged to negotiate with the opposition parties for getting sufficient support for the proposal. By supporting a legislative resolution introduced by one or more opposition parties, the government was able to avoid the postponement of the legislative proposal under consideration (Helander 1997: 12–13).

EU legislation and especially directives usually require the amendment of national legislation. This legislation is enacted in normal order. Before attending Council meetings, ministers inform the Grand Committee of the items on the agenda and the positions that Finland's representatives intend to take in the Council. Council meetings are attended by the minister responsible for the administrative sector in question. The Foreign Affairs Committee has the same right to be kept informed when it comes to the common foreign and security policy as the Grand Committee has in other EU affairs.

Output

As a consequence of the EU-membership, the decision-making processes of the Finnish parliament have been reformed. Have these reforms led to changes in the main focus of the parliamentary output? And if so, is it possible that such change has renewed the internal power structure of the parliament?

During the last three decades the general activity profile of the parliament is characterized by stability rather than dramatic changes. A comparison between the decade before the EU membership and the decade after the membership shows, on the whole, no EU-related activity effect in parliament. Consequently, the general assumption that EU has increased the activity in parliament is false. However, as to certain parliamentary activities an EU effect is quite obvious.

The number of government proposals on average per year has in fact decreased after EU membership. The number of interpellations per year has been almost the same for many decades. However, as to motions, dramatic changes have occurred. There is a marked decrease in the number of petitionary as well as budgetary motions during the last decade. Moreover, the number of oral questions has decreased and the number of written questions has increased during the last decades. However, whether these changes have anything to do with the EU membership, is difficult to evaluate.

Table 1. Number of cases according to type of activity and period (average per year)

Type of activity	1983–94	1995–2012	Change
Government proposals	279	240	– 39
Interpellations	3,8	3,7	– 0,1
Motions			
– legislative motions	124	146	+ 22
– petitionary motions	941	201	– 740
– budgetary motions	2010	1086	– 924
Oral questions	304	197	– 107
Written questions	622	1068	+ 446

Source: Raunio & Wiberg 2014: 22–23

Has the activity profile of single special committees changed during recent decades? The first major observation is that the total number of committee reports has not increased after Finland became an EU-member. During the period 1980–94 the committees wrote 331 reports on average per year. During the period 1995–2012 the corresponding number was 263. In other words, the number of committee reports went down with 25 per cent.

However, the number of reports varies a lot between the single committees. In fact, two committees dominate the picture before EU membership as well as after. Moreover, it is the same two committees that are dominant, the Finance Committee and the Social Affairs and Health Committee. During the first period about 40 per cent of all reports came from these two committees. The Finance Committee alone gave on average almost 100 reports per year during the period of 1980–94. However, during the later period the Finance Committee gave on average per year only 43 reports, still being the most active single committee in this respect.

Table 2. Number of committee reports according to committee and period (average per year)

Parliamentary committee	*1980–94*	*1995–2012*	*Change*
Constitutional Law Committee	27	9	– 18
Foreign Affairs Committee	24	17	– 7
Finance committee	96	43	– 53
Audit Committee	X	6	
Administration Committee	22	25	+ 3
Legal Affairs Committee	13	20	+ 7
Transport and Communications C.	9	19	+ 10
Agriculture and Forestry Committee	21	15	– 6
Defence Committee	4	3	– 1
Education and Culture Committee	22	15	– 7
Social Affairs and Health Committee	41	40	– 1
Commerce Committee	24	27	+ 3
Committee for the Future	X	–	
Employment and Equality Committee	12	13	+ 1
Environment Committee	16	11	– 5
Total	*331*	*263*	*– 84*

X = the committee did not yet exist
Source: Raunio & Wiberg 2014: 20–21

The number of reports by the Constitutional Law Committee has decreased dramatically as well. Before EU membership this committee delivered 27 reports on average per year. During the EU era this number has dropped to nine reports only. As to the Transport and Communications Committee the development is the opposite. The number of average annual reports has increased from nine to nineteen during these decades. Once again, whether this and other major changes in the report output of the committees are related to EU membership or not is difficult to assess. Anyhow, the assumption that the EU membership has increased the work of the parliamentary committees in the form of more committee reports is just an illusion.

When it comes to statements produced by parliamentary committees, the pattern of activity is totally different from that of the committee reports. Until 1995 the committees wrote on average only 69 statements per year. The corresponding figure for the period 1995–2012 is 290 statements. In other words, after Finland became an EU member, the parliamentary committees have produced on average four times more statements than before EU membership. Obviously, this dramatic change in the number of statements, can mainly bee considered to be an EU effect. According to the working procedures regarding EU matters, the Grand Committee often asks special committees to deliver statements to the Grand Committee.

Before EU membership one committee was dominant regarding the annual number of statements. At that time, the Constitutional Law Committee delivered about 25 per cent of all parliamentary statements. All the other committees delivered only a few statements per year. After 1995 the activity pattern changed dramatically. All committees started to write much more statements than earlier. The Constitutional Law Committee is still the leading committee in this respect, but three other committees in particular have become highly active as statements producers. Almost half of all statements are nowadays delivered by the Constitutional Law Committee, the Finance Committee, the Administration Committee and the Commerce Committee. The lowest activity is displayed by the Committee for the Future, the Defence Committee, the Audit Committee and the Foreign Affairs Committee.

Usually the committees try to attain an agreement in their reports and statements. This implies that compromises are possible

Table 3. Number of committee statements according to committee and period (average per year)

Parliamentary committee	1980–94	1995–2012	Change
Constitutional Law Committee	17	43	+ 26
Foreign Affairs Committee	2	9	+ 7
Finance committee	6	30	+ 24
Audit Committee	X	6	
Administration Committee	7	29	+ 22
Legal Affairs Committee	3	19	+ 16
Transport and Communications C.	2	21	+ 19
Agriculture and Forestry Committee	6	24	+ 18
Defence Committee	2	6	+ 4
Education and Culture Committee	3	14	+ 11
Social Affairs and Health Committee	6	16	+ 10
Commerce Committee	3	28	+ 25
Committee for the Future	X	4	
Employment and Equality Committee	5	16	+ 11
Environment Committee	7	25	+ 18
Total	69	290	+ 211

X= the committee did not yet exist
Source: Raunio & Wiberg 2014: 18–19

to reach between the representatives of government and opposition parties. However, the development during the last decade shows that such compromising has become more difficult for the political parties.

Since 2000 the element of reservations to reports and dissenting opinions to statements has increased significantly. At the end of the 1990s only about ten per cent of the committee reports and statements included a reservation or a dissenting opinion. Ten years later this share had been doubled (Mattila 2014: 128–130). This development is interesting, but quite difficult to interpret. It indicates an increasing tension between government and opposition parties. On the other hand, this development might also contribute to more alert and animated plenary sessions in the future.

Debates

The plenary session is Finland's most important forum for political debate. Parliament has several opportunities to bring matters of current significance before a plenary session. They include oral questions during the weekly question hour, interpellations, topical discussions, and announcements by the prime minister. Individual MPs also submit written questions to the minister whose sphere of competence covers the matter (Pesonen & Riihinen 2002: 159). All these devices are important to ensure political openness and the proper functioning of democracy. In particular, the question hour provides an occasion for timely debate between the government and the opposition.

For example, the Speaker's Council may decide that a debate be held in plenary session to allow for the representatives to put questions to ministers (question time). The Speaker shall give the floor to MPs for brief questions and to ministers for responses as he or she sees fit (Parliament's Rules of Procedure, section 25). A written question, directed to a minister, must have a defined content and must be answered within 21 days (section 27). Moreover, a MP may propose that a debate be held in plenary session on a given topic issue. The Speaker's Council decides whether such a debate will be held or not (section 26).

Compared to the Anglo-Saxon tradition the plenary sessions in Finland have been few, short and formal. As time passed, the focus on the committees became stronger and the plenary sessions lost their position as an important arena for public debate and decision making. Not until the 1990s were the plenary sessions revived. When the parliamentary rule was stabilized, the party leaders and the ministers returned to parliament and the speeches regained their persuasive power (Nousiainen 1998: 175, 195).

As a side-effect of the EU scrutiny in the Finnish parliament the standards of ministers and leading politicians were raised. The internal sources of information have grown and the knowledge level among the MPs has improved. In combination with the fact that nowadays the media are much more present in parliament the debates in plenary sessions have been vitalized. Therefore, even the Finnish parliament has to greater extent become a debating parliament. Thirty years ago the element of debate was almost completely missing in the Finnish parliament. That is not the case anymore.

Despite the fact that the parliament now is more powerful than ever, the parliament is overshadowed by surplus governments (Raunio & Wiberg 2014: 11). Unlike the Scandinavian model, Finland has a long and strong tradition of surplus majority coalitions. After the war no less than 59 per cent of the Finnish governments have been of this kind. Together with Italy, Finland is the promised land of surplus majority coalitions. These two countries have produced half of all the surplus majority coalitions in Western Europe (Isaksson 2013: 136–140; Gallagher *et al.* 2011: 433–435).

By contrast, Sweden, Norway or Denmark have not had a single surplus majority coalition after the war. In these countries single-party minority cabinets have been predominant; in Denmark minority coalitions as well. In fact, 45 per cent of all single-party minority cabinets in Western Europe after the WWII can be traced to these three Scandinavian countries (Gallagher *et al.* 2011: 433–435).

Conclusions

In the literature a distinction is often made between two basic concepts of legislative assembly in pluralist democracies: *working* parliaments and *debating* parliaments. A clear distinction between these two types cannot be made. However, a parliament can be considered to be of the 'working' variety if the significant policy deliberation takes place largely outside the plenary sessions. The Nordic parliaments can be considered as 'working parliaments' as a consequence of the fact that all Nordic countries have specialist standing committees systems (Arter 1999: 213–215).

The centrality of the specialist committees has underlined and reinforced the predominant and preferred role of Nordic parliamentarians, namely that of *expert*. According to Norton's classification of legislative assemblies into policy-making, policy-influencing and policy-legitimising bodies, all the Nordic parliaments may be placed in the category of *policy-influencing assemblies,* meaning that the assemblies can transform policy but only by reacting to executive initiatives (Arter 1999: 241–242; Heywood 1997: 306).

The fundamental shape of the Finnish parliament has obviously changed during the last decades. The essence of this transformation is a result of the more powerful position of the parliament and the adaptation to EU membership.

On a general level the range of the parliamentary authority has expanded when parliament has taken control over essential presidential powers. The most important of these is the authority over government formation. In a parliamentary system government formation should explicitly be a task for the parliament. In addition, parliamentary control has been extended to domains that earlier were out of the reach of the parliament. When the power domains of the government have increased, the controlling functions of the parliament have increased as well. Above all, this refers to the reforms of dissolution of parliament and decision making in the field of foreign policy.

On the other hand, it is obvious that the EU membership has restricted the power of the parliament. However, it must be emphasized that this development has taken place in all EU member states, not only in Finland. The extent of this lost power is difficult to estimate. Anyway, the Finnish system for dealing with EU issues in parliament seems to be quite flexible and smart compared to other EU countries. Above all, the parliamentary connection and control of EU-issues seems to be stronger than in other EU-countries. It seems obvious that Finland successfully has tried to minimize the damages of the power lost to Brussels.

In a parliamentary system the government is, of course, dependent on the confidence of the parliament. However, in many ways the parliament is de facto dependent on government. The relations between parliament and government are, above all, determined by the type of government in office. In Finland surplus majority coalitions are common, though the demand for large parliamentary coalitions has decreased. Until 1992 a parliamentary minority with one third of the parliament seats was able to postpone an approved proposal. By doing this the opposition was able, in fact, to retard or even to block the legislation proposed by the government (Helander 1997: 12–13). This mechanism intensified the Finnish consensus and blurred the line between government and opposition. The abolishment of the mechanism has created more apt circumstances for normal majority parliamentary rule to work. In addition, the divide between government and opposition has become more distinct (Raunio & Wiberg 2014: 29–30).

Despite this reform, the element of consensus has continued in terms of surplus governments. A more common use of minimal-winning governments would create a broader and stronger opposition in parliament. In the committee work, the influence of the opposition parties would probably increase, at least occasionally. Moreover, a more manifest opposition would vitalize the political debate in parliament further. The plenary sessions would to a greater extent become a place of public debate on an equal basis between government and opposition. The elements of a policy-debating as well as a policy-making parliament would be strengthened. If this were to be the case, the Finnish parliamentary system would, again, move closer to the Scandinavian form of parliamentary rule.

References

Anckar, D. (1984*). Folket och presidenten. En författningspolitisk studie.* Helsingfors, Finska Vetenskaps-Societeten.

— (1990). Finland: Dualism och konsensus. In E. Damgaard (ed.), *Parlamentarisk forandring i Norden.* Oslo, Universitetsforlaget: 131–175.

Arter, D. (1999). *Scandinavian politics today.* Manchester, Manchester University Press.

— (2006). *Democracy in Scandinavia. Consensual, majoritarian or mixed?* Manchester and New York, Manchester University Press.

Damgaard, E., (ed.) (1990). *Parlamentarisk forandring i Norden.* Oslo, Universitetsforlaget.

Damgaard, E. (2008). Cabinet Termination. In K. Strøm, W. C. Müller & T. Bergman (eds.), *Cabinets and Coalition Bargaining. The Democratic Life Cycle in Western Europe.* Oxford, Oxford University Press: 301–326.

Davidsson, L. (2004). *Kammare, kommuner och kabinett.*

Stockholm, SNS Förlag.

De Winter, L. (1995). The Role of Parliament in Government Formation and Resignation. In H. Döring (ed.), *Parliaments and Majority Rule in Western Europe.* Frankfurt, Campus Verlag: 115–151.

De Winter, L. & Dumont, P. (2008). Uncertainty and Complexity in Cabinet Formation. In K. Strøm, W. C Müller & T. Bergman (eds.), *Cabinets and Coalition Bargaining. The Democratic Life Cycle in Western Europe.* Oxford, Oxford University Press: 123–158.

Gallagher, M., Laver, M. & Mair, P. (2001). *Representative Government in Modern Europe. Institutions, Parties, and Governments.* New York, McGraw-Hill Higher Education.

— (2011). *Representative Government in Modern Europe.* New York, McGraw-Hill Higher Education.

Hague, R. & Harrop, M. (2007). *Comparative Government and Politics. An Introduction*, Houndmills, Palgrave Macmillan.

Helander, V. (1997). Legislative Resolutions in the Finnish Eduskunta. In G.-E. Isaksson (ed.), *Inblickar i nordisk parlamentarism.* Meddelanden från Ekonomisk-statsvetenskapliga fakulteten vid Åbo Akademi, Ser. A:470. Åbo, Åbo Akademi: 1–21.

Helander, V. & Pekonen, K. (2007). Eduskunnan vahvistuva valiokuntalaitos. In V. Helander, K. Pekonen, J. Vainio & T. Kunttu, *Valiokunnat lähikuvassa. Suomen Eduskunta 100 vuotta, osa 7.* Helsinki, Edita: 10–138.

Heywood, A. (1997). *Politics.* London, Macmillan Press.

Isaksson, G-E. (2001). Parliamentary Government in Different Shapes. *West European Politics* Vol. 24, 4: 40–54.

— (2005). From Election to Government: Principal Rules and Deviant Cases. *Government and Opposition* Vol. 40, 3: 329–357.

— (2013). *Regering eller opposition? Regeringsbildningar i Norden och i Västeuropa under sex årtionden.* Stockholm, Santérus Förlag.

Jansson, J.-M. (1992). *Från splittring till samverkan. Parlamentarismen i Finland.* Borgå, Söderströms.

— (1999). Från regeringsformen till Grundlagen. *Historisk Tidskrift för Finland* 84: 538–559.

Jyränki, A. & Nousiainen, J. (2006). *Eduskunnan muuttuva asema. Suomen Eduskunta 100 vuotta, osa* 2. Helsinki, Edita.

Laver, M. & Schofield, N. (1990). *Multiparty Government. The Politics of Coalition in Europe.* Oxford, Oxford University Press.

Lijphart, A. (1994). Presidentialism and Majoritarian Democracy: Theoretical Observations. In J. J. Linz & A. Valenzuela (eds.), *The Failure of Presidential Democracy. Comparative Perspectives.* Volume 1. Baltimore, Johns Hopkins University Press: 91–105.

Lindman, S. (1979). *Presidentens ställning. Fyra uppsatser och en efterskrift.* Meddelanden från Stiftelsens för Åbo Akademi Forskningsinstitut, Nr 45. Åbo, Åbo Akademi.

Linz, J. J. & Valenzuela A., (eds.), (1994). *The Failure of Presidential Democracy. Comparative Perspectives.* Volume 1. Baltimore: Johns Hopkins University Press.

Mattila, M. (2014). Valiokuntalaitos. In T. Raunio & M. Wiberg (eds.), *Eduskunta. Kansanvaltaa puolueiden ja hallituksen ehdoilla.* Helsinki, Gaudeamus: 119–131.

Mattila, M. & Raunio, T. (2002). Government Formation in the Nordic Countries: The Electoral Connection. *Scandinavian Political Studies* Vol. 25, 3: 259–280.

Mitchell, P. & Nyblade, B. (2008). Government Formation and Cabinet Type. In K. Strøm, W. C. Müller & T. Bergman (eds.), *Cabinets and Coalition Bargaining. The Democratic Life Cycle in Western Europe.* Oxford, Oxford University Press: 201–236.

Müller W. C. & Strøm, K. (2000). *Coalition Governments in Western Europe.* Oxford, Oxford University Press.

— (2000). Conclusion. Coalition

Governance in Western Europe. In W. C. Müller & K. Strøm (eds.), *Coalition Governments in Western Europe*. Oxford, Oxford University Press: 559–592.

Noponen, M. (1989). Kansanedustajan toimi, sen hoitotapa ja kehitys. In M. Noponen (ed.), *Suomen kansanedustusjärjestelmä*. Porvoo, WSOY: 165–224.

Nousiainen, J. (1998). *Suomen poliittinen järjestelmä*. Juva, WSOY. —(2006). *Eduskunnan muuttuva asema. Suomen Eduskunta 100 vuotta, osa 2*. Helsinki, Edita.

Persson, T. (2008). Book reviews. The Presidentialization of Politics: A Comparative Study of Modern Democracies. *Democratization* Vol. 15, 2: 433–435.

Pesonen, P. & Riihinen, O. (2002). *Dynamic Finland. The Political System and the Welfare State*. Helsinki, Finnish Literature Society.

Poguntke, T. & Webb, P. (eds.), (2005). *The Presidentialization of Politics. A Comparative Study of Modern Democracies*. Oxford, Oxford University Press.

Raunio, T. (2008). Parlamentaarinen vastuu ulkopolitiikkaan: Suomen ulkopolitiikan johtajuus uuden perustuslain aikana. *Politiikka* Vol. 50, 4: 250–265. — (2011). Semi-presidentialism and the Dual Executive in EU Affairs: What Can We Learn from the Finnish Experience? In T. Persson & M. Wiberg (eds.), *Parliamentary Government in the Nordic Countries at a Crossroads. Coping with Challenges from Europeanisation and Presidentialisation*. Stockholm, Santérus Academic Press: 301–325.

Raunio, T. & Wiberg, M. (2014). Johdanto. Eduskunta Suomen poliittisessa järjestelmässä. In T. Raunio & M. Wiberg (eds.), *Eduskunta. Kansanvaltaa puolueiden ja hallituksen ehdoilla*. Helsinki, Gaudeamus: 7–38.

Saalfeld, T. (2008). Institutions, Chance, and Choices: The Dynamics of Cabinet Survival. In K. Strøm, W. C. Müller & T. Bergman (eds.), *Cabinets and Coalition Bargaining. The Democratic Life Cycle in Western Europe*. Oxford, Oxford University Press: 327–368. —(2009). Intra-party conflict and cabinet survival in 17 West European democracies, 1945–1999. In D. Giannetti & K. Benoit (eds.), *Intra-Party Politics and Coalition Governments*. London, Routledge: 169–186.

Strøm, K. & Budge, I. & Laver M. J. (1994). Constraints on Cabinet Formation in Parliamentary Democracies. *American Journal of Political Science* Vol. 38, 2: 303–335.

Wiberg, M. & Mattila, M. (1997). Committee Assignments in the Finnish Parliament 1945–1994. In G.-E. Isaksson (ed.), *Inblickar i nordisk parlamentarism*. Meddlanden från Ekonomisk-statsvetenskapliga fakulteten vid Åbo Akademi, Ser. A: 470. Åbo, Åbo Akademi: 221–244.

The Changing Balance of Power between President and Cabinet

HEIKKI PALOHEIMO

International literature has traditionally categorized the Finnish political system as semi-presidential, with the executive functions divided between an elected president and a cabinet that is accountable to the parliament. From the 1980s on, the semi-presidential division of power became under pressure and gradually changed towards a parliamentary system. There have been both external and internal pressures contributing this development.

The semi-presidential style of government adopted in the first years of independence was a result of social developments before Finnish independence, intentions of the conservatives to counter the revolutionary pressures of the socialist labour movement, and of compromises between conservative and liberal politicians concerning the division of power between different government institutions. Conservatives wanted to have a monarchy or at least an executive vested with strong powers. Liberals were in favour of parliamentary democracy.

In the semi-presidential system, there was a divided executive (Nousiainen 1971). The president had large independent powers. The government (cabinet) headed by the prime minister, and responsible to the parliament, runs the daily business of the executive. The president was the effective head of the executive. Governments were in many instances subordinate to the president. The power of the president varied according to political situations without any changes in the constitution. Some presidents wanted to use their powers in full, some wanted to leave a bigger and more important political role for the government.

In the old semi-presidential regime, the president was elected by an electoral college (Nousiainen 1971: 239–251). Every sixth year, citizens elected 300 electors to elect the president for the nation. The president had supreme executive powers. For the general government of the state, there was the plenary meeting of the government (cabinet) or the council of state (*valtioneuvosto*), as it is called in Finnish constitution. It is headed by the prime minister and is politically responsible to the parliament (*eduskunta*).

According to the old constitution (Act 94/1919), the president appointed governments, presented government bills to parliament, ratified laws approved by parliament, issued decrees, led Finnish foreign policy, appointed judges to the supreme court, the supreme administrative court and courts of appeal as well as senior civil servants, was the head of the armed forces, could grant pardons, had the right to dissolve the parliament and call premature general elections, and to convene extraordinary sessions of the parliament. These duties included legislative, executive, and judicial powers.

In the semi-presidential era, the division of power in the Finnish political executive varied from one period to another without there necessarily being any changes in the constitution. The Finnish semi-presidential system was, As Dag Anckar (2000) has put it, like a buffet table for the presidents. It was up to the president to choose which constitutional powers vested in the president they wanted to choose from the constitutional buffet table for their active use. Some presidents have been quite moderate in using their powers, leaving much room for the parliamentary side of the executive body. Some others have used their powers more actively. President Kekkonen was, as Anckar puts it, a *gourmand*. But none of the Finnish presidents have been real ascetics in using the powers of the president, not even those presidents who have had a highly parliamentary ethos.

Table 1. Presidential elections in Finland

Year	Name of president	Party of president	Method of election	Supporting coalition
1919	Dr. Kaarlo J. Ståhlberg	Liberal	Elected by parliament	Liberals Agrarians Social democrats
1925	Dr. Lauri Relander	Agrarian	Election by t electoral college	Agrarians Conservatives Swedish

1931	Mr. Pehr E. Svinhufvud	Cons	Election by electoral college	Conservatives Agrarians Part of Swedish
1937	Mr. Kyösti Kallio	Agrarian	Election by t electoral college	Agrarians Social democrats Part of Liberals
1940	Mr. Risto Ryti	Liberal	Elected by electoral college of 1937	Almost all parties
1943	Mr. Risto Ryti	Liberal	Elected by electoral college of 1937	Almost all parties
1944	Marshall C.G.E Mannerheim	non partisan	Elected by parliament	Almost all parties
1946	Dr. Juho K. Paasikivi	Cons	Elected by t parliament	Most parties
1950	Dr. Juho K. Paasikivi	Cons	Election by electoral college	Conservatives Social democrats Swedish
1956	Dr. Urho Kekkonen	Agrarian	Election by electoral college	Agrarians People's democrats Part of Liberals
1962	Dr. Urho Kekkonen	Agrarian	Election by electoral college	Agrarians Conservatives Liberals Swedish
1968	Dr. Urho Kekkonen	Centre	Election by electoral college	People's democrats Social democrats Centre party Liberal Swedish
1974	Dr. Urho Kekkonen	Centre	Kekkonen's term of office was extended with four years by a law passed by parliament	Most parties
1978	Dr. Urho Kekkonen	Centre	Election by electoral college	People's democrats Social democrats Centre party Swedish Conservatives
1982	Dr. Mauno Koivisto	Social democrat	Election by electoral college	Social democrats People's democrats
1988	Dr. Mauno Koivisto	Social democrat	Election by electoral college	Social democrats Conservatives
1994	Mr. Martti Ahtisaari	Social democrat	Direct election by the people	
2000	Mrs. Tarja Halonen	Social democrat	Direct election by the people	
2006	Mrs. Tarja Halonen	Social democrat	Direct election by the people	
2012	Mr. Sauli Niinistö	Cons	Direct election by the people	

Source: Pietiäinen 1992; Mylly 1993; Turtola 1993; Väyrynen 1994; Paloheimo 1994; Statistics Finland 2002; 2012.

During the semi-presidential era, prime ministers could not assume the role of a national leader in the same way as their colleagues in pure parliamentary systems. Instead, their role was to supervise the day-to day politics taking into consideration the policy preferences of both parliament and president, and, especially after the Second World War, accepting president's sovereign leadership in foreign policy. With good reasons, some governments with their prime ministers could be called the president's governments.

In 1944–1946, prime minister J.K. Paasikivi was the incontestable leader of Finnish foreign policy, his goal being to improve Finnish relations with the Soviet Union. When he was elected president, in 1946, he monopolised foreign policy leadership (Turtola 1993). Paasikivi's successor, president Urho Kekkonen (1956–1981) followed the same tradition (Väyrynen 1994). When Kekkonen was president he gradually increased his power in domestic affairs, too. In this period the power of the president was in its highest (Arter 1981: 219–234; Anckar 1990). Kekkonen became so actively involved in party disputes that the president gradually became vulnerable to open criticism. From the latter half of Kekkonen's presidency on, presidents have been publicly criticised in the media just as any other politicians.

The combination of the president's prerogatives to appoint cabinets, to influence the party composition of the cabinet, to dismiss a cabinet indirectly by dissolving the parliament, and his role as a gate keeper in selecting single ministers, made the Finnish president in the 1970s an almost omnipotent head of the state. The power of the Finnish president in the 1970s was greater than that of the president in any democratic presidential system. In a presidential regime, there is always the system of checks and balances between legislature and executive. But in Finnish politics, parliamentary party groups were humble since they were familiar with the role of the president as a gate keeper in cabinet formation and also in terminating cabinets by calling a premature general election. It made David Arter (1981) wonder whether Kekkonen's rule was not a case of enlightened despotism.

There have been nine non-partisan caretaker cabinets. All these cabinets have clearly been cabinets of the president. Prime ministers in stable majority coalitions have secured more independence in relation to the president. Before the Second World War, and still in the 1950s, the coalition capacity of Finnish political parties was low, minority cabinets were typical and the average life span of the cabinets was about one year. As a result, cabinets were weak, and prime ministers were left in shadow compared to the president. From the 1960s on, the coalition capacity of Finnish parties increased, and as a result, majority cabinets became typical, and the life span of cabinets began to increase. In the 1960s and 1970s, there were typically two cabinets during an electoral term. From the 1980s on, all the cabinets have been majority coalitions, and in most cases cabinets have been in office over the whole electoral term.

This development strengthened the political power of prime ministers in the Finnish political system. Between 1972 and 1987 Kalevi Sorsa, the leader of the Social Democratic Party, was the prime minister in four different cabinets. The combined tenure of his cabinets was almost ten years. He was a strong prime minister and succeeded in raising the power of the prime minister in relation to the president both in domestic issues and in foreign policy. The basis of his powerful position as prime minister was a result of the increased coalition capacity and coalition elasticity of political parties, as well as the increased role of the Social Democratic Party in Finnish political life. But as late as 1987 president hand-picked a new prime minister (Harri Holkeri, in office 1987–1991) from political reserve against the intentions of party leaders.

The strong position of the president in the 1970s was followed by a counterblow in the 1980s. Combined with the rising coalition capacity and coalition elasticity of political parties it increased the parliamentary ethos in political parties, so that political parties, parliament and the next president, Mauno Koivisto (1982–1994), were willing to reform Finnish constitution towards a normal parliamentary system. President Koivisto gave his support to gradual reforms that were made in the constitution. He supported reforms aimed at connecting presidential decision-making closely to decision-making in the cabinet; as a result, the prerogatives of president were to some extent reduced. According to the rhetoric of president Koivisto: if we can make important decisions either by a single decision-maker or jointly by a group of people, it is better to make them jointly.

Three decades of reforms

During the presidency of Koivisto several incremental amendments were made in the constitution to reduce the powers of the
president and to strengthen the functioning of the parliamentary
system. From 1991 on, the president had to chart the opinions of
the chairman of the parliament and the party groups in parliament
before the appointment of a new government and before major
changes were made in the composition of the government (Act
1074/1991). This was a tradition that had been used for decades,
but now it was made compulsory according to the constitution.

From 1991 on, president could not dismiss the cabinet without a
vote of no confidence by the parliament or initiative of the cabinet
(Act 1074/1991). President could not dissolve the parliament and
order a premature general election without the initiative of the
prime minister (Act 1074/1991). This amendment clearly reduced
the power of the president over the cabinet. Before this amendment
the president could always exert pressure on the cabinet, as he could
appeal directly to the people by dissolving parliament.

The president's veto on legislation was weakened in 1987.
Parliament could override the president's legislative veto in the
diet of the following year, whereas earlier it could be done only
after next general election (Act 575/1987). From 1988 on, the same
person may be elected president for no more than two consecutive
terms of office. It was a clear response to Kekkonen's 25 years in
office.

In the 1980s, the system of electing the president was criticized.
According to the criticism, the election of the president in the
electoral-college included too much logrolling connected to the
power game between political parties. At the same time, there arose
discussion on the need for increasing direct citizen participation in
politics (Sänkiaho 1990). As a result of these pressures, government
gave a bill to reform the electoral system of presidential elections.
The new election law (Act 1074/1991) went into effect in 1991.
From 1994 on, presidents have been elected with a direct two stage
run-off election. If none of the candidates has received a majority
of the votes cast, a new election shall be held between the two candidates with the most votes. This reform also raised some criticism.
The point of the critics was that a direct popular election of the
president would make him even more independent and his role even

more important, which is against the objectives of other reforms made in the constitution (Paloheimo 1994: 122). It is evident that the introduction of direct popular presidential election later intensified new demands to reduce the powers of the president.

Finland's entry to the European Union (EU) increased demands to reduce the powers of the president (see the chapter by Raunio). In EU issues, there is no clear borderline between foreign policy and domestic policy. Had the president been responsible for leading Finnish policies in the EU, the president's powers would have increased in areas that traditionally have been domestic issues (economic policy, welfare policy) and mainly the responsibility of the cabinet. The other alternative was to make the cabinet responsible for Finnish EU policy. In this case, power of the cabinet would grow at the expense of the president, and the Finnish political system move closer to a normal parliamentary system.

The latter alternative was chosen. When Finland entered the European Economic Area (EEA) in 1994 and the European Union (EU) in 1995, new sections were written to the old constitution (Act 116/1993). These new sections made cabinet responsible for the national preparation of issues to be decided in the EU. They also made it compulsory for the cabinet to inform the parliament beforehand on Finnish policy stances in EU issues. The president is still responsible for other areas of Finnish foreign policy. This division in foreign policy leadership was also incorporated into the new constitution in 2000.

It was typical in this period of parliamentarisation from the 1980s on that coalition capability of the parties was high. Cabinets were strong and stable. All cabinets have been majority coalitions and with some exceptions they have been in office over the whole electoral term. In the 1950s, Finnish cabinets were the most unstable in the Nordic countries, and with Italy, the most unstable among European democracies. From the 1980s on, Finnish cabinets have been most stable among the Nordic countries.

As a result of reduced presidential powers, stability of coalitions, and an increased parliamentary ethos, cabinets have been much stronger than earlier, and during the presidency of Martti Ahtisaari (1994–2000) prime ministers challenged the president as the effective executive leader. In 1994, prime minister Esko Aho had a dispute with president Ahtisaari over Finnish representation

at EU summits. President Ahtisaari wanted the president to represent Finland at EU summits. According to prime minister Aho it
was clear that prime minister should participate. As a compromise,
both president and prime minister participated. This practice made
the division of labour between president and prime minister at EU
summits somewhat blurred.

In March 2000, a totally new constitution went into force (Act
731/1999). It codified the amendments made in the old constitution
in the 1990s, reduced the powers of the president further and continued to strengthen features typical of a parliamentary system. The
new constitution cut off most of the prerogatives of the president
that were typical of the earlier semi-presidential system. In 2012 one
more amendment reduced the powers of the president even further.
According to this amendment (Act 1112/2011) the prime minister
represents Finland at the meetings of the European Council. Prime
ministers are now important negotiators in international arenas.
All these factors strengthen the real power of cabinet and the prime
minister. When cabinets also typically survive over the whole electoral term, we can say that governments in contemporary Finland
are both stable and strong.

The new constitution eliminates all real powers of the president
in the formation of a new cabinet. Parliament elects the prime
minister, who is thereafter appointed to the office by the president.
Before prime minister is elected, the parliamentary party groups
negotiate on the political programme and composition of the
government. President appoints other ministers in accordance
with a proposal made by the prime minister (section 61). Rules
on the resignation of the cabinet as well as on the dissolution of
the parliament restate the amendments made in 1991 (sections 64
and 26). This way of bargaining and forming a new government
increases the real powers of the prime minister. After succeeding
in the process of forming a majority coalition in a parliament with
different ideological cleavages the prime minister rises to be the
clear effective executive head of the country. In most cases, he or
she is also the party leader of the largest party in the parliament.

The president's right to make changes in government bills has
been abolished. In the first years of the new constitution, the president still formally delivered government bills to parliament, but
he/she was tied to the proposal of the cabinet. From 2012 on, the

president does not have even this formal duty anymore. Cabinet, headed by the prime minister, presents government bills to the parliament (Act 1112/2011, section 58).

The parliament may override over president's veto in legislation without delay. If the president does not in three months countersign a law passed in the parliament, it is returned to the parliament. If the parliament readopts the act without material alterations, it goes into force without the president's confirmation (section 77).

The new constitution retains the duality in the leadership of Finnish foreign policy that was established when Finland entered the European Union. According to the new constitution, the foreign policy of the nation is directed by president in co-operation with the government. But on the other hand, government is responsible for the national preparation of decisions to be made in the European Union, and decides on concomitant Finnish measures, unless the decision requires the approval of parliament. Parliament participates in the national preparation of decisions to be made in the EU (section 93).

This arrangement may suggest that Finland has not yet evolved into a fully parliamentary model in this policy domain. The principle in the division of labour between president and cabinet seem clear. However, as the EU develops the borderline between EU matters and other foreign policy issues is becoming increasingly blurred. As a result, a constitutional crisis could be possible if both parts of the executive claim the right to have the final say. In practice, these kind of crises are not probable, at least not highly probable, because there is a highly consensus-prone culture in Finnish foreign policy decision-making. Some tensions remain, however. It became evident in 2014 when policies concerning the Ukraine crisis were discussed. The EU made joint decisions concerning sanctions against Russia. In Finland, some politicians thought that Finland should stay in the line with other EU member states, while some others emphasized the importance of Finnish bilateral relations with Russia, which clearly lies in the area of president's prerogatives.

In the new constitution, the appointment of civil servants is mainly the duty of the government with its ministries. In this area, the powers of the president have been reduced to a very limited group of highest level civil servants, mainly judges and army officers. The president is still the commander-in-chief of the armed forces, and may grant a full or partial pardon from a penalty imposed by a court of law (sections 105 and 128).

To sum up, as a result of the new constitution, the Finnish political system is a parliamentary system with some remaining rudiments of the earlier semi-presidential system. In foreign policy there is a strong tradition of looking for a consensus between the parts of the executive. In domestic policies, the president cannot assert him/herself over the cabinet. A summary of the prerogatives of parliament, government and president according to the new constitution was presented in the introductory chapter of this book.

Government formation

The new constitution totally parliamentarised the process of forming a new cabinet (Paloheimo 2003). The president no longer has any active role in cabinet formation. The new rules increase the power of the parliament and that of the prime minister. After the general election, parliamentary party groups will negotiate on the forming of the new cabinet. A formateur will be selected by the parliamentary party groups. It is probable, but not quite necessary, that the party leader of the largest parliamentary party will lead the first attempt to form a cabinet. The *formateur* negotiates with the parliamentary party groups. Based on these negotiations he or she decides on the party composition of the new cabinet. After successful negotiations concerning the program of the cabinet and the distribution of the portfolios, the parliament nominates the *formateur* as the prime minister. The president then appoints the prime minister based on the nomination by parliament. Other ministers are appointed by the president based on the proposal of the prime minister.

Between the World Wars, most of the Finnish cabinets were minority coalitions or even single party minority governments. After the Second World War, majority coalitions became more common, but still governments were quite unstable. In the 1950s, the average life span of cabinets was less than one year (list of governments in table 2). In the 1960s, the average life span of the cabinets rose to about two years, and from 1983 on, all but three governments have been in office over the whole electoral term.

Until the 1980s, the traditional left-right dimension played an important role in the formation of coalition governments. Cabinets were typically closed coalitions on the left-right dimension. Majority coalitions were either centre-right coalitions (Cent + Swe + Lib + Cons), centre-left coalitions (Left + Soc.dem + Cent and possibly smaller centrist parties), so called red soil coalitions where the Social Democrats and the Centre Party were the main cabinet parties, and in one case (Fagerholm II in 1956) a majority coalition spanning from Social Democrats to Conservatives. In this one-dimensional coalition game, the Centre Party was the median party. It was a necessary partner in all majority coalitions. Before 1987, not a single majority coalition was formed without the Centre Party as a member of the governing coalition.

From the 1980s on, other kinds of cleavages have risen in importance (Grönlund & Westinen 2012). Urbanization has underlined the cleavages between urban and rural areas. Enlarging international co-operation and changes in the international arena after the cold war gave rise to different opinions and goals in foreign policy and international co-operation. Figure 1 gives a rough presentation of the position of political parties in this multidimensional coalition game. From 1987 on, there have been three key players in Finnish government formation, Social Democratic Party (Soc. dem.), Centre Party (Cent), and Conservatives (Cons). After each general election, two out of these three parties have formed the cabinet with some smaller parties, while the third of the above-mentioned parties has stayed in opposition. Smaller parties have been in office even in those cases where the two bigger coalition partners have gained a minimal winning position without any smaller partners. Bigger parties have often wanted cabinets to include smaller parties that they feel ideologically close to. The Social Democrats have often been willing to include the Left Wing Alliance (Left) or the Green League (Greens) or both in the government. The Conservatives, on the other hand, have favoured the Swedish People's Party (Swe) and the Christian Democrats (CD) as minor coalition partners. As a result, in the era of majority coalitions, all Finnish cabinets have been oversized coalitions at the time of their appointment. However, four cabinets (Sorsa III in 1982, Aho in 1994, Katainen in 2014, and Stubb in 2014) have then

Table 2. Governments in Finland 1944–2015

N:o	Date of nomination	Days in office	Prime Minister	Party of PM	Coalition type
29	Nov.17, 1944	151	J.K. Paasikivi II	Cons	qualified majority
30	April 17, 1945	343	J.K. Paasikivi III	Cons	qualified majority
31	March 26, 1946	856	M. Pekkala	Left Party	qualified majority
32	July 29, 1948	596	K.A. Fagerholm I	Soc. dem.	single-party minority
33	March 17,1950	306	U.K. Kekkonen I	Agr/Cent	minority coalition
34	Jan. 17, 1951	246	U.K. Kekkonen II	Agr/Cent	surplus majority
35	Sept. 20, 1951	658	U.K. Kekkonen III	Agr/Cent	surplus majority
36	July 9, 1953	131	U.K. Kekkonen IV	Agr/Cent	minority coalition
37	Nov. 17, 1953	169	S. Tuomioja	Lib	caretaker
38	May 5, 1954	168	Törngren	Swe	surplus majority
39	Oct. 20, 1954	500	U.K. Kekkonen V	Agr/Cent	minimal winning
40	March 3, 1956	450	K.A. Fagerholm II	Soc.dem.	surplus majority
41	May 27, 1957	186	V.J. Sukselainen I	Agr/Cent	minority coalition
42	Nov. 29, 1957	148	R. von Fieandt	non partisan	caretaker
43	April 26, 1958	125	R. Kuuskoski	non partisan	caretaker
44	Aug. 29, 1958	137	K.A. Fagerholm III	Soc.dem.	qualified majority
45	Jan. 13, 1959	913	V.J. Sukselainen II	Agr/Cent	single party minority
46	July 14, 1961	273	M. Miettunen I	Agr/Cent	single party minority
47	April 13, 1962	311	A. Karjalainen I	Agr/Cent	minimal winning
48	Feb. 18, 1963	572	R. Lehto	non partisan	caretaker
49	Sept. 12, 1964	622	J Virolainen	Agr/Cent	minimal winning
50	May 27, 1966	665	R. Paasio I	Soc.dem.	qualified majority
51	March 22, 1968	783	M. Koivisto I	Soc.dem.	qualified majority
52	May 14, 1970	62	T. Aura I	Lib	caretaker
53	July 15, 1970	471	A. Karjalainen IIa	Cent	qualified majority
54	Oct. 29, 1971	117	T. Aura II	Lib	caretaker
55	Feb. 23, 1972	194	R. Paasio II	Soc.dem.	single-party minority
56	Sept. 4, 1972	1012	K. Sorsa I	Soc.dem.	minimal winning
57	June 13, 1975	170	K. Liinamaa	Soc.dem.	caretaker
58	Nov. 30, 1975	304	M. Miettunen II	Cent	qualified majority
59	Sept. 29, 1976	228	M. Miettunen III	Cent	minority coalition
60	May 15,1977	545	K. Sorsa II	Soc.dem.	qualified majority
61	May 25, 1979	1001	M. Koivisto II	Soc.dem.	surplus majority
62	Feb. 19, 1982	315	K. Sorsa IIIa	Soc.dem.	surplus majority

	Dec. 31, 1982	126	K. Sorsa IIIb	Soc.dem.	minimal winning
63	May 6, 1983	1455	K. Sorsa IV	Soc.dem	surplus majority
64	April 30, 1987	1216	H. Holkeri a	Cons	surplus majority
	August 28, 1990	241	H. Holkeri b	Cons	surplus majority
65	April 26, 1991	1159	E. Aho a	Cent	surplus majority
	June 28, 1994	289	E. Aho b	Cent	minimal winning
66	April 13, 1995	1463	P. Lipponen I	Soc.dem.	qualified majority
67	April 15, 1999	1463	P. Lipponen II	Soc.dem.	qualified majority
68	April 17, 2003	68	A. Jäätteenmäki	Cent	surplus majority
69	June 24, 2003	1395	M. Vanhanen I	Cent	surplus majority
70	April 19, 2007	1160	M. Vanhanen II	Cent	surplus majority
71	June 22, 2010	365	M. Kiviniemi	Cent	surplus majority
72	June 22, 2011	1017	J. Katainen a	Cons	surplus majority
	April 4, 2014	81	J. Katainen b	Cons	surplus majority
73	June 24, 2014	94	A. Stubb a	Cons	surplus majority
	Sept. 26, 2014	245	A. Stubb b	Cons	minimal winning
74	May 29, 2015		J. Sipilä	Cent	minimal winning

Source: Governments and ministers since 1917 listed on the website of the Finnish Government http://valtioneuvosto.fi/en/government/history/governments-and-ministers.

eroded during their life span when a member of the coalition has resigned due to policy disagreements. But even these cabinets have secured their position as a majority coalition.

Both the results of general elections and the importance of current policy issues have affected the dynamic of this tripartite coalition game. When issues of international integration have been at the top of the agenda, the Social Democratic Party and the Conservative Party have been closer to each other than to the Centre Party. When welfare state and redistribution issues have been at the centre of attention, the traditional left-right cleavage dominates coalition formation, and increases the probability of a coalition that is closed on the left-right dimension. In these cases the Centre Party stands in the median position, and no majority coalition can be built without its participation. From 1987, five cabinets out of nine have been closed coalitions on the left-right dimension (Aho, Jäätteenmäki, Vanhanen I and II, Kiviniemi). Five cabinets

International orientation
Orientation towards national centres

CONS

SDP   GREENS   SWE

Left   Right
    LEFT   CD

CENT
TF

National orientation
Orientation towards national peripheries

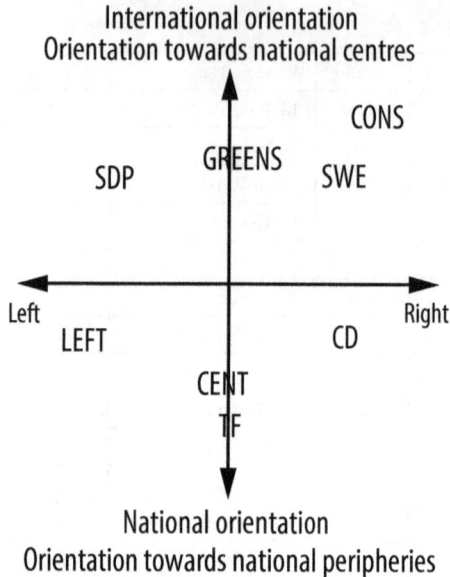

SDP = *Social Democratic Party*
CENT = *Centre Party*
CONS = *National Coalition Party (conservatives)*
LEFT = *Left Wing Alliance*
GREENS = *Green Alliance*
SWE = *Swedish People's Party*
CD = *Christian Democrats*
TF = *The Finns Party*

Figure 1. Finnish political parties on a three-dimensional policy space.

have been open coalitions on the left-right dimension (Holkeri, Lipponen I and II, Katainen, and Stubb).

In most Western European countries, the fragmentation of the party system has to some extent increased during recent decades. This is the result of the rise of populist parties (Norris 2005). The same has happened in Finland, too (Paloheimo 2012). In the general election 2011 the Finns Party won 19 per cent of the vote and became the third largest party in parliament. The shares of conventional left, centre and right-wing parties declined. Negotiations on government formation lasted over two months, which clearly exceeded the typical duration of about one month.

Division of power between president and cabinet

Within the Finnish divided executive there are still two kinds of sessions: *presidential sessions of government*, where the president takes the chair and makes his or her decisions based on cabinet proposals; and *plenary meetings of cabinet* headed by the prime minister. At *presidential sessions*, each issue on the agenda is presented by the minister concerned, but no voting occurs. As in a pure presidential system, the president has the sole right to make the decision in these cases, and is not tied to the opinion of the government. However, the contrary is the case in respect of *plenary meetings of cabinet*. There decisions are made collegially, sometimes putting issues to vote, but typically, pursuing inter-party consensus.

In foreign policy, both president and cabinet enjoy their own prerogatives, which may seem to suggest that Finland has still not evolved into a fully parliamentary model in this policy domain (see the chapter by Raunio). Before 2012, Finland sent both president and prime minister to EU summits. In the French case, the president often alone represents France, when he is supported by a majority in the National Assembly. In the Finnish case, the division of power in international affairs might be regarded as the Achilles' heel of the constitution. The principle seems clear enough: the cabinet should take the lead in EU matters, while the president should take the lead in other international affairs. But the borderline between the two is becoming increasingly blurred as the EU develops. This gives rise to the prospect of a constitutional crisis should the Finnish President and cabinet ever disagree on certain foreign policy matters, with both parts of the executive claiming their right to have the final say (Jyränki 2000). There have still been pressures to remove the remains of semi-presidentialism in foreign affairs especially due to the further integration in the EU. Based on a constitutional amendment that went into force in 2012 (Act 1112/2011), Prime minister now represents Finland in the European Council. Moreover, any unresolved disagreements between president and cabinet in the area of foreign policy shall be left to the parliament to decide.

The President may assert him- or herself over the cabinet in appointing highest level civil servants. In a couple of cases, president Halonen has appointed top-level civil servants against the express wishes of the cabinet. But this prerogative of the president was limited further by a constitutional amendment in 2012 (Act

1112/2011). The president no longer has the authority to appoint even top-level civil servants in the line organisation of the public administration. The idea is that in the line organization of public administration all civil servants serve the government; as a result, the cabinet should have the power to nominate its own servants.

All presidents have had their own styles of preparing, making and implementing policy decisions. President Kekkonen (1956–81) was eager to build an informal inner circle of his own (Apunen 1984; Väyrynen 1994). He appointed his close trustees to various strategic positions in the civil service, and then, in the preparation of government policies, often had contacts and gave orders to his entrusted civil servants without informing cabinet ministers. In some cases, ministers found out later that they had not been informed about policy orders given by the president to civil servants. In formal decision-making president Kekkonen also every now and then made decisions against the will of the cabinet.

The next president, Koivisto (1982–94), wanted to have a closer co-operation with the cabinet (Paloheimo 1994; Majander 2013). He said that when he was prime minister (1979–81) during Kekkonen's last turn in presidency, it was confusing to find that he should have known something he did not know. President Koivisto also put more stress on consensus-prone decision-making with the cabinet. This clearly increased the actual political power of the cabinet in political decision-making.

Martti Ahtisaari rose to the presidency (1994–2000) without any active background in party politics. He was a member of the Social Democratic Party, and had done his career as a civil servant in the ministry of foreign affairs. His reputation was based on his achievements in international crisis management. His knowledge of domestic affairs was thin, and in several policy issues he was overrun by the cabinet (Väyrynen 2013). Ahtisaari also had disagreements with the cabinet on Finnish representation at the summits of the European Union. Ahtisaari tried to strengthen his position by organizing a cabinet of his own in the office of the president. This tradition of having a cabinet in the office of the president has been used after the presidency of Ahtisaari. The tensions between president Ahtisaari and the government increased political parties' willingness to prepare and enact a new constitution (Act 731/1999) that reduced powers of the president. President Ahtisaari did not like the government's eagerness to reduce the powers of the president, but he did not have the authority to prevent these changes.

Due to tensions between president Ahtisaari and the Social Democratic Party, the party did not even ask president Ahtisaari to stand for presidency in the next election. In the presidential election in 2000, the Social Democratic candidate, foreign minister Tarja Halonen was elected. She again had her own style of presidential leadership (Lehtilä 2013; Tiilikainen 2013). Questions of sustainable development, inequality, poverty on the global level, and the position of women in society were prominent on Halonen's policy agenda. The traditionally quite realist foreign policy style turned somewhat towards a more idealist policy stance. In preparing of this more idealist foreign policy Halonen involved a small group of like-minded politicians and civil servants. As a result, there were occasionally tensions between president and top-level civil servants of the ministry of foreign affairs.

From 1982 to 2012 Finland had a president with a Social Democratic background. Before that all Finnish presidents had a centre, liberal or conservative political background. The period of presidents Koivisto, Ahtisaari, and Halonen was the high tide of Finnish Social Democracy. It was an uninterrupted 30-year period of Social Democratic presidents. During this period the Social Democrats were in cabinet for 22 years, and there was a Social Democratic prime minister for 13 years.

During this 30-year period the support for the Social Democratic Party in parliamentary election declined from 27 per cent in 1983 to 19 per cent in 2011, and the combined support for Social Democrats and Left Party declined from 40 to 27 per cent. In the presidential election 2012 the Conservative candidate Sauli Niinistö was elected. In the second round of the election a majority of the typical voters of the centre-right parties gave their support to Niinistö. As president, Niinistö has taken some steps back towards the so-called realist foreign policy. In issues of security policy, he stresses co-operation between Western European nations. In the Ukraine crisis from 2014 onwards both president and cabinet supported joint EU actions, but the president also had bilateral discussions with Russian leaders.

Division of power between parliament and cabinet

The Finnish parliament has mainly been a policy-influencing assembly (Heywood 2013: 323–325; Arter 2008: 193–208), in line with most parliamentary systems. During earlier decades, two factors strengthened the power of parliament in relation to the cabinet. Until the 1970s, governments were mostly weak and unstable. Moreover, all the way the early 1990s, one third of the MPs could effectively veto legislation, which strengthened the power of the opposition in relation to government. However, with the stabilization of majority cabinets and the concomitant loss of opposition power to delay legislation, the Finnish parliament has effectively become an executive-dominated assembly that exerts but marginal influence on most issues. About 99 per cent of legislation is based on government bills, and ministers' supporters in parliament are active in supervising the legislative timetable (Paloheimo 2002). Virtually all private legislative initiatives taken by MPs fail. The high tide of parliament's power vis-à-vis the executive now occurs during the formation of new governments. During such periods, parliamentary party groups can make policy proposals, which, if included in the programme of the new government, become politically binding.

Even when majority governments are in office, parliament is not totally subordinate to the cabinet. The prime minister and other ministers always have to monitor reactions among their parliamentary party groups (Paloheimo 2002). Ministers in a coalition government usually have to be sensitive to reactions in parliament. Tensions in the parliament often also increase tensions between the partners of the coalition cabinet. Any major changes in government bills must be based on discussions between cabinet ministers and leaders of parliamentary party groups of the governing parties.

The rising role of prime minister can be seen in his/her activity in the general debates of the parliament. In the 1970s and in the 1980s, some prime ministers appeared in parliament only a couple of times a year. From the 1990s on, prime ministers have addressed the general meetings of the parliament more than one hundred times annually (Murto 1994; Aula 2003: 96–98).

Division of power within the cabinet

Decision-making inside the government may be organized in many different ways. In some countries, the prime minister is the main decision-maker. In some others, most decisions are made collegially at cabinet meetings. And still others use ministerial governance where ministers as heads of their ministries or departments make a large part of the decisions in the name of the government. The Finnish tradition of decision-making has been very centralized and collegial. Most decisions have been made collegially at the plenary meeting of the cabinet, while minor departmental issues have been decided by individual ministers (Nousiainen 1975). For a number of decades, the work load of the cabinet has increased dramatically. In the first decades of Finnish independence, ministers could sit at the plenary meeting of the cabinet in order to discuss and modify single paragraphs of government bills and decrees. When the work load increased governments had unofficial preparatory discussions at the so-called evening class of the cabinet, and the plenary meeting of the cabinet became more of a formal arena of decision-making.

As a result of the rising work load, cabinet decision-making was decentralized in the mid-1990s, and the scope of individual ministerial governance expanded correspondingly. Thus, whereas in the late 1980s about 2000 decisions a year were made at cabinet plenary meetings, since the late 1990s, this number has fallen to between 500 and 700 (Statistics Finland 2002: 555). In any case, as the number of issues on the agenda has risen continuously since the 1960s, informal arenas of decision-making have become more important, while plenary meetings have been left as an arena of formal decision-making.

Along with the decentralization of cabinet decision-making some new kinds of policy instruments were developed (Tiili 2008). One of them was frame budgeting. Earlier, the expenditures of the ministries were allocated in detail to different sections of the ministry according to the purpose of the expenditure. With the new system of frame budgeting ministries have more freedom to allocate budget expenditures given to the ministry within the budget limits of the ministry. Another novelty was a programme-based view of policy-making. With time, government programmes have become increasingly important. Still in the 1960s, government programmes

Table 3. Decisions made by the President in the Government

	1997	2000	2005	2010
Government proposals, ratification of laws	500	429	455	596
Other affairs concerning the Parliament	33	17	18	14
Decrees	415	124	52	70
Personnel affairs	248	94	83	64
International affairs	160	102	69	98
Åland affairs	80	14	13	22
Affairs concerning the Government	6	10	2	3
Naturalisations	991	–	–	–
Pardon petitions	230	176	20	19
Life saving medals	1	22	–	–
Honorary titles	201	218	2	3
Public service medals and other decorations	974	1214	2	3
Others	4	8	8	1
Total	3843	2428	724	893

Source: Statistical Yearbook of Finland.

Table 4. Decisions in Plenary Meetings of the Cabinet

	1997	2000	2005	2010
Personnel affairs	168	150	213	171
Norm decisions	135	35	4	6
Government resolutions (decrees)	–	279	287	259
Administrative decisions	–	–	17	20
Decisions in principle/plans	22	25	12	27
Secondary organisations	107	139	73	73
Financial steering	91	82	63	63
Licences	53	17	23	25
Reports and communications to the Parliament	5	4	6	13
Parliament's communications	–	8	21	20
President of the Republic/Government	14	17	24	19
Incomes agreements/collective bargaining agreements	1	1		
Government statements	65	82	55	56
International and European Union affairs	–	28	39	59
Others	15	5	14	4
Total	676	872	851	815

Source: Statistical Yearbook of Finland.

typically consisted of about five pages. From the 1980s on, the length of government programmes has increased dramatically. The programme of Matti Vanhanen's first cabinet was 56 pages, that of his second cabinet 82 pages. The length of the programme of Jyrki Katainen's cabinet was 89 pages.[1] These modern cabinet programmes are packages of comprehensive policy plans over the whole electoral term.

The change from collegial to ministerial decision-making has had several effects on the working of the government. As individual ministers gained increased powers in decision-making in their own policy areas, their activities had to be controlled. In a single party cabinet this is typically the responsibility of the prime minister. In a coalition government this monitoring and control has to done collectively with the coalition parties.

In contemporary Finland, cabinet committees and special ministerial groups play an important role in the preparation of government policy. There are four or five permanent ministerial committees. In 2014 there were four cabinet committees: cabinet committee on foreign and security policy, cabinet committee on European Union affairs, cabinet finance committee, and cabinet committee on economic policy. There were also 12 working groups of the cabinet for the following policy areas: educational policy, social and health policy, energy and climate policy, basic social services, transport and communications policy, Russian affairs, fight against the shadow economy, internet security, integration and migration policy, monitoring work on the Government foresight report, and Sami affairs.

Typically, each coalition party is represented on each cabinet committee and in most of the working groups. The latter function as watchdogs of multi-party cohabitation by monitoring individual ministers' policy development: their brief is to ensure that individual ministerial power does not endanger the carefully constructed political balance that was crafted during the formation of the governing coalition and the negotiation of a detailed government programme. The prime minister also plays a vital part, since he heads all the permanent cabinet committees, and his

1   Government programmes since 1917 on the website of the Finnish government: http://valtioneuvosto.fi/en/government/history/government-programmes-since-1917.

role has come to resemble that of the managing director of a major corporation; s/he coordinates government activity and seeks to ensure that the spirit of the coalition agreement is adhered to.

Since 2000, the prime minister and his/her office have also gained power by taking on the responsibility for coordinating the preparation of policy relevant to the EU, a task transferred from the Ministry of Foreign Affairs. This role tends to increase bilateral connections between the Prime Minister's Office and specific ministries, but EU membership also underlines the importance of those ministers that have major responsibilities in the EU Council of Ministers, such as the Minister of Finance. The increased coordinating task of the prime minister is reflected in the growing resources available in his or her office. Thus, in 1990 there were approximately 150 civil servants working in the Prime Minister's Office, while in 2014 this number is about 250 – a growth rate of 67 per cent in fourteen years.[2]

From the 1990s on, a kind of informal inner cabinet operates in Finland (Murto 1994; Murto *et al.* 1996). This inner cabinet consists largely of the leaders of the coalition parties. They occupy the most important government committees and ministerial working groups and in this way supervise the functioning of ministerial governance. The core of this inner circle consists of the prime minister and the leader of the second major coalition party. These are the two 'biggest hitters' in Finnish government, and any informal understandings they might reach can seriously restrict the bargaining power of smaller coalition parties.

In sum, the Finnish style of governance is a mixture of eroded formal presidential rule, weakened cabinet government, and increased ministerial governance, supervised by a growing network of government committees and ministerial working groups. The prime minister lies at the centre of this network and, in the increasing realm of EU matters, s/he is also the key actor in a new set of bilateral relationships with other decision-makers. Finnish cabinets remain strongly partified in many ways, but there is no doubt that the prime minister enjoys significantly greater power and autonomy than previously.

2   Facts about the personnel of the Prime Minister's Office,
    see http://vnk.fi/en/personnel.

The rising power of the prime minister in the cabinet is based on his/her new autonomy in relation to the president, his/her active informal role in building the daily agenda of the government, his/her importance in settling of internal cabinet disputes (a job that was earlier often done by the president), and his/her role as the conductor in the making of Finnish EU policy.

Reasons for government resignation

There have been several reasons for the resignation of governments (table 5). There are parliamentary reasons, such as general election, lack of support in the parliament, and vote of no confidence. There are reasons internal to the government. And thirdly, there are reasons based on relations with the president. Between the World

Table 5. Reasons for cabinet resignation 1945–2015

Reason for resignation	1917–1944	1945–1981	1982–2015	1917–2015
Parliamentary reasons				
General election	1	4	9	14
Lack of support	7	2	0	9
Vote of non-confidence	3	1	0	4
Enlargement of coalition	0	1	0	1
Government reasons				
PM becomes president	4	2	1	7
resignation of PM	1	3	3	7
Disagreement in government	2	6	0	8
Presidential reasons				
Disagreement with president	3	2	0	5
Presidential election	1	2	0	3
Foreign policy reasons	4	2	0	6
Caretaker governments	2	7	0	9
Total	28	32	13	73

Source: Own calculations.

Wars cabinets often resigned as a result of a lacking support in the parliament, and in three cases a vote of no confidence in the parliament. After the Second World War, internal tensions in the cabinet became a more typical reason for government resignation. Between 1953 and 1975 there were also seven caretaker governments which were appointed by the president due to the insufficient coalition capacity of political parties.

From the 1980s on, the profile of government resignations has changed dramatically. In most cases, cabinets have been in office over the whole electoral tern, and resigned following a general election that has been organized at the normal time. The last premature general election was called in 1975. In 1982 the government resigned when prime minister Koivisto was elected president. The prime minister has resigned once as a result of lacking support in the parliament (Jäätteenmäki 2003), and twice because of personal reasons (Vanhanen 2010, Katainen 2014).

The popularity of the government and the electoral success of parties in office are highly dependent on the cyclical situation of the economy. Figure 2 describes these dependencies. The contiguous line in the graph presents annual growth of the volume of gross domestic product (GDP) based on national accounts. The dotted line is an aggregated variable for the satisfaction of citizens with the performance of the current government. It is based on surveys where respondents are asked how satisfied they are with the performance of the government. In the poll offered the following response alternatives: 1) mainly satisfied, 2) mainly not satisfied, and 3) cannot say. The combined measure in the graph is the difference between mainly satisfied and mainly not satisfied respondents. When this variable has positive values, this indicates that there were more respondents that where mainly satisfied with the performance of the government than respondents who were mainly dissatisfied. When the variable displays negative values, this indicates that there were more respondents that were mainly not satisfied. The combined electoral success of all the governing parties is presented with bars. It is the summed up change in the percentage share of all government parties.

There seems to be a very close connection between economic growth and people's satisfaction with government performance. When the economy expands, satisfaction with government per-

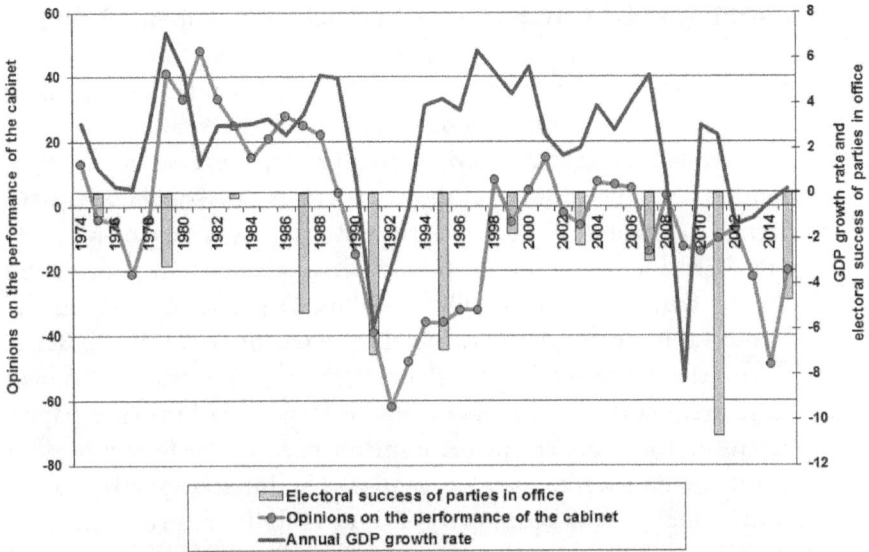

Figure 2. Economic growth, citizen opinions on the performance of the government and the combined electoral success of the governing parties 1974–2015

Source: Finnish Voter Barometer Surveys. Finnish Social Science Data Archive; National Accounts Statistics. Statistics Finland; Election statistics. Statistics Finland.

formance increases. When there is recession, satisfaction declines. During or after deep economic recessions, the governing parties have faced the biggest losses in their combined electoral support. In the general elections of 1991 and 1995, the combined loss of the parties in office was about seven percentage points. In the general election in 2011, it was almost eleven points. The main winner in the general election 2011 was the populist Finns Party with its highly critical policy stance towards the European Union and towards the bailout packages for Greece and other countries in economic crisis.

Citizen expectations about political leadership

In many European democracies, there has been debate about the personalization of politics and the rising role of political leaders. According to several writers, the personal role of party leaders has become more important in their parties, and the personal role of prime ministers as leaders of their governments has increased (Foley

1993; Poguntke & Webb 2005). Michael Foley, Thomas Poguntke and Paul Webb talk about the presidentialization of politics, as the role of prime ministers in parliamentary democracies increasingly resembles the role of presidents in presidential systems.

In Finland, there has been, at least partly, a reverse trend (Paloheimo 2005). The powers of the president as a personal leader have been reduced, and the powers of the government as a collective body have been increased. The trends of personalization in politics will also be found in Finland. The visibility of prime minister in the media has increased dramatically during recent decades. Still in the 1960s, the name of the president of the republic was mentioned more frequently in the pages of the largest nation-wide paper. From the 1980s on, the prime minister has bypassed the president in the media (Murto 1994: 364-365). The internationalization of politics increases the personal role and visibility of prime minister in politics. The stabilization of government coalitions increases the tenure of governments, which again increases the power and visibility of the prime minister. According to Lauri Karvonen's detailed analyses, the assumption that individual politicians and politicians as individuals have come to mean much more for voter behaviour and party choice is however, overstated both in the media and also in parts of the research literature (Karvonen 2010).

On the system and elite level, the Finnish political system has changed from a semi-presidential to a nearly parliamentary one, and the prime minister is in most issues the real executive head. On the mass level, semi-presidential expectations are prominent. The Finnish Business and Policy Forum EVA has in several opinion surveys polled citizen opinions concerning the power of about 20 different social institutions. Respondents have been asked to present their view the power of these institutions. Alternatives have been: 1) too much power, 2) suitable power, 3) too little power.

Table 6 presents citizen opinions on the power of the president and that of the government from 1986 to 2006. In all the surveys in Table 6, a large majority of the respondents have been satisfied with the amount of power of the president as well as that of the government. However, in all the surveys, the number of respondents thinking that president has too little power clearly exceeds the number of respondents thinking that president has too much power. As concerns the power of the government, in each survey

Table 6. Citizen opinions on the power of president and government, 1986–2006

	1986	1988	1990	1998	2002	2006
	%	%	%	%	%	%
President of the republic						
Too much power	7	10	11	21	7	7
Suitably	72	74	75	64	68	62
Too little power	21	16	14	16	26	30
Per cent together	100	100	100	100	100	100
(n)	(2430)	(2459)	(2338)	(2154)	(2092)	(1923)
Government						
Too much power	25	35	52	28	26	14
Suitably	68	60	44	66	71	80
Too little power	7	5	4	7	4	7
Per cent together	100	100	100	100	100	100
(n)	(2410)	(2441)	(2317)	(2135)	(2076)	(1923)

Source: Finnish Business and Policy Forum EVA. National opinion surveys.
Archived in the Finnish Social Science Data Archive FSD: FSD1080 (1986),
FSD1081 (1988), FSD1082 (1990), FSD1086 (1998), FSD1262 (2002),
FSD2292 (2006).

there are more respondents thinking that government has too much power compared to those who think that government has too little power. In the age of the new constitution, the proportion of those respondents that are satisfied with the level of power of the government has risen. But at the same time, the proportion of those who think that the president has too little power has increased. In the survey conducted in 2006, 30 per cent of the respondents thought that the power of the president is too limited. A large part of the population is unhappy with the reduction of presidential powers and would like to have a more semi-presidential regime.

In another 2006 survey, the following statement was tested: 'The power of the president in decision-making should be increased'. A majority of the respondents agreed totally or at least partly. In Table 7, results on this question are presented broken down by gender, age, education and respondent's knowledge of politics. Citizens with a low level of education are more willing to increase the power of the president compared to those having a high level of education. People with a poor knowledge of politics are more willing to

Table 7. The power of the president in political decision-making should be increased: citizen opinions in 2006

	Totally agree, per cent	Partly agree, per cent	Party disagree, per cent	Totally disagree, per cent	Total, per cent	(n)
All	21	33	30	16	100	(891)
Gender						
Men	25	29	25	21	100	(437)
Women	17	36	35	12	100	(454)
Age						
18–34	22	37	33	9	100	(211)
35–49	16	33	35	16	100	(249)
50–64	21	32	27	20	100	(257)
65–	25	29	24	21	100	(174)
Education						
Primary level	36	38	16	10	100	(177)
Lower secondary level	25	35	25	15	100	(184)
Higher secondary level	17	32	36	15	100	(397)
University level	6	24	41	29	100	(128)
Political knowledge						
Poor	27	40	24	9	100	(335)
Average	18	33	35	14	100	(254)
Good	17	25	33	26	100	(302)

Political knowledge is a sum variable of several items measuring respondent's knowledge on political facts.

Source: Finnish Social Science Data Archive, FSD2131 (2006).

increase the power of the president compared to those with a good knowledge of politics. People with a low level of education or poor knowledge of politics have a more positive view of strong personal political leadership compared to those having a high education or good knowledge of politics.

Citizen opinions on the proper type of the democratic regime seem to vary. Some people are more satisfied with the recent changes towards a parliamentary style of executive than some others. A large part of the people would like to have a more powerful presidency than is normal in parliamentary democracies. Those wanting a president with extensive independent powers are typically less educated, working class people who are dissatisfied with the functioning of democracy and the possibilities of citizens to have a say in politics, and dissatisfied with political parties. Those who are satisfied with a parliamentary style of executive where the president has limited powers only are typically well-educated middle class people who have more confidence for political parties as important actors in democracy.

Citizen expectations on a strong presidency have a clear effect on the direct presidential elections in Finland. No candidate who supports a purely parliamentary political system can win presidential elections. Because of citizen expectations about a strong presidency, only candidates wanting to have a fairly strong presidency can make it to the second round of the election. As a result, there will be presidents who want to have an active role as executive heads. However, under the present constitution, presidents cannot any more be the kind of effective executive heads as they were under the old constitution. The present constitution paves the way for the prime minister to be the effective executive head. As a result, especially in foreign affairs there is some rivalry between president and prime minister on the role of the effective executive head.

Based on changes in the Finnish constitution strengthening the prerogatives of parliament and government at the expense of the president, we could expect that voting turnout in parliamentary elections would have risen and, by the same token, fallen in presidential elections. However, the contrary seems to be the case. During the semi-presidential era, voting turnout in presidential elections was always lower compared to the parliamentary elections of the time. The situation changed with the presidential election of 1982. In that election, a new president (Koivisto) was elected after the 25 year tenure of Kekkonen. This election was turning point. After that voting turnout in presidential elections has always been higher than that of the parliamentary elections, notwithstanding the reduced powers of the president.

In her comparative analysis on parliamentary democracies Margit Tavits (2009) has found that voting turnout in parliamentary elections is statistically lower in countries with direct presidential elections compared to countries with indirect presidential elections. She does not give much in the way of a theoretical explanation of this empirical result. One explanation of this paradoxical situation may be found in the varying clarity of political accountability and political alternatives. Voting turnout is higher in elections where it is clear to the voters who is accountable for the policies during the past electoral term (Bengtsson 2002: 103–119). Voting turnout is also higher in elections where the alternatives in the election clearly differ from each other (Bengtsson 2002: 120–127). In Finland, as in many other parliamentary democracies, governments are multiparty coalitions, and in the Finnish case, from the 1990s on, almost any kind of coalition has been politically possible. As a result, it is not very clear who is responsible for the policies of the past electoral term. In parliamentary election campaigns, parties do not tell the citizens which of the other parties they are willing to co-govern with after the election. As a result, it is not clear for the citizens what the real alternatives in the parliamentary elections are. In presidential elections the picture is clearer. It is clear who is responsible of the decisions made by the president during the past presidential term. Compared to the parliamentary elections, the alternatives are clearer, too, and in the second round of the election, in quite a polarized way. All this encourages citizens to use their franchise in presidential elections. It is possible that this contextual difference between presidential and parliamentary elections also increases people's willingness to give more power to the president contrary to the wishes of the political elite.

Conclusion

Since the early 1980s, the regime type of Finnish political system has gradually changed from a semi-presidential to a parliamentary or at least nearly parliamentary political system. This process culminated in the enactment of a totally new constitution in 2000. The new constitution codified amendments made to the old constitution in the 1990s, reduced the powers of the president further and continued to strengthen features typical of a parliamentary system. The new constitution cut off most of the powers of the president that were typical of the earlier semi-presidential system. The president still retains some independent powers, especially in foreign affairs, excluding Finnish relations with the European Union.

Changes in the international context and in Finland's position in it have been the most important factors behind the regime change. The collapse of the Soviet Union made possible the abandonment of personalized presidential leadership in foreign policy. Finnish membership in the European Union has facilitated foreign policy decision-making on a parliamentary basis. In the domestic arena, the increased coalition capacity and coalition elasticity of political parties paved the way for more stable cabinets with less internal erosion.

In contemporary Finland, cabinet is the key player in policy making, and the prime minister the effective executive head. Cabinets in contemporary Finland are majority coalitions, and with some exceptions their life span covers the whole electoral term. With the growing tasks of the public sector and the crowding of political agendas, decision-making in the government has changed. Until the 1990s, decision-making in the Finnish cabinet was collegial. A large part of decisions were made collegially at the plenary meeting of the cabinet. From the 1990s on, government decision-making has been decentralized, and a large part of decisions are nowadays made by single ministers. In a multi-party coalition, ministerial working groups are used to keep an eye on the decision-making of single ministries. Party leaders of the governing parties are also always ministers in contemporary Finnish governments. They are the informal inner circle of the cabinet with the responsibility of finding compromises when there are disagreements between the coalition partners.

While on the system level the Finnish political system has changed from a semi-presidential to a parliamentary one, there has not been a similar change in the civic culture of the nation. A large segment of voters, maybe even half of them, agree with the notion that the power of the president in political decision-making should be increased. As a result, the winning candidate in presidential elections always has to be in favour of quite an active presidency. This keeps at least minor conflicts between parliamentary and semi-presidential ethos alive in political decision-making.

References

Act 94/1919. The Constitution Act of Finland, with later amendments.

Act 731/1999. The Constitution of Finland (see http://www.om.fi/constitution/ 3340.htm).

Anckar, D. (1990). Democracy in Finland: The Constitutional Framework. In J. Sundberg & S. Berglund (eds.), *Finnish Democracy*. Jyväskylä, Finnish Political Science Association: 26–50.

— (2000). Jäähyväiset semipresidentialismille, *Politiikka* Vol. 42, 1: 9–14.

Apunen, O. (1984). Tilinteko Kekkosen aikaan. Ulkopoliittinen valta ja vallankäyttö Suomessa. Helsinki, Kirjayhtymä.

Arter, D. (1981). Kekkonen's Finland: Enlighted Despotism or Consensual Democracy. *West European Politics* Vol. 4, 3: 219–234.

— (2008). *Scandinavian Politics Today*. Second edition. Manchester and New York, Manchester University Press.

Aula, M. K. (2003). Eduskunta Suomen poliittisessa järjestelmässä. In P. Saukkonen (ed.), *Paikkana politiikka*. Acta politica 26. University of Helsinki, Department of Political Science.

Bengtsson, Å. (2002). *Ekonomisk röstning och politisk kontext. En studie av 266 val i parlamentariska demokratiere*. Åbo, Åbo Akademi University Press.

Foley, M. (1993). *The Rise of the British Presidency*. Manchester, Manchester University Press.

Grönlund, K. and Westinen J. (2012). Puoluevalinta. In Sami

Borg (ed.), *Muutosvaalit 2011*. Oikeusministeriö, Selvityksiä ja ohjeita 16/2012: 156–188.

Jyränki, A. (2000). *Uusi perustuslakimme*. Turku, Iura nova.

Karvonen, L. (2010). *The Personalisation of Politics. A Study of Parliamentary Democracies*. Cocchester, ECPR Press.

Lehtilä, H. (2013). *Tarja Halonen. Paremmat maailman puolesta*. Helsinki, Tammi.

Majander. M. (2013). Mauno Koivisto – Yksinäinen sheriffi, filosofikuningas. In S. Tiihonen *et al.* (eds.), *Presidentti johtaa. Suomalaisen valtiojohtamsien pitkä linja*. Helsinki, Kustannusosakeyhtiö Siltala: 213–235.

Murto, E. (1994). *Pääministeri. Hallintohistoriallisia tutkimuksia 13*. Helsinki, Painatuskeskus.

Murto, E., Väänänen, P. & Ikonen, R. (1996). *Sisäpiirit EU-Suomessa. Unioni ja uudet eliitit*. Helsinki, Edita.

Mylly, J. (1993). *Tasavallan presidentit. Svinhufvud, Kallio*. Porvoo, Weilin+Göös.

Norris, P. (2005). *Radical Right. Voters and Parties in the Electoral Market*. New York, Cambridge University Press.

Nousiainen, J. (1971). *Finnish Political System*. Cambridge, Harvard University Press.

Nousiainen, J. (1975). Valtioneuvoston järjestysmuoto ja sisäinen toiminta. In *Valtioneuvostonhistoria 1917–1966*, vol. III. Helsinki, Valtion painatuskeskus: 217–390.

Paloheimo, H. (1994). *Tasavallan presidentit. Koivisto.* Porvoo, Weilin+Göös.
— (2002). Pääministerin vallan kasvu Suomessa. *Politiikka* Vol. 44, 3: 203–221.
— (2003). The Rising Power of Prime Minister in Finland. *Scandinavian Political Studies* Vol. 26, 3: 219–243.
— (2005). Finland: Let the Force Be with the Leader – But Who Is the Leader? In T. Poguntke and P. Webb (eds.), *The Presidentialization of Politics. A Comparative Study of Modern Democracies.* Oxford, Oxford University Press: 246–268.
— (2012). Support for Populist Parties in the Nordic Countries. In C. Anckar and D. Anckar (eds.), *Comparison, Regimes, Elections. Festscrift for Lauri Karvonen.* Åbo, Åbo Akademi University Press: 335–353.
Pietiäinen, J.-P. (1992). *Tasavallan presidentit. Ståhlberg, Relander.* Helsinki, Weilin+Göös.
Poguntke, T. & P. Webb (eds.) (2005). *The Presidentialization of Politics. A Comparative Study of Modern Democracies.* Oxford, Oxford University Press.
Statistics Finland (2002). *Statistical Yearbook of Finland 2002.* Helsinki, Statistics Finland.
Statistics Finland (2012). *Statistical Yearbook of Finland 2012.* Helsinki, Statistics Finland.
Sänkiaho, R. (ed.) (1990). *People and Their Polities.* Jyväskylä, The Finnish Political Science Association.

Tavits, M. (2009). *Presidents with Prime Ministers.* Oxford, Oxford University Press.
Tiili, M. (2008). *Ministers as strategic political leaders? Strategic political steering after NPM reforms in Finland.* Acta politica 34. University of Helsinki, Department of Political Science.
Tiilikainen, T. (2013). Tarja Halonen. Presidentti puolustuskannalla. In S. Tiihonen *et al.* (eds.), *Presidentti johtaa. Suomalaisen valtiojohtamisen pitkä linja.* Helsinki, Kustannusosakeyhtiö Siltala: 258–277.
Turtola, M. (1993). *Tasavallan presidentit. Ryti, Mannerheim, Paasikivi.* Espoo, Weilin+Göös.
Väyrynen, R. (1994). *Tasavallan Presidentit: Kekkonen.* Porvoo, Weilin+Göös.
Väyrynen, R. (2013). Martti Ahtisaari. Diplomaatista poliitikoksi. In S. Tiihonen *et al.* (eds.), *Presidentti johtaa. Suomalaisen valtiojohtamisen pitkä linja.* Helsinki, Kustannusosakeyhtiö Siltala: 237–256.

No Definite Decline. The Power of Political Parties in Finland: A Focused Analysis[1]

LAURI KARVONEN

Comparative literature on political parties is characterized by a peculiar duality. On the one hand, there is the 'decline of parties' thesis, according to which parties are past their prime when it comes to engaging and convincing citizens. On the other, hand, the very same sources often cite James Bryce's (1921: 119) statement 'parties are inevitable. No one has shown how representative government could be worked without them' (Dalton & Wattenberg 2002: 3; Webb 2002: 1; Dalton *et al.* 2011: 3). In a cogent comparative analysis of how parties organize democracy, Russell J. Dalton, David M. Farrell and Ian McAllister (2011, ix) summarize their findings in the following way:

> In part, we agree that some features of partisan politics suggest a pattern of decline – such as decreasing party membership, declining turnout, and fewer citizens identifying with a political party. But these changes in citizens' connections with parties have not been paralleled by a similar decline in parties' performance of their institutional roles in democracy. Rather, political parties generally adapt to changing social and political circumstances to retain their preeminent role in the democratic process.

To put it differently: while research indicates that parties face increasing difficulties when it comes to winning the hearts and minds of citizens, they seem to cling successfully to institutional-

1   The author wishes to thank Seppo Tiihonen for valuable comments.

ized political *power*. It is the latter aspect that forms the focus of the present study. Its aim is to examine whether and how the power of political parties in the Finnish political system has changed in the course of the past four decades. Stated in this laconic manner, the task may appear huge. The time period to be covered is long, and the Finnish system is characterized by a large number of parties. Power itself can be defined and exercised in numerous ways; political parties may be influential concerning certain channels of power while they may lack access to others. All of this goes to say that producing general statements about the power of parties presents a formidable challenge.

Consequently, while retaining the ambition to present an analysis of parties in general rather than a given party, this study must be focused in order to make the task manageable. First, the concept of power must be delineated in a way which is both theoretically reasonable and operationally sound. Second, it must be applied to the sphere of parties; what is meant by the notion that parties have or lack power? Moreover, the study looks for change and continuity over roughly a forty-year period. Why this time-frame was chosen deserves to be discussed. Finally, the empirical focus of the study must be presented and justified. What concrete phenomena should we examine if the ambition is to compare the relative power of parties over time?

The concept of power: choice of theoretical focus

Few concepts are as central to political analysis as that of power; few concepts are, at the same time, as essentially contested. Briefly, at least the following three phases can be distinguished in the literature. In the postwar decades, focus was largely on what we might term *substantive power*, above all, the ability to influence the content of political decisions. Whose will was reflected in the concrete substance of political decisions such as laws and government programs? Gradually, this research spearheaded by scholars such as Robert Dahl received criticism from, *e.g.*, Peter Bachrach and Morton S. Baratz. Pointing at what might be called the covert face of power they argued that the ability to avert decision merited as much attention as the study of decisions themselves. *Non-decision making, i.e.*, the exclusion of certain issues from the sphere of political decision-making was seen as a highly potent instrument. Finally, as of the 1980s in particular, discursive power – or *hegemonic power* as it is sometimes called – has been a focus of the debate on political power. In this view, power is very much a matter of being able to define the linguistic perspectives of political discourse. The power over words is often synonymous with the power over the minds of citizens (for an overview, see Göhler 2009).

Each of these perspectives may contribute valuable insights into the forms and nature of political power. The present study, nevertheless, clearly leans towards the first one. It looks for change and continuity in the power wielded by parties over two important sets of *decisions*: government (cabinet)[2] formation and the process leading up to the annual central government budget. While acknowledging the potential inherent in alternative perspectives on political power, we argue that substantive decisions belong to the core of the political process.

Empirical focus

The empirical scope of the study is defined by two central factors: the temporal focus on the period from the 1970s until today, and the substantive focus on government formation and the budgetary process. A few words are in order about both of these choices.

The general literature on political parties (Dalton *et al.* 2011: 6–7; Merkl 1970: 105–110; Seiler 1986: 60–65) lists several functions that parties fulfil in the political system. Parties aggregate individual preferences and propose programmatic or ideological alternatives. They mobilize citizens as voters and party members. They recruit candidates and officeholders. They represent the views of their constituents in elected assemblies. They govern by making decisions and directing government bureaucracy.

If we were to ask experts on Finnish politics to name the time when the power and influence of political parties in Finland peaked, many of them would probably point to the 1970s. The newly

---

2   The expressions 'government formation' and 'cabinet formation' will be used interchangeably throughout this study.

introduced public party finance helped boost the organizational networks of parties represented in parliament (Djupsund 1990: 24–34). The major parties were involved in a process whereby government employment – often even menial jobs of no political importance – was filled on the basis of party political affiliation (cf. Heiskanen 1977: 251). These decisions were frequently made in the form of large package deals through which the major parties agreed how the spoils were to be divided between them. Moreover, for a while registered parties even had a legal monopoly on the nomination of candidates in elections (1969–1975). It is no wonder that contemporary analysts characterized Finnish public administration as 'partified' (Ståhlberg 1979) and spoke of 'omnipresent parties' (Helander 1983).

On the other hand, the lively debate about 'neo-corporatism' pointed to a diminished role for the parliament as a result of the incomes policy deals forged by the labor market organizations in cooperation with the government. Parliament was expected to pass large pieces of legislation that were in fact agreed upon by employer and employee organizations as part of collective wage agreements. Certainly, it could be argued that these corporatist arrangements limited the influence of parties in major social and economic issues (Kyntäjä 1993: 125–133).

No comprehensive account for the role of parties since those years has been presented. Still, there seems to be a sense that parties have been on the wane in recent decades (Mickelsson 2009: 12; Paloheimo & Raunio 2008: 209–212; Wiberg 2008: 181–182). Not only have figures on voter turnout, party membership and party identification plummeted. Parties have retreated from parts of the pervasive politicization of lower-level government jobs. In more general terms, political actors are claimed to have lost influence to the market, to EU institutions and to independent public authorities such as central banks and courts. Consequently, it is interesting to inquire whether this development is reflected in the phenomena that form the substantive focus of the present study.

So why government formation and central government budgets as substantive focus? Clearly, this limits the perspective to two party functions: recruitment and governance. The choice has been guided by several considerations. Government formation and the budgetary process are crucial from the point of view of the parties' ability to influence the substance of political decisions. Moreover, it is important to focus on phenomena that carry an indisputable political weight throughout the period. It is hard to deny that government formation and the budgetary process are at the core of politics in a system such as the Finnish one. In parliamentary politics, the difference between insiders and outsiders is marked. Cabinet parties – particularly when the cabinet is backed by a majority in parliament – have dramatically stronger means at their disposal than do opposition parties. By the same token, the annual central government budget is the single most important instrument in deciding 'who gets what' as a result of the political process. In good times as well as in austerity, the budget incorporates the major decisions on how public money is to be spent. Equally important, these two phenomena are recurrent and retain their legal status and their general format throughout the period. In other words, focusing on them steers clear of the problem of comparison between apples and oranges. Many alternative foci – say, comparing single pieces of legislation – would easily be influenced by the fact that we would not be comparing 'the same thing' over time.

It must be underlined that the aim is not to study *which parties* have power over the two phenomena but *whether* the power of parties appears to have changed over time. It is parties versus other actors that are at the centre of attention, not parties compared to one another.

Analysis

Government formation

What does 'power over government formation' mean?

The process of government formation starts when a previous government leaves office, either due to a parliamentary election or for some other reason, such as a cabinet crisis or a vote of no confidence in parliament. The formation process is completed when all cabinet ministers have been appointed and the new cabinet has assumed its day-to-day operations as a collective body. Between these two points in time, several important decisions have been made. These concern functions that may or may not be clearly separable in terms of who does what and when; however, they all must be fulfilled in order for a new government to be formed. In a fragmented multi-party system such as the Finnish one, each function, each step on the way is potentially decisive for the outcome. It is the influence over how these steps are taken that determines the power of parties and other actors over government formation (*cf.* De Winter & Dumont 2008).

The first phase of the process is an investigative one: on what basis in terms of parties (and possibly individual ministers) can a cabinet be formed? Who is willing to govern together with whom? Can a majority cabinet with regard to parliamentary backing be accomplished or must a minority cabinet be formed? The person responsible for this process, which frequently takes place behind the scenes, is sometimes called the *informateur*. When the general political conditions for government formation have been charted, a person may be chosen as government *formateur*.[3] This is normally the politician who is expected to become the Prime Minister of the new cabinet. His or her task is to conduct detailed negotiations about the party composition and program of the new government as well as the division of cabinet posts between parties. Still another step involves the selection of the individual ministers. When these individuals have been selected they need to be formally appointed and sworn into office. Depending on constitutional provisions and parliamentary practice, the cabinet may then directly assume its responsibilities without a formal blessing on the part of the parliament (negative parliamentarism). If positive parliamentarism is the rule, the government and/or its program must receive the explicit support of a parliamentary majority before the cabinet can assume its duties.

Each of the phases of the cabinet formation process may either be a matter for the parties to agree on among themselves and internally, or they may be influenced by actors outside the sphere of political parties. Constitutional provisions or parliamentary custom may provide other government institutions, notably the Head of State (president or monarch) with substantial influence. Powerful actors outside the government sphere – such as moneyed interests or foreign powers – may exert considerable *de facto* influence over the party composition and personnel of cabinets.

---

3   For these twin concepts, see Biesheuvel-Vermeijden (2013).

Cabinets in the 1970s and 2000s

Table 1. Cabinets in Finland in the 1970s and 2000s

Prime minister	Date of appointment	Duration in months	Party composition	Type of government
1970s				
Teuvo Aura	May 1970	2	–	Non-partisan
Ahti Karjalainen	July 1970	15	Cent, Lib, Swe, Left P	Majority coalition
	As of March 1971		Cent, Lib, Swe, Soc dem	
Teuvo Aura	October 1971	4	–	Non-partisan
Rafael Paasio	February 1972	6	Soc dem	Single-party minority
Kalevi Sorsa	September 1972	33	Soc dem, Lib, Swe, Cent	Majority coalition
Keijo Liinamaa	June 1975	6	–	Non-partisan
Martti Miettunen	November 1975	10	Cent, Lib, Swe, Soc dem, Left P	Majority coalition
Martti Miettunen	September 1976	7	Cent, Lib, Swe	Minority coalition
Kalevi Sorsa	May 1977	24	Soc dem, Lib, Cent, Swe, Left P	Majority coalition
	As of March 1978		Soc dem, Lib, Cent, Left P	
Mauno Koivisto	May 1979	33	Soc dem, Swe, Cent, Left P	Majority coalition
2000s				
Paavo Lipponen	April 1999	48	Soc dem, Cons, Swe, Green, Left P	Majority coalition
	As of May 2002		Soc dem, Cons, Swe, Left P	
Anneli Jäätteenmäki	April 2003	2	Cent, Swe, Soc dem	Majority coalition
Matti Vanhanen	June 2003	45	Cent, Swe, Soc dem	Majority coalition
Matti Vanhanen	April 2007	38	Cent, Cons, Swe, Green	Majority coalition

Note: Includes cabinets that were appointed in 1970–79 and 2000–2009 or whose time in office primarily occurred in these decades. A new cabinet is considered to have been formed if at least one of the following criteria is fulfilled: a) There was a parliamentary election b) A new prime minister was appointed c) A cabinet's majority/minority status was altered. Minor reshuffles, including changes in party composition that did not alter a cabinet's majority/minority status do not signify a 'new cabinet'. Based on Nousiainen (2006: 355–357) and the listing of governments and ministers since 1917 on the website of the Finnish government http://valtioneuvosto.fi/en/government/history/governments-and-ministers.

Parties: Lib = Liberal People's Party. Swe = Swedish People's Party. Soc dem = Social Democratic Party. Left P = Finnish People's Democratic League (1970s), Left Alliance (2000s). Cons = National Coalition Party. Cent = Centre Party. Green = Green League. Christ = Christian Democratic Party.

In terms of cabinets, the political landscape in Finland looked radically different in the 1970s as compared to the situation three decades later. There were ten cabinets in the 1970s and only four in the 2000s. This means that average government longevity was much higher in the latter decade, a little over 33 months as compared to 14 months in the seventies.

There is also a difference in terms of the party composition of cabinets. One of the major parties, the Conservatives, remained outside cabinet politics throughout the 1970s (in fact all the way up to 1987). In the 2000s, it participated in two of the four cabinets. Moreover, cabinets in the 1970s were composed of parties that were adjacent to each other on the left- right scale. In other words, the typical cabinet[4] during this period consisted of ideologically 'connected' parties (*cf.* Gallagher *et al.* 2001: 345). The opposition was therefore normally either to the left or to the right of the cabinet. In the 2000s, two of the coalitions were of this type while two others were not. In these latter cases, both the cabinet and the parliamentary opposition were clearly divided ideologically.

Another conspicuous difference concerns government type. In the 1970s there were both minority cabinets and nonpartisan caretaker cabinets; no such cabinets occurred in the 2000s. All governments in the 2000s had the backing of a solid majority in parliament. In fact, they were oversized majority cabinets in that they contained more parties than was necessary in order to secure a bare majority of the parliamentary seats.

The practice of cabinet formation

The constitutional change concerning cabinet formation was described in Isaksson's chapter above. As will be seen in this section, the blueprint of the Finnish constitutions offers quite an accurate account of political reality in Finland both in the 1970s and thirty or forty years later.

The intricate game of the 1970s

Up until the 1950s, Finnish presidents used their powers on government formation to varying degrees. Some adopted an active stance

4   Not including nonpartisan cabinets.

while others limited themselves to a more formal role (Laakso 1975: 208–263). During the prolonged presidency of Urho Kekkonen (1956–1981), the potential inherent in the 1919 constitution began to be utilized to its fullest extent (Nousiainen 2000: 338–347). During his first six-year term, Kekkonen faced staunch opposition from an alliance of two major parties, the Social Democrats and the Conservatives. In the course of the 1960s, he established his position as the largely unquestioned centre of political power in Finland. Arguably, his power peaked in the 1970s. While one cannot understand his ascendancy without reference to his personal ambition and leadership qualities, it would have been impossible without the powers granted to the president by the 1919 constitution. Besides the powers concerning cabinet formation, the president's sovereign role as the leader of Finnish foreign policy was used to discipline parties, politicians and public opinion. A party or politician deemed by him to be a risk for Finnish-Soviet relations could not count on being included in a cabinet, irrespective of popular following.

Cabinet formation in the 1970s was anything but straightforward, which is why it is demanding to give a concise account of the processes that led to the formation of the numerous cabinets during that decade. The essential facts[5] are presented in Timeline 1; after that, the main features are summarized in the form of enumerated conclusions.

TIMELINE 1. FINNISH CABINETS IN THE 1970S

Aura 1. The history of government formation in the 1970s starts with a failure to form a political cabinet at all. In the parliamentary elections that year, the Conservatives and the Rural Party emerged victorious. Both parties were perceived to be critical of Kekkonen. Kekkonen gave the conservative leader Juha Rihtniemi the formal task to investigate the conditions for a partisan cabinet. The word 'formal' must be underlined. Rihtniemi failed to form a cabinet, and in May the president appointed a nonpartisan cabinet led by Teuvo Aura, Mayor of Helsinki. The cabinet largely consisted of Kekkonen's personal

---

5   This account draws heavily on Jansson (1992: 147–161), Laakso (1975: 265–294), Murto (1994: 100–111), Nousiainen (2006: 241–281), and Arter (1987: 89–96).

trustees. It was in office a couple of months, while Kekkonen had K-A. Fagerholm, a Social Democrat and a former Prime Minister investigate on what basis a partisan cabinet might be formed. Fagerholm proposed a broad majority coalition including the Rural Party but excluding the Conservatives. Kekkonen agreed, except for the Rural Party that was to be kept out. He handpicked Ahti Karjalainen, a Centre Party notable but not the party leader, as prime minister.

Karjalainen. The majority coalition led by Karjalainen was in office for fifteen months, which is a fairly long time given the fact that it was basically in a constant state of crisis. In March, 1971, the Communists[6] whom Kekkonen had insisted be included in the cabinet walked out and were replaced by additional social democratic ministers. By autumn the cabinet had nevertheless reached the end of its road due to a crisis related to agricultural policy. Kekkonen told Karjalainen that he would dissolve parliament if the crisis was not solved. But to no avail. The cabinet resigned and new elections were scheduled for early March, 1972.

Aura 2. Aura was again called upon to form a nonpartisan cabinet pend-ing election results. These did little to alter the political constellations. In an exceptional move, the president ordered the leaders of the five parties of the Karjalainen cabinet to assemble in his office; the aim was to compel them to resume office anew under Karjalainen. This time, the party leaders did not budge, and the president had to appoint a social democratic minority cabinet led by Rafael Paasio.

Paasio. The Paasio cabinet was feeble in terms of parliamentary support; it could not count on more than 55 of the 200 members of parliament. Important and controversial issues related to pensions policy and the Finnish free trade agreement with the EEC were on the agenda. There was no way a narrow minority cabinet could resolve these issues on its own. In July, 1972, after six months in office, Paasio tendered the

6   The Finnish Communist Party was not represented in parliament and cabinet directly but through an organization called the Finnish People's Democratic League (FPDL). The FDPL was a joint organization of communists and left wing socialists, with the communists forming the majority. For the sake of simplicity, the present analysis uses the term "communist' to refer to all FPDL members.

resignation of his cabinet. Negotiations between the Social Democrats, the Centre Party, the Liberals and the Swedish People's Party failed to produce a consensus on the pension issue. To break the stalemate, Kekkonen resorted to one more exceptional move. He walked into a Centre Party Delegation meeting and plainly ordered the party to toe the line in the pension question. This tipped the balance within the party and a majority cabinet under social democratic party secretary Kalevi Sorsa was appointed in September, 1972.

Sorsa 1. The Sorsa cabinet ushered in a period of rarely witnessed stability in Finnish politics. It was in office for nearly three years and was able to carry out several major reforms. The oil crisis originating from the 1973 war in the Middle East gradually created pressures within the coalition. By April, 1975, Kekkonen had drawn his conclusions. He wrote a somber letter to leading cabinet members indicating that he had lost faith in the cabinet and was intent on dissolving parliament.

Liinamaa. Sorsa having resigned at the end of May, Kekkonen appointed a caretaker cabinet led by Keijo Liinamaa. As the early elections held in June brought about little change in parliamentary constellations, the Liinamaa cabinet was to hold office no less than six months. Although the president publically admonished the parties to agree on a majority coalition the stalemate was not broken. What followed was the most spectacular move on the part of Kekkonen when it comes to cabinet formation. In late November, 1975, he sent a letter to the leaders of all centrist and left wing parties to meet with him to discuss the cabinet issue. When these leaders arrived they realized that the 'talks' would be held in front of an army of reporters and T V cameras. Standing in line with the entire nation watching, the seasoned parliamentarians were rebuked like a band of naughty youngsters. The president told them that the nation was facing a state of emergency due to heightened unemployment. A coalition cabinet with merely one item on its agenda – to combat unemployment – was therefore to be formed within three days. The humiliated politicians saw no exit except the one offered by the president.

Miettunen 1. Once again, a personal trustee of the president was called upon to assume the prime ministership. Martti Miettunen, a provincial governor and a long-time Centre Party notable, formed a majority coalition consisting of the centrist and left wing parties, including the communists. The Conservatives were once more left outside the cabinet. The Miettunen cabinet was a forced marriage replete with insurmountable contradictions from its inception. The communists refused to go along with the sales tax hike the other cabinet parties considered necessary. Miettunen saw no alternative but to resign. Kekkonen refused to accept his resignation and persuaded the cabinet parties to allow the communists to vote against the government on the sales tax issue. Even this highly unorthodox method proved insufficient to rescue the cabinet. By September, 1976, the social democrats were also on a collision course with their bourgeois cabinet partners concerning the budget. Even the president seemed to have run out of options to rescue the cabinet. Once again, Finland stood without a majority cabinet.

Miettunen 2. Kekkonen ordered Miettunen to stay put and form a centrist minority cabinet. The president also told Miettunen to conduct the cabinet operations so as not to alienate the left wing parties and thereby preclude their future government participation. However, in order to be able to pass the budget for 1977 Miettunen was compelled to do seemingly just that. He negotiated a deal with the Conservatives and the Christian League in order to create a majority for his budget proposal. Far from producing the reaction Kekkonen had feared, this highly temporary agreement raised the specter of a more permanent *rapprochement* between the bourgeois parties in the eyes of social democrats and communists. A series of negotiations ensued; in these, the left wing parties presented no insurmountable demands. A government based on centrist and left wing parties was formed in May, 1977; Kalevi Sorsa, by then chairman of the Social Democratic Party, was appointed prime minister.

Sorsa 2. The Sorsa cabinet was in office for two years, all the way up to the 1979 parliamentary election. Although the small Swedish Party left the negotiations due to a disagreement on economic policy, the Sorsa cabinet was basically reinstated in March, 1978.

Koivisto. The 1979 elections signified another victory for the Conservatives who gained 12 new seats in parliament. Although the president asked conservative Harri Holkeri to act as *informateur* at the beginning of the cabinet formation process, this task was again purely formal. Too few other parties were willing to co-govern with the conservatives. The result was new Centre-left cabinet headed by another social democrat, Mauno Koivisto. It was in office the rest of the decade and well into the next.

What, if anything, can be concluded about the power of parties on the basis of this account? The overall conclusion must be that *parties as collective actors – and, indeed, as representatives of the people – remained peripheral when it came to crucial decisions about government formation* (and survival). There were a number of characteristic patterns and elements that affected the position of parties negatively:

1. The various tasks in the cabinet formation process were seldom clearly separated from each other. Sometimes *informateurs* and *formateurs* were selected, while in other cases it is difficult to pinpoint the persons who were actually in charge of investigating the alternatives and negotiating the coalition. At times the president chose to give such tasks to persons he did not really wish to have as cabinet leaders; when Conservative leaders were used as *informateurs* this simply served to humiliate them. Frequently, he himself played the main role from beginning to end. It was therefore difficult for parties to forge clear strategies for cabinet formation.

2. Election results were of limited importance. In a fragmented multiparty system such as Finland, it is often difficult to have election winners form cabinets; parties that gain new seats may very well be at odds with each other on most issues. However, in the 1970s election results seemed to matter particularly little. The strong electoral showing of the Conservatives did not help the party. The two spectacular victories of the Rural Party were similarly of no avail. In a way, the democratic chain of delegation was broken. It mattered little whom the people chose to reward in elections; the key to government power laid elsewhere.

3. Parliamentary doctrine views nonpartisan caretaker cabinets as a final resort in a crisis. Kekkonen, however, used this option widely as part of his overall strategy (Laakso 1975: 287–292; Nousiainen 2006: 279).

4. Formal position in the party hierarchy meant little. Only two of the prime ministers in the 1970s were party leaders when they were appointed. Both were social democrats; Paasio in 1972 and Sorsa in 1977. More often than not, what mattered was how Kekkonen himself viewed the individuals he chose to appoint (*cf.* S.Tiihonen 1990a: 239). Several of the prime ministers – and this was not limited to the leaders of caretaker cabinets – were his personal trustees. These individuals did not necessarily feel bound by the collective will of their parties when accepting the job.

5. The above also largely applies to the selection of numerous other cabinet ministers. The choice of Foreign Minister was always contingent on Kekkonen's will; he handpicked the persons for this position (Laakso 1975: 294). Depending on cabinet composition and the political situation he could also actively influence the choice of other ministers. He was particularly active when it came to the selection of minister from his own former[7] party, the Centre Party. Equally important, he let it be known that certain individuals should not be on the list of ministers (*cf.* Myllymäki 2010: 81; Nousiainen 2006: 279). This blacklisting was of course not official, but the political elite were aware of it and took care not to suggest ministers unacceptable to the president.

6. The use of foreign policy arguments to influence government formation and the choice of ministers was frequent. The president took care not to do it too often, at least in public. Those who were viewed as his unofficial spokesmen in the public debate used this instrument more freely. The Conservatives as party were portrayed as a risk for Finland's friendly relations with the Soviet Union, as were numerous individual politicians.

7. Kekkonen used unexpected and spectacular moves to influence the parties. Parties and leaders were often taken by surprise and even humiliated in public. This led to a behavior based on 'anticipated reactions'; it was not wise to do things that might cross the president. Often, therefore, Kekkonen

---

7   It is customary that a new president withdraw from party membership when taking office.

had his way without having to do very much. If needed, however, he did not refrain from bold actions.

8. In an important sense, government formation begins when a previous cabinet hands in its resignation. Kekkonen also influenced cabinet formation by terminating cabinets. Sometimes cabinets resigned when he told them their time was up. Sometimes he had to use his constitutional power to dissolve parliament and call for new elections. Kekkonen used this power more frequently than any other president in Finnish history.

Stability in the 2000s

TIMELINE 2. FINNISH CABINETS IN THE 2000S

Lipponen. The cabinet led by Paavo Lipponen that was in office until the 2003 parliamentary election was appointed in April, 1999. It was therefore the last cabinet to be formed before the new constitution was enacted. However, it was neither constitutionally nor politically formed under the same conditions as the cabinets of the 1970s. The post-Kekkonen era had witnessed a growing consensus among parties about the need to limit the powers of the president. The result was a series of partial constitutional amendments. They were incorporated in the 2000 constitution. By April it was also apparent that the new constitution with its detailed parliament-centred provisions for government formation would be supported by an overwhelming majority. It was passed merely two months after Lipponen took office. The Lipponen cabinet – a 'rainbow coalition' including parties from the Conservatives on the right to the Greens and the Left Alliance – governed throughout the parliamentary period up to the 2003 election. The Greens left the cabinet in May, 2002, due to the cabinet's decision to grant a concession for a new nuclear plant. The cabinet's majority status was, however, not altered.

Jäätteenmäki. The 2003 elections and the subsequent cabinet formation process took place under the new constitution. In 2002, moreover, the parties in parliament had agreed on a specification of the constitutional provisions on government formation. According to the agreement, the formation process after an election is initiated by the leader of the

largest party in parliament. The agreement was not incorporated into
the blueprint of the constitution, but it does constitute a powerful
common-law specification of it (Nousiainen 2006: 322; Wiberg 2009:
18). The 2003 election was a tight race between the Social Democrats
and the Centre Party who both gained in terms of vote shares and
parliamentary seats. The latter emerged as the largest party with a
thin margin. In accordance with the 2002 agreement, Centre Party
leader Anneli Jäätteenmäki took the initiative in the negotiations on a
new cabinet. The Centre Party and the Social Democrats fairly swiftly
agreed on a cabinet consisting of the two parties plus the Swedish
Party. In April, 2003, the cabinet led by the first female prime minister was appointed by the first female president Tarja Halonen. But
this was not to be. In the final phase of the campaign, Jäätteenmäki
had launched an offensive against Lipponen challenging his conduct
of talks with the White House about Finland's role in the coalition
against Iraq. In turn, she was criticized for using classified diplomatic
material in an election campaign. Her denial of this led to investiga-
tions where her veracity was called into question. By June, 2003, the
affair had snowballed to such an extent that Jäätteenmäki was compelled to resign both as prime minister and as Centre Party leader.[8]

Vanhanen 1. The crisis was, however, limited to Jäätteenmäki personally.
The Centre Party selected Matti Vanhanen as her successor as party
leader, and the parliament went on to elect him prime minister. The
party composition of the cabinet was not affected, and the personnel
changes were kept to a minimum. The Vanhanen cabinet was in office
until the 2007 election.

Vanhanen 2. The 2007 election was a victory for the Conservatives who
gained no less than ten new seats, while the Social Democrats lost
eight seats. The Centre Party lost four seats, but less than two per cent
in terms of vote shares, and remained the largest party in parliament.
The Social Democrats preferred to remain in opposition while the victorious Conservatives were willing to co-govern with the Centre Party.
These two major parties were joined by the Greens and the Swedish
Party in a four-party coalition. The tenure of this cabinet came increasingly to be marked by scandals related to campaign financing, whereby

8   For an account in English, see Pesonen (2004).

the Centre Party in particular came into bad light. Vanhanen's decision in 2010 to step down as party leader and prime minister – officially due to health reasons – is frequently explained with reference to this issue.

Kiviniemi. Vanhanen was replaced by Mari Kiviniemi, who headed the otherwise intact cabinet until the 2011 election.

Cabinet formation in the 2000s stands out as a reversed image of the processes in the 1970s; the role of parties is central. The main features in the 2000s are:

1. The process of cabinet formation is tied to the will of the parliamentary majority; the president has the role of formal appointer.
2. Elections matter. The party that has the highest number of parliamentary seats takes the initiative in the coalition bargaining process. This increases the likelihood that that party will conquer the prime ministership. Consequently, elections today are much more a vote on who should be the next prime minister than they were in the 1970s.
3. Party hierarchy matters. In the normal case, it is the leader of the largest party who becomes prime minister. The leaders of the other coalition parties – especially those of major parties – occupy the other prestigious cabinet posts. Moreover, and in contrast to the 1970s, only individuals who are centrally placed in party organizations (normally MPs) are appointed as ministers. In sum, deliberations within parties are decisive when determining the personnel of cabinets.
4. Cabinets are stable. No cabinet has resigned *in toto* in the 2000s. Even the two cases where a prime minister resigned between elections serve to underline overall stability in contrast with the 1970s. The frequent cabinet formations between elections in the 1970s signified severe political crises and cabinet breakdowns. Change of prime minister in the 2000s was not a sign of a general crisis. From the point of view of overall parliamentary constellations, all cabinets in practice remained in office throughout the four-year period between elections. The parliament has not been dissolved a single time. A 1991 constitutional amendment, later incor-

porated in the 2000 constitution, deprived the president of the sovereign right to dissolve parliament. Instead, he/she can only do it at the initiative of the prime minister. Here, too, important constitutional powers have been transferred from the president to the parliamentary sphere.

5. Only broad majority cabinets have occurred. Not a single minority cabinet, let alone a caretaker cabinet, has been in office.

6. With stable cabinets, it makes sense to try to implement a long-term agenda. Cabinet programs are today much more detailed than in the 1970s and they guide government policy in an entirely different way (Wiberg 2009: 19–21). In the 1970s, politicians did not expect cabinets to survive more than perhaps a year, which made it less meaningful to compose a detailed program, let alone feel bound by it.

Why have parties become more powerful?

Government formation in the 2000s is entirely in the hands of political parties. Deliberations between and within parties decide which parties form the cabinet, how cabinet posts are divided within the coalition, what will be included in the cabinet program and which individuals will be appointed as cabinet ministers. Heightened party power also means increased voter influence. Election results are important when it comes to deciding the likely prime minister of the post-election cabinet. All of this stands in a stark contrast to the 1970s.

To say that this change is due to constitutional reform is of course true, but it is not a particularly strong explanation. The reformed constitution is in itself a result of changes that have pervaded Finnish politics at large. These changes explain both why constitutional change was possible and why parties have gained power over the government formation process. The political transformation that made constitutional reform possible was due to three strongly interrelated factors: a more consensual pattern in Finnish society at large, learning from the excesses of the Kekkonen era and change in Finland's international environment.

The president-centred political practice in the 1970s was partly a result of the conflictual atmosphere that characterized interparty relations and seriously incapacitated parties as central actors. This political culture was in turn largely a reflection of a high level of conflict in Finnish society at large, especially in the labor relations field. In the first three postwar decades, Finland had one of the highest levels of industrial conflict in the Western world (Mitchell, B.R 2007: 186–7). Gradually, however, labor market actors realized that this did not work to anyone's benefit. A more consensual pattern ensued signified by a long series of comprehensive wage agreements. By the late 1970s, the main parties too were ripe for more consensual politics. Thanks to this approach, the parties reconquered much of the political space that the president had been able to exploit until the late 1970s.

Along with this change, a stronger sense emerged among parties and politicians that the practices under Kekkonen had perverted Finnish parliamentarism. Immediately after Kekkonen's resignation, and strongly supported by his successor Mauno Koivisto, a parliamentarization of political practice was initiated (Paloheimo 2003: 220; 2005: 249). Reforms of constitutional blueprint soon followed (Arter 2006: 89). For new generations of politicians, it was increasingly apparent that parties had to a high degree let themselves be marginalized in the 1970s.

The change in the Soviet Union as of Mikhail Gorbachev in the mid-1980s and the subsequent collapse of the communist empire constitute a historical dividing line for Finnish politics. The 'Soviet card' had been used repeatedly to influence Finnish domestic politics, including cabinet formations, in the Kekkonen era. To what extent the Soviet Union had actively sought to do so, and to what extent this instrument was used by Finnish actors to influence the domestic power struggle is still a highly controversial issue. Elsewhere, I have argued that Kekkonen was more motivated by domestic politics than has often been claimed (Karvonen 2003). This view is also supported by the fact that the parliamentarization of Finnish politics started right after Kekkonen's resignation while the Soviet Union was still a potent superpower. In the present context, however, this is not a central point. The fact remains that foreign policy, for whatever reason, *had* been used to influence cabinet formation; as of Gorbachev this was no longer an efficient strategy.

By bolstering the position of the cabinet in the increasingly important European affairs, Finland's membership in the EU has indirectly contributed to the strengthening of parties in the cabinet formation process (see chapter by Raunio in this volume). However, the first important steps towards a parliamentarization of Finnish politics had been taken long before Finland's decision to enter into the Union.

Central government budgets

Politics comes with a cost. Parties and candidates make promises to their constituents and generally work to improve the conditions of those groups whose support they depend on in elections. Parties therefore have a strong stake in the annual central government budget. This is the chief channel through which campaign promises can be fulfilled and policy goals financed. From the point of view of budgetary balance and financial sustainability, parties irrespective of political orientation may present a risk. In simplistic terms, left wing parties promise increased publically-financed welfare; their policies tend to *increase public spending* levels. Right wing parties are more likely to make promises about lower taxes; if implemented, their policies tend to put a strain on government finance by *decreasing revenue*. This schematic claim is generally supported by comparative research on the association between the political makeup of governments and levels of public spending. The correlations are, however, normally rather modest; all parties live in a reality where the overall development of government spending and revenue is determined by economic trends (Dalton *et al.* 2011: 207; Blais *et al.* 1993; Blais *et al.* 1996).

Parties frequently disagree on what, and how much of it, should be in the budget. Here, however, the focus is not on *which parties* influence the budget. Naturally, in a democracy large parties are expected to have more influence than small parties. If the system is a parliamentary one, government parties are expected to be more influential than opposition parties, at least if the cabinet holds a majority in parliament. Neither is the primary aim to determine whether governments spend or tax more or less from year to year. In a single-country study it is not sensible to compare spending itself simply because the effects of economic trends and path dependence cannot be controlled for. Rather, the interesting question is whether *changes in the legal and institutional framework and practice have affected the power of parties over budgets as compared to other actors.*

Many kinds of actors can compete with parties and politicians when it comes to influencing budgets. Organized interests, such as labor market and industrial associations, may at least indirectly exert a considerable influence. Their view is partial: they want more money for certain things, perhaps less for some others. The European Union may influence the budgetary process in several ways. Parties may also face competition from domestic actors who worry about financial sustainability and macroeconomic stability. Central banks and the government finance bureaucracy are among these; unlike interest organizations, these actors are supposed to represent a holistic view of what is in the public interest. It is the balance between parties and these various actors that determines the power of parties over the budgetary process.

The central government budget is an annual decision on government expenditure and revenue for the coming fiscal year. Due to its temporal scope, a budget in itself is not a long-term program. However, it is only through budgets that such programs can be put into practice. Naturally, long-term social and economic objectives are far from the only goal of parties when they try to influence government budgets. According to a classical notion, parties and MPs always strive to further the particular interests of their constituents. This may result in what is known as pork barrel politics, characterized by the predominance of territorially and socially confined benefits over holistic political goals.

Potential channels of party influence

In most democratic systems, constitutions define legislative assemblies as central institutions in budgetary matters; at least formally, parliaments have 'the power of the purse' (*cf.* Blondel 1995: 256; Hague & Harrop 2001: 225). The Finnish system is no exception in this respect. Parliaments offer several channels for party power in handling the budget. Parties may form majorities necessary for approving budgets or introducing changes in the government budget bill. They may work through parliamentary committees, whether they be called Finance Committee or Appropriations Committee. There may be mechanisms of minority protection enabling parties without a parliamentary majority to exert an influence. Finally, parties may influence budgets through the activity of their individual MPs. Budgetary motions are an instrument that is available to

MPs in many legislative assemblies (Arter 1984: 293–302).

Cabinet parties have an array of additional ways to try to influence the size and content of the government budget. Cabinets submit the budget bill to parliament collegially, in the name of the entire cabinet. If a cabinet consists of one party only, it may be fairly easy for the party in question to leave its mark on the budget. In coalition cabinets, ministers are rarely equal in the budgetary process. Key ministers, such as the prime minister or the minister of finance are normally more influential than other ministers when it comes to overall decisions. The minister of finance has the advantage of being the head of the bureaucracy that plays a key role in the administrative preparation of the budget. Other ministers may have central roles in the budgets of their respective sectors.

Parties hold the key to *decisions* about the budget. It is only through a decision by a cabinet that a government budget bill can be sent to parliament. It takes a sufficient number of MPs, who are also party representatives, to pass, amend or reject a budget. Decisions of this kind are but a part of the story. Budgets have to be *prepared* before they can be decided on; after formal decisions they must be *implemented*. Both in the preparation of budgets and in their implementation, the role of the government finance bureaucracy is central. External actors can also in many ways influence the conditions surrounding the budget. If the government is involved in large-scale corporatist cooperation with labor market organizations, agreements among the latter may contain elements that compel the government to adjust the budget to these. The European Union and the European Monetary Union (EMU) also impose restrictions on government spending and thereby affect the budgets of member states.

The constitutional framework

Both the 1919 and the present constitution stress the sovereign role of the parliament in deciding about the annual budget. However, the dominant interpretation of constitutions has confined the role of the parliament to a line-by-line scrutiny of the items and sums included in the budget bill. Parliament cannot alter the introductory argumentation for the budget, nor its overarching goals (P. Tiihonen 1989: 5). As the budget is presented in the form of a government bill to parliament it will have to be approved at the cabinet plenary meeting and adopted at a State Council meeting with the president. From a formal constitutional point of view, therefore, cabinet and parliament stand out as the focal points of budgetary power.

This is not to say that important constitutional reforms have not been carried out. Among these are several from the late 1980s and early 1990s. They have enhanced the flexibility of net budgeting and multi-year budgeting and removed some important requirements for qualified majorities in parliament (S. Tiihonen 2012: 214–215).

However, constitutions have been silent about the preparatory process leading up to the budget bill. The planning and negotiations preceding the bill have mainly been regulated by lower-level ordinances and established practice. The administrative preparation of the budget has been seen as being of 'technical' nature and therefore not in need of formal codification. This has consistently been the position of the Ministry of Finance (FIM). Also, the legal status of the detailed *ex ante* control of budgetary spending – a central instrument in planning and monitoring budgets until the 1980s – was never determined clearly (P. Tiihonen 1989: 2–5).

Preparing a budget

1970s

Up until the mid-1960s, the appropriations included in the budget were determined in negotiations between FIM and the sectoral ministries on the basis of plans and petitions from the latter. From then on and until the end of the 1980s, the final agreement on the budget was hammered out at the drawn-out cabinet budget session in late August/early September. Whatever was undecided after the sector-wise negotiations was resolved here. Cabinet ministers and finance ministry top officials were the key participants at the session. It was on the basis of this session that the cabinet budget bill to parliament was determined. The preparation phase was shrouded in secrecy (Heikkinen & Tiihonen 2010: 336–339).

2000s

The frame budgeting introduced in 1991 altered the preparation of budgets considerably. In March each year, the cabinet decides the financial scope of the budget by determining a quantitative frame for individual ministerial sectors. This budget frame decision is also

presented to parliament. Based on the frame, the ministries prepare
detailed sectoral budgets that are submitted to FIM in May. The
ministry presents its budget proposal on the basis of the materials
submitted by the various ministries; this occurs in late July or early
August. The cabinet budget session is held a few weeks later. Focus
is, unlike in the 1970s, not so much on a line-item scrutiny as on
politically and financially significant issues and remaining con-
troversies. The session is usually completed in about two days, as
opposed to 4–5 days in the 1970s (Wiberg 2009: 46–48; Heikkinen
& Tiihonen 2010: 336–354).

The sectoral budget proposals are considered to be public documents from the instance that FIM has presented its budget proposal.

Decision

1970s

When the cabinet plenary meeting had agreed on a budget proposal
and it had been presented at the joint meeting with the president,
the budget bill was submitted to parliament. After an introductory
general debate the bill was sent to the parliament financial committee along with any budget motions from individual MPs. Based on a
scrutiny by its various sections the committee presented its budget
proposal. At this plenary meeting, a general debate was followed by
a line-by-line scrutiny of the proposal. If the committee proposal
was not adopted, it was sent anew to the committee. The plenary
then adopted the budget on the basis of the revised report by the
financial committee, either by accepting the committee's sugges-
tions or revising them before the final decision. After this, the president signed the budget and the minister of finance countersigned
it, whereupon it was promulgated in the official legislative record
(Nousiainen 1970: 459–464; 1980: 329–333).

2000s

The cabinet decision on the budget frame is reported to parliament.
In 2000, the report was submitted in the form of a Government
Statement. As such a statement is always followed by a vote in
parliament this practice actually meant that the cabinet tested its
parliamentary confidence when submitting its frame decision. This
practice was abandoned in favour of submitting the budget frame
as a Government Report which is followed by a debate but no vote

in parliament (Wiberg 2009: 46–48; Heikkinen & Tiihonen 2010: 336–354).

Parliamentary procedure is largely similar to that in the 1970s. The plenary meeting and the financial committee interact in basically the same way as earlier. However, the formal promulgation of the adopted budget is handled by the parliament (Jansson 2000: 170).

Monitoring, control

1970s

The *ex ante* control of budgetary compliance and spending ('list control') was the core of the control system. This control was performed by FIM and the Cabinet Finance Committee. Decisions condoned by FIM were carried out according to the standpoint of the individual ministry. Matters challenged by FIM were decided either on the basis of a proposal from FIM ('B-list'), or if this was not accepted by the ministry in question, brought to the Cabinet Finance Committee ('A-list'). The Committee and FIM thus controlled sectoral budgetary discipline great detail (P. Tiihonen 1989: 76–81).

2000s

Reforms since the 1990s have introduced performance-based budgeting and given individual ministries and agencies greater leeway in the use of sectoral appropriations. Focus has shifted from line-item budget controls to efficiency and targets (S. Tiihonen 2012: 190–191, 217).

Analysis

The above descriptive account for the constitutional and procedural aspects of budget-making provides a necessary background for an analysis of the power of parties in this area, but it tells us relatively little about the actual power relations and possible changes in them over time. Additional evidence must be brought in before conclusions can be drawn.

As the final decision rests with the parliament, parliament in theory has the sovereign power to change the budget. The difference in terms of the total value of appropriations between the government bill and the final budget adopted by parliament provides

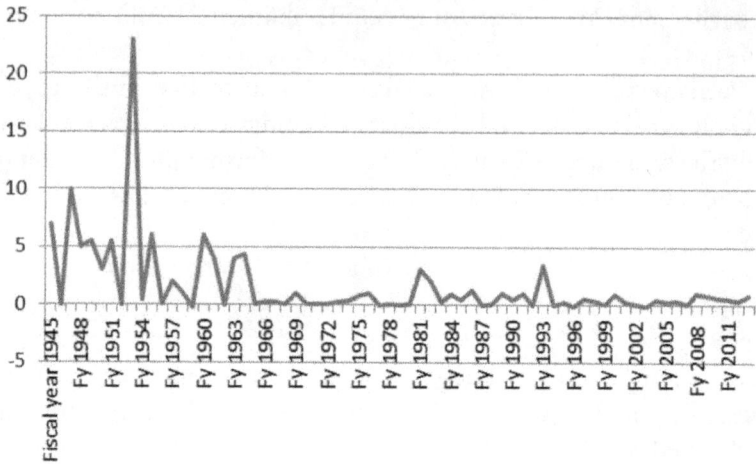

Figure 1. The difference between the government budget bill and the budget approved by parliament, 1945–2013. Per cent of total value of appropriations.

Source: Wiberg 2006: 234; website of the Finnish parliament, government budget proposals 2013 http://web.eduskunta.fi/Resource.phx/riksdagen/riksdagsarbetet/ statsbudgeten/index.htx.

a rough measure of the extent to which parties in parliament have done so (Figure 1).

Until the early 1960s, major interventions by parliament were common. Parties in parliament frequently agreed on considerable additions to the budget proposed by cabinet. As of the mid-1960s such amendments became much rarer, although deviations of up to about three per cent of the total amount have occurred a few times since then. Overall, however, parliament as an *independent* channel of budget-making has not really existed for half a century. Given the present focus on the 1970s and the 2000s, it is interesting to note that these periods look remarkably alike. The 1970s witnessed a number of important welfare reforms initiated by the first Sorsa cabinet in particular. Evidently, parliament saw little need of expanding the proposed budgets further.[9] In the 2000s, frame budgeting restricts the parliament's room to manoeuver. In

---

9 The 1966 left-wing majority cabinet led by Rafael Paasio brought about an important change in Finnish politics. The specter of continued leftist governance compelled the Conservatives to give up their resistance against expansionist welfare policies.

fact, the cabinet *a priori* determines a margin that parliament is not to exceed.

Motions by individual MPs have not been a main channel of influence. MPs submit budget bills in order to draw attention to matters important to their constituents rather than to influence the content of the budget itself. Already by the 1970s, less than two per cent of the individual bills were approved by parliament (Nousiainen 2006: 260).

In one important sense, parliament has declined when the 1970s are compared with the 2000s. Until the early 1990s, a third of the members (67 MPs) could defer any legislative bill beyond the next election. As budgets gave rise to legislation that was important from the point of view of their implementation, this mechanism gave the legislative minority a potentially powerful bargaining chip in the budgetary process. When the mechanism was scrapped via reforms in 1992 and 1995 strongly supported by FIM, the role of parliament as an independent institution in the budgetary process was clearly played down (Jansson 2000: 170).

While the parliament's formally sovereign role in deciding the annual budget is important from the point of view of democratic legitimacy, the shape and size of the budget are largely determined before it reaches parliament. The question about the power of parties must therefore be answered with reference to the preparatory phases of the budgetary process.

In order for parties to have a substantial influence through the cabinet, cabinets must be sufficiently strong. A cabinet that lacks a majority in parliament or is beset with chronic conflicts will hardly be able to use budgets as an efficient policy tool. Transient cabinets cannot formulate credible programs for sustained reform; sufficient cabinet longevity is the *condition sine qua non*. Cabinets in the 1970s were typically short-lived and suffered from internal turmoil. Most of them were hard pressed to produce a budget at all; long-term economic programs were simply out of their reach. The plans to link budget-making to medium-term planning – much in vogue throughout the period – remained pious hopes for lack of political continuity (Isaksson 1980; S. Tiihonen 1990b: 286–288). Individual sectors faced the intrusive *ex ante* control with FIM as a central actor. This made it difficult for sectoral ministers to exert sustained influence over budgets (S. Tiihonen 2012: 190–191).

The importance of stability is vividly illustrated by the Sorsa cabinet in 1972–1975 which was the strongest cabinet during the period. Not only did it govern much longer than the average cabinet in the 1970s; it was able to launch important reforms that required major budget appropriations. The axis of power in this government lay between the social democratic Prime Minister Sorsa and the Minister of Finance, Johannes Virolainen of the Centre Party. Through their ability to agree on major issues they controlled the cabinet agenda and persuaded both their respective parties and the other cabinet members to go along. More than in the case of any other cabinet, the Sorsa-Virolainen cooperation exerted extensive influence in budget matters as well (cf. Jansson 1992: 152; Nousiainen 2006: 245). It was a matter of highly centralized power; the role of these key actors was not matched by other ministers. Meanwhile, parties were reluctant to face the political consequences of the economic measures that the situation brought about by the development after the oil crisis called for.

By the 2000s, cabinets had the stability and parliamentary strength required for long-term undertakings. As cabinets normally remain in office throughout the four-year period, their programs constitute an important starting point for the annual budget frames. With the transition from meticulous *ex ante* controls to performance-based budgeting, individual ministers have gained influence over the spending priorities of their sectors[10] (S. Tiihonen 2012: 217). Simultaneously, a centralization of cabinet power has taken place. Members of key cabinet committees, the Cabinet Committee on Economic Policy and the Cabinet Finance Committee in particular, have an advantage over other ministers. Ad hoc meetings of the leaders of cabinet parties – a central instrument for political consensus – represent a second type of centralization. In both these arenas, the prime minister and the Minister of Finance are present in two important capacities: as key ministers in regard of economic policy and as party leaders (cf. Wiberg 2009: 43–46).

While contemporary cabinets have widely better conditions for influence than in the 1970s, cabinets in the 2000s are not necessarily alike. Their political makeup makes a difference. When cabinets

10 However, sectoral ministries still complain about meticulous FIM control (Tiili 2008: 80–100).

consist of numerous and ideologically diverse parties a continuous search for compromises marks the agenda. This may play into the hands of actors perceived as neutral in terms of intra-party rivalry, the government finance bureaucracy in particular.

Contemporary analyses of the 1970s (Tandem 1977: 438–440) and of the 2000s (Wiberg 2009: 46–47) as well as accounts that cover longer periods (S. Tiihonen 2012: 232–233) all stress the paramount importance and influence of the Ministry of Finance in the budgetary process. In the 1970s, the transient nature of governments – with the exception of the first Sorsa cabinet – underlined the role of FIM as the guarantor of continuity. Cabinets that could perhaps only count on a few months in office had limited means to make an impact. Instability went hand in hand with a phenomenon that characterized this period:

> During this time of political instability and economic crisis, political parties did not compete for the portfolio of Minister of Finance. This meant that the political and practical leadership of the Ministry was given into the hands of civil servants of the Ministry or its former civil servants: in 1975 former Budget Chief Heikki Tuominen served as Minister of Finance; in 1976 the post was in the hands of former Permanent State Secretary of the Ministry Paul Paavela and in 1977 former Budget Chief Esko Rekola was appointed to the post. (S. Tiihonen 2012: 173).

Parties were reluctant to face the political consequences of the economic measures that the development after the oil crisis called for. The bureaucrats-turned-finance-ministers were of course more likely to toe the cautious macroeconomic line preferred by the ministry rather than putting forth bold partisan initiatives. Given the chronic internal disagreements among cabinet parties this line was probably more acceptable politically than any alternative course. The *ex ante* control system furnished FIM with a superior position in day-to-day processes.

By the 2000s, the *ex ante* system had been scrapped. Moreover, it had become unthinkable that the Minister of Finance be anything but the leader of one of the main cabinet parties. Although the institutional and procedural conditions for a strengthened party power seem to be at hand, the impression is that FIM has retained and even strengthened its role as a 'super ministry' (Heikkinen &

Tiihonen 2010: 486–488). In the negotiations about the budget frame, FIM successfully reminds sectoral ministries about the expenditure and deficit limits agreed on in the cabinet program. Nothing which is not included in the frame with a clear financing plan has a real prospect of being included in the final budget (Tiili 2008: 80–100). The procedure tilts towards FIM. Three departments within the ministry, with the Budget Department as the final gatekeeper, scrutinize the frames for each sector. Perhaps more than anything, however, external factors have boosted FIM's position.

The 1970s were the golden age of corporatism. While party politics was unstable, an impressive series of comprehensive labor market deals were struck during this period. Wage agreements formed the core, but they also had far-reaching consequences for politics at large. To facilitate the deals, government committed itself to social and economic legislation agreed on by the central organizations (Kyntäjä 1993: 133–154). This legislation presupposed major budget appropriations. Thus, parties not only surrendered much of the political initiative to the organizations; they also had to accept that budgets and legislation were de facto decided in labor market negotiations (P. Tiihonen 1989: 16–17; S. Tiihonen 2012: 186).

Corporatism has clearly waned since the 1990s. Central agreements alternate with deals on the level of industrial sectors; their effect on legislation and budgets has diminished. Instead, Finland's participation in the European Union has emerged as a highly important external force. Membership in EMU eliminated a major rivalry between FIM and the Bank of Finland (the Finnish central bank). The EMU and the EU Growth Pact have created fiscal rules with significant effects on budgets. These rules reflect macro-economic goals that have long guided FIM's work. It is indisputable that the Europeanization of Finnish politics has strengthened the ministry's position as the actor that largely controls the politics of budget-making (Heikkinen & Tiihonen 2010: 487; S. Tiihonen 2012: 215).

Paradoxically, then, the 'super ministry' seems to have found ways of asserting its powerful position in widely varying circumstances. In the volatile political environment of the 1970s, it stood for continuity and partly replaced what was supposed to be partisan control. Its position was also rooted in the detailed control and monitoring of spending practiced during that period. In the 2000s, it fares well in the orderly world created by stable majority cabinets with a commitment to long-term programs and frame budgeting, and the macroeconomic discipline ordained by the EU and the EMU. (See the chapter by Murto for an analysis of the role of the Ministry of Finance, particularly its civil servants.)

Parties and budgets: conclusions

Central government budgets in the 2000s are shaped in conditions that differ widely from those in the 1970s. *Yet, on balance, the general conclusion is that the power of parties has changed surprisingly little.* Parliament as an independent actor was not prominent in the 1970s; no change was to be noted in this regard three or four decades later. Opposition parties lost an important channel of influence in the 1990s, when the right for a parliamentary minority to defer legislation was abolished. The stable majority cabinets of the 2000s have a strongly improved capacity to pursue coordinated and consistent economic policies compared to the transient cabinets of the 1970s. They do this, however, in a context marked by the globalization of the economy and the heightened influence of the EU's fiscal rules over the budgets of member states.

Still, it is clear that the prolonged period of stable majority parliamentarism has entailed changes in party influence as well. Those parties that occupy the posts of prime minister and finance minister have a stronger access to the budgetary process than other parties. Other ministers have some leeway in determining spending priorities in their respective sectors, but their possibilities to alter the overall structure of frame budgets remain limited. The one actor that has been able to assert its influence in changing circumstances – and in fact reinforced its position – is the Ministry of Finance. The internationalization of economy and politics has boosted FIM's position.

This is not to say that parties are powerless in the face of Europeanization and FIM's successful adjustment to it. Stable majority cabinets can control the budgetary agenda if the political will is there. The propensity to form oversized and ideologically highly heterogeneous cabinets, however, sets limits to what cabinets can agree on in terms of economic policies and budget appropriations. This very heterogeneity is one of the keys to the powerful position of the Ministry of Finance in Finnish politics.

Conclusion

The case of Finland certainly does not gainsay the conclusion by Dalton et al cited at the outset. Turnout in parliamentary elections has dropped some fifteen per cent since its peak in the 1960s. Party membership since 1980 has declined from nearly sixteen per cent to about eight per cent of the electorate – incidentally, the change in Finland is almost exactly the West European average (van Biezen *et al.* 2012: 43–46). Electoral volatility has increased. In the late 1970s, more than three out of four voters voted for the same party as in the previous election; by the 2000s, party loyalty was down to around sixty per cent.[11]

On the other hand, the present analysis indicates no overall 'decline of parties' when it comes to key policy decisions. In the case of cabinet formation, parties control this vital process in an entirely different way than in the turbulent and president-centred setting of the 1970s. As to budget-making the picture is less clear-cut. Clearly, the Europeanization of economic policy has made important parts of the budgetary process contingent on standards set by the EU and the EMU; it is difficult for Finnish parties to influence these rules unilaterally. For the government agency responsible for the general management of the budget, the Finance Ministry, the European fiscal rules have been *gefundenes Fressen*. Still, parties are by no means powerless. On balance, it is fair to say that party power is at least on the same level as three or four decades ago.

The stabilization of parliamentary politics and the constitutional reform strengthening the role of parliament and cabinet constituted important preconditions for a stronger role for parties and elections when it comes to cabinet formation. There is still another step parties need to take if they wish to reinforce their positions more generally. That step would mean a move away from the heterogeneous coalitions of today towards clearer ideological coalition alternatives. This would not only strengthen the resolve of cabinet parties when it comes to shaping budgets and policies. It would most probably also increase their credibility in the eyes of the citizens.

11   Calculated on the basis of data available at www.fsd.uta.fi (FSD 1102, 1005, 1260, 2269 and 2653).

References

Arter, D. (1984). *The Nordic Parliaments. A Comparative Analysis.* London, C. Hurst & Co.
— (1987). *Politics and Policy-Making in Finland.* Brighton, Sussex, Wheatsheaf Books.
— (2006). *Democracy in Scandinavia. Consensual, Majoritarian or Mixed?* Manchester, Manchester University Press.

Biesheuvel-Vermeijden, J. (2013). *The Formation of the Dutch Cabinet: Control and Transparency.* Quito, Inter-Parliamentary Union/ Association of Secretaries General of Parliaments/ Communication.

Blondel, J. (1995), *Comparative Government. An Introduction.* London, Prentice Hall / Harvester Wheatsheaf.

Blais, A., Blake, D. & Dion, S. (1993). Do Parties Make a Difference? Parties and the Size of Government in Liberal Democracies, *American Journal of Political Science* Vol. 37, 1: 40–62.
— (1996). Do Parties Make a Difference? A Reappraisal, *American Journal of Political Science* Vol. 40, 2: 514–520.

Bryce, J. (1921). *Modern Democracies.* London, Macmillan.

Dalton, R. J., Farrell, D. M. & McAllister, I. (2011). *Parties & the Democratic Linkage. How Parties Organize Democracy.* Oxford, Oxford University Press.

Dalton, R. J. & Wattenberg, M. P. (2002). Unthinkable Democracy. Political Change in Advanced Industrial Democracies. In R. J. Dalton & M. P. Wattenberg (eds.), *Parties without Partisans.*

Political Change in Advanced Industrial Democracies. Oxford, Oxford University Press: 3–18.

De Winter, L. & Dumont, P. (2008). Uncertainty and Complexity in Cabinet Formation. In K. Strøm, W.C. Müller & T. Bergman (eds.), *Cabinets and Coalition Bargaining. The Democratic Life Cycle in Western Europe.* Oxford, Oxford University Press: 122–157.

Djupsund, G. (1990). Organisa-tionsstrukturen i finländ-ska politiska partier. In G. Djupsund & L. Svåsand (eds.), *Partiorganisationer. Studier i strukturer og processer i finske, norske og svenske partier.* Åbo, Åbo Academy Press: 13–40.

Göhler, G. (2009). 'Power to' and 'Power over'. In S.R. Clegg & M. Haugaard, (eds.), *The SAGE Handbook of Power.* Los Angeles, SAGE: 27–39.

Hague, R. & Harrop, M. (2001). *Comparative Government and Politics. An Introduction.* Houndmills, Basingstoke, Hampshire, Palgrave.

Heikkinen, S. & Tiihonen, S. (2010). *Hyvinvoinnin turvaaja. Valtionvarainministeriön historia 3.* Helsinki, Edita.

Heiskanen, I. (1977). Julkinen, kollektiivinen ja markki-naperusteinen. Suomalaisen yhteiskunnan hallintajärjestelm-ien ja julkisen päätöksenteon ja hallinnon kehitys ja kehittäminen 1960– ja 1970-luvuilla. Helsinki, Deta 31/1977.

Helander, V. (1983). De allestädes närvarande partierna? In L. Karvonen & U. Lindström,

(eds.), *Bakom och bortom partier.*
Meddelanden från Stiftelsens för Åbo
Akademi forskningsinstitut. Nr 88.
Åbo, Åbo Akademi: 131–134.

Isaksson, G-E. (1980). KTS-*planer-*
ing: ideal och verklighet. En studie
kring utfallet av ett statligt planer-
ingssystem. Åbo, Åbo Akademi:
RESPO 45/1980.

Jansson, J.-M. (1992). *Från splittring*
till samverkan. Parlamentarismen
i Finland. Borgå, Söderström &
C:O Förlags AB.

Jansson, J.-M. (2000). *Från regerings-*
formen till grundlagen. Helsingfors,
Söderström & C:O Förlags AB.

Karvonen, L. (2003). Kekkonens
ställning. Fyra kritiska test. *Finsk*
Tidskrift 8–9: 573–588.

Kyntäjä, T. (1993). *Tulopolitiikka*
Suomessa. Tulopoliittinen diskurssi ja
instituutiot 1960-luvulta 1990-luvun
kynnykselle. Helsinki, Gaudeamus.

Laakso, S. (1975). *Hallituksen muo-*
dostaminen Suomessa. Tutkimus
HM 36 § :n taustasta, genetiikasta,
tulkinnasta ja soveltamiskäytän-
nöstä. Vammala, Suomalainen
lakimiesyhdistys: nro 110.

Merkl, P. H. (1970). *Modern*
Comparative Politics. New York,
Holt Rinehart & Winston.

Mickelsson, R. (2009).
Johdanto. In R. Mickelsson
(ed.), *Puolueiden tulevaisuus.*
Helsinki, Oikeusministeriö –
Justitieministeriet: 8–14.

Mitchell, B. R. (ed.), (2007).
International Historical Statistics.
Europe 1750–2005. Basingstoke,
Palgrave Macmillan.

Murto, E. (1994). *Pääministeri.*
Suomen pääministerin
rooli 1917–1993. Helsinki,
Hallintohistoriakomitea &
Painatuskeskus: nro 13.

Myllymäki, A. (2010). *Suomen*
pääministeri – presidentin varjosta
hallitusvallan käyttäjäksi. Helsinki,
Talentum.

Nousiainen, J. (1970). *Suomen poliit-*
tinen järjestelmä. Porvoo, WSOY.
—(1980). *Suomen poliittinen järjest-*
elmä. Juva, WSOY.
— (2000). From Semi-Presidentialism to Parliamentary
Government: Political and
Constitutional Development in
Finland. In L. Karvonen & K.
Ståhlberg, (eds.), *Festschrift for*
Dag Anckar on his 60th Birthday
on February 12, 2000. Åbo, Åbo
Akademi University Press: 337–352.
— (2006). Suomalainen parla-
mentarismi. In A. Jyränki & J.
Nousiainen, *Eduskunnan muut-*
tuva asema. Suomen eduskunta 100
vuotta. Helsinki, Edita: 180–335.

Paloheimo, H. (2003). The Rising
Power of the Prime Minister in
Finland. *Scandinavian Political*
Studies Vol. 26, 3: 219–244.
— (2005). Let the Force Be
with the Leader – But Who
Is the Leader? In T. Poguntke
& P. Webb (eds.), *The*
Presidentialization of Politics. A
Comparative Study of Modern
Democracies. Oxford, Oxford
University Press: 246–268.

Paloheimo, H. & Raunio, T. (2008).
Suomen puolueiden nykytila ja
tulevaisuuden haasteet. In H.
Paloheimo & T. Raunio (eds.),
Suomen puolueet ja puoluejärjest-
elmä. Porvoo, WSOY: 209–219.

Pesonen, P. (2004), Dangerous
Curves in Finnish Politics:
A Sweet Victory and a Sour
Honeymoon, *Tidsskrift for*
Samfunnsforskning Vol. 45, 2:
273–293.

Seiler, D.-L. (1986). *De la com-
paraison des partis politiques*. Paris,
Economica.

Ståhlberg, K. (1979). Den
partipolitiska förvaltningen,
Finsk Tidskrift 4–5: 206–219.

Tandem. Tasa-arvion ja demokratian tutkimus (1977).
*Demokratian rajat ja rakenteet.
Tutkimus suomalaisesta hallitsemistavasta ja sen taloudellisesta
perustasta*. Porvoo, WSOY.

Tiihonen, P. (1989). *Budjettivalta.
Budjettisäännökset ja suun-
nittelukäytäntö*. Helsinki,
Lakimiesliiton kustannus.

Tiihonen, S. (1990a). *Hallitusvalta.
Valtioneuvosto itsenäisen Suomen
toimeenpanovallan käyttäjänä*.
Helsinki, VAPK-kustannus.

– (1990b). *Talouden ylivalta*.
Helsinki, Valtion painatuskeskus
/ Hallintohistoriakomitea.

– (2012). *The Ministry of Finance.
Two Hundred Years of State-
Building, Nation-Building & Crisis
Management in Finland*. Helsinki,
Suomalaisen kirjallisuuden seura.

Tiili, M. (2008). *Ministers as Strategic
Political leaders? Strategic Political
Steering after NPM Reforms
in Finland*. Acta Politica 34.
Department of Political Science,
University of Helsinki.

Van Biezen, I., Mair, P. & Poguntke,
Th. (2012). Going, going...
gone? The Decline of Party
Membership in Contemporary
Europe. *European Journal of
Political Research* Vol. 51, 1: 24–56.

Webb, P. (2002). Introduction:
Political Parties in Advanced
Industrial Democracies. In P.
Webb, D.M. Farrell & I. Holliday
(eds.), *Political Parties in Advanced
Industrial Democracies*. Oxford,
Oxford University Press: 1–15.

Wiberg, M. (2009). *Hallitseeko hallitus?* Sastamala, Kunnallisalan
kehittämissäätiö.

–(2006). *Politiikka Suomessa*.
Porvoo, WSOY.

– (2008). Puolueet eduskunnassa
ja hallituksessa. In H. Paloheimo
& T. Raunio (eds.), *Suomen puolueet ja puoluejärjestelmä*. Porvoo,
WSOY: 163–184.

Intra-Party Power: The Ascendancy of Parties' Public 'Face'?

VESA J. KOSKIMAA

When trying to understand why political parties do what they do and how they do it, their internal power configuration is a key factor (Lawson 1990: 108). The distribution of organizational power affects how parties formulate policies, run campaigns, join governments and work in parliament. Viewed from another angle, the organizational 'power map' (Panebianco 1988) sets boundaries for the party leadership's ability to manoeuvre in the political market. The fewer competing power concentrations exist, the greater is his/ hers ability to react to changes in political climate.

Power distributions can fluctuate over time, and it has been argued that today traditional class-mass parties are transforming into small, flexible and centrally controlled electoral-professional 'agencies' (Panebianco 1988; Katz & Mair 1995; 2002). The organizational model that is under a threat of extinction, the mass party, was born along with universal suffrage at the beginning of the 20th century. To collect greatly enlarged resources (money and votes) and to advance the working class cause, an internally representative organization that pinnacled around central office and democratically elected party executive was created. Old bourgeois cadre parties had centred around their parliamentary party groups, but in mass parties an 'elected bureaucracy' emerged as the true power holder whose main task was to control the party's parliamentary arm. Eventually, in order to survive, or perhaps just to look fashionable, old elite parties had to form mass organizations, too (Katz & Mair 2002: 117–122). By the 1970s most European mainstream parties looked fairly similar in their basic organizational features. Whether they really worked similarly is another question.

Today, according to the most prominent party theory (the cartel party model), the hierarchic representative mass party is more or less dead. Contemporary parties are characterized by the unrivalled 'ascendancy of the party in public office' (elected representatives and their support teams, from now on PPO) and the concomitant 'relegation' of 'the party on the ground' (the field organization that manifests in party congress and council, from now on POG) and more importantly 'the party in central office' (central office and the national executive committee, from now on PCO). These party 'faces' relate to certain functions whose relative importance has changed over time. Activity in the public domain, most importantly in the national parliament and in the media, now forms the basis of parties' *modus operandi*, while traditional party work in local communities has become significantly less important. Changed priorities have turned the POG vacuous while the PCO has transformed into a 'media agency' whose main purpose is to support the PPO. It has lost its independent leadership role. (Katz & Mair 1992; 1993: 599–600; 1995; 2002: 113, 122–133; 2009: 763; Katz 2005: 98–99; Manin 1997) Power-wise, parties have become unipolar.

Katz and Mair's story leans heavily on the so-called environmental adaptation theory of party change, which suggests – in an evolutionary manner – that when parties encounter changes in their 'electoral environments', they have to respond to them by changing accordingly or they will perish (see Appleton & Ward 1997, Ishiyama 1999 and Harmel 2005). Because established parties rarely die, the hypothesis seems to suggest that parties are becoming more similar[1].

The story pays little attention to historical party-type differences, for example between parties in cadre/elite and mass traditions (Duverger 1954. It is also a well-established fact that parties tend to behave conservatively – especially when it comes to organ-

---

1   Katz and Mair (2002: 130) do note that new organizational innovations are
      best conceived as 'items on a menu' from which parties can choose. But they
      also argue that party change is ultimately set forth by external pressures, inter-
      nal choices being merely the 'immediate' reason for change.

izing (Duverger 1954; Panebianco 1988; Müller 1997). In Katz and Mair's story party change looks almost *too easy*.

It must be kept in mind that the organizational characteristics of parties are embedded on decades (if not centuries) of heritage, and their rules that lean on the principle of democracy are not easy to alter (Paloheimo & Raunio 2008: 216). If historical differences in parties' democratic sentiments are acknowledged, some parties might be able to transform more fluidly than others because their leaders face less opposition. Fairly recent cross-country evidence shows that inter-party differences explain parties' organizational choices better than cartelizing pressures (Detterbeck 2005; 2008). Especially social democratic parties have struggled to adapt to modern demands (Kitschelt 1994).

To shed light on this problem in the Finnish case I will analyse two interrelated questions: 1) has the party in public office become the dominant party 'face' in Finnish parties? 2) Do significant inter-party differences still exist? The questions will be addressed by analysing three sets of measures that tap the power distribution between parliamentary party groups and extra-parliamentary party organizations, concrete manifestations of the PPO and the PCO. Their powers are viewed as proxies of a more general development.

I will begin by examining the distribution and use of parties' financial and staff resources, moving from general comparison of PCO and PPO strength towards a more specific analysis on how PCOs use their resources. As Katz and Mair (2002) point out, the ascendancy of the public dimension is not just about the PPO's getting more resources; it is about fundamental change in the *modus operandi* of parties. This calls for changes in PCOs too. If parties have adopted an electoral-professional style that is associated with the thesis, we should witness substantial increases in electoral and publicity spending – which favours the PPO – and decreases in traditional party work. The official financial statements and annual reports of parties are used as data source.

Secondly, I will analyse the transformation of parties' formal power structures by measuring how much the extra-parliamentary party's power over the parliamentary group has changed over time (for coding scheme see Appendix 1). Lastly, following Katz and Mair (1993), I will investigate who controls the party's central leadership organ by measuring the number of MPs in national executive committees (NEC) of the parties. All measures cover a time-span from the early 1980s to the early 2010s.

The measures have a dual nature. As Pedersen argues concerning party rules, they can be interpreted either as power resources that empower someone to do something, or as symbolic reflections of past power struggles (Pedersen 2010: 744). This applies to resources and positions, too. Resources enable their possessor to do certain things he would not otherwise be able to do, but the mere existence of a certain distribution mirrors wider agreement in the party community since the distribution is a product of parties' internal mechanisms. The composition of the NEC is also decided in a vote in party congress. If the share of MPs is high it does not only mean that they are powerful within the NEC; it also signifies a more general acceptance of the principle.

To take potential party-type variation into account and provide some grounds for generalization I will compare the development of three parties that represent different organizational ideal types[2]. The Social Democratic Party of Finland (SDP) is considered as an exemplar of socialist mass party type that has traditionally valued its extra-parliamentary organization over the parliamentary party group and focused on a wide range of activities in local and regional settings. The National Coalition Party (from now on NCP), the largest conservative party in Finland, plays the role of parliament-born bourgeois cadre party that has historically valued its parliamentary arm over the extra-parliamentary organization and focused mostly on electioneering. Lastly, The Greens of Finland (Greens) work as 'control' case: they have endorsed an 'ultra-democratic' ethos, but disliked institutionalization and bureaucracy – common characteristics of the social democratic representative 'pyramid'. Because they were born in a time when media politics was strengthened in Finland (1988), it is interesting to see which route they chose: to become mainly a parliamentary oligarchy or to ensure grassroots viability in extra-parliamentary arenas.

The chapter is organized as follows. First, in order to provide a context I will sketch out a short historical overview of the development of the parties under investigation. We shall see that Finnish

---

2   A similar classification of Finnish parties has been used previously for example by Lane and Ersson (1987).

parties have converged ideologically and organizationally over the years, but the extent of similarity is debated. Macro-studies emphasise similarities while studies that seek in-depth viewpoint highlight fundamental differences. In the case of intra-party power distribution no conclusive evidence exists. Secondly, I will provide an overview of those major changes in the Finnish political landscape that should have affected the power structures of parties. I will show that there is a plethora of reasons to expect the emergence of the theorized trajectory. After the context is set I will present the analysis and main findings and finally discuss them in light of parties leadership cultures, which could explain some of the observed variation. I will draw insight from my qualitative in-depth analysis of intra-party decision-making in the 1980's, which employs accurate archival data from real decision-making processes (party organs' minutes from 1983 and 1987 government negotiations, mostly verbatim) and in-depth elite interviews (3 former party chairs and deputy-chairs). I will attempt to provide some persuasive conclusions by combining macro and micro perspectives.

Enlargement, institutionalization and convergence of Finnish parties

Early development of Finnish major leftist and rightist forces, the SDP and the NCP, reflects the basic distinction of organizational ideas that was presented in detail by Duverger (1954). The general strike of 1905 ignited the institutional change from estate rule to parliamentary governance. As a reaction to the universal suffrage, the SDP expanded rapidly. Membership increased and already in 1906 the party erected the representative 3-layer organization (local, regional and national) that it continues to employ today. It proved highly successful: the first parliamentary elections in 1907 brought them 37 per cent of the vote. The NCP that was formed in 1918 as a merger of two parliamentary-born elite factions was organized in a loose cadre fashion far into the 1900s. Local clubs were activated mainly during election times and membership activity was weak. While the SDP strongly advocated sectional interests, the NCP claimed to represent the whole nation (Soikkanen 1975, Höltta 1984, Leino-Kaukiainen & Uino 1994). These objectives correspond to the classic forms of political representation: the delegate model where the representative is merely a vessel for previously decided objectives and the trustee model where he maintains autonomy to manoeuvre (Pitkin 1967). It has been argued that at this point in history the former surpassed the latter which was considered as a relic from times of a very limited electorate (Manin 1997). Interestingly, contemporary parties are, more than anything, interested in the 'common good'.

The SDP wanted to take over the state by democratic means. After the law of municipal elections (1917) made them free for competition, it begun to occupy council and committee and this led to a heavy 'partification' of municipal politics. For a long time the NCP rejected to join the game, but after the wars it created a strong organizational network too. By the 1970s significant Finnish parties had developed fairly equal member bases (Sundberg 1994: 159–163). To enjoy all of the public benefits, parties had to maintain certain sub-organizations like youth clubs and women's unions. Still, however, in the third quarter of the past century the NCP was heavily characterized by the strong role of its parliamentary party. Overall party activity on the right was still generally weaker too. (Mickelsson 2007: 204–205; Rantala 1982) Organizational convergence appears to have been, at least to some extent, confined to concrete structures, which are of course lot easier to change than 'deep structures', *i.e.*, the organizational culture.

In the 1970s parties ceased to grow and they were 'standardized', legally and practically. Compared to the rest of Scandinavia, contemporary Finnish parties are exceptionally regulated (Sundberg 1997). The general law on parties, the Party Act was enacted in 1969 and it greatly reduced the heterogeneity in the organizational realm (Wiberg 2000: 166). Before it parties could freely choose how to run their organizations, but the Party Act explicitly forbade undemocratic practices. To the parties' relief, as it later turned out when membership fees started to decrease, the Act also introduced public subsidies that unified the parties' revenue logic. Political activity generally cooled down: a passionate drive to change society was replaced by standardized representation in various arenas (Sundberg 1994: 159–163; 1997: 102–106). At the same time, possibly without even knowing it, parties begun to distance themselves from society.

In the turn of 1960's ideological convergence took root in the form of 'catch-allism'. A famous indication of this was when the third historically significant party, the Agrarian Union changed its name to Centre Party in 1965 in the midst of a rapid process of industrialization and urbanization. The NCP manifesto showed a clear catch-all spirit already in 1957 and even the SDP fought over the issue whether to become a 'general party' or not. However, it was widely conceived as an interest party until the 1980's. (Mickelsson 2007: 188, 233) In 1987 SDP introduced a new manifesto that was significantly milder than the previous one (from 1952). It still made some use of the word 'socialism', but overt class conflict had disappeared and the manifesto gave acceptance to the capitalist system. This made the SDP officially a contemporary centre-leftist party. That same year it formed the first 'blue-red' government with NCP. Since then this has been established as normal form of cooperation along with bourgeois (NCP and Centre Party) and 'red ochre' (SDP and Centre Party) coalitions. Since 1980s Finnish parties have not entered government in order to fight for sectional interests, but to form long-term national politics (Wiberg 2008: 177). Nowadays it is inconceivable that a main party would justify its aims by referring to certain fractions of society. Everything has to be, at least publicly, done for the 'common good'. In this sense the left wing has followed the right.

The most visible change in the organizational realm is the gradual erosion of 'field' organizations. The number of members, local branches and auxiliary organizations started to diminish in early 1980s. The accumulated number of party members in the five largest parties in Finland peaked in 1980 (565 000); 26 years later it had dropped almost by half (330 000). The battle against this erosion gave birth to new organizational ideas around the turn of the 1990s. Both main parties stressed the importance of leadership and the panic erupted in major leadership shuffles. (Mickelsson 1999: 286–287; 2007: 245, 258–260) Still, all parties continue to employ the three-tier model the SDP adopted in 1906. No major innovations have been introduced.

The organizing of the ecological movement represents an interesting new development. Its central goal (along with environmental concerns, of course) was to fight against the bureaucratization of political movements. It was heavily influenced by the first European

Green party, the German Greens, who had wanted to prove Robert Michels' (1915) 'iron law of oligarchy' wrong (Poguntke 1987). As the movement gained electoral strength around mid-1980s (still as informal consortium of ideological and local clubs) need for real organization became a hot topic. The majority of activists were against it because they believed the party would become an end in itself – as had happened in old parties, they argued. Freewheeling anti-partyists believed in spontaneous and antiauthoritarian association and promoted informality as organizing principle. In late 1987, after a group of radical ecologists split from the movement to form their own party the MP Pekka Haavisto wrote an influential letter where he explicitly proposed to form a party organization to avoid future turmoil and to keep the group viable in the policy domain. Surprisingly, the group reacted positively to Haavisto's relatively conservative idea. The Green Party was registered few months later. In a few years it fully adopted the traditional three-tier model. The Greens were originally highly susceptible towards representative democracy but in 2006 they considered it – and parties – necessary (Mickelsson 2007: 72–73, 253–256, 260).

The 'grand narrative' of Western parties seems to apply fairly well to Finnish parties, but it is harder to say how power distributions have changed. Only one Finnish study has scrutinized them over time. Surprisingly, it found that the formal autonomy of the PPO decreased during the period studied (1960–1990) because parliamentary parties links with PCOs became more fixed after the Party Act and they lost some old prerogatives to take part in PCO work. Consequently, party secretaries (leaders of the central office) gained rights to participate in parliamentary meetings and established a firm PCO presence in the PPO. While the introduction of public subsidies increased the resources of parliamentary parties significantly (their own 'office aid' was introduced already in 1967) the financial and staff resources of central organizations continued to rise steadily until the late 1980s as well. Field organizations (POG) clearly stagnated already before 1990s. Professionalization and nationalization of party work made local branches highly dependent on national parties (Sundberg 1994: 173–176; see also Paloheimo & Raunio 2008: 212).

Erosion of parties grassroots activity is hardly news anymore. Party memberships have plummeted all over Europe for decades and no signs of turning the tide are in sight (Biezen, Mair & Poguntke 2012). This does not, however, automatically mean that all competing power centres are gone. A few thousand activists in an institutionalized, well-established extra-parliamentary organ can make the life of the PPO harder because many key decisions are still, at least formally, under democratic control. As Duverger (1954) argued, the size and shape of parties' formative parts is not the main thing that differentiates parties, it is how the formative parts are bound together, and what their roles and prerogatives are. If the powers of subunits are respected, they can still have an effect on parties' destinies.

In this vein Sundberg (2003: 129–159) has suggested that Scandinavian parties have taken on a 'democratic-professional' form: while 'professional assets have replaced voluntary assets, and public assets replace private assets', members still rule parties via representative intra-party mechanisms. They are 'the ultimate rulers in a democratic organization' and it's in their hands to 'hire and fire party bureaucrats and to decide whether to buy or not to buy professional aid from external sources'. It has also been suggested that parties have become 'modern electoral organizations' as the role of the prime minister role has expanded due to constitutional reform (Paloheimo 2007: 265). Following Sundberg's line of though, this can only happen through member approval.

To stir up expectations even more, some evidence indicates that serious party-type specific differences might still prevail. Sundberg (1997: 109–114) found that in spite of heavy state regulation the distribution of formal power within Finnish parties still varied significantly in the mid-1990s, from 'extremely egalitarian to the extremely hierarchical'. As rules too are results of intra-party negotiations, one might wonder where the motivation comes from. The answer might lie deeper. Mickelsson's (1999: 286–287) longitudinal analysis of the SDP's and the NCP's 'self-perceptions' indicates that despite that some features have converged fundamental differences that are based on different basic values (individuality in the NCP and communality in the SDP) still exist. The mass party identity has always been very important to the SDP while the NCP has never let go of its emphasis on statesmanship and personal skill. When it comes to intra-party procedures in the SDP, a communal ethos is still heavily supported (Mickelsson 2007: 267–268).

Changing the party's organizational course should be harder in parties that grant legitimate decision-making power to their sub-units. While POG erosion is a fact, there is not much evidence to support the decay of PCOs. They still enjoy larger subsidies than PPO's and they control parties formal decision-making procedures so they have potential to leave their mark on organizational development. If they decide to halt the party's transformation to 'electoral-professionalism', this might become a problem for the leadership. The SDP is especially vulnerable to this problem because current pressures demand a change against its historical self-understanding (as mass organization based on equality and hierarchical representation). Because conservatives have generally valued pragmatism over orthodoxy in ideological and organizational matters (von Beyme 1985) and individual leadership over equality the NCP should be better suited for transformation.

Changing political environment demands changes in parties

The Finnish political system has changed a great deal during the period studied, and as these changes relate directly to explanatory factors suggested by Katz and Mair (2002), there are good reasons to expect that the public face of Finnish parties has been strengthened.

First of all, Finland's constitutional voyage from strong presidential government to parliamentarism has empowered parties by increasing the significance of parliamentary work and making the prime minister the key player (Arter 1999: 231–232, 237; 2006: 131–132; Paloheimo 2007).[3] Alongside with constitutional reform Finnish politics has become strongly 'governmentalized'; i.e., significant oppositional parties have become extinct and most parties join governments in recurring intervals.[4]

Another factor that should strengthen public 'face' is the fact that party leaders are no longer dependent on the willingness of

---

3   See Introduction and chapters by Isaksson, Karvonen and Paloheimo about the effects of constitutional reform.

4   For the development of cabinet politics, see chapters by Isaksson, Karvonen and Paloheimo.

party members to pay dues. Today, public subsidies are parties' main source of revenue (Wiberg 2006: 62; 2008: 183) and Finnish parties are the most dependent on state money in the Western world (Pierre, Svåsand and Widfelt 2000: 13–14). Subsidies are in fact so generous that parties could survive without members (Wiberg 2006: 62) and therefore they are now much less dependent on mass organization (Sundberg 2003: 149). PPOs seem to have been strengthened staff-wise too. The amount of ministerial special assistants has continued to grow, in 1997 every MP got a personal assistant, and in 2005 a state secretary system was consolidated to relieve ministers' workload. Especially the ministerial 'entourages' have grown significantly. (Wiberg 2006: 218–222; 2008: 180). Here, as was pointed out before, the interesting question is how PCOs have used their increased resources. If parties' *modus operandi* has changed, it should be reflected in PCO spending, too. In absolute terms they still get more.

Katz and Mair argue that the weakening of traditional political participation and the emergence of personalized 'media politics' supports the PPO 'ascendancy'. Mediatization of politics places public office holders in the limelight and nationalizes electoral competition making it also more centralized. Professionalization of campaign work depoliticizes PCOs by replacing the activist stratum that is the only potential source for intra-organizational counter-power (Katz & Mair 2002). 'Audience democracy' makes organizations more dependent on luminous personalities and it blurs the boundaries between party decisions and actors' freedom to manoeuvre (Manin 1997).

Electoral turnout in Finland has declined for decades; 20 per cent less of the electorate participate nowadays as compared to the 1960s (Paloheimo & Raunio 2008: 210). The number of party memberships and local party units has decreased, too. At the same time hints of a more personalized style of politics are emerging (Karvonen 2009: 121–122; 2010). For example top candidates have increased their votes (Borg & Paloheimo 2009: 17). These changes are reflected in the media which started to commercialize in the early 1980s. Since then 'mass appeal' has become the primary objective and journalists are now constantly seeking personalized angles on politics (Herkman 2012, 187–195). According to Paloheimo (2007: 263–264), politics and media today react in real time so politicians can no longer supress and reveal information when it suits them. Increased complexity, technicality and the sheer volume of political issues enhance the evolution.

Politics has also become internationalized, furthering the complexity even more. Especially the emergence of the EU has blurred traditional political boundaries (Arter 1999: 239). According to Raunio (2002; 2008: 195–196, 203) supranational cooperation makes PPOs stronger because information flows through the parliament and not through party organs, and parties (especially when they are in government) have to react quickly. The delegate model with its emphasis on intra-party scrutiny seems to be too slow for contemporary complex media politics. This causes a serious problem for political responsiveness – at least inside parties that wish to 'advise' their representatives in advance.

The distribution of organizational resources: from regional representation to the national public sphere?

Since 1960s the growth rate of parties' main income source, public subsidies, has favoured PPOs although party aid to PCOs is still over four times larger. Over the years party aid has decupled, parliamentary 'office aid' to party groups has multiplied 80 times. Its average annual growth rate is twelve per cent against six per cent for party aid. (Koskimaa 2010: 61–67.[5]) While the party aid has merely retained its value against inflation, the value of 'office aid' has actually increased (Venho 2008). In the new millennium most parliamentary group budgets show surplus – parties cannot even spend all of it.

5   This study deals only with SDP. While it does not describe overall development accurately, it does provide a rough estimate because both subsidies are paid according to the party's electoral success and the numbers were calculated from overall sums that are divided between parties.

PPG staff, total

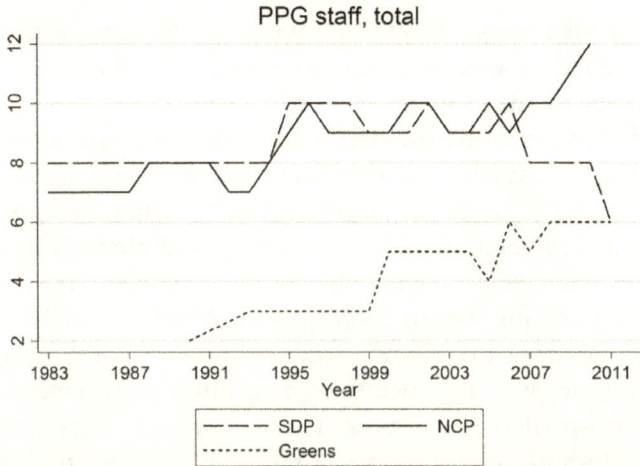

Figure 1. Total number of full-time employees in parliamentary group offices

Comparison of staff numbers in central and parliamentary offices shows similar tendencies. As Figure 1 shows, staff sizes in group offices have increased over time. The Greens' parliamentary office staff has tripled, which is due to the fact that the personnel was recruited during this period. The NCP has doubled its parliamentary workforce during the period studied, but the SDP's office has not grown very much over time; the 2007 electoral loss even decreased it a bit. Overall, however, investment in the parliamentary arena is visible, in money as well as manpower.

Staff, total

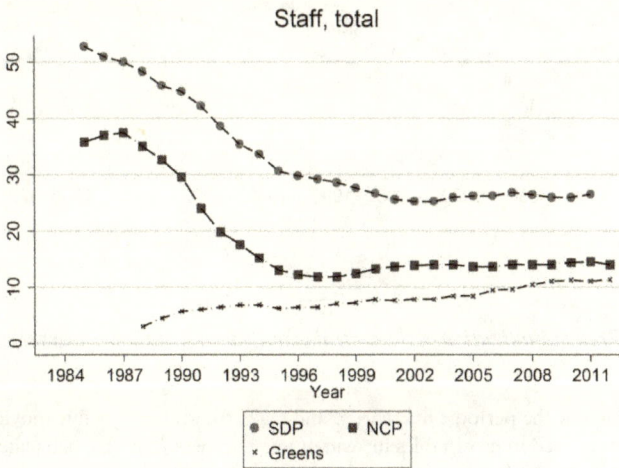

Figure 2. Total number of full-time employees in central offices

The opposite is true of parties' central offices: they have generally become smaller[6]. The downhill trend began around the turn of the 1990s, along with the major depression that cut back party subsidies and rapid changes in information technology. One computer has replaced ten typewriters and therefore these numbers cannot be treated as direct measures of power. But because new technology has affected parliamentary offices too, the overall picture suggests that parties – as a whole – tend to favour the parliamentary sphere. Almost the same number of people works in NCP's and Green's offices. Considering the big difference in their electoral strength this magnitude probably meets the minimum requirements of focused extra-parliamentary work. The SDP's central organization is still significantly larger. Its extra ten employees relate to five per cent larger personnel spending (compared to the NCP) and it amounts to 372 409 EUR from the SDPs 1992–2012 average total expenditure. This is roughly the double of what the party has spent on publicity in the new millennium (on yearly average).

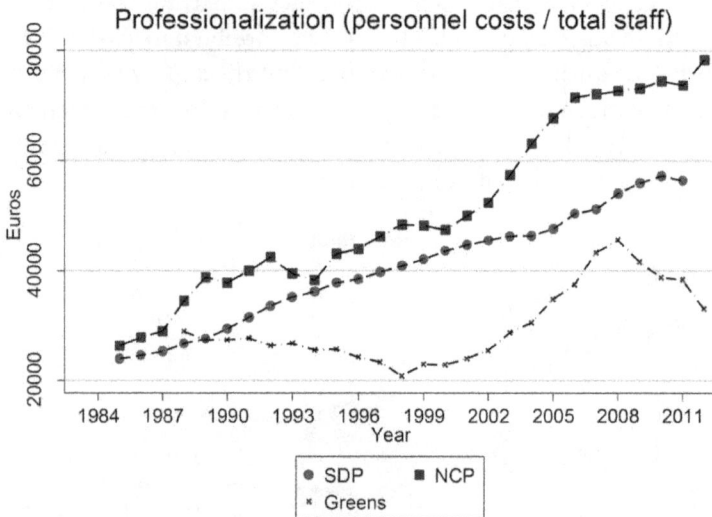

Figure 3. Professionalization of the central office (average wage per worker)

---

6   To even out the periodic fluctuation and make trends more visible moving aver-
    ages were used in most tables instead of raw numbers. They are calculated as
    follows: $(1/5)^*[x(t-2) + x(t-1) + 1^*x(t) + x(t+1) + x(t+2)]$; $x(t)$ = the equalized
    variable.

Professionalization is a key factor in contemporary theories of party change: professionals are expected to replace 'party men' and depoliticize party organizations. As figure 3 shows, average wages have gone up, but party specific differences exist too. In the NCP the average wage remained slightly above the SDP's average until the turn of the millennium. From there, the curve rises steeply. Around this time the NCP adopted the centralized, image-centred and professional electoral party style that it is now known for. In 2004, after the loss in 2003 elections, young and dynamic Jyrki Katainen (then 32 years of age) became the chair. Already in 2006 the party almost succeeded in bringing in the first NCP president in 50 years. In 2007 parliamentary elections Katainen led the NCP to its all-time second best result finishing second (only one seat behind Centre Party) and in 2011 NCP became the largest party in parliament for the first time in its history, making Katainen prime minister. One year later Sauli Niinistö of the NCP won the presidential election.

It is worth noticing how rapidly the NCP executed the change. The SDP too had an explicit intention to become professionalized already in 1992 (according to annual reports), but no such attempts are visible in the data. Yearly increases resemble annual index raises. As the total staff numbers have also remained at the same level since the mid-1990s, it seems that the SDP has not really become professionalized or at least its development has been significantly slower. The data for the Greens, on the other hand, indicate that most of their staff works on a quasi-voluntary basis. Considering their nature as a 'lifestyle party' and their heavy reliance on public money this might actually be their only way to survive.

To find out whether parties direct their organizational resources towards electoral-professional activities or traditional party work I divided the central office staff into two categories: political planning, publicity plus elections, and associational staff[7]. A general trend towards electoral-professionalism exists (Figure 4), but so do

---

7   Categorization is based on parties own classification schemes and titles. Planning and publicity includes (but is not limited to): planners, publicists, media workers and permanent electoral staff. Associational work includes: district officers, trade union specialists, municipal secretaries and other auxiliary liaisons.

Staff, planning & publicity (% / total staff)

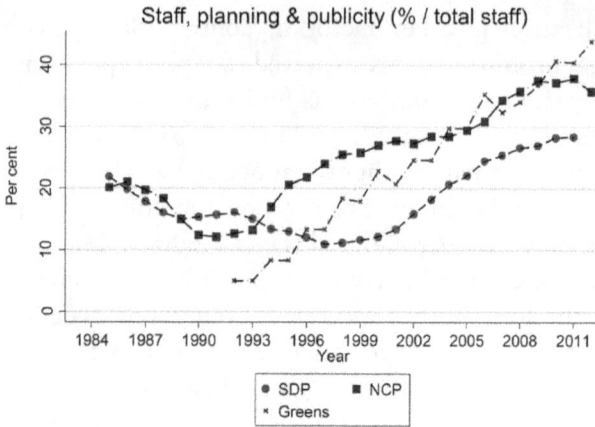

Figure 4. Relative share of full-time workers in political planning, elections and publicity

substantial party-wise differences. Apparently in the early 1990s
the NCP and Greens started to pay a lot attention to media politics–
almost as if they knew that 'audience' democracy was emerging.
In the SDP this realization took ten more years and it is still not
fully executed. At the turn of the millennium, when the NCP was
reaching the 30 per cent mark, the SDP was just beginning its climb
from the ten per cent level. Although the SDP did catch the train
eventually, almost ten years later, a significant difference remains.
The 2005–2010 average for the SDP is 26 per cent, for the NCP 36
per cent and for the Greens 32.5 per cent. This difference is even
more evident in party spending on publicity (Figure 5).

Publicity costs (% / total costs)

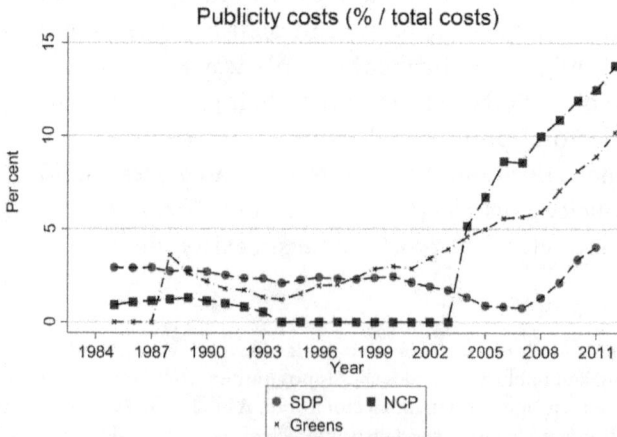

Figure 5. Relative share of money invested in publicity

Parties started to pay attention to publicity only in the 2000s, but since then spending has generally increased. The NCP started a very steep climb after the turn of the millennium, spending almost fifteen per cent of its total expenditure on publicity towards the end of period studied. The SDP came later and with a smaller effort, spending less than five per cent at the end of the period. When parties press subsidy was released in 2008, the NCP immediately transferred significant amounts from the party press to its internal media, but in the SDP it took two years to do anything and the party continued to direct ten per cent more to its old papers. This represents a clear difference in party preferences. The aggressiveness of the NCP's rise in the early 2000s resembles the work of an autonomous entrepreneur. The Greens preferences are the clearest signs of the emergence of media politics: In 2011 a whopping 53.9 per cent of their central office workers worked in media, planning and elections and over 12 per cent out of their total expenditure went to publicity. Overall, parties new emphasis on media politics is clearly visible.

The other side of the story is a decrease in traditional party work. Surprisingly, however, there are no signs of a general trend. Parties' investments in traditional work have remained fairly unchanged. The SDP has always put significant emphasis on it and it continues to do so (averaging over 20 per cent of its total workforce), while the NCP has never during the period studied employed more than

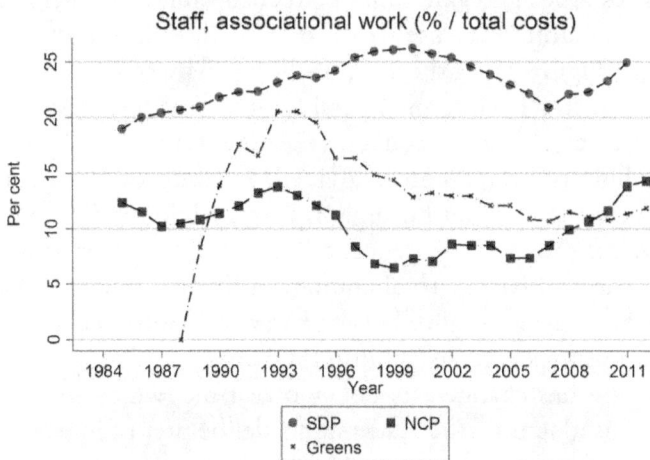

Figure 6. Relative share of full-time workers in traditional mass party tasks

ten per cent in mass party tasks. Here, too, the Greens converge with the NCP after the quick rise in the early 1990s that was caused by a rapid increase in subsidies that followed their huge victory in 1991 elections (from four seats to ten) and the young party's eagerness to 'engage with the people'. 'The Green bus' initiative brought the party leadership to several happenings around the country and the 'Magic winter' conference assembled young citizens in the Wanaja castle. Combined, these events ate roughly about ten per cent of the party's total budget. After them, Greens have not held similar mass events.

Another way to assess support to traditional party work is to measure the central parties they allot to regional subunits. The legal minimum for regional district subsidies was from 1987 until 2007 eight per cent of total. Between 2008 and 2011 the quota was twelve per cent and in 2012 it dropped to 10 per cent. The SDP has always paid significantly more than the legal threshold, on average 37.6 per cent of its party aid. Unsurprisingly, the NCP has paid less, on average only 16.6 per cent. The Greens have paid only the legal minimum.

There are two other ways to support the 'field': parties can channel a share of membership fees back to the subunits, and they can pay district workers' salaries. Because in the latter case the central party maintains a direct hold of the subunit, the best way to assess districts' independent resources is to focus on 'freely usable allowances', the aggregate sum of direct subsidies and membership fees that subunits may use freely, or at least without any explicit demands (Figure 7). In the SDP, the lion's share of its membership fees are directed back to membership organizations. According to party statutes the party council (the representative of the POG) decides how the total sum is divided. In 2009 only 20 per cent was directed to the central organization, while district and local organizations received 80 per cent. Because direct district subsidies are also substantial, the total amount of 'freely usable allowances' is fairly high, averaging well over 20 per cent of total expenditure. It has, however, decreased a bit in the 2000s.

The NCP has changed its policy over time, which in itself can be taken as a sign of the leadership's deliberate attempt to make the most of limited resources. Until the turn of 1990's the PCO paid, along with direct aid and membership fee returns, district

Freely useable allowances to subunits (% / total)

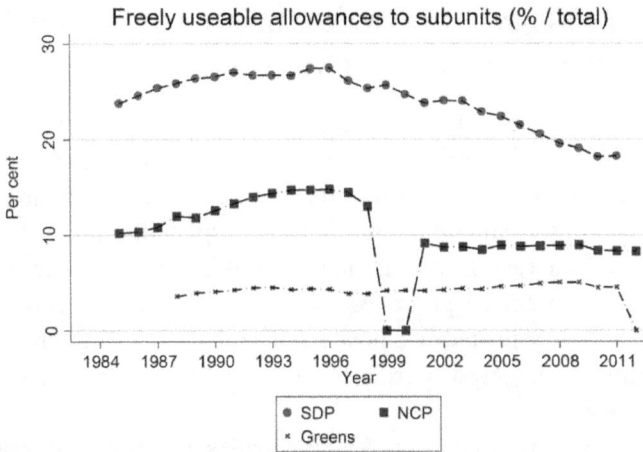

Figure 7. Central organization's total financial aid to subunits (per cent out of total expenditure)

salaries. When it stopped doing so, it increased direct aid (peak in early 1990's). In 1997 district offices salaries reappeared to central party's financial statements and direct district subsidies plummeted. At the beginning of the millennium the party also centralized its membership fee system and kept reducing 'freely usable allowances' (now only direct district aid). While the party continues to pay direct district aid and possibly some portion of membership fees, by centralization of district personnel and membership revenue system significantly reduced the autonomy and power of its subunits and moved the party towards electoral-professionalism. In times of nationalized politics (see Caramani 2004) the absence of field organizations' financial leverage and the ability to coordinate things from the centre gives the party leadership great powers to manage the organization according to its own desires. In 2008 the NCP formed a business conglomerate. According to annual report the aim was to strengthen the centres' steering powers over its constituent elements (the party and two media agencies the party owns).

In the NCP the party leadership has been able to change the organization relatively quickly to meet the needs of electoral-professionalism in audience democracy. In contrast, SDP's changes have been markedly smaller and slower. At least to some extent this likely results from subnational parties wider financial leverage.

Formal power relations reflect historical characteristics – except where there are no historical characteristics

Due to their availability and comparability party statutes have formed the most popular source in party power studies. While rules do not describe real power relations perfectly, they are likely to correspond to reality reasonably well – especially in highly institutionalized parties. Because they are public they cannot deviate too much from actual practices. (Pedersen 2010: 744; Bille 1997: 47.) Party actors probably know their rights and Finnish culture is generally considered as relatively amenable when it comes to obeying rules.

Katz and Mair (1992: 6–8) view rules symbolically: not as concrete descriptions of decision-making system, but as mirrors of party culture that provide continuity and limit conflicts. Pedersen (2010) adds that they can also be viewed as resources, especially in times of conflict.

Figure 8 shows the development of the aggregated formal power of central party organizations over parliamentary groups (for detailed information see Appendix 1). In the SDP the PCO has always had a significantly stronger hold over its parliamentary arm compared to the NCP and the Greens, which – once again – show considerable similarity. Only in the Greens has the balance changed significantly. Again, this is not very surprising because the party was formed during this period. But the direction of change is surprising: the central party organization has been strengthened *vis-à-vis* its parliamentary arm. As for the NCP, the PPO has been strengthened somewhat; in the SDP the distribution has remained virtually unaltered.

Perhaps the most important intra-party decision, whether a party decides to join or abstain from a governmental coalition, is a good example of deep inter-party differences between two main cases. In the NCP, the PCO rules do not mention anything about negotiators. Until 2003 the PPO rules assigned the task to its chairmanship and to the PCO's negotiators, but in 2003 this rule was removed leaving the issue formally open. According to a standard interpretation (Pedersen 2010) the non-existence of rule leaves the PPO – the lawfully elected body that represents voters – the upper hand. On the decision the rules only state that the issue needs to

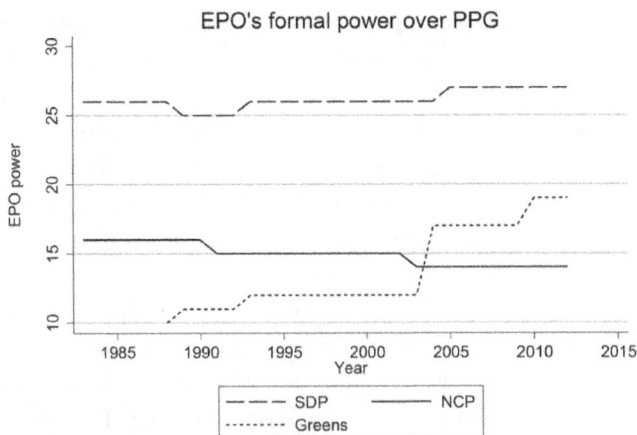

Figure 8. PCO's control over parliamentary party groups

be 'negotiated and decided' at a joint meeting of the party council and the parliamentary group. It is not specified who decides (the parliamentary group, council or both), nor does it say anything about procedure.

In the SDP the procedure is more specified and it assigns the ultimate power to extra-parliamentary organs. The parliamentary group gets to appoint members to a negotiating group but the majority is on the PCO side (assuming that party leader is a representative of the PCO). It is explicitly stated that the party council defines party's stance on the cabinet program, decides whether party joins a cabinet or not and who will represent the party in cabinet. It may also transfer all its powers to the party executive (and it normally does so). Nonetheless, all relevant aspects of the decision are in the hands of the extra-parliamentary party. The parliamentary group is involved in crafting the final proposal and it also can make an independent statement to the council, but it has no voting power over the issue.

The Greens have come up with a halfway solution: the decision is made at a joint meeting of the council and the parliamentary group where every participant has one vote. Because the Green council is always larger than the parliamentary party group, the extra-parliamentary organization can overturn the negotiators' decision if it is able to act in concert. This actually happened in 2011.

When it comes to policies, the SDP's rules are fairly specific about the chain of command: party organs decide and parliamentary party group executes. It is clearly stated that the PPO's task is to pursue policies that are mentioned in the party programs. In the 1980s the parliamentary group even maintained a formal sub-organ to supervise that all of the most important motions found in the party's concrete program become submitted. Back then the NCP was not very different (although it did not have a similar sub-organ). Eventually, however, the rule to follow concrete policies was dropped from the PPO's statutes and was replaced by more vague 'support for objectives that reflect the party's principles'. In 2003, programmatic work was dropped from the tasks of the PPO's committee group, leaving NCP rules devoid of any formal indication that parliamentary group drives the party's policies. Parliamentary group's constitutional independence in still explicitly stated.

Perhaps the most interesting – and telling – component in party rules concerns information. In the SDP the PCO has after wars enjoyed extensive rights to participate in the parliamentary party's meetings, including the 'working committee' that acts as its executive branch. Up until 2005 every member of council and executive had an automatic right to be present at parliamentary group meetings. The party secretary who runs the central office has enjoyed a right to participate also in working committee meetings since the 1960s. In the NCP the council has never had the right to be present at PPO meetings, and from the executive only chairs are automatically allowed. Both groups present annual reports to their extra-parliamentary organs. In the SDP they are processed and discussed in the council, in the NCP they are only submitted to a hearing. It makes at least a symbolical difference whether the extra-parliamentary party is seen as something that engages in scrutiny, or just hears out what the PPG has been doing.

The Greens have never established any formal information channels, although the annual report of the party includes a brief section about the parliamentary party group. This information, however, is something that anyone could read in the news. The Green parliamentary party has always reserved itself the absolute right to control who attends its meetings – no one has an automatic right even to listen. The party has always prided itself for denying imperative mandates – this is made explicit in its rules. When the party was formed, the autonomous status of the parliamentary group was considered natural. But as the graph shows, the extra-parliamentary organization has clearly grown stronger over time.

According to a former party chair, aspirations to strengthen formal party institutions might be forming among younger Green generations (interview in autumn 2013). While the upward trend in the 1990s might have been caused by the gradual formalization of the organizational procedures in a new party, the PCO has continued to strengthen in the 2000s. In 2004, the PCO's negotiating powers in government formation were made formal and the PCO created rules for sanctioning individual members, including MPs. These measures represent traditional methods of extra-parliamentary influence, and in a party that has always emphasised MP autonomy they reflect a change in the PCO's self-understanding. Considering the 'hyper-democratic' ethos of the Greens, this might not be very surprising after all. In a party with a small but devoted activist membership it makes sense to strengthen units that are likely to counter parliamentary elites.

Sundberg (1997) has noted that party rules are not changed often; this is clearly the case here too. But the persistence is more important. It suggests that the SDP activists want to continue to keep tighter grip of their PPO whereas the NCP's PCO has not succeeded in doing so. In fact it continues to lose strength. To be sure, these changes are minor (party's weakening in the formation of negotiating group and the waning of concrete policy link between the PCO and the PPO), but considering their direction they can be quite seamlessly connected to the general argument. Changes or the ability to resist them do not only make someone stronger; the movement, or the lack of it, is itself a sign of different underlying organizational power structures.

MP's in national executive committee: controlling the leading party organ, or signalling its importance?

The third traditional indicator of intra-party power balance is the locus of 'the ruler'. While some analysts have suggested focusing on party chairs' loyalties (Heidar & Koole 2000) it is difficult to measure and therefore the control of central party organs has become the standard tool. The national executive committee (NEC) takes care of a party's ongoing work, prepares policies for other organs, announces their meetings and manages working groups. It is also the official 'home' of the party chair and therefore usually thought to be the most important sub-organ. Following Katz and Mair (1993) analysts have relied on fairly straightforward measurement and interpretation: count the MPs in NECs and view a high amount as a sign of parliamentary control (for example Biezen 2000: 398–399; Enyedi & Linek 2008: 461, 468).

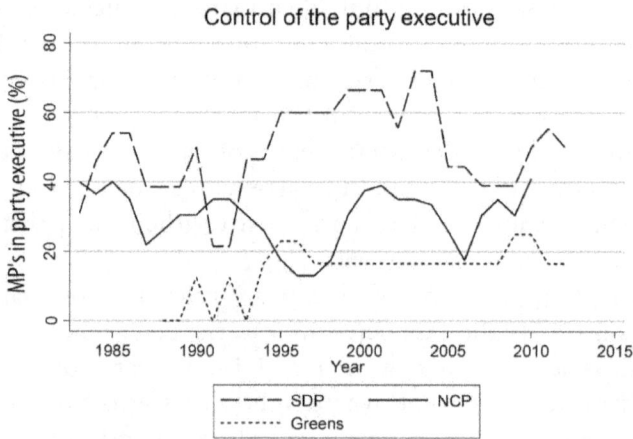

Figure 9. Parliamentary representatives in parties' national executive committees

If we want to hold on to the general argument about historical party type-specific differences that has been developed during the course of this study, Figure 9 requires a new interpretation. Not only are the upward trends missing, but parties' positions on the vertical scale run contrary to theoretical expectations. The SDP, a party hailing from a class-mass tradition where PCO control over the parliamentary arm is a well-established historical characteristic (at least in the party folklore), has clearly the highest over-time average of parliamentarians on its national executive committee. Although the relative amount of MPs exceeds the 50 per cent level only half of the time, the all-time average (49.6 per cent) is nevertheless very high. To make things even stranger, the NCP that averages roughly at 30 per cent has throughout the research period had an explicit rule that prevents over 50 per cent MP representation in the NEC. The Greens do not make things easier: low levels of public office holders in the NEC would make sense in an institutionalized democratic party (like the SDP) where it would be considered a counterweight to the PPO and a way to affect its functioning between elections. But the PPO should be the main force in new parties that are not yet institutionalized, as van Biezen (2000) has theorized.

In her own study van Biezen (2000: 410–413) found that this is the case, but only when power balance is measured with this indicator. Every other indicator (rules and resources) pointed towards PCO dominance. To explain the apparent discrepancy (to my knowledge) she suggests that analytical distinction and theoretical conflict between these organs might not reflect the reality too well and the relationship is more complex. van Biezen reasons that parties are probably dominated by a small elite that works 'in the intersection' of these faces to root cohesiveness that is still a valuable asset in party work. Although new democracies are certainly different playing fields than established ones like Finland, her hypothesis opens a way to more nuanced interpretation. My interviews and qualitative in-depth data on intra-party decision making processes support the idea that intra-party power is not mainly about a constant struggle between the parliamentary and extra-parliamentary 'faces'. Therefore the idea that MPs 'infiltrate' the PCO to control it does not sound feasible. After all, it is the party congress (in the SDP) or council (in the NCP) that decides about its composition.

If the NEC is the prominent decision-making authority in the SDP, it makes sense to bind a significant number of representatives to its work. According to one veteran who played a very central role in the SDP in the 1980s, the national executive committee was a place where the party's 'best forces' gathered to solve political problems (interview conducted in the fall of 2013). But as records show, most of these 'best forces' were also MPs (the chairman, party secretary and deputy chairs, etc.). This challenges the caricature where the PCO is solely comprised of extra-parliamentary actors who unidirectionally try to control the PPO. Instead, it is more realistic to view it as a 'command centre' where leaders from different 'faces' meet, decide on central issues and positions and foster cohesion.

But what about the NCP? If the NEC is a 'command centre' it certainly does not make sense that in a party that has historically emphasised the role of the PPO the MP representation in it is so low, and formally regulated. My guess is that these contradictory observations simply signify that NECs perform different duties in different parties. This in fact parallels the 'common knowledge' on party organizational types: only in parties that hail from socialist class-mass tradition is the NEC 'the ruler'. The NCP NEC is elected by the party council and not the congress so its composition strongly reflects regional interests. It sounds ludicrous to assume that a historically parliamentary-heavy party would vest its highest decision-making authority in the hands of regional councillors. It is more plausible that in 'internally' created cadre parties effective decision-making power lies in somewhere else, possibly in the parliament. At least in the late 1980s the NCP parliamentary group played significantly larger role when the government was formed, compared to the NEC.

If this still holds, it makes a major difference to intra-party power relations. The SDP NEC is an assembly that is elected at the party congress, by the party's subnational delegates. This gives the party membership a direct channel to influence intra-party decision-making. If the power in the NCP lies within the parliamentary group, it effectively avoids extra-parliamentary control because it is elected by voters, not party activists.

The public 'face': varying degrees of power increase

It is clear that some developments in Finnish parties mirror the 'ascendancy of the party in public office' thesis presented by Katz and Mair. Change is most visible in the development of parties' resources. 'Office aid', the public subsidy to parliamentary party groups has increased way more rapidly than extra-parliamentary organizations' 'party aid' (although the latter is still larger in absolute terms). While the latter has merely retained its value, the former has increased. In line with this, staff sizes in parliamentary group offices have increased while parties' central offices have become smaller. Also, publicity-related spending and staff investments in electoral-professional work have increased throughout the party-type spectrum. I view these as reactions to changes in parties' media environment that follow from rapid advancements in information technology. As such, they do enhance the role of public office holders and it is not difficult to predict what the future will look like. Following Paloheimo (2007) and analysts in the field of political journalism (for example Niemi 2014), it does seem that future political battles will be fought, to increasing extent, in a 'virtual agora' where professional politicians have to be ready to present and defend their views on complex issues in real time without consulting a party-wide 'pow-wow' in advance.

This does not mean, however, that every party is able to adapt to these pressures simultaneously. As Heidar and Saglie (2003: 220) pointed out after analysing organizational change in Norway, 'parties may change in the same direction but within different modes'. This is clearly the case in Finland, too. Significant differences in party spending, formal power structures and PCO control persist. It certainly looks as if some underlying 'deep structure', a party culture if you will, acts as a weight that defines how much and how rapidly the 'surface level' (spending strategies, organizational roles and processes) is able to transform[8].

It is important to notice that it is not only the size of the weight that matters, its shape is crucial too. Some shapes work better in specific winds. It is not a surprise that the Social Democrats dominated Finnish politics in the golden age of mass politics. For leader-centred NCP the idea of empowering the grassroots probably seemed less palatable, which might explain why their transformation into a mass party was confined mostly to formal structures. Fortunately from an NCP point of view, in contemporary personalized media politics, after decades of decrease in traditional political participation no one expects such things anymore.

The National Coalition Party has quickly transformed into a true electoral-professional organization. It has reduced its central office staff to a small group of highly professionalized personnel and doubled the workforce in its parliamentary office. It has also channelled more and more money into political planning and publicity and it has effectively decreased the relevance of its subunits by tying them tightly under the wings of central organization. It has also slowly released the PCO's formal hold over the parliamentary group – a link that was not very strong to begin with. Judging by the role and composition of its NEC it seems like organizational

---

8   In this study the best empirical reflection of 'deep structure' is party rules that symbolize significant differences in PCO vs. PPO-relations.

power escapes 'field' control effectively. This is a good example of how the deep structure conditions surface level development. Historical emphasis on the public domain makes it easy to channel new resources to it – without fears of interference from below. This also is evident in the speed of the change.

NCP's historical main rival, the SDP, has had more problems in transforming into a PPO-dominated 'media agency'. At the end of the research period its central office was still characterized by relatively large and non-professionalized staff that worked more often with traditional mass party tasks than with media politics. Its emphasis on subnational party work still consumed almost 20 per cent of the total income while investments to publicity remained at the five per cent level. Formally, the Social Democratic parliamentary group is still significantly more tightly tied to their extra-parliamentary party organization. Also, as their NEC still seems to be the main locus of intra-organizational power, transformation to electoral-professionalism becomes even harder. Some 20 years ago Herbert Kitschelt (1994: xiii) argued that in order to compete successfully, social democratic parties need to get beyond their 'programmatic, organizational, and electoral legacies'. The SDP's electoral record from the past 30 years suggests that this has not occurred. As it is generally believed that fundamental ideological differences have lost their flavoor (and therefore are unable to explain electoral fortunes), the answer might lie in a stiff organizational imperative that restrains the leadership.

The development of the Greens resembles the NCP's evolution in many ways. This gives additional empirical support to van Biezen's (2005) idea that newly formed parties tend to emulate established parties in a 'periodic' fashion. This study might add that they seem to emulate successful contemporary parties. The Greens were born as a radical grass-roots movement, but they quickly adopted adequate measures to survive in the contemporary electoral-professional climate. European Green parties have been observed to aim at maintaining their original spirit without losing electoral competitiveness (Burchell 2001). They have not built a large bureaucracy or a vast ground organization. Instead, they have directed most of their resources to electioneering and publicity – enhancing their public 'face' that is still formally relatively autonomous from the PCO. Some signs suggest, however, that the

PCO is becoming stronger. Especially the relatively large change in the formal distribution of power signals that significant forces are forming below the PPO level.

In the spring of 2011 the Greens caused two events that have not been witnessed in Finnish party politics before. First, their council overturned the parliamentary party's idea to join a government coalition. This was more than a whim of mind or a rebellious act. The party had previously decided, reluctantly, to enter cabinet negotiations. But when the original line up crashed and a new one that was based on a traditional bourgeois coalition was introduced, the council acted. In other words: they had clear political preferences and they fought for them. A little later the party also elected a new chairman in open membership ballot. Although the ballot was not formally binding, central party figures said it would have been very hard to reject the verdict at the party congress that formally appointed the chair. As democratizing innovations are probably hard to overturn, this is likely to become the norm for the Greens.

These procedures set a new standard for Finnish intra-party politics. The combination of 'ultra-democratic' activist spirit and institutions that have real power might provide a solution to the crisis of mass parties. As programmatic work has lost most of its meaning due to catch-allism that leads to indigestible abstraction, and concrete decisions by party congresses lack actual impact because modern politics work predominantly in a reactive fashion (Manin 1997), the only way to save the democratic component in party politics might be to confine it to major decisions like membership ballots on leadership and government formation (German SPD already tried the latter after the 2013 federal elections). This strategy would grant real decision-making power to the diminishing but active grassroots while maintaining a high level of leadership autonomy that is mandatory in contemporary media politics. In fact, while POGs have lost their numeric strength, their formal powers in party leadership selection have been upgraded in many parties (Scarrow 1999; Cross & Blais 2011). As party activists especially in small countries like Finland often work close to one another, these procedures are likely to prove contagious – especially if they prove effective.

References

Appleton, A. R. & Ward, D. S. (1997). Party Response to Environmental Change: A Model of Organizational Innovation. *Party Politics* Vol. 3, 3: 341–362.

Arter, D. (1999). *Scandinavian Politics Today*. Manchester, Manchester University Press.

— (2006). *Democracy in Scandinavia: Consensual, Majoritarian or Mixed?* Manchester, Manchester University Press.

Beyme, K. (1985). *Political Parties in Western Democracies*. New York, St. Martin's Press.

Bille, L. (1997). *Partier i Forandring*. Odense, Odense Universitetsforlag.

van Biezen, I. (2000). On the Internal Balance of Party Power: Party Organizations in New Democracies. *Party Politics* Vol. 6, 4: 395–417.

— (2005). On the Theory and Practice of Party Formation and Adaptation in New Democracies. *European Journal of Political Research* Vol. 44, 1: 147–174.

van Biezen, I., Mair, P. & Poguntke, T. (2012). Going, going, ... gone? The Decline of Party Membership in Contemporary Europe. *Party Politics* Vol. 51, 1: 24–56.

Borg, S. & Paloheimo H. (2009). Johdanto. In S. Borg & H. Paloheimo (eds.), *Vaalit yleisödemokratiassa: Eduskuntavaalitutkimus 2007*. Tampere, Tampere University Press: 13–27.

Burchell, J. (2001). Evolving or Conforming? Assessing Organisational Reform Within European Green Parties. *West European Politics* Vol. 24, 3: 113–134.

Caramani, D. (2004). *The Nationalization of Politics: the Formation of National Electorates and Party Systems in Western Europe*. Cambridge, Cambridge University Press.

Cross, W. & Blais A. (2011). Who selects the party leader? *Party Politics* Vol. 18, 2: 127–150.

Detterbeck, K. (2005). Cartel Parties in Western Europe? *Party Politics* Vol. 11, 2: 173–191.

— (2008). Party Cartel and Cartel Parties in Germany. *German Politics* Vol. 17, 1: 27–40.

Duverger, M. (1954). *Political Parties: Their Organization and Activity in Modern State*. London, Methuen.

Enyedi, Z. & Linek L. (2008). Searching for the Right Organization: Ideology and Party Structure in East-Central Europe. *Party Politics* Vol. 14, 4: 455–477.

Gibson, R. & Harmel R. (1998). Party Families and Democratic Performance: Extraparliamentary vs. Parliamentary Group Power. *Political Studies* Vol. 46, 3: 633–650.

Harmel, R. (2005). Party Organizational Change: Competing Explanations? In K.R., Luther, & M.-R. Ferdinand (eds.), *Political Parties in New Europe*. Oxford, Oxford University Press: 119–142.

Heidar, K. & Koole R. (eds.) (2000), *Parliamentary Party Groups in*

European Democracies: Political Parties Behind Closed Doors. London, Routledge.

Heidar, K. & Saglie J. (2003). Predestined Parties? Organizational Change in Norwegian Political Parties. *Party Politics* Vol. 9, 2: 219–239.

Herkman, J. (2012). Politiikan media-ajulkisuus Kekkosen jälkeen. In K. Paakkunainen (ed.), *Suomalaisen politiikan murroksia ja muutoksia.* Helsinki, Helsingin yliopisto, Politiikan ja talouden tutkimuksen laitos: 187–208.

Hölttä, Outi (1984): Suomen Puolueiden Organisaatiot Vuosina 1918–39. *Poliittinen historia*, sarja C. Turun yliopisto: Turku.

Ishiyama, J. T. (1999). The Communist Successor Parties and Party Organizational Development in Post-Communist Politics. *Political Research Quarterly* Vol. 52, 1: 87–112.

Janda, K. (1980). *Political Parties: A Cross-National Survey.* New York, The Free Press.

Karvonen, L. (2009). Politiikan henkilöityminen. In S. Borg, S. & H. Paloheimo (eds.), *Vaalit yleisödemokratiassa: Eduskuntavaalitutkimus 2007.* Tampere, Tampere University Press: 94–125.
— (2010). *The Personalisation of Politics. A Study of Parliamentary Democracies.* Colchester, ECPR Press.

Katz, R. (2005). The Internal Life of Parties. In K.R., Luther & M.-R. Ferdinand (eds.), *Political Parties in New Europe.* Oxford, Oxford University Press: 87–118.

Katz, R. & Mair P. (1992). *Party Organizations: A Data Handbook on Party Organizations in Western Democracies, 1960–90.* London, Sage.
— (1993). The Evolution of Party Organizations in Europe: The Three Faces of Party Organization. *The American Review of Politics* Vol. 14, 4: 593–617.
— (1994). *How Parties Organize. Change and Adaptation in Party Organizations in Western Democracies.* London, Sage.
— (1995). Changing Models of Party Organization and Party Democracy: The Emergence of the Cartel Party. *Party Politics* Vol. 1, 1: 5–28.
— (2002). The Ascendancy of the Party in Public Office: Party Organizational Change in 20th Century Democracies. In R. Gunther, J. R. Montero. & J. J. Linz (eds.), *Political Parties: Old Concepts and New Challenges.* Oxford, Oxford University Press: 435–459.
— (2009). The Cartel Party Thesis: A Restatement. *Perspectives on Politics* Vol. 7, 4: 753–766.

Kitschelt, H. (1994). *The Transformation of European Social Democracy.* Cambridge, Cambridge University Press.

Koskimaa, V. (2010). *Kiinni, Irti: SDP:n Eduskuntaryhmän ja Ulkoparlamentaarisen Puolueen Suhteen Muutos Vuosina 1960–2010.* Master's Thesis (125 p.). Tampere, University of Tampere.

Lane, J.-E. & Ersson S. (1987). *Politics and Society in Western Europe*. London, Sage.

Lawson, K. (1990). Political Parties: Inside and Out. *Comparative Politics* Vol. 23, 1: 105–119.

Leino-Kaukiainen, P., & Uino, A. (1994). *Suomalaiskansallinen Kokoomus: Suomalaisen Puolueen ja Kansallisen Kokoomuspuolueen historia vuoteen 1929. Osa 1.* Helsinki, Suomen kansalliskirja.

Manin, B. (1997). *The Principles of Representative Government.* Cambridge, Cambridge University Press.

Michels, R. (1915). *Political Parties: A Sociological Study of the Oligarchical Tendencies of Modern Democracy.* New York, The Free Press.

Mickelsson, R. (1999). *Samanlaiset ja erilaiset puolueet: Retoriikka- ja diskurssianalyyttinen tutkimus kokoomuslaisten ja sosiaalidemokraattien jäsenlehdissä ilmaisemista käsityksistä omista puolueistaan vuosina 1965–1995.* Academic Dissertation. Turku, University of Turku.

— (2007). *Suomen puolueet: Historia, muutos ja nykypäivä.* Tampere, Vastapaino.

Müller, W. C. (1997). Inside the Black Box: A Confrontation of Party Executive Behaviour and Theories of Party Organizational Change. *Party Politics* Vol. 3, 3: 293–313.

Niemi, M. K. (2014). *Kaksi tietä huipulle. Media ja puoluejohtajuus Suomessa naisten noususta populismin aaltoon* (Pathways to the Top. Media and Party Leadership in Finland from Women's Breakthrough to the Wave of Populism). Academic dissertation. Turku, Department of Politics, University of Turku.

Paloheimo, H. (2007). Finland: Let the Force Be with the Leader. But Who Is the Leader? In Poguntke, T. & Webb P. (eds.), *The Presidentialization of Politics.* Oxford, Oxford University Press: 244–266.

Paloheimo, H. & Raunio T. (2008). Suomen puolueiden nykytila ja tulevaisuuden haasteet. In H. Paloheimo & T. Raunio (eds), *Suomen puolueet ja puoluejärjestelmä.* Helsinki, wsoy: 209–219.

Panebianco, A. (1988). *Political Parties: Organization and Power.* Cambridge, Cambridge University Press.

Pedersen, H. H. (2010), How Intraparty Power Relations Affect the Coalition Behaviour of Political Parties. *Party Politics* Vol. 16, 6: 737–754.

Pierre, J., Svåsand, L. & Widfeldt A. (2000). State Subsidies to Political Parties: Confronting Rhetoric with Reality. *West European Politics* Vol. 23, 3: 1–24.

Pitkin, H. (1967). *The Concept of Representation.* Berkeley, University of California Press.

Poguntke, T. (1987). New Politics and Party Systems: The Emergence of a New Type of Party? *West European Politics* Vol. 10, 1: 76–88.

Rantala, O. (1982). *Suomen Puolueiden Muuttuminen 1945–1980.* Helsinki, Gaudeamus.

Raunio, T. (2002). Why European Integration Increases Leadership Autonomy Within Political Parties. *Party Politics* Vol. 8, 4: 405–422.

— Euroopan integraation vaikutus Suomen puoluejärjestelmään. In H. Paloheimo & T. Raunio (eds), *Suomen puolueet ja puoluejärjestelmä*. Helsinki, WSOY: 185–208.

Scarrow, S. (1999). Parties and the Expansion of Direct Participation Opportunities: Who Benefits? *Party Politics* Vol. 5, 3: 341–362.

Soikkanen, H. (1975). *Kohti kansanvaltaa 1: Suomen Sosialidemokraattinen Puolue 75 vuotta, osa 1 1899–1937*. Helsinki, Suomen Sosiaalidemokraattinen Puolue.

Sundberg, J. (1994). Finland: Nationalized Parties, Professionalized Organizations. In R. Katz & P. Mair (eds.), *How Parties Organize: Change and Adaptation in Party Organizations in Western Democracies*. London, Sage: 158–184.

— (1997). Compulsory Party Democracy: Finland as a Deviant Case in Scandinavia. *Party Politics* Vol. 3, 1: 97–117.

— (2003). *Parties as Organized Actors: The Transformation of the Scandinavian Three-Front Parties*. Helsinki, The Finnish Society of Sciences and Letters.

Venho, Tomi (2008): *Piilotettua julkisuutta. Suomalaisen puolue- ja vaalirahoituksen avoimuusintressi normeissa ja käytännöissä*. Doctoral dissertation. University of Turku: Turku.

Wiberg, M. (2000). The Partyness of the Finnish Eduskunta. In K. Heidar & R. Koole. (eds.), *Parliamentary Party Groups in European Democracies: Political Parties behind Closed Doors*. London, Routledge: 161–176.

— (2006). *Politiikka Suomessa*. Helsinki, WSOY.

— (2008). Puolueet eduskunnassa ja hallituksessa. In H. Paloheimo & T. Raunio (eds), *Suomen puolueet ja puoluejärjestelmä*. Helsinki, WSOY: 163–184.

Appendix 1:

CODES FOR FORMAL RULES (inspired by Janda 1980, Sundberg 1997, Gibson & Harmel 1998, van Biezen 2000, and Pedersen 2010)

General criteria: 1) objective: to what extent is extra-parliamentary organization (EPO) able to control/affect parliamentary party groups (PPG) work? 2) Scale: no rule (PPG autonomy) – congress/ referendum – council – government (EPO control). 3) Codes reflect real options and variation. 4) Both rule sets (party and parliamentary group rules) are treated as equal parts of a whole.

- A1) Government formation, decision: to what extent can the EPO affect decision to join or abstain from government? 1: PPG decides (no formal role to the EPO), 2: decisions have to be made in PPG-EPO joint meeting, no formal decision rules, 3: joint meeting, equal weight to both organs, 4: joint meeting, single vote for every participant (EPO's natural majority), 5: EPO decides

- A2) Government formation, negotiators: who negotiates about government formation? 1) No formal regulations (formal PPG autonomy), 2) joint participation, only PPG defined; 3) joint participation, explicit equal weight; 4) joint participation, EPO domination; 5) only EPO

- B) Candidate selection: to what extent is the EPO able to affect candidate selection in parliamentary elections? 1) Membership ballot, no possibility for EPO interference, 2) membership ballot – EPO can change a portion of the candidates, but not the best half; 3) membership ballot – EPO can change a portion of candidates to others who were up for election; 4) membership ballot – EPO can freely change a portion; 5) membership ballot – the EPO can change all candidates

- C) Leadership selection: to what extent can the EPO affect PPG's leadership selection? 1) PPG decides; 2) EPO can suggest a candidate

- D) Policy: to what extent can EPO have a say on PPG's policy positions? 1) No formal decision-makers in the EPO, no defined tasks for the PPG; 2) specifically designated decision-maker in the EPO, no defined tasks for PPG, 3) EPO organs are specifically defined as decision-makers, PPG works according to party's principles; 4) EPO organs are specifically defined as decision-makers, PPG's explicitly defined purpose is to carry out programs of the party; 5) EPO organs are specifically defined as decision-makers, PPG's explicitly defined purpose is to carry out programs of the party, and specific organ takes care that this happens

- E) Information: to what extent is the PPG obliged to share information with the EPO? 1) PPG reports annually, no automatic rights for EPO to participate in the PPG; 2) PPG reports annually. EPO has limited rights to participate (only chairman in basic meetings and PPG executive); 3) PPG reports annually, EPO inspects. EPO has limited rights to participate (only chairman in basic meetings and PPG executive); 4: PPG reports annually, EPO inspects. EPO has automatic and vast rights to participate (every organ involved, in basic meetings and PPG executive)

- F) Sanctioning: to what extent can the EPO sanction PPG or its individual members? 1) The sanctioning of MPs is carried out by the PPG, 2: The sanctioning of MPs is carried out by the PPG, but the EPO can suggests a sanction, 3) EPO can suspend individual member if he/she has seriously damaged the party (vague); 4) central EPO organs have explicit right to suspend members who have acted against party's interests. Suspended member loses his rights to act as official at party organs (incl. PPG) and is not eligible for candidacy in elections

Passing through the Eye of the Needle – Individual Electoral Success in Finnish Parliamentary Elections

ÅSA VON SCHOULTZ

(*née Bengtsson*)

When in search of political power the most established channel for individuals is the electoral one. It is via election to public office a citizen can gain access to decision-making power over central aspects of society. The possibility to reach a position as an elected representative is, however, always conditioned by the electoral system. In most systems, individual politicians will need to pass two main hurdles in order to gain access to a position as a Member of Parliament (MP). The first one is *nomination*, which requires trust and support within the party organisation. The second is *election* which involves winning the support of voters. The importance of each of these two thresholds for individual candidates aiming at becoming elected varies substantially between electoral systems.

In electoral systems with proportional representation (PR) the first hurdle is often considered as the most vital one. This is due to the fact that PR is frequently combined with a closed or mixed list where candidates are placed in a ranked order on the ballot. Under these conditions the most important step towards becoming elected is to be placed high enough on the ballot, and the rationale for those seeking political power is hence to focus on party internal relations and support. The election itself is less vital from an individual perspective since candidates share a common goal of maximizing the total party vote.

In an electoral system such as the Finnish one, which uses an open list PR-system (OLPR), nomination is to be considered only as the first step in a highly competitive selection process where power lies in the hands of the voters. In the Finnish OLPR-system the candidates nominated by parties are presented to voters without internal rank ordering, and the personal votes each candidate receives fully determine which candidate/s will represent a given party in Parliament. The Finnish electoral system has been described as one of the most candidate-centred in the world (Raunio 2005) with very high incentives for individual campaigning (Shugart 2001: 83).

Under open lists the study of electoral success at the individual level can provide important information to the access to political power. Despite this, the accumulated knowledge of the mechanisms that shape the electoral performance of candidates under these conditions is still relatively scant (Bergman *et al.* 2013). The aim of this chapter is to build on the previous, relatively scant, research within the field and to provide a general overview of which kind of candidates that are successful in the Finnish context. This involves analyses of the success value of a wide set of vote earning attributes such as experience, reputation and localism. Moreover, a specific emphasis will be on how gender and age shape electoral fortunes. The analyses are performed on a data set consisting of 5 022 candidates that are competing for a parliamentary seat in four consecutive Finnish elections, during the period 2003–2011.

The chapter is organized as follows: I begin with a brief presentation of the Finnish electoral system and then move on to a discussion of the literature on personal vote-earning attributes and electoral success under OLPR. This is followed by a presentation of analytic design and empirical analyses. I conclude with a discussion of the results and their implications.

A candidate- and party-centred system

From an institutional perspective, Finland constitutes an interesting case with an electoral system that combines the use of a proportional formula and multimember districts with a strong degree of candidate-centeredness. Karvonen (2014) summarizes the most important aspects of the systems as the following: 1. It is a *proportional* system 2. It is a *list* system 3. It includes *compulsory preferential voting*.

The first aspect highlighted by Karvonen is proportionality. The 200 seats in the Eduskunta (Riksdagen in Swedish) are distributed in 15 constituencies using the D'Hondt method. Except for Finland's only single member district, the autonomous Åland Islands, the number of seats distributed within each constituency is determined by the number of Finnish citizens residing in the district six months prior to the elections. In the 14 constituencies situated on the mainland there is a sizable variation in the number of seats distributed. In the parliamentary election in 2011 district magnitude ranged from 6 to 35. Over the years the variation in district magnitude between different constituencies has increased. The corresponding figures for the general election in 1962 were 9–20 (Borg & Paloheimo 2009).

While no fixed electoral threshold is applied, the effective threshold varies extensively from one constituency to another according to the number of seats distributed. In the parliamentary election 2007, the effective threshold ranged from 2.9 to 14.3 per cent in the various constituencies (*ibid.*). Due to the increasingly different prerequisites within the country in terms of chances of becoming elected, there has been a continuous discussion on how to develop the electoral system, and in particularly on how to increase the overall level of proportionality. Parties have, however, had a hard time reaching consensus on the most suitable alternative and in 2013 the Eduskunta opted for minor revision, by merging four of the smallest constituencies into two, and hence lowering the effective threshold in these merged constituencies.[1]

The second aspect that Karvonen highlights is that it is a list system, which implies that the system as such is party-centred. The votes given to individual candidates are pooled at the party level in each constituency, and the total number of votes determine the amount of seats allocated to each party (Cox 1997). Parties can decide to join forces and form electoral alliances at the constituency level, but the number of candidates nominated by an alliance (a

---

[1]　Kymi and South Savo will be merged into Southeast Finland with 17 seats and North Savo and North Karelia will be merged into Savo-Karelia. After the merger they are expected to have 17 and 16 seats to distribute, respectively. See the site on electoral districts on the elections website of the Ministry of Justice, http://www.vaalit.fi/fi/index/vaalit/eduskuntavaalit/vaalipiirit.htm.

joint list) may not exceed the maximum number of candidates for a single party. During the last five elections (1995–2011) the number of alliances has varied from 14 to 48, hence there are on average between 1 and 3.4 alliances per constituency in the multimember districts at the Finnish mainland.

The third of Karvonen's fundamentals – compulsory preferential voting – is what differentiates the Finnish systems from most other PR systems. In order to cast a vote one has to vote for a specific candidate, and the ranking of the candidates running for each party is determined solely by the amount of votes each candidate receives (Reynolds *et al.* 2005). The ballot paper only contains an empty circle in which voters write the number of their preferred candidate (see Figure 1). Parties generally present their nominated candidates in alphabetic order, even though this is not a legal requirement (Raunio 2005: 478). Candidates can be nominated for election in any district (Kuitunen 2008), but due to a decentralised nomination process, cross-constituencies nominations tend to be rare. Parties are allowed to nominate a maximum of 14 candidates or, if district magnitude exceeds 14, the amount of representatives to be elected (Raunio 2005: 477). During the last three parliamentary elections a total of just above 2,000 candidates has been nominated in the 15 constituencies.

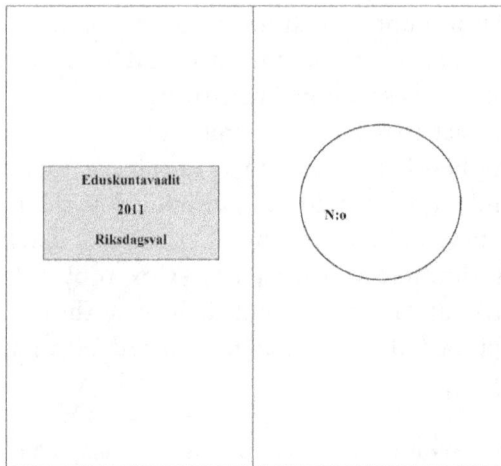

Figure 1. A ballot paper in a Finnish parliamentary election

Attracting a personal vote

When parties refrain from ranking candidates, the candidates that are to become elected are fully determined by the voters, creating a high level of intra-party competition at the constituency level. In order to win a seat, individual candidates have binary incentives; they need to maximise the total amount of votes given to the party, as well as their personal share of the votes.

The election is hence not only fought *between* but also *within* parties. Alongside with nationally oriented political debates between parties and their leading politicians, there are constituency based battles, where candidates running for the same party compete to get the most votes (Lutz & Selb 2014).

In order to be successful in the dual competition imbedded in the OLPR-system, candidates need to cultivate a 'personal vote' along with a 'party vote'. According to Cain *et al.* (1987) a personal vote is the portion of the vote derived from a politician's personal characteristics, experience, or record of constituency service. The 'personal vote' can hence be earned by behaviour, for example by constituency service, or by the general profile of the candidate, such as his or her experience or reputation. A partisan vote, in turn, is the share of the votes won by the candidate's party label and is a collective good shared by all candidates running for the party (Cox & McCubbins 1993).

How do candidates go about attracting a personal vote and to stand out compared to their intra-party competitors, and what kinds of attributes are rewarded by voters? Previous studies on candidate-centred elections and personal vote-earning attributes (PVEA) have mainly focused on the aspect of locality, such as local roots and political experience from the local level (Tavits 2010; Shugart *et al.* 2005; see also Gallagher 1985; Marsh 1985; Gorecki & Marsh 2009). The underlying argument put forward in this literature is that local ties function as information shortcuts for voters confronted with a large amount of candidates to choose from.

Locality

While cues to party choice often come in terms of nationally expressed party platforms, it is more likely that information about candidates involves local or narrow considerations that are of easily digested nature (Shugart *et al.* 2005). Factors that are easy to grasp and that can be used as a proxy for 'knowing the area and its interests' are hence applied by voters. From the perspective of candidates, the strategy of trying to win a seat with the use of locality as a vote-earning attribute can be considered as cost and time efficient, since it implies emphasising the connection to subgroups of constituents, rather than trying to appeal to all voters (Shugart 2008); an aspect that indeed is likely to be more important in larger districts. Simply put, this suggests that locality matters for voters and locality is used by candidates to attract votes. And it matters more if there are many candidates to elect and to choose from.

In the Finnish context, several aspects speak in favour of an important local perspective in national politics. The geographical representativeness of the 200 MPs in the Eduskunta can be considered as very good. Although MPs on the Finnish mainland are elected from 14 relatively large constituencies (varying from 6 to 35 seats)[2] they did in the 2011 election represent as many as 113 different municipalities (of a total of 336). Moreover, data presented in the study by Shugart *et al.* (2005) indicate that the extent of local PVEAs is widespread among Finnish MPs. Among the MPs elected in 1999 almost 60 per cent were native to the district where they were nominated and close to 85 per cent had experience in lower-level elected office within their district. Moreover, when asked about their views on representative roles and foci, Finnish voters, as well as their elected representatives, tend to downplay the role of parties and emphasise the importance of the local perspective (Bengtsson & Wass 2011; Esaiasson & Heidar 2000). Considering the emphasis given to locality it is not unexpected that politicians from urban areas are overrepresented in the Finnish Parliament (Paloheimo 2007: 357). In sum, it appears to be an electoral advantage to be resident in a municipality with many, rather than fewer voters.

There seems to be little doubt that locality is an important aspect of election campaigns where the level of intra-party competition is high. However, the argument presented above by Shugart *et al.* (2005) and Tavits (2010) about easily digested personal candidate information does not necessarily imply that locality is

2   This number excludes the single member constituency of Åland Islands.

the only vote-earning attribute that can be used by candidates in order to distinguish themselves from their co-partisans, or as cues by voters to find their preferred candidate. Although local ties represent a common interpretation of the personal vote (Desposato & Petrocik 2003) and locality is likely to be a cost efficient way to earn votes, there are other attributes that can be used in intra-party competitive situations. According to the definition of the personal vote given by Cain *et al.* (1987) presented above, a personal vote can imply much more than locality, for example a politician's personal characteristics or experience in other arenas than local office.

In fact, recent research in the Finnish context, as well as in other candidate-centred systems indicates that candidates use (or would benefit from using) several other means in order to cultivate a personal vote. For example a recent study by Berggren and colleagues (2010), inspired by studies from the American context (Todorov *et al.* 2005), demonstrates that looks are of importance in order to be electorally successful. While good looks are difficult to classify and study without the type of experimental design utilised by Berggren and his colleagues, there are other means to cultivate a personal vote, means that are easier to control for in more conventional studies, using standard statistical techniques. The factors discussed below are connected to two important aspects; reputation and experience.

Celebrities

One of the most well-known ways to cultivate a personal vote, and one frequently discussed in critical terms in the Finnish context, is to have earned public recognition before entering the field of politics (Marshall 1997; Bennett 2011). 'Celebrity candidates' is a recognised concept in Finnish politics (Karvonen 2010), used in order to describe candidates that are well-known from other areas of public live, for example from media or sports, when entering the field of politics. To be recognized from other contexts has been considered an advantage in the electoral arena, not least for rookies (Arter 2009), since these candidates tend to receive more extensive and favourable media coverage (Abramowitz & Segal 1986). In the Finnish parliamentary election of 2007 as many as 15 per cent of the rookies could be classified as celebrity candidates (Arter 2009).

A track-record from other areas can be considered as one of the attributes that is easiest to digest for voters, although it is not necessarily an attribute that all voters find equally attractive.

Experience

A more well-established theory is that of incumbency advantage. An large number of studies have demonstrated that being an incumbent is an effective vote-earning attribute, both from an inter- and intra-party perspective (see Erikson 1971; Garand & Gross 1984; Gelman & King 1990; Alford & Brady 1993). The incumbency effect is however considered to be smaller in PR multi-member districts with open lists than in single-member districts (Maddens *et al.* 2006). This is supported by data from Finland, where the level of intra-partisan defeats has been relatively high, while the level of inter-partisan defeats has tended to be been substantially lower (Arter 2009). Although weaker than in single member districts the incumbency advantage in Finnish politics still seem to be substantial. During the period 1962–2003, 85 per cent of MPs on average ran for re-election with an average success rate of 76 per cent (Paloheimo 2007: 334). Independently of the relative weight of the incumbency advantage in a comparative perspective, it is safe to say that incumbency is one of the most important PVEAs a candidate can exhibit. Incumbency signals valuable political experience, incumbents tend to be more well-known than non-incumbents, and the effect is likely to be enhanced in systems with distinct incentives to cultivate a personal vote due to a higher level of constituency work.

Building on the theory of incumbency advantage, it seems plausible that there are other types of high-rank positions that function as valuable assets in electoral competition. Assignments as minister or a position as party leader are obvious positions that inevitably entails a great deal of media exposure, which in turn increases personal reputation. These types of positions are likely to be valuable PVEAs for candidates that can contribute to electoral success.

Demographics

Another interesting aspect is the extent to which extent certain demographic characteristics are to be considered an advantage or disadvantage when it comes to winning the support of voters and competing against co-partisans. Here we find that the impact of gender has received attention in previous studies and it has been suggested that the general underrepresentation of women in politics is less acute in larger electoral districts (Matland & Brown 1992; Rule 1987). It has also been proposed that women might have an advantage in open list systems, particularly if there are fewer women than men running (Rule 1994; Shugart 1994).

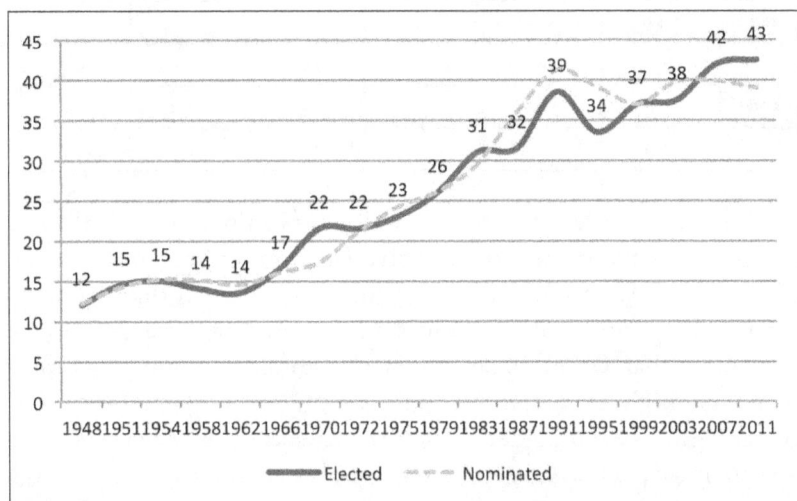

Figure 2. Share of women elected and nominated in Finnish parliamentary elections 1948–2011

In line with the trend in most advanced democracies, the number of nominated and elected women in Finnish elections has increased substantially over the years (Figure 1). The share of women in the Eduskunta has increased from less than 15 per cent in 1948 to around and above 40 per cent in the new century (2003–2011). The share of female nominees has developed in accordance. The supply side, *i.e.* the number of female candidates running for election does seem to be of importance for how many women succeed in becoming elected. The tendency for women to be on average more successful in districts which elect a large number of MPs, does, however, indicate that the success of women is not only a matter of supply, but rather that the electoral system shapes the prerequisites for female candidate success (Paloheimo 2007: 355).

Table 1. Mean age among male and female candidates and elected mps, 1995–2011

	MEN			WOMEN		
	Candidates	*Elected*	*Diff*	*Candidates*	*Elected*	*Diff.*
1995	45,6	49,1	3,5	42,9	43,3	0,4
1999	47,7	50,0	2,3	44,3	43,1	−1,2
2003	48,6	51,8	3,1	44,5	43,6	−0,9
2007	48,9	51,9	3,0	44,6	44,1	−0,4
2011	46,9	50,8	4,0	45,0	45,7	0,7
Total	47,5	50,7	3,2	44,3	44,0	−0,2
N	6362	615		4062	385	

Looking at gender differences among nominated and elected according to age during the last five elections it becomes evident that parties have a tendency to nominate older men than women. During the period male nominees were on average 3 years (47.5 vs 44.3) older than female. The tendency to nominate younger women than men might be a strategic choice on the part of parties since the age gap grows even bigger among those elected. After voters have had their say, the average difference between successful male and female candidates is close to 7 years. Hence, while the average male MP is 51 years old, the equivalent age for a female MPs is 44 years.

So far several different types of attributes or mechanisms that candidates can use in order to attract a 'personal vote' or - to put it the other way around – mechanisms that are rewarded by voters when they make up their minds about which candidate they will vote for, have been highlighted. Locality in terms of *local roots* and *local level electoral experience* tend to be rewarded by voters, and political experience from the office at stake, *i.e. incumbency* is generally considered as the most valuable attribute a candidate can display. Likewise other types of *high-rank positions* which signal experience and competence are likely to be highly valued by voters. The *celebrity* factor, *i.e.* being famous from outside the political arena is also often claimed to be an electoral advantage in an open list system. Other aspects that will be disentangled in the empirical section of the chapter are the effects of *gender* and *age*.

Finally, it is worth noticing that not all of the more than 2000 Finnish candidates that on average are nominated in a parliamentary election, enter the race with the goal or expectation of becoming elected. In order to maximize votes for the party list, parties have the incentive to nominate as many candidates as allowed (*i.e.* 14 or more), even though they expect only to win one or a few seats.[3] In large districts such as the constituency of Uusimaa (Nyland), where the amount of seats available for competition is as high as 35 and parties hence are allowed to nominate the same amount of candidates, parties are expected to nominate 35 candidates even if they know that they only stand a chance of winning one or a few seats. According to Paloheimo (2007), four different kinds of candidates can be identified in Finnish elections: *incumbents* seeking re-election, *challengers* with an actual prospect of becoming elected, *career-builders* who utilize the election campaign to enhance their reputation and increase for future contests, and finally *top-up candidates* who are nominated to attract support of specific subgroups of voters but without posing a threat to the 'main' candidates (see also Carty *et al.* 2003; Arter 2013). The last category of top-up candidates is hence used by parties in order to make sure that all potential voters can identify a suitable candidate on the list, mainly in terms of socio-demographic background or residence.

Research design

Data

In order to study the electoral success value of different personal vote-earning attributes complemented by contextual aspects such as size of municipality, an extensive data base including electoral data at the candidate level from four consecutive Finnish parliamentary elections (1999, 2003, 2007, 2011), combined with biographical

---

3   Naturally there are also many candidates representing parties without the chance of winning a single seat, who participate mainly to promote their political agenda within the frame work of the election campaign.

data for individual candidates as well as district and party level data, is utilized.[4] The main sources used to gather data are websites with official electoral statistics.[5] These have been supplemented with information from other relevant sources when needed.[6] The data base consists of over 8 300 candidates for the four years of interest. In this study a sub-population of candidates running for lists which succeeded in winning at least one parliamentary seat are included[7], which reduces the number of candidates to 5 022.

Electoral success

The most relevant measure of success is of course if the individual candidate becomes an elected MP or not. Another interesting way to conceptualise electoral success is the number of personal votes a candidate receives. Since votes are pooled at the party level, and seats are distributed according to the total number of votes each party obtains, a recurrent feature of the Finnish electoral system is that individual candidates with a high number of votes are not elected, while candidates that attracted a smaller number of votes are pulled through by more popular co-partisans. The candidates that are rewarded by voters are hence not always successful in becoming elected. A widened scope of the study to include the more general question of which candidates are rewarded by voters makes it interesting to extend the analyses to look at preference votes. Preference votes should, however, be contextualised at the party and constituency level, since the electoral behaviour of voters to a large extent is influenced by party labels, and the total number of votes cast varies extensively between constituencies. In the following analyses three different operationalisations will be applied;

---

4   The data were collected within the framework of the NSF-founded project *The Intraparty Dimension of Representation* lead by Matthew S. Shugart, University of California, Davis. I thank Mattias Karlsson for excellent work with the data collection.

5   The most frequently employed sources are: Ministry of Justice, Finland (www.vaalit.fi) and statistics of Finland (www.tilastokeskus.fi).

6   Newspaper searches were conducted in order to code celebrity status of candidates.

7   The candidates running for election within the single member district of the Aaland Islands are also excluded from the analyses.

a dummy variable indicating if the candidate got elected or not, the total number of preference votes, and the share of the total party vote in a constituency a candidate receives.

Personal vote-earning attributes

The independent variables of the study involve several different types of personal vote-earning attributes. The first two are related to the importance of locality, or the local ties of candidates. These are measures of incumbency at the local level, *i.e.*, if the candidate currently holds local office in the municipality in which the candidate is resident, and if the candidate was born within the constituency in which he or she is running for election.[8] The next group of vote-earning attributes is related to experience. The first one is incumbency, *i.e.* if the candidate holds a position as elected Member of Parliament or not. Included is also a variable indicating if the candidate has held a position as MP during a previous term. The third variable measures if the candidate holds a leadership position within the party at the national level which is likely to make them well known to voters; for example a position as minister, party leader, party secretary or vice leader the party. The third variable to measure experience is a position as leader at the regional level within the party. The last vote-earning attribute included in the analysis is a variable of celebrity status.[9] All variables are measured as dummy variables.

Other aspects that will be included in the empirical analyses, but that are not to be considered as vote-earning attributes in the classical sense are age and gender. In the multivariate analyses age will be included in two different forms, in its original form and as age squared in order to control for an expected curvilinear pattern indi-

8   The municipality is the lowest local level in Finland and the amount of municipalities is as high as 336 (www.kunnat.net), although the amount has decreased substantially during the last five years. Each constituency entails between 1 (Helsinki) and 43 (Vaasa, Oulu) municipalities. In order to appeal to subgroups of voters based on local ties within a constituency the municipality-level is most often the obvious point of departure. The municipality in which candidates are resident is displayed on the ballot.

9   A celebrity that manages to become an elected Member of Parliament loses his or her status as celebrity in the following election.

cated by Paloheimo (2007: 356), where he shows that the youngest (<29 years) and oldest (>60 years) age groups are systematically underrepresented in the Finnish Parliament.

Individual electoral success in Finnish parliamentary elections

As was mentioned previously, all candidates do not enter the election with the same expectations. Some are highly merited, well known and ambitious. Others agree to be nominated out of loyalty to the party and have the more limited goal of attracting the votes from a small group of local supporters and as such contribute to the total party vote.

If divided according to vote-earning attributes it becomes obvious that these types of top-up candidates constitute close to 40 per cent of the candidates found on the lists of parties or alliances which succeed in winning at least one seat in the 1999–2011 elections. These candidates are not rewarded by voters and have a very low chance of winning a parliamentary seat (2 per cent).

The largest group of candidates is the one which exhibits the most common vote-earning attribute, that is being an incumbent at the municipality level. In this group the probability of winning a seat is six per cent. Among the group of candidates which exhibits several vote-earning attributes (eight per cent), but without being incumbents or celebrities the success rate is above one out of four (27 per cent). Celebrity candidates, often described as a somewhat questionable side-effect of open list systems, constitute merely one per cent of all candidates. They do, however, on average tend to be relatively successful with a 30 per cent chance of becoming elected. The most successful group is as expected what can be considered the most experienced candidates, *i.e.* incumbent MPs who constitute 13 per cent of all candidates and have a close to 80 per cent chance of becoming re-elected.

While Table 2 presents certain types of candidates, the next step is an overview of the average success value of each of the seven vote-earning attributes as well as age and gender, presented in Table 3. The probability of winning a seat, the average number of preference votes and the share of the list total won by each group of candidates

Table 2. Individual electoral success a personal vote-earning attributes

| | WINNING A SEAT | PREFERENCE VOTES | | | |
	%	No. preference votes	% preference votes on list	(n)	% of all candidates
No vote-earning attribute	2.3	838	2.6	(1831)	37
Local level incumbency (only)	6.1	1607	4.5	(2071)	41
Quality candidate	27.2	2995	8.3	(423)	8
Celebrity (only)	29.9	3155	7.1	(67)	1
Incumbent MP	77.8	6469	16.8	(630)	13
Total	15.8	2074	5.7	(5022)	100

NOTE: 'Quality candidates' are candidates who are not Incumbent MPs but exhibit some other attribute than local level incumbency. 'Celebrities' are candidates who lack other attributes than being a celebrity. 'Local roots', *i.e.* having been born in the district, is not included as a personal vote-earning attribute. Only candidates running for a list with P>0 are included in the analyses.

are displayed alongside with the difference between the groups of comparison. Once more it stands clear that one of the most powerful attributes a candidate can display in order to be become elected is the position as an incumbent MP. The most successful candidates are however the once that belong to the even more exclusive group of politicians with experience from party-leadership positions at the national level. These candidates are to be considered an elite within the party consists of party leaders, deputy leaders and candidates with experience as minister or as party secretary; all of which attracts plenty of media attention, which naturally can be beneficial when it comes to attracting personal votes.

An interesting, but far less successful category of candidates is the one is the one with non-incumbent candidates with previous experience as an MP. This group hence consists of candidates that have chosen to take a break from the Parliament or who have failed to receive sufficient support to become re-elected in a previous election. Although they have plenty of experience, the average success rate for candidates belonging to this group rate is below 40 per cent, compared to just above 15 among all candidates.

The two attributes that are often highlighted as important in the literature on the personal vote are local-level experience and local

Table 3. Individual electoral success in different groups (winning a seat, no. of preference votes, share of the preference votes the preference votes received by the list in constituency)

| | WINNING A SEAT | PREFERENCE VOTES | | (n) |
	%	no. pref. votes	% pref. votes/ list	
Total	15.8	2074	5.7	(5 022)
Gender				
Men	16.9	2 154	5.9	(2 829)
Women	14.4	1 972	5.5	(2 193)
Diff	2.5	182	0.4	
Age				
18–29	4.4	1 104	3.2	(620)
30–39	15.9	2 114	5.9	(917)
40–49	15.5	2 140	5.7	(1 456)
50–64	20.3	2 372	6.5	(1 836)
65+	13.0	1 666	5.1	(193)
Diff *	15.9	1 262	3.3	
Local level incumbency				
Yes	19.9	2 480	7.0	(2 837)
No	10.5	1 548	4.0	(2 185)
Diff	9.4	932	3.0	
Born in constituency				
Yes	17.2	2 218	6.0	(2 745)
No	14.2	1 902	5.3	(2 243)
Diff	3.0	316	0.7	
Incumbent MP				
Yes	77.8	6 469	16.8	(630)
No	6.9	1 444	4.2	(4 392)
Diff	70.9	5025	12.6	
Previous MP				
Yes	38.6	4 084	10.0	(158)
No	15.1	2 009	5.6	(4 864)

Diff	23.5	2 075	4.4	
Leader position at the national level				
Yes	82.2	8 044	20.8	(163)
No	13.6	1 876	5.2	(4 794)
Diff	68.6	6 168	15.6	
Leader position at the regional level				
Yes	26.0	2 779	8.2	(173)
No	15.4	2 054	5.6	(4 784)
Diff	10.6	725	2,6	
Celebrity				
Yes	29.2	3 014	6.5	(106)
No	15.5	2 054	5.7	(4 916)
Diff	13.7	960	0.8	

NOTE: Only candidates running for a list with P>0 are included. 'Leader position at the national level' includes prominent positions such as minister, party leader, party secretary or deputy leader of the party. * The difference displayed is the between the age groups with the most and least successful candidates, *i.e.* 50–64 and 18–29.

roots. Clearly local level incumbents have an advantage compared to others, with a nine percentage point higher probability of becoming elected than candidates without this attribute. This attribute is, however, often combined with other beneficial qualities, and as was demonstrated in Table 3 the chance of winning a parliamentary seat when only being an incumbent at the local level is relatively low. Having local roots, *i.e.* being born in the constituency where one is nominated for election, appears to have a limited effect on electoral success in the Finnish context.

Concerning the socio-demographic variables, age and gender, we find that men on average have a slight advantage over women, but that the effect of age is more substantial. The age group which is the on average most successful in the Finnish context is the second oldest with candidates aged 50 to 64 where the average success rate is 20 per cent. Voters tend to be far less interested in electing candidates below the age of 30. In this category only four per cent of the candidates became elected.

While these descriptive statistics in groups are revealing they do not provide the full picture. Within each of the groups displayed in Table 3 we find candidates with different portions of other important attributes. In order to single out the effect of each of the individual attributes a multivariate test is necessary, that is a model in which all attributes are included alongside with socio-demographic characteristics. Moreover, both models presented in Table 4 include an interaction term with age and gender in order to outline in more detail how these aspects influence electoral success in tandem. Since access to power is of central interest to the chapter the most important aspect of electoral success is the chance to become elected. An analysis of the number of preference votes candidates receive is, however, also included. Since the first model has a binary dependent variable measuring if the candidate succeeds in becoming elected (1) or not (0) it is analysed with binary logistic regression. The second model where the dependent variable is the number of preferential voters received, is analysed with OLS linear regression. This model also includes an extra independent variable to control for the total number of votes given to the list. In both models robust clustered standard errors are applied to control for the nested structure of the data within constituencies of different size (*i.e.* different levels of district magnitude). As in the bivariate section above, comments are concentrated on the model with the binary outcome variable (winning a seat or not).

The results are perhaps not surprising, but they are substantial. All of the seven vote-earning attributes included in the analysis alongside with age and gender contribute to increase the probability that a candidate will win a seat, and the indicative proportion of variance accounted for is above 40 per cent. This by no means suggests that the attributes included in the analysis are the only ones that candidates use in order to win the support of voters, but it does show that these factors that are relatively easily accessible and measurable posits considerable explanatory power.

Most of the findings in the bivariate analysis presented in Table 3 survive the multivariate test. When controlling for all other variables in the model, however, the effect of the most valuable attributes related to experience appears even stronger. Outstanding in this respect is a position as Member of Parliament. The fact that incumbents are extraordinarily successful when they seek re-election is widely recognised in the literature (even though often assumed to be weaker in multimember compared to single-member districts). Finland is no exception in this respect; when

Table 4. The effect of personal vote-earning attributes on the probability of winning a seat (binary logistic) and the number of preference votes won (OLS)

	Winning a seat (or loosing			No. of preference votes won		
	OR	p	(s.e)	b	p	(s.e)
Local level incumbency	1.64	***	(0.19)	370.64	***	(67.30)
Local roots (born in const.)	1.31	*	(0.14)	260.92	***	(54.32)
Incumbent MP	54.15	***	(6.02)	4090.22	***	(175.03)
Previously served as MP	12.04	***	(2.49)	2455.98	***	(523.83)
Leadership, nat. level	10.40	***	(3.10)	3379.90	***	(645.56)
Leadership, reg. level	2.10	**	(0.57)	542.81	**	(88.68)
Celebrity	9.91	***	(2.12)	1550.40	***	(353.90)
Age	1.12	**	(0.04)	85.16	***	(14.07)
Age^2	0.99	***	(0.00)	−1.12	***	(0.17)
Gender	0.25	**	(0.10)	−731.06	**	(153.21)
Gender*Age	1.03	**	(0.01)	18.48	***	(3.25)
Number of votes won by list				0.02	***	(0.00)
Constant	0.00	***	(0.00)	−1363.84	***	(239.15)
Pseudo R^2 / Adj. R	0.42			0.49		
N	4923			4923		
χ^2 / F-sign.	2920.59	***		438.91	***	

NOTE: Table entries are odds ratios and b-coefficients with standard errors in parentheses; * p≤ 0.05, **p≤0.01, **p≤0.001. Only candidates running for a list with P>0 are included in the analyses. Robust clustered standard errors are applied in order to control for the nested structure of the data in terms of district magnitude.

controlling for the other variables included in the model the odds of an incumbent to become re-elected are 54:1. Candidates who have previously served as MPs also have an electoral advantage, with the odds of becoming elected being 12:1.

The other two experience-related attributes, a prominent position within the party at the national or the regional level, also have a noteworthy success value. The odds for a candidate with a national-level leadership position to win a seat are 10:1. These relatively exclusive positions (held by only 3 per cent of all candidates), often attract a substantial amount of media attention, which clearly comes with a benefit. A leadership position within the party at the regional level is far less impressive in the eyes of the voters, with the odds of 2:1 for these candidates to become an elected Member of Parliament.

It is also clear that the frequently criticized celebrity candidates, candidates who have gained recognition in other areas of public life – for example from media or sports – before entering the field of politics, hold an advantage compared to others. The odds that a candidate with celebrity status will outperform another candidate are 10:1. As was shown in the descriptive section above, celebrity-candidates should, however, be considered a marginal phenomenon since they only make out a total of one per cent of the candidates included in the study.[10] All in all, 31 out of 800 MPs elected in 1999–2011 had a celebrity background.

Far lower success value is found for the two locality factors included the model, local level incumbency and local roots (born in the constituency). The odds of a candidate holding a seat at the municipality to win a seat are 1.6:1. The corresponding advantage of having local roots, *i.e.* being born in the constituency is 1.3:1. Given that locality is frequently referred to as a very important vote-earning attribute in open list systems, these can be considered as very moderate effects. An important contributing factor to the low success value of these factors is, however, the fact that these types of characteristics are highly valued by parties when nominating candidates. During the period 1999–2011, as many as 56 per cent of all candidates running for parliament (for a list which won at least one seat), were local-level incumbents, and 55 per cent of all candidates were native to the district in which they were nominated. Yet another aspect which speaks in favour of the importance of local ties is the fact that cross-constituency nominations are relatively rare.[11]

The multivariate analysis also allows for more detailed analyses of how electoral success is shaped by gender and age interactively. In order to facilitate the interpretation of the findings the relation-

---

10   This figure refers to celebrity candidates who lack other vote earning attributes than their status as a celebrity.

11   Among the MPs elected in 2011, only four were elected from a constituency where they were not resident. Moreover, all of these four candidates were elected form the constituency of Uusimaa (Nyland), which surrounds the capital of Helsinki and is part of the same metropolitan area. The four MPs in question were all residents in Helsinki (constituting a constituency of its own).

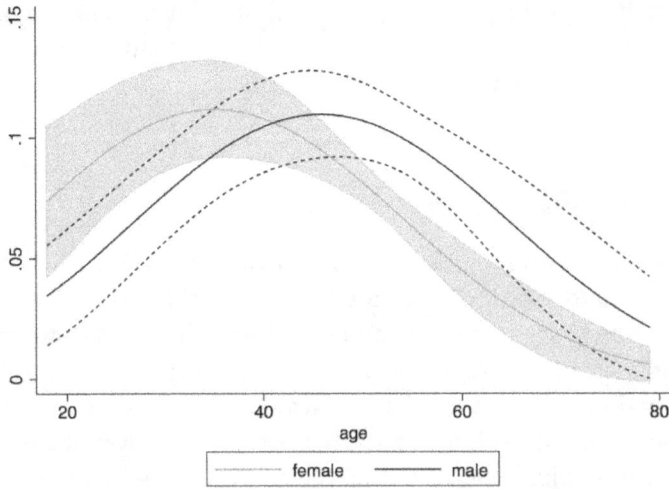

Figure 3. The estimated probabilities of becoming elected for female and male candidates at different ages

ship is presented in Figure 2. The graph outlines the probability of becoming elected for women and men at different ages, while all other variables that are included in the analysis are set at their mean value. The line in dark grey represents the probabilities for men at different ages and the line in a lighter shade represents the corresponding information for women. Clearly female and male candidates peak at different ages in terms of their chances of becoming elected. For female candidates the probability is the highest at 35 and for male candidates at 46. The graph also shows that age is an important factor when it comes to determine which gender has an electoral advantage. Among candidates younger than 41 women have a higher probability of becoming elected, while there is an advantage for male candidates above the same age.[12]

The analysis of the second dependent variable, the number of preference votes received, more or less confirms the results discussed above, but the interpretation is perhaps more straightforward. The b-coefficients presents the success value of each vote-earning attribute in terms of the average number of preference

12 It should however be noted that the confidence intervals only are separated between the age 54 and 66, the age at which the gender effect is statistically significant.

votes won if displaying the specific attribute. An incumbent MP hence on average (holding all other variables constant) wins more than 4000 votes more than non-incumbents.

Concluding discussion

The Eduskunta is a powerful arena in Finnish society, and the most travelled road to gain political influence at the national level is without doubt to try to become an elected Member of Parliament. Parties as collective actors are of course important in political decision-making, and it is the parties' collective support that determine the composition of governments and the overall course of politics. Individual MPs are, however, of importance from many different angles. Parties as such are not anonymous collective bodies, but rather constituted by individual politicians, among whom MPs belong to the elite. Which candidates become elected does hence not only have a great impact on the process of law-making in Parliament; it also sets a mark on the internal development of parties. Moreover, prominent positions such as government ministers are to a large extent recruited from the pool of incumbent MPs. By gaining seats in Parliament, individual politicians have access to considerable power, although they command a mandate which is on many accounts constrained by the position of the party they represent.

Thanks to the open list system applied in Finnish elections, where the election of candidates is fully determined by voters, the study of individual electoral success deals directly with access to political power. The analyses presented in this chapter have clearly demonstrated that the most valuable attribute a candidate can exhibit in order to increase his or hers chances of becoming elected, is experience. Incumbent MPs are superior when it comes to attracting votes, and this puts challengers in a far less advantageous position. Other types of positions or experience that increase the reputation of a candidate, such as prominent leadership positions within the party or former experience as an MP, are also of value in the selection process. Another factor which can facilitate election is if the candidate has gained a reputation from other areas of life; this is often referred to as *the celebrity factor* in Finnish politics. Being a celebrity indeed significantly increases the chances to become elected. The overall impact at the system level is, however, relatively minor considering that these types of candidates on average only constitute one per cent of all elected M Ps.[13]

The overall impact of locality, which has been much highlighted in the literature on the personal vote is however relatively minor. Being an incumbent at the local level and having local roots does indeed increase the overall electoral performance of candidates, but since these aspects are very common they are usually not sufficient to get an on other accounts unexperienced candidate elected to Parliament.

The effects of gender and age disentangled in the analyses are also interesting. On average female candidates have a slight disadvantage compared to men, but both voters and parties tend to favour younger female candidates compared to their male competitors. First we find that the female candidates nominated for election are on average three years younger than their male equivalents. After the election process the age difference grows close to seven years. The multivariate analysis confirmed this pattern and revealed that the probability for female candidates to become elected peaks at 35, while the corresponding age for men is 46. This analysis also indicated that female candidates have a slight electoral advantage over men at ages below 41, while the opposite is the case among older candidates.

This chapter has aimed at opening up the black box of individual candidate success in Finnish politics. It is, however, important not only to highlight the merits of the approach but also to reflect on its limitations. Clearly, the types of personal vote-earning attributes included in the analyses presented in this chapter do not provide the full story of how elections are fought and won at the individual level. Other types of personal characteristics such as charisma, rhetoric abilities and looks are likely to be important pieces of the puzzle. Moreover, politics is not only about being someone, it is also very much about achievements and ideas. The political accom-

---

13 This figure represents celebrity candidates without any other personal vote-earning attribute. The total share of celebrity candidates for the four years of interest in this study is two per cent.

plishments at different levels and the ability to inspire voters during the election campaign are likely to be of great importance for a candidate's chance of becoming elected; these questions remain, however, outside the scope of this study. This said, the chapter has hopefully advanced our understanding of what it takes to gain access to political power in the Finnish context.

References

Abramowitz, A.I. & Segal, J. (1986). Determinants of the Outcomes of U.S. Senate Elections. *Journal of Politics* Vol. 48, 2: 433–439.

Alford, J. R. & Brady, D. W. (1993). Personal and Partisan Advantages in U.S. Congressional Elections, 1846–1990. In L.C. Dodd & B. I. Oppenheimer (eds.), *Congress Reconsidered*. Washington, CQ Press: 153–169.

Arter, D. (2009). Money and Votes: The Cost of Election for First-Time Finnish MPs. *Politiikka* Vol. 51, 1: 17–33.
— (2013). The 'Hows', not the 'Whys' or the 'Wherefores': The Role of Intra-party Competition in the 2011 Breakthrough of the True Finns. *Scandinavian Political Studies* Vol. 36, 2: 99–120.

Bengtsson, Å. & Wass, H. (2011). The Representative Roles of MPs: A Citizen Perspective. *Scandinavian Political Studies* Vol. 34, 2: 143–167.

Berggren, N., Jordahl, H. & Poutvaara, P. (2010). The looks of a winner: Beauty and electoral success. *Journal of Public Economics* Vol. 94, 1–2: 8–15.

Bergman, M. E., M. S. Shugart & K. A. Watt. (2013). Patterns of intraparty competition in open-lists & SNTV systems. *Electoral Studies* Vol. 32, 2: 321–333.

Borg, S. & Paloheimo, H. (2009). Vaalipiirin koon vaikutus vaaliosallistumiseen. In S. Borg & H. Paloheimo (eds.), *Vaalit ja yleisödemokratiassa. Eduskuntavaalitutkimus 2007.* Tampere, Tampere University Press: 243–278.

Cain, B., Ferejohn J., & Fiorina, M. (1987). *The Personal Vote: Constituency Service and Electoral Independence*. Cambridge, Harvard University Press.

Carty, R. K., Eagles, D. M. & Sayers, A. (2003). Candidates and Local Campaigns. *Party Politics* Vol. 9, 5: 619–636.

Cox, G. (1997). *Making Votes Count: Strategic Coordination in the World's Electoral Systems*. New York, Cambridge University Press.

Cox, G. & McCubbins, M.D. (1993). *Legislative Leviathan: Party Government in the House*. Berkeley, University of California Press.

Desposato, S. W. & Petrocik, J. R. (2003). The Variable

Incumbency Advantage: New Voters, Redistricting, and the Personal Vote. *American Journal of Political Science* Vol. 47, 1: 18–32.

Erikson, R. (1971). The Advantage of Incumbency in Congressional Elections. *Polity* Vol. 3, 3: 395–405.

Esaiasson, P. & Heidar, K. (eds.) (2000). *Beyond Westminster and Congress: The Nordic Experience.* Kent, Ohio State University Press.

Gallagher, M. (1985). Social Backgrounds and Local Organization of Members of the Irish Dail. *Legislative Studies Quarterly* Vol. 10, 3: 373–394.

Garand, J. C. & Gross, D. A. (1984). Changes in the Vote Margins for Congressional Candidates: A Specification of Historical Trends. *American Political Science Review* Vol. 78, 1: 17–30.

Gelman, A. & King, G. (1990). Estimating the Incumbency Advantage without Bias. *American Journal of Political Science* Vol. 34, 4: 1142–1164.

Gorecki, M. & Marsh, M. (2009). Not just friends and neighbours: the effects of canvassing on vote choice in Ireland. Paper presented at the ECPR General Conference, Potsdam, Sept. 2009.

Karvonen, L. (2010). *The Personalisation of Politics. A study of Parliamentary Democracies.* Colchester, ECPR Press. — (2014). *Parties, governments and Voters in Finland. Politics under Fundamental Societal Transformation.* Colchester, ECPR Press.

Kuitunen, S. (2008). Vaalit ja ehdokkaiden asettaminen. In H. Paloheimo & T. Raunio (eds.), *Suomen puolueet ja puoluejärjestelmä*. Helsinki, WSOY: 109–133.

Lutz, G. & Selb, P. (2014). Lone fighters: Intraparty competition, interparty competition, and candidates' vote seeking efforts in open-ballot PR elections. *Electoral Studies* Vol. 39, 329–337.

Maddens, B., Wauters, B., Noppe, J. & Fiers, S (2006). Effects of Campaign Spending in an Open List PR System: The 2003 Legislative Election in Flanders/Belgium. *West European Politics* Vol. 29, 1: 161–168.

Matland, R. & Brown, D. D. (1992). District magnitude's effect on female representation in US state legislatures. *Legislative Studies Quarterly* Vol. 17, 4: 469–492.

Marsh, M. (1985). The voters decide? Preferential voting in European list systems. *European Journal of Political Research* Vol. 13, 4: 365–378.

Marshall, P. D. (1997). *Celebrity and power: fame in contemporary culture.* London, University of Minnesota Press.

Paloheimo, H. (2007). Eduskuntavaalit 1907–2003. In A. Ollila & H. Paloheimo (eds.), *Kansanedustajan työ ja arki.* Helsinki, Edita: 173–369.

Raunio, T. (2005). Finland: One Hundred Years of Quietude. In M. Gallagher & P. Mitchell (eds.), *The Politics of Electoral Systems.* Oxford, Oxford University Press, 471–493.

Reynolds, A., Reilly, B. & Ellis, A. (2005). *Electoral System*

Design: The New International
IDEA Handbook. Stockholm,
International Institute for
Democracy and Electoral
Assistance.

Rule, W. (1987). Electoral systems,
contextual factors and women's
opportunity for election to
Parliament in twenty-three
democracies. *Western Political
Quarterly* Vol. 40, 3: 477–498.

— (1994). Parliaments of, by
and for the people: Except for
women? In W. Rule & J. F.
Zimmerman (eds.), *Electoral
systems in comparative perspective:
Their impact on women and minorities.* Westport, CT, Greenwood
Press: 15–30.

Shugart, M. S. (1994). Minorities
represented and unrepresented.
In W. Rule & J. F. Zimmerman
(eds.), *Electoral systems in comparative perspective: Their impact on
women and minorities.* Westport,
CT, Greenwood Press: 31–44.

— (2001). Electoral "Efficiency"
and the Move to Mixed-Member
Systems. *Electoral Studies* Vol. 20,
2: 173–193.

— (2008). Comparative
Electoral Systems Research:
The Maturation of a Field and
New Challenges Ahead. In M.
Gallagher & P. Mitchell (eds),
The Politics of Electoral Systems.
Oxford, Oxford University Press:
25–56.

Shughart, M. S., Valdini, M. E.,
Suominen, K. (2005). Looking
for Locals: Voter Information
Demands and Personal
Vote-Earning Attributes of
Legislators under Proportional
Representation. *American Journal
of Political Science* Vol. 49, 2:
437–449.

Tavits, M. (2010). Effect of Local
Ties on Electoral Success and
Parliamentary Behaviour. The
Case of Estonia. *Party Politics* Vol.
16, 2: 215–235.

Todorov, A., Mandisodza, A.,
Goren, A. & Hall, C.C. (2005).
Inferences of Competence
from Faces Predict Election
Outcomes. *Science* Vol. 308, 5728:
1623–1626.

Power Relationships Between Ministers and Civil Servants

EERO MURTO

It is commonplace to argue that the role of civil servants has strengthened at the expense of democratically elected office-holders. There is a rich body of literature on the accountability of bureaucracies, with much of this scholarship emphasizing the expansion of bureaucracy and the difficulties governments, individual ministers and parliaments face in controlling the activities of civil servants or governmental agencies. This research indicates that bureaucratic discretion or empowerment has increased in recent decades, with the more detailed nature of issues on the political agenda and the internationalization of politics contributing to this development. Hence achieving both more central or hierarchical leadership and horizontal coordination inside the executive branch and the cabinet have become more pressing concerns for governments across the democratic world. (*E.g.*, Weber 1946; Dunleavy 1991; Huber 2000; Huber & Shipan 2002; Peters 2009; Dahlström *et al.* 2011.)

This chapter examines the balance of power between politicians and civil servants in Finland, and how that relationship has changed from the late 1970s to the early 2010s. The central question asked is whether the most significant political decisions are influenced more by politicians or by bureaucrats. Formally, of course, the power lies with the politicians, the MPs and the cabinet ministers. Actual power and influence, on the other hand, are a sum of various factors, in which situational factors and persons have a central role. However, civil servants always have the power of expertise. Measuring real-life power relations is in any case problematic, certainly not least when examining bureaucracy, as ministerial civil servants are always in the end accountable to the government.

Power always includes a relationship – in this case the relationship between civil servants and politicians. Political power refers to the ability or possibility to influence other individuals' political behaviour. According to Max Weber (1946) civil servants should not practice politics, but only govern impartially. Weber viewed that the honour of civil servants depends on the ability to carry out the orders of her or his superiors even when they are against her personal views or even erroneous. Political decision-making power and public administration are clearly separated: politicians make the political decisions, which the civil servants implement. (Bendix 1962: 290–328) In the daily life of modern ministries, Weber's clear-cut puritanism is practically impossible.

Robert A. Dahl (1971) in turn speaks of 'influence terms' which he uses to refer to power, influence, control, persuasion, might, strength, and force. Influence can be based both on formal positions and the authority and jurisdiction that these give, as well as on informal factors, such as competence, capability, or charisma (Lasswell & Kaplan 1950: 23; Ruostetsaari 1992: 37). Michel Foucault on the other hand emphasises action and discourse, partly at the expense of structures and institutions (Foucault 1998: 67; Foucault 2000: 343–345). All these approaches are relevant for studying power relations between politicians and civil servants.

This chapter is also a study of elites and role behaviour. Elite refers to persons who can regularly influence significant societal decisions through their strategically central positions. For Mosca (1939), the 'political class' consists of those who formally make policy decisions and of those who influence their content. (Moyser & Wagstaffe 1987; Etzioni 1970; Putnam 1976; Zannoni 1978; Ruostetsaari 1992, 2003; Etzioni-Havely 1993) Here is again a direct link to politicians and civil servants: cabinet ministers and MPs decide, civil servants wield influence. Finally, it is important to make the distinction between roles and role behaviour. Ministers and civil servants have their formal roles regardless of their personalities, but the individual persons occupying same positions can have very distinct role behaviours (Biddle & Thomas 1966).

Research questions and data

The issues to be decided by the government are formally resolved either in the cabinet plenary session or in the ministries. All these issues are prepared in the relevant ministry. Ministers must often make decisions on extensive issues whose concrete content they may not be familiar with. Hence ministers are not able to act without civil servants – it would be completely impossible. Because the issues are abundant, often complex and demand profound knowledge, the politicians simply do not have the time to carefully weigh the different alternatives, whereas it is the full-time job of civil servants to examine the issues. Often they are the ones delineating the alternatives that will be discussed and in this way shape the final outcome. Perhaps approximately 90 per cent of the daily tasks in the ministries are routine matters. Based on the author's long-standing practical experience as civil servant and as an observer, it can be concluded that ministers have nothing to say about them – no matter which government coalition or minister is in power. However, the real test of bureaucratic influence is in the remaining ten per cent of issues, those that are politically more salient and where ministers are more actively involved.

The analysis is structured around the following questions: Has the power of top level civil servants changed during recent decades? Has the increase in the number of political advisors influenced the power relationships between ministers and civil servants? Has the increased scope and specificity of the government programmes influenced the relationship? Does the power of ministers in relation to civil servants depend on cabinet duration, coalition structure, or the minister's length of term? Are ministers primarily representatives of their parties or figureheads of their ministries? How has the system of rapporteurs that has replaced committees and working groups influenced the balance of power? In addition, attention is paid to the role of female civil servants and the impact of globalization and the European Union (EU) on power structures inside the executive branch.

The main data consists of a survey carried out in 2012 which focused on the politicians and civil servants views of their roles. The survey was sent also to those working close to the politicians and civil servants, such as representatives of media, businesses, trade unions, and employers' organisations. The sample was 1 212

persons, out of whom 1 140 persons received the survey by email
and 72 by mail (a total of 784 men and 428 women): 379 ministry
civil servants, 145 other civil servants, 213 persons with background
as minister or MP, 94 ministers' political advisors, 48 members of
party organizations, 69 representatives of businesses, 50 representatives of trade unions and employers' organisations, and more
than 200 media representatives. The response rate was 36 per cent.
Of the respondents 52 per cent belonged to the age group 51–65
years, 33 per cent were under 50 years old and 15 per cent were
more than 65 years old. The respondents were guaranteed anonymity – only their age, gender and work background were reported in
the survey. Additionally, dozens of persons, again on the basis of
anonymity, have been interviewed. The research also benefits from
the author's first-hand experience of over 25 years as a civil servant
and as a participatory observer.[1]

Empirical analysis

Civil servants versus political power – basic determinants

The power of civil servants has been strong throughout the research
period: a total of 40 per cent think that the power of bureaucrats has
been enhanced, one-third view that it has remained unchanged and
only 17 per cent think that the role of civil servants has decreased
(Figure 1). It is also clear that regardless of the time period, strong
ministers have been strong also in relation to civil servants whereas
weak ministers have in turn been effectively controlled by strong
civil servants. The following statements were considered to explain
the empowerment of civil servants most (Figure 2): 'civil servants'
expertise vs. ministers' inexperience' (81 pe rcent), 'civil servants
remain in place while politicians come and go' (70 per cent) and
'the quantity and complexity of issues have increased' (70 per cent).
The internationalisation of politics and economy, as well as the civil

---

1   Since 1988 as a civil servant in the Ministry of Trade and Industry / the
     Ministry of Employment and the Economy in various positions such as senior
     advisor, ministerial advisor, director of planning, director of finance, and
     budget counsellor.

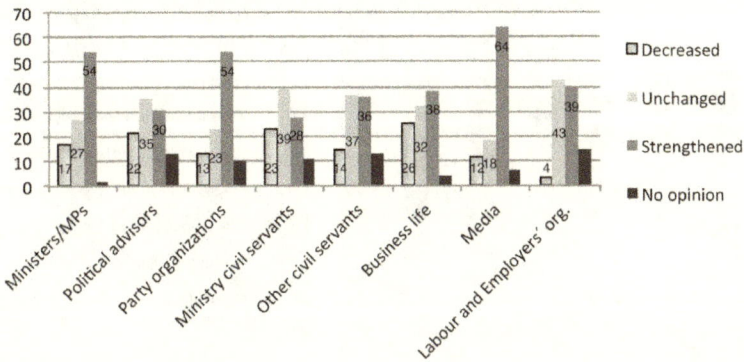

Figure 1. Changes in the power of top civil servants in comparison with the power of ministers during recent decades (per cent).

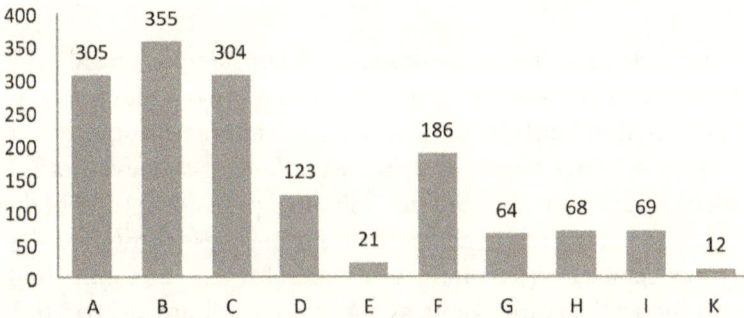

Figure 2. Key factors that strengthen the role of civil servants (number of respondents). Possible to select four factors (all respondent groups).

A = Civil servants remain in place while politicians come and go
B = Civil servants' expertise vs. ministers' inexperience
C = The quantity and complexity of issues have increased
*D = Civil servants have a genuine role in controlling the political agenda
    and the preparation of issues*
E = Civil servants take care of things; ministers are only figureheads of the ministries
F = The internationalisation of politics and economy
*G = Ministers have freedom to act independently, which at the same time strengthens
    the role of civil servants in policy formulation within the ministries*
H = Political advisors are weak in relation to experienced civil servants and experts
I = Political state secretaries (since 2005) have not reduced the power of civil servants
K = Other

■ Other or no opinion

Substance issues of various ministries

● Foreign affairs (generally)

EU affairs at the level of ministries

EU affairs at the level of government

Economic affairs (generally)

Budget affairs at the level of ministries

Budget affairs at the level of government

Ministers/MPs: 32, 38, 32, 17, 36, 49
Political advisors: 33, 57, 22, 15, 28, 46
Party organizations: 36, 39, 26, 31, 36, 44
Ministry civil servants: 58, 47, 28, 31, 22, 34
Other civil servants: 49, 43, 32, 21, 31, 45
Business life: 51, 40, 19, 26, 34, 45
Media: 51, 45, 32, 26, 28, 46, 40
Labour and Employers' org.: 54, 54, 18, 11, 43, 39

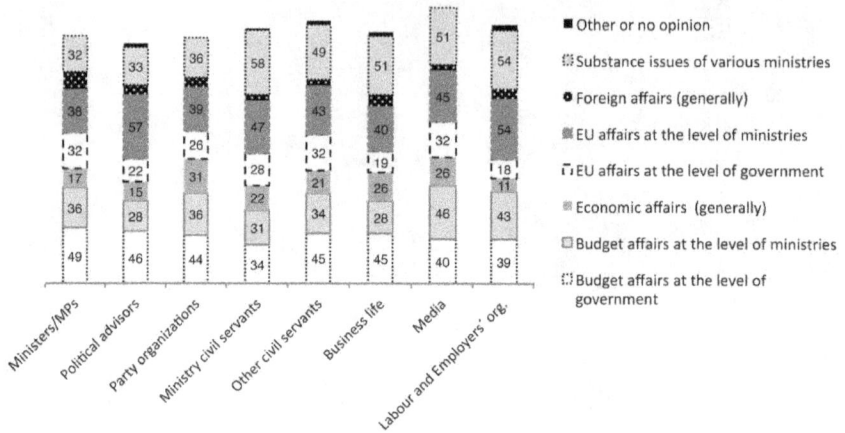

Possible to select more than one policy area.

Figure 3. Policy areas where the role of civil servants is at its highest (per cent).

servants' role in preparing issues are also considered central.

Turning into variation between policy areas (Figure 3), the power of civil servants is considered greatest in the substance issues of various ministries (50 per cent), EU affairs at the levels of government and ministries (combined share of 73 per cent) and budget affairs at the levels of government and ministries (combined share of 73 per cent). Furthermore, at a general level, economic affairs are emphatically pointed out as a key area of bureaucratic influence. Overall, the fact that ministers can act fairly independently in their own jurisdictions has enhanced the power of the civil servants in the ministries. Above them, there is 'just' the minister. The power of the civil servants is also robust in EU affairs, because preparing these issues is in all instances in the hands of the expert civil servants – and in most cases the individual ministers or the cabinet merely rubber-stamp the documents or national positions prepared in the ministries (see the chapter by Raunio).

We can also observe some trends that have worked in the other direction, enhancing the power of politicians. According to the survey two such central factors are (1) the longer duration of governments (53 per cent) as ministers have more time to get acquainted with the issues; and (2) the detailed nature of the government programmes (58 per cent) which works against 'solo acts' of civil servants. The 'quality' of ministers correlates only marginally with the power of the civil servants. Instead, the increase in the number of ministers' political advisors has an impact, with one-third of respondents viewing that these party-political posts have weakened the influence of civil servants. Nearly 90 per cent agree that the minister's person – persona, competence and experience – influences strongly the power relationship. Ultimately, this is the most significant determinant. Over half of the respondents also consider the minister's portfolio as an essential factor, and approximately one-third view the minister's position in her own party as important.

Almost all respondents think that in their activities, the ministers defend or push through policies prepared by the civil servants in their ministry. 94 per cent of the ministers or MPs, 96 per cent of the political advisors and 89 per cent of the civil servants of ministries fully or partly agree with this statement. Two-thirds also partly agree and one-third fully agrees with the statement that in their activities, the ministers advance the political agendas of their parties within the framework of the government programme. This can be interpreted as consolidation of party politics and individual ministers: the minister and political advisors have more time to learn the issues and practices. Power is, after all, also a function of time. Even the minister's competence requirements have become greater, because governments have essentially been in office throughout the entire parliament term since the early 1980s (see the chapter by Paloheimo). Thus, politicians have been able to catch up with the civil servants in matters of substance.

Superiority of the civil servants of the Ministry of Finance

All respondent groups view that the power of civil servants is greatest in the Ministry of Finance. 95 per cent fully or partly agree on the supremacy of the power of the Ministry of Finance's civil servants – including 94 per cent of the politicians. It is clear that, through budgetary frameworks and money allocations, the Ministry of Finance's civil servants are able to guide the operation of the other ministries and the entire government. This central role of the Ministry of Finance is criticised both by politicians and by the civil servants of other ministries. It is argued that when a politician or a new civil servant starts working in the Ministry of Finance and opens the ministry's door, his or her own party or other background is instantly replaced by that of the 'Ministry of Finance party'.

In budgetary matters, the government reigns supreme as its proposal for the annual budget is approved basically as such by the Eduskunta. Within the government, the role of Finance Minister's civil servants is equally sovereign in preparing the budget. The power of civil servants is based on the fact that the budget proposal is drawn up piece by piece in the administration. Power slips to those who have the time to examine the issues. These people are the budget officials of the ministries, and above them is the Ministry of Finance's budget department. When the budget proposal comes to the stage of political decision-making, the preparation work has been so thorough that changes are difficult to make (see the chapter by Karvonen).

In 1991, the government for the first time adopted the use of budgetary frameworks, and this further empowered the Ministry of Finance's civil servants. Politicians continually describe the budget frameworks as restrictions on their activity. The election promises made to the citizens become secondary right after the elections when the reality of the national economy is presented by the civil servants to the politicians. The negotiations on the first budget framework of each four-year electoral term underline the weak position of democratically elected office-holders in relation to the Ministry of Finance's civil servants.

The government's Cabinet Committee on Economic Policy used to be called 'the government's economic affairs insiders'. Headed by the prime minister, the committee has representatives from each cabinet party. The Ministry of Finance's top civil servants are the permanent experts of the committee and they also form the committee secretariat. The Ministry of Finance civil servants are in the committee as gatekeepers and as grey eminences as they also are in the Cabinet Finance Committee. When the Cabinet Committee on Economic Policy is in favour of a proposal, it is usually also the final cabinet decision. If the other ministries want to influence the proposals, they normally approach the civil servants in the Ministry of Finance, not the politicians. According to the survey the finance minister (49 per cent), Ministry of Finance's civil servants (48 per cent) and prime minister (46 per cent) are considered nearly equally strong in the operation of the committee. The influence of the other ministers (10 per cent) in the committee is considered marginal.

Government programme and political agenda

Government programmes have in recent decades become much longer and more detailed, structuring the work of the cabinet and committing the coalition partners to commonly agreed objectives and priorities (see the chapter by Paloheimo). The past few governments have been nearly stifled by the specificity of their programmes. When the government coalition consists of several parliamentary parties and sometimes from both extremes of the political spectrum, deviating from the programme is nearly impossible.

Whose penmanship do we see most in the government programme? The 'worst case scenario' is that the programme is drafted by civil servants, as the media would often have us believe. In such a case –government policy would be in reality decided by bureaucrats. However, from the perspective of parliamentarianism and democracy, the survey results are comforting, with 47 per cent viewing the role of politicians as more central in drawing up the government programme. 13 per cent saw that the civil servants are more important, whereas 18 per cent considered both sets of actors to be equally significant. Nonetheless, even when formulating the government programme, the Ministry of Finance civil servants are thought to have a clearly stronger role than the other civil servants. This is most evident in the framework and appropriation sections of the programme. Sometimes their statements are included as such in the programme or its appendices. Such bureaucratic influence was at its peak during the heavy recession of the early 1990s, but since then the influence of the civil servants has clearly decreased and the weight of the politicians has increased.

While the government programme influences to a large extent also the political agendas of the ministries, new issues come and go constantly. But who influences the preparation and content of these political agendas? According to the survey two-thirds views that in preparing the political agenda, the politicians have clearly more power than the civil servants. The politicians (ministers / MPs) and civil servants share this perception. Only a small minority of five per cent thinks that the role of civil servants is stronger. A large part of political issues are ultimately linked to the state budget or budgetary frameworks, which is why the Ministry of Finance civil servants are also in this context seen to have a greater role than other civil servants.

The interviews and the author's participatory observation suggest that the power of civil servants is in fact stronger than what the survey responses indicate. Regardless of the detailed government programme, it is chiefly the civil servants who introduce new themes to the agenda – preparation of new issues is constantly underway. Although the individual ministers are responsible for implementing the government programme in more detail than before, every time a new minister enters her ministry for the first time, she is faced with a long list drafted by the civil servants consisting of issues in which 'the minister's input is urgently required'.

Countering the power of civil servants – political aids and fixed-term positions

The prime minister was assigned his own political secretary in the 1930s, but the other ministers had to wait until 1972. After that the number of political aids has increased quite substantially. In the beginning of 1993, the cabinet ministers had 24 advisors. As of 2005, ministers have been entitled to their own political state secretaries, and all ministers who are MPs have their personal parliamentary assistants. In 2013 the government ministers (N = 19) had 149 aids, although not all of them were so-called political aids.[2]

Depending on the minister, the state secretaries and special advisors have at times exerted strong influence. They often select the material that reaches the minister, partly watch who has access to the minister, and carry out assignments given by the minister. Sometimes the civil servants have difficulties dealing with the advisors 'who think he or she is the minister' (interviews). Only 16 per cent of the survey respondents agreed with the statement 'special

2   P. Ahokas, 'Ministerien avustajakunta on kaksinkertaistunut: Jyrki Kataisen hallituksen ministereitä avustaa 149 ihmistä', *Helsingin Sanomat* 20.7.2013.

advisors / political state secretaries are no match to experienced civil servants with expertise'. It can thus be said that, from the perspective of making public policy, the power of civil servants has been successfully curtailed with the help of political aids.

Adopting the system of political state secretaries was a long and controversial project. The object of the reform was to strengthen political control and at the same time to curtail the power of civil servants. Prime Minister Harri Holkeri was the first to have a political state secretary in 1989. At the time, there was insufficient support for extending the system to the other ministries, but after that the topic was actively discussed until the state secretary system was established. For a long while, the debate also included a system of deputy or assistant ministers, with the right-wing parties favouring the deputy minister system, while the parties on the left preferred the state secretaries.

The central public justification among those in favour of enhancing the political capacity of ministers was the increased workload resulting from EU membership, but in actual fact, decreasing the power of civil servants was the strongest factor behind the reform. The top civil servants of the ministries, the permanent secretaries, were dismayed and rejected the idea of political state secretaries. They feared for their positions, thinking that a 'political tornado' will take over the ministries. The fact that the state secretaries would be in the middle between the ministers and the traditional 'unbiased' civil servants was considered a problem. The matter proceeded slowly for years until finally the government proposal on establishing the offices of state secretaries to the ministers was submitted to the Eduskunta in 2002 (HE 270/2002 vp). However, the Constitutional Law Committee (PeVM 13/2002 vp) unanimously proposed that the government proposal should be rejected. The idea was reintroduced two years later. The new proposal (HE 142/2004 vp) underlined that the permanent secretaries would continue to lead their ministries, and now it received the needed parliamentary approval.

First political state secretaries were appointed in 2005. According to a gentleman's agreement between governing parties, civil servants from the ministries were not appointed as state secretaries, because a sudden promotion bypassing the entire official hierarchy would have caused problems within the ministries. These state secretaries are appointed for the term of the minister. Each government determines whether there is need for state secretaries. A state secretary assists and represents the minister according to the minister's instructions. The permanent secretary, in turn, directs the ministry. Unlike the permanent secretaries, permanent under-secretaries or director generals, the state secretaries do not possess any official decision-making power.

The reform has angered particularly the senior civil servants, partly because it has confused the internal preparatory work carried out in the ministries. Many think that instead of lightening the unreasonable workload of the ministers as was the intention, most state secretaries are just special advisors with a better salary and a finer title (interviews). In the daily life of the ministry, the civil servants often see no real difference between state secretaries and special advisors. The recruitment of the state secretaries has also received criticism as 'most of them have been less qualified than most special advisors'. It is apparent that the system of state secretaries leaves room for interpretation. The border between the preparatory work of the civil servants and political decision-making has not necessarily always been clear, but it has always existed. Now the state secretaries are interfering with this preparatory work and their role is causing confusion in the hierarchy and division of labour of central administration (interviews). However, only 16 per cent of the survey respondents agreed with the statement 'the practice of state secretaries has not achieved its goals and has not decreased the power of the top civil servants'. Hence, the power of civil servants is constrained to some extent through the system of state secretaries.

The increase in the number of political advisors in the ministries becomes evident through the fact that the number of civil servants involved with political actors has also clearly increased. Earlier, the minister's contacts with civil servants were primarily made through the permanent secretary and partly director generals. Now political advisors and expert civil servants are in direct contact with each other. Therefore, a larger number of civil servants are now involved with 'political' preparatory work. This implies that role of permanent secretaries and, in some cases, of general directors has weakened – and that of the expert civil servants has been enhanced (interviews).

In addition to the system of state secretaries, another reform aiming at weakening the power of civil servants was the introduction of fixed-term appointments. Before the early 2000s, the positions were usually permanent. The argument was that fixed-term contracts would facilitate stronger political control of civil servants. This goal has been at least partly achieved, but not without negative side effects. Not surprisingly, towards the end of their contracts, the civil servants are perhaps too cautious in dealing with the minister, for example through not presenting policy alternatives that differ from the minister's preferences.

Political appointments

In the appointment of top officials of both the state and municipalities, the political background of the candidates has typically been a key variable: the more senior the office, the more political parties have affected the appointment. In the municipalities, no attempt is often made to hide the political nature of appointments, unlike in state administration. By the 1960s public administration gained increasing political significance and attracted the attention of political parties. Actual political appointments began in earnest after the 1966 elections under a cabinet led by Social Democrats. Political appointments were made in massive scale in the 1970s. Large appointment packages were formed in which each of the largest parties had their quotas, but some positions were also reserved for the smaller parties. In those days, attitudes toward the politicisation of administration varied. The left-wing parties were largely in favour of 'representative bureaucracy', *i.e.* appointing people according to political grounds, whereas the centre-right parties were more in favour of emphasising merit-based appointments (Rantala 1982: 53). By 1977, just under one-third of the top positions in the ministries and approximately half of those in other major public agencies were held by the two main governing parties, the Social Democrats and Centre Party (Gronow *et al.* 1977: 40–41).[3]

Officially, political appointments do not exist. After allegedly political appointments, the responsible minister will declare that

---

3   These appointment packages included so-called 'overcoat offices', where a civil servant appointed on political grounds received an 'overcoat' person, appointed simultaneously to a similar or slightly lower position, from the other main government party.

the 'most competent' person was appointed. The differences in opinion largely depend on whether the party is in the opposition or in the government. Politicians have said frankly that it is important to have reliable party people in the bureaucracy, not least because this enables the parties often to by-pass the ordinary routes of influence (interviews). However, the number of political appointments has clearly decreased. A new trend has appeared in which the government no longer handles appointments collectively. Beginning with the Social Democratic-led 'rainbow' coalitions (1995–2003), it has become unofficial practice that individual ministers handle appointments in their own jurisdictions.

In the survey 91 per cent of the respondents considered political appointments to be purely motivated by party-political influence, *i.e.* to have a member of one's party influencing the preparatory work of civil servants and ensuring the presence of the party in the public administration. Although it is impossible to calculate the exact numbers, one could say that over the past decades the parties can be ranked as follows regarding their level of political appointments: 1) Social Democrats, 2) Centre Party, 3) National Coalition, and 4) Swedish People's Party and Finnish People's Democratic League /Left Alliance. The Social Democrats come first especially because of their high number of appointments in the early part of the examination period. Naturally, everything depends on which parties are in the government at any given time. As soon as the National Coalition was able to join governments again in 1987, it began playing the same game. The Centre Party has been able to maintain a steady pace of appointments given its regular presence in the cabinet.

Committees, working groups, rapporteurs and consultants

Since the end of the 1990s the ministries have witnessed a boom of rapporteurs and consultants. On the other hand, preparing policy through broader committees (including MPs) has nearly completely ended. Committees have over the recent decades been primarily replaced by working groups, with hundreds of them cooperating each year. Increase in the number of working groups is linked to the vanishing community spirit of the government. The ministries are largely separate from one another, with the respective ministers manages only the affairs of their own fields of competence. The working groups are established inside individual ministries, and ministers can appoint a person of her choice as a rapporteur to examine a specific issue.

The borderline between rapporteurs and consultants is blurry. One might ask whether the state is outsourcing its expertise. Essentially both rapporteurs and consultants are paid outsiders telling the government what to do. (Kuusela & Ylönen 2013; interviews). They also weaken the power of civil servants through reducing their role in policy formulation. Many in the bureaucracy also feel that relying on rapporteurs and consultants is an expression of distrust towards civil servants. Half of the survey respondents think that rapporteurs have had a genuine and necessary role in preparing issues. Around 40 per cent feel that the rapporteurs enhance the role of the minister, which is logical as the ministers carefully screen the rapporteur candidates. One-fifth thinks that rapporteurs have clearly weakened the position of civil servants. However, only just over 10 per cent consider the role of rapporteurs completely unnecessary. In the interviews, however, the rapporteurs were considered completely unnecessary to a much larger extent.

Female civil servants

While the role of women has become much stronger in Finnish politics in recent decades (see the chapter by Niemi), similar progress has been much slower in public administration. Ministers are often very inexperienced, but reaching the higher ranks of the bureaucracy takes time. Appointing women to top positions only really began in the 1990s. Gender differences are also present in the corporate world. Although the so-called 40 per cent equality recommendations are in force for executive boards, in 2013 only three women were the heads in the 58 corporations wholly or partly owned by the Finnish state.

In 2000, the share of women in the top leadership positions of state administration was approximately 12 per cent. In 2012 approximately half of the staff in state administration were women, but that share was much lower among the top civil servants (28 per cent). The system of permanent secretaries began in the early days of independence, but it took more than 70 years (in 1995) for the first woman to be appointed as a permanent secretary. In 2014, six of the permanent secretaries of the ministries were women and five were men. At the level of director generals of the ministries, the development has been similar, but the ministries differ greatly. In 2014, 16 of the 52 director generals of ministries were women (31 per cent), whereas in 2005 the corresponding figure was only 16 per cent. In the early part of the research period, the figure was nearly zero. Women are more commonly found in lower level management duties such as communications, personnel administration, or in economic and general administration. The slow introduction of women into leadership positions is basically due to the fact that women entered the state bureaucracy in large numbers only a few decades ago, and even their educational qualifications were lower than among the male population. Nowadays the situation is reversed, as the share of women with the higher level of education is larger than that of men. The younger the age group, the larger the share of women among those with a university degree.

The survey also examined the reasons for the relatively low presence of women in key bureaucratic positions. The respondents pointed out that in addition to a 'glass ceiling' blocking women's advancement, female civil servants may not prioritise job promotion to the same extent as their male colleagues. Interestingly, no females came up when the respondents were asked to name strong permanent secretaries, other top civil servants or ministers from the past three decades.

Concluding discussion

The greatest weakness of the Finnish governments is their seemingly insurmountable sectorial division. The cabinet no longer makes decisions as a collegial body, because the official plenary sessions of the government simply rubberstamp things that have been agreed upon in advance in the ministerial committees or in the individual ministries. And because ministers enjoy fairly free reign in their fields, this development has in fact enhanced the power of the civil servants of the ministries. In their daily work, the ministers and their political aids are alone with the civil servants.[4]

4   Finnish governments have since the turn of the millennium invested resources
    in improving coordination and strategic planning inside the cabinet and the

Formal decisions belong to politicians, but the actual power of the civil servants depends on a variety of factors such as the issue area, the economic outlook, or the personal skills and motivation of the minister. In central issues, the minister usually adopts the stance of the civil servants and not the other way around. The policy interests or daily routines of each substance ministry change fairly little when the minister changes. The minister must adapt to it in order to survive in office. Ultimately, the most decisive determinant in terms of balance power is the person holding each position, and this applies especially to ministers. In the survey nearly 90 per cent agreed that it is the minister's personality and competence which influences most the relationship between civil servants and the minister.

However, a large consensus prevails on the powerful role of the Ministry of Finance civil servants. Most ministers and MPs even think that through budgetary frameworks and appropriations the bureaucrats in the Ministry of Finance essentially guide the operation of the entire government. The powerful role of the Ministry of Finance is of course understandable, as there has to be coordination between and above the demands of the sectoral ministries. The role of the civil servants is very strong also in the other ministries in matters pertaining to the budget and budgetary framework. One could generalise by saying that the tougher the times, the harder it is for the politicians to find a way forward without strong guidance from the civil servants. The power of civil servants is also robust in EU affairs.

The number of ministers' political advisors has continued to increase. The most significant change is the system of political state secretaries adopted in 2005. These developments have in turn weakened the input of civil servants. At the same time the role of the permanent secretaries of the ministries has decreased. Political appointments have not lost their significance, in part because parties want their representatives to influence the preparatory work

---

entire executive branch. Hence the governments appointed since 2003 have tried to improve horizontal coordination inside the government, mainly through government's intersectoral policy programmes (that were used from 2003 to 2011) and other coordination instruments such as various government strategy documents or the budgetary frameworks (Kekkonen & Raunio 2011).

of the civil servants. The move towards fixed-term positions has also strengthened political control, but the stronger influence of political parties or ministerial aids have also created tensions in the ministries. Political control manifests itself also through the highly influential government programme, the formulation of which is driven more by party political preferences than by civil servants. In terms of policy preparation, broader committees whose membership included MPs and politicians have been nearly completely abandoned. Instead, policy reforms and new laws are planned inside individual ministries in working groups or envisioned by rapporteurs or even consultants.

To conclude, the power of civil servants has without any doubt seen strong throughout the research period. Among the factors contributing to the influence of civil servants are policy expertise, the quantity and complexity of the matters on the agenda, the internationalisation of politics and economy, particularly through EU membership, as well as the simple fact that civil servants are career bureaucrats whereas cabinet ministers normally change every four years. Hence longer cabinet duration since the early 1980s coupled with the higher quality of ministers that enjoy more staff resources has curtailed the influence of civil servants. (See also Tiihonen 2006; Murto 2014.)

Political control is in a way always incomplete, which is why there is no simple answer to whether the ministries are controlled by the ministers or the civil servants. Their relationship is one of necessary interdependence, and the locus of power in the relationship varies depending on the persons, issues and situations. Ministers depend on their civil servants and the civil servants on their minister.

References

Bendix, R. (1962). *Max Weber. An Intellectual Portrait.* New York, Anchor Books.

Biddle, B. & Thomas, E. (eds.) (1966). *Role Theory. Concepts and Research.* New York, Wiley.

Dahl, R. A. (1971). *Johdatus politiikan tutkimukseen.* Helsinki, Tammi.

Dahlström, C., Peters, B.G. & Pierre, J. (eds) (2011). *Steering from the Centre: Strengthening Political Control in Western Democracies.* Toronto, University of Toronto Press.

Dunleavy, P. (1991). *Democracy, Bureaucracy, and Public Choice.* London, Harvester Wheatsheaf.

Etzioni, A. (1970). Power as a Societal Force. In J. P. Olsen (ed.), *Power in Societies.* New York, Macmillan: 18–28.

Etzioni-Halevy, E. (1993). *The Elite Connection: Problems and Potential of Western Democracy.* Cambridge, Policy Press.

Foucault, M. (1998). *Seksuaalisuuden historia. Tiedontahto. Nautintojen käyttö. Huoli itsestä.* Finnish transl. Kaisa Sivenius. Helsinki, Gaudeamus.

— (2000). The Subject and Power. In J. D. Faubion (ed.), *Power: The Essential Works of Michel Foucault 1954–1984.* Vol. 3. New York, The New Press: 326–348.

Gronow, J., Klemola, P. & Partanen, J. (1977). *Demokratian rajat ja rakenteet. Tutkimus suomalaisesta hallitsemistavasta ja taloudellisesta perustasta.* Tasa-arvon ja demokratian tutkimus Tandem. Juva, WSOY.

Huber, J. D. (2000). Delegation to civil servants in parliamentary democracies. *European Journal of Political Research* Vol. 37, 3: 397–413.

Huber, J. D. and Shipan, C. R. (2002). *Deliberate Discretion? Institutional Foundations of Bureaucratic Autonomy.* Cambridge, Cambridge University Press.

Kekkonen, S. & Raunio, T. (2011). Towards Stronger Political Steering: Program Management Reform in the Finnish Government. In C. Dahlström, B. G. Peters & J. Pierre (eds), *Steering from the Centre: Strengthening Political Control in Western Democracies.* Toronto, University of Toronto Press: 241–260.

Kuusela, H. & Ylönen, M. (2013). *Konsulttidemokratia. Miten valtiosta tehdään tyhmä ja tehoton.* Helsinki, Gaudeamus.

Lasswell, H. & Kaplan, A. (1950). *Power and Society.* New Haven, Yale University Press.

Mosca, G. (1939). *The Ruling Class.* New York & London, McGraw-Hill.

Moyser, G. & Wagstaffe, M. (1987). Studying Elites: Theoretical and Methodological Issues. In Moyser, G. & Wagstaffe, M. (eds.), *Research Methods for Elite Studies.* London, Allen & Unwin: 1–24.

Murto E. (2014). *Virkamiesvaltaa? Ministerien ja virkamiesten väliset valtasuhteet Suomessa viime vuosikymmenien aikana.* Tampere, Tampere University Press.

Peters, B.G. (2009). *The Politics of Bureaucracy: An Introduction to Comparative Public Administration.* 6th edition. London, Routledge.

Putnam, R. D. (1976). *The Comparative Study of Political Elites.* Englewood Cliffs, Prentice Hall.

Rantala, O. (1982). *Suomen puolueiden muuttuminen 1945–1980.* Helsinki, Gaudeamus.

Ruostetsaari, I. (1992). *Vallan ytimessä. Tutkimus suomalaisesta valtaeliitistä.* Helsinki, Gaudeamus.
— (2003). *Valta muutoksessa.* Helsinki, WSOY.

Tiihonen, S. (2006). *Ministeriön johtaminen: Poliittisen ja ammatillisen osaamisen liitto.* Tampere, Tampere University Press.

Weber, M. (1946). *From Max Weber: Essays in sociology.* Translated, edited, and with an introduction, by H. H. Gerth and C. W. Mills. New York, Oxford University Press.

Zannoni, P. (1978). The Concept of Elite. *European Journal of Political Research* Vol. 6, 1: 1–30.

The Effect of EU and Internationalization on the National Division of Power

TAPIO RAUNIO

Recently an increasing number of scholars have investigated the impact of globalization and particularly of European integration on national political systems. Most of this literature has focused on whether the European Union (EU) alters the balance of power between domestic actors. The EU creates new exit, veto, voice and informational opportunities for domestic actors and therefore changes the opportunity structure for exerting political influence. A key argument in this literature is that global and regional integration empower the executive branch vis-à-vis the parliament, and that within the government, particularly prime ministers (PM) and other portfolios with a strong international dimension have become more accentuated. Moreover, through the centrality of technical expertise in the EU and in international organisations, the true winners of internationalization have arguably been bureaucrats and organized private interests at all levels of government and not cabinet members or MPs.

However, in Finland the impact of internationalization and European integration has been particularly profound, as they acted as a catalyst for constitutional change from the early 1990s onwards, providing a major exogenous factor for reducing the powers of the president and strengthening parliamentary democracy. The adjustment to the post-Cold War context and to the demands of EU membership went hand in hand with a comprehensive revision of the Finnish constitution. Since relations with the Soviet Union were, at the top level, primarily based on negotiations between the

Finnish president and the leaders in the Kremlin, the dissolution of the Soviet empire reduced the importance of such personalized foreign policy leadership. Given that all of the then EU countries, with the exception of France, were parliamentary regimes, it was perceived that having the president represent Finland in the EU would constitute 'an anomaly' in the Union (Kinnunen 2003: 22). It was thus argued that there was a poor fit between a president-led system and the demands of EU membership, with the PM and the government better positioned to co-ordinate national EU policy and to represent Finland in Brussels. This question was very important also in terms of parliamentary accountability as the president has no obligation to inform the Eduskunta.

Without constitutional change, the president would have led national integration policy and would have been Finland's main representative at the European level. Already Finland's membership in the European Economic Area (EEA) would have implied, in accordance with a strict interpretation of the constitution, the inclusion of the entire EEA policy in the competence of the president. The constitution had therefore to be amended in order to enable the participation of the parliament and the government in EEA matters. The result was first an addition to Section 33 of the Form of Government Act, and finally, the whole Section was modified in the new unified constitution that entered into force in 2000[1]. This amendment (Section 33a) purported to balance the division of powers between the president and the government in EEA matters and to prevent the powers that by definition belonged to the sphere of domestic policy from being transferred to the president.[2]. The importance of the amendment increased when Finland joined the Union. Section 33 of the Form of Government Act was applied to Finland's EU membership in the sense that as a part of his general foreign policy leadership, the Common Foreign and Security Policy

---

1   The Constitution of Finland, 11 June 1999 (731/1999).
2   'The Parliament shall participate in the approval of those decisions taken by international organs which according to the Constitution require the consent of the Parliament in the manner stipulated by the Parliament Act. The Council of State shall decide on the approval and implementation of the decisions covered by the subsection 1 if the decision does not require the Parliament's approval and does not because of its substance necessitate that an order is issued.'

(CFSP) as well as amendments to the EU treaties were interpreted to belong to the president's jurisdiction while other EU matters belonged to the government. According to Section 93 of the new constitution the government is responsible for EU policy with foreign policy leadership shared between the president and the government:

> The foreign policy of Finland is directed by the President of the Republic in co-operation with the Government. However, the Parliament accepts Finland's international obligations and their denouncement and decides on the bringing into force of Finland's international obligations in so far as provided in this Constitution. The President decides on matters of war and peace, with the consent of the Parliament.
>
> The Government is responsible for the national preparation of the decisions to be made in the European Union, and decides on the concomitant Finnish measures, unless the decision requires the approval of the Parliament. The Parliament participates in the national preparation of decisions to be made in the European Union, as provided in this Constitution.
>
> The communication of important foreign policy positions to foreign States and international organizations is the responsibility of the Minister with competence in foreign affairs.

This constitutional reform forms the backbone of this chapter, the aim of which is to examine the impact of global and particularly European integration on the division of power between and within Finnish national political institutions. While the chapter draws on quite extensive empirical material, the purpose is nonetheless to provide a 'bird's eye view' of the overall influence of internationalization on national politics. The next section analyses how European integration has affected legislative-executive relations, with the third section focusing on distribution of power inside the cabinet and the executive branch. The fourth section in turn investigates the dual leadership in foreign affairs. The main argument is that the post-Cold War context and EU membership have contributed significantly to domestic developments that were already underway without any external factors – strengthening of parliamentary democracy, bureaucratization, and reducing the powers of the president. Moreover, Finnish political agenda and room of manoeuvre are increasingly influenced and constrained by regional and global integration and more specifically by the agendas of EU institutions.[3]

Legislative-executive relations

European countries have joined the EU and global agreements in order to benefit from regional and global integration. But while member states can certainly benefit from EU membership economically and politically, Europe also acts as a significant constraint on national democracy. Though there is no scholarly consensus about the extent to which European integration impacts on the work of domestic legislatures, it is nonetheless generally agreed that European integration and the consistent empowerment of the EU have presented a major challenge to national parliaments. According to the so-called 'deparliamentarization' thesis, the development of European integration has led to the erosion of parliamentary control over the executive branch (*e.g.* Moravcsik 1994; Raunio & Hix 2000).

The argument about deparliamentarization is based on constitutional rules and on the political dynamics of the EU policy process. The EU member states have transferred policy-making powers to the European level in a broad and significant range of questions, and as a result, parliaments have directly lost influence. With the partial exception of Treaty amendments and other issues decided by unanimity, the influence of national legislatures in EU affairs is mainly limited to scrutinizing the Commission's initiatives and to influencing the government that represents the country at the European level. The increased use of qualified majority voting in the Council, which means that individual governments can find themselves in the losing minority, and the often complicated bargaining in the Council and the European Council in turn make it difficult for

3   The chapter draws on previous research by the author. Unless specifically mentioned, the data consists of interviews with parliamentary and government civil servants, MPs and ministers and Eduskunta and government documents. For detailed information on data sources, please consult the literature referred to in the chapter.

national parliaments to force governments to make detailed ex ante commitments before taking decisions in Brussels. The main point is that national governments represent their countries in European and global negotiations, and hence this results in informational asymmetries between the executive and the legislature. Given the dominance of this deparliamentarization thesis in scholarly work and political debate, it is not surprising that national parliaments are often labelled as the main 'losers' or 'victims' of European integration (Goetz & Meyer-Sahling 2008; Raunio 2009).

EU membership presented thus a challenge for the Eduskunta, concerned not to see its new-won powers weakened as a result of the political dynamics of regional integration. Adaptation to European integration within the Eduskunta started already in 1990 when the Foreign Affairs Committee demanded that the parliament have access to information and can influence national policy in EEA decision-making. The goal was to guarantee the Eduskunta as powerful a position in EU decision-making as is possible for any national legislature. Here the Eduskunta studied closely the work of the existing scrutiny systems in the national legislatures, particularly that of the Danish Folketinget. The Eduskunta appreciated the regular appearance of Danish ministers in the European Affairs Committee (EAC), but saw that the sectoral committees were not really utilized in the processing of EU matters in the Folketinget. Also many MPs were against centralizing EU matters to the EAC as that might have created an 'elite' group of deputies that would alone decide European issues. The Eduskunta also noted that the Folketinget became involved rather late in EU matters (basically before the decisive Council meeting), and hence identified a need for a system that would facilitate a more proactive role for the Eduskunta. (Jääskinen 2000; Raunio 2007a, 2015)

Decentralization to committees before EAC *mandating*

There is no doubt that the institutional rules established for parliamentary scrutiny of EU matters work rather well. The scrutiny model of the Eduskunta has five main strengths: the position of the parliament is regulated in the constitution; the Eduskunta gets relatively early involved in the processing of EU matters; the parliament enjoys basically unlimited access to information from the government; ministerial hearings in the EAC for Brussels-bound ministers; and the regular involvement of specialized committees (Jääskinen 2000). The design of the parliamentary EU scrutiny system has been 'path-dependent' in the sense that it is based on two features central to Eduskunta: committees and information rights. In fact, the Eduskunta (2010: 14) itself has remarked that the scrutiny model was purposefully designed so that it would resemble as much as possible the parliamentary procedures for processing domestic legislation. The only real difference is that the specialized committees report to the Grand Committee, the EAC of the Eduskunta, and not to the plenary.

The parliamentary EU scrutiny system is primarily geared towards scrutinizing the government position and mandating Brussels-bound ministers. The Grand Committee and the Foreign Affairs Committee are the main committees responsible for European questions. The former coordinates parliamentary work in EU affairs while the latter is responsible for EU's foreign and security policy and Treaty amendments. The Grand Committee is in a powerful position because it is the EAC – and not the plenary – that mandates the government in EU affairs. The Grand Committee convenes normally on Wednesday and Friday afternoons. It has enjoyed high status in the parliament since Finland joined the EU, and among its members are chairs of standing committees and leaderships of the party groups. Like the other committees, the Grand Committee meets behind closed doors. The Eduskunta has argued that the confidentiality of committee deliberations facilitates government accountability, but it also means that the electorate receives very little information about party positions in European matters.[4]

The constitution (Section 96) defines the parliament's role in EU matters as follows:

---

4   This lack of openness was noted by a visiting delegation from the British House of Commons. According to Matthew Kirk, the UK ambassador to Finland, the visitors had been particularly struck about the strong consensus among Finnish politicians, the broad cooperation between the government and the opposition in EU affairs, and that in an otherwise transparent society such a high share of parliamentary work is conducted behind closed doors. Annamari Sipilä, 'Suomen eduskunta antoi briteille mallia EU-asioiden käsittelyssä', *Helsingin Sanomat* 23.3.2005.

The Parliament considers those proposals for acts, agreements and other measures which are to be decided in the European Union and which otherwise, according to the Constitution, would fall within the competence of the Parliament.

The Government shall, for the determination of the position of the Parliament, communicate a proposal referred to in paragraph (1) to the Parliament by a communication of the Government, without delay, after receiving notice of the proposal. The proposal is considered in the Grand Committee and ordinarily in one or more of the other Committees that issue statements to the Grand Committee. However, the Foreign Affairs Committee considers a proposal pertaining to foreign and security policy. Where necessary, the Grand Committee or the Foreign Affairs Committee may issue to the Government a statement on the proposal. In addition, the Speaker's Council may decide that the matter may be taken up for debate in plenary session, during which, however, no decision is made by the Parliament.

The Government shall provide the appropriate Committees with information on the consideration of the matter in the European Union. The Grand Committee or the Foreign Affairs Committee shall also be informed of the position of the Government on the matter.

European issues are introduced in the Eduskunta as either U-matters, E-matters or as government bills, with the latter dealing with the domestic implementation of directives, EU Treaties and other EU legislation. The government must inform the Eduskunta without delay of any proposal for a Council decision. These U-matters are usually Commission's legislative proposals that fall within the competence of the parliament. The government must also send the Grand Committee information on the preparation of any issue relating to the EU that might belong to the competence of the Eduskunta. According to Section 97 of the constitution the Grand Committee 'shall receive reports on the preparation of other matters in the European Union'. In these E-matters the government delivers a report to the Grand Committee, either upon request from the EAC or on its own initiative. E-matters are sent to relevant specialized committees who may decide – but are not required – to issue a report to the Grand Committee. If a specialized committee reports on an E-matter, the Grand Committee normally sends the report to the relevant ministry. Typical E-matters are

Commission's legislative initiatives that fall outside the jurisdiction
of the Eduskunta and non-legislative documents published by the
Commission (*i.e.*, green and white papers and other Commission's
consultative papers). Other E-matters include reports on Finland's
integration policy or on court cases concerning Finland in the
Court of Justice of the European Union (CJEU).

The processing of EU draft acts begins with the government
sending a formal letter to the Speaker. The letter includes at least
a summary of the proposal, an evaluation of its legal basis and
relation to the subsidiarity principle, the timetable for processing
the matter, and the (tentative) position of the government. Hence
the Eduskunta does not normally receive from the government the
relevant EU documents (such as the full texts of the Commission's
legislative proposals). Instead, scrutiny is primarily based on the
government letter which focuses on explaining the cabinet's position on the matter. Obviously the Eduskunta, like all national
parliaments, receives the Commission's draft acts and other EU
documents directly from the EU institutions. The Speaker for-
wards the matter to the Grand Committee and requests the competent specialized committee or committees to give their opinion
to the Grand Committee. The majority of U-matters are processed
by more than one specialized committee. The specialized committees must according to the constitution report on U-matters to the
Grand Committee, but in less salient questions at least some committees basically just indicate their position briefly in the minutes
of the committee meeting – for example, that the committee agrees
with the government position (Eduskunta 2010: 30).

The share of committee time spent on European matters has been
relatively high. Data from 2004 and 2008 (surveys of committee
clerks) showed that there was considerable variation between the
committees, with this variation primarily driven by the allocation
of powers between the national and European levels. Committees
on Education and Culture and Future were least burdened by EU
matters, while in the Environment, Commerce, and Agriculture and
Forestry Committees European questions comprised half or more
of the meeting time. Basically all respondents emphasized the difficulties involved in giving exact or even rough estimates, as national
issues often have a European dimension. Many of the committees
– such as the Finance Committee – also utilize sections where EU

matters appear more frequently than in actual committee meetings. This variation applies also to reports produced by the committees to the EAC, with particularly Legal Affairs, Finance, Agriculture and Forestry, Commerce, Environment, Administration, and Transport and Communications Committees producing actively opinions on EU matters. The Eduskunta (2005: 14–15) has estimated that nearly half of all items processed by it are EU matters. That same report also noticed that the workload of committees, measured by the number of agenda items, had roughly doubled as a result of EU membership. (Raunio & Wiberg 2010: 83–85)

It has been estimated that in approximately 90–95 per cent of the cases the Grand Committee agrees with the opinion of the specialized committee, with the latter in turn having agreed with the government position. After debating the issue, the Grand Committee formulates a position, which is a parliamentary recommendation, not a formal decision, in the form of a summary from the chair. Normally the Grand Committee produces a written opinion or oral statement only in more salient matters or when it wants to make amendments to the government position. In other matters the EAC simply gives its consent or agrees with the government position. In order to enhance the ability of the Eduskunta to monitor and guide government behaviour in the Council, an effort is made to formulate the view of the EAC before the consideration of the matter begins in the preparatory organs of the Council. It can be asked whether even this is perhaps too late. After all, the Eduskunta's participation in the matter normally begins after the Commission has published the initiative and after it has already been processed domestically in the ministries and in the government. Hence the Eduskunta (2010: 26) has emphasized the need to become involved already at the stage when the Commission is preparing its initiatives.

The Grand Committee convenes, usually on Fridays, to hear ministers about Council meetings scheduled for the following week. In foreign and security policy matters the ministerial hearings are in the Foreign Affairs Committee. The ministers must give the EAC the chance to express its opinion on all matters before final decisions are taken in the Council. After Council meetings the EAC receives a report on the Council meeting. Ministers must be also prepared to appear before the Grand Committee and to explain in detail any deviations from the given policy guidelines. In practice the minister normally reports on the previous Council meeting when appearing next in the Grand Committee. Advance scrutiny of Council agenda items means, in most cases, discussing the relevant issues and their implications. Actual voting instructions are only given at the final stage of the process and constitute a very small per cent of all instructions. The Grand Committee usually does not impose very strict mandates, thus leaving ministers a certain amount of freedom of manoeuvre. More important is to define the range of outcomes acceptable to the EAC, with the government then also having the possibility to use this as a bargaining chip in Brussels. This is reflected in the behaviour of the Finnish government in the EU, which has mainly been characterized by flexibility and the desire to build compromises. Moreover, the Grand Committee focuses its scrutiny on selected issues: the overwhelming majority of European matters does not cause any controversy or are not even debated by the EAC.

According to Section 97 of the constitution

> The Foreign Affairs Committee of the Parliament shall receive from the Government, upon request and when otherwise necessary, reports of matters pertaining to foreign and security policy. Correspondingly, the Grand Committee of the Parliament shall receive reports on the preparation of other matters in the European Union. The Speaker's Council may decide on a report being taken up for debate in plenary session, during which, however, no decision is made by the Parliament. The Prime Minister shall provide the Parliament or a Committee with information on matters to be dealt with in a European Council beforehand and without delay after a meeting of the Council. The same applies when amendments are being prepared to the treaties establishing the European Union. The appropriate Committee of the Parliament may issue a statement to the Government on the basis of the reports or information referred to above.

Hence the PM has the obligation to inform the Grand Committee both beforehand and afterwards of European Council meetings, appearing before the EAC the same way as other cabinet ministers do before Council meetings. Since December 2006 the government has provided written reports on European Council meetings to the Eduskunta, both before and after the meetings. The PM also informs the Foreign Affairs Committee about foreign and security policy matters discussed in the European Council. If needed, the PM and the government are also in contact with the Grand Committee during the actual European Council meeting. Such contacts can be required particularly if new issues or initiatives appear on the agenda of the European Council in the course of the meeting. Government bills on amendments to EU Treaties are handled by the Foreign Affairs Committee, but the Grand Committee is the primary committee responsible for monitoring government behaviour in Intergovernmental Conferences (IGC).

As indicated above, the informational rights of the Eduskunta in EU matters are very strong. Section 47 of the constitution is particularly important in terms of the specialized committees' access to EU information. The right of the Grand Committee and the Foreign Affairs Committee to receive information on EU matters is instead based on Sections 96 (U-matters) and 97 (E-matters) of the constitution. The constitutionally regulated, basically unlimited, access to information is an essential prerequisite for effective parliamentary scrutiny. This access to information is especially relevant regarding E-matters and ministerial hearings in the EAC. However, good access to information has also resulted in information overload, with MPs often pointing out the problems involved in identifying important EU issues or in understanding the documents that are often quite technical and detailed. Also the Eduskunta has regularly noted that the information arrives in the parliament too late to allow meaningful deliberation, with the government failing to inform the Eduskunta 'without delay' as the constitution stipulates.

Consensus behind closed doors

With parliamentary activity focusing on government scrutiny, it is not very surprising that the approach of Finnish MPs towards inter-parliamentary cooperation has so far been fairly passive. Finnish parliamentarians and civil servants obviously take part in the various interparliamentary activities, particularly in the Conference of Parliamentary Committees for Union Affairs of Parliaments of the European Union (COSAC), but it would be wrong to say that there is much enthusiasm in the Eduskunta towards such networking. The Eduskunta's permanent representative in Brussels monitors the work of the EU institutions, focusing particularly on the European Parliament (EP). The same attitude applies to the Early Warning Mechanism (EWM) introduced by the Lisbon Treaty (2009) whereby national parliaments are involved in monitoring the application of the subsidiarity principle. The implementation of the EWM has not necessitated any real reforms in the Eduskunta as the subsidiarity check is integrated into the standard model of EU scrutiny. Overall, the Eduskunta has emphasized that it participates in EU governance through controlling the government, not through direct links with EU institutions. Indeed, the Eduskunta (2010) has explicitly stated that it views any direct links between national parliaments and EU institutions as problematic, emphasizing that domestic legislatures participate in EU politics indirectly through controlling their governments. The Eduskunta has even argued that at the EU level there is only the one Finnish position as approved by Eduskunta; the government and the Eduskunta do not have separate, independent positions on EU matters.

The Eduskunta has made rather limited use of Finnish members of the EP (MEPs), primarily due to the fact that the Eduskunta has not seen them as particularly essential channels of information or influence. Finnish MEPs are not allowed to attend the meetings of the Grand Committee, and only recently the EAC has invited some individual MEPs to give testimony. Also the specialized committees have made little use of the MEPs. But while there is not much institutionalized cooperation between the MEPs and the Eduskunta, the former are in regular contact with their parties' party groups (and their EU sections or working groups) and EAC members. Indeed, most of the Finnish MEPs are closely involved in the work of their national parties, and thus they can provide parties information on European matters (in most parties at least one MEP belongs to the executive party organs). It appears that such intra-party links have gradually become stronger over the years. (Ruostetsaari 2003; Raunio 2007b)

The processing of EU matters in the Eduskunta has been consensual and pragmatic. Particularly noteworthy has been — at least until the euro zone crisis — the lack of conflict, or even tension, between the government and the Eduskunta on the one hand, and between the government and the opposition on the other hand. Committee scrutiny of EU issues has differed from the processing of domestic legislation in the sense that the government–opposition dimension has not played the only significant role in either the EAC or in specialized committees. The main goal is understood to be to achieve parliamentary, and thus national, unanimity or at least broad consensus (see the next section).[5]

This emphasis on consensus achieved in committees has impacted on the role of plenary. In EU affairs the plenary can become involved both before and after decisions are taken at the European level. The Speaker's Council can decide that proposals for EU decisions be debated in the plenary, but in such cases the chamber is not entitled to make formal decisions. Plenary stage is also required when the implementation of EU laws or Treaties requires legislation. However, plenary involvement in European matters was, at least until the euro crisis, very limited. Debates focused almost exclusively on 'high politics' matters such as Treaty amendments, Finland's EU presidencies, single currency, and security and defence policy, including decisions concerning Finland's participation in EU-led crisis management operations (Koivula & Sipilä 2011). European Council meetings are not normally debated in the plenary, either ex ante or ex post. (Raunio & Wiberg 2010: 85–86; Auel & Raunio 2014)[6]

This limited role of the plenary is probably explained by a combination of institutional choices and the interests of political parties – which are obviously related as parties control the parliamentary agenda and design the legislature's rules of procedure (Auel & Raunio 2014). The main explanation for the brevity of plenary debates is the role accorded to the Grand Committee as it coordinates parliamentary work in EU issues and speaks on behalf of the Eduskunta in such matters (with the exception of those

5   Interestingly, when Finnish and Swedish MPs were asked in a survey carried out in 2001/2002 who should have influence in domestic EU decision-making, Swedish MPs placed the electorate in second place (with the cabinet) after the parliament, whereas Finnish MPs placed the electorate in eighth position after the various national political institutions (Ahlbäck Öberg & Jungar 2009).

6   However, interviewed Eduskunta civil servants also emphasised strongly that it is increasingly difficult to draw a clear line between national and EU issues and that often the most important European debates take place in the context of matters that are categorised as domestic issues. For example, debates on the Baltic Sea, climate change, environment, agriculture, and human rights have been strongly related to the role of EU in such questions (Eduskunta 2010: 35).

questions that specifically require plenary approval). This con-
tributes to the Eduskunta essentially only debating 'high politics'
EU matters in the chamber. However, the decision to delegate
EU affairs almost completely to the EAC and other committees
is, of course, an intentional decision of political parties who have
designed a scrutiny system for EU affairs which aims at the effective scrutiny of the government and is geared towards achieving
a broad domestic elite consensus behind closed doors rather than
making EU affairs a matter of public party competition. One of
the reasons is that for a smaller EU member state speaking with a
strong and united national voice at the European level (arguably)
strengthens its bargaining position. In addition, parties are not
only internally divided over Europe, the gap in opinion between
the parties and their voters is also large, which presents a problem
especially for the three 'core' parties of recent decades: Centre,
National Coalition, and the Social Democrats (Mattila & Raunio
2005, 2012). As European matters produce disagreement within
and among parties, public debates on the floor might damage the
parties by highlighting these internal cleavages.

The low involvement of the plenary means that while the Eduskunta deserves credit for establishing an effective committee-based
system of parliamentary scrutiny, the debating function of the parliament has remained marginalized in European matters (Auel &
Raunio 2014). However, the euro zone crisis and the 2011 elections
have certainly changed the situation, bringing at least a temporary
end to this domestic depoliticization of Europe. Since the outbreak
of the euro crisis the fate of the single currency, and European
integration more broadly speaking, have appeared repeatedly on
the plenary agenda, with many debates lasting several hours each.
These parliamentary debates, many held in connection with euro
crisis-related interpellations, are thus arguably the first time when
the government has really been forced to justify and defend its EU
policies in the public – and when the opposition has attacked the
cabinet publicly over the handling of EU matters.[7] It also appears

---

7   Between 1995 and 2014 a total of 72 interpellations were tabled. Before 2010
    two were EU-related, with both of them dealing with Common Agricultural
    Policy and its impact on Finland (the interpellations were from 1998 and 2003).
    However, since the outbreak of the euro crisis the opposition has tabled five

that the euro zone crisis has at least partially changed the consensual mode of EAC decision-making. Voting has become more common in the Grand Committee, with the votes reproducing the government-opposition cleavage characterizing plenary decision-making, and with the losing opposition minority adding its dissenting opinions to the statements and minutes of the EAC and the specialized committees. Much of this activity is explained by the strategies of The Finns Party. (Raunio 2015).

When scholars have ranked the effectiveness of the various parliamentary EU scrutiny mechanisms, the Eduskunta is without exception categorized as one of the strongest parliaments (*e.g.* Maurer & Wessels 2001; Raunio 2005; Karlas 2012, Winzen 2013; Hefftler *et al.* 2015). The Finnish scrutiny model has also been exported abroad. At least the parliaments of the Baltic countries, Hungary and Slovenia examined it closely when preparing for EU membership, adopting several features of the Finnish mechanism to their own scrutiny models. Particularly the decentralization of scrutiny to specialized committees increases the ability of the whole Eduskunta to influence the government. The active scrutiny of EU matters has arguably improved the overall dialogue between the government and the Eduskunta, thus strengthening parliamentary accountability also in domestic issues (Jääskinen 2000: 131–132). The regular appearance of ministers before the Grand Committee has also had a positive impact on the internal work of the government, leading to improved policy coordination within the cabinet and among the ministries and forcing the ministers to study the issues more thoroughly than might otherwise be the case.

It is thus plausible to argue that the 'deparliamentarization' effect of internationalization has not been as strong in Finland as in most other EU member states. Nonetheless, it must be stressed that the formulation of national EU policy is very much government-driven – as indeed is the case in domestic policy as well. The Eduskunta usually agrees with the government position. In certain more controversial issues, notably the processing of Economic and Monetary Union (EMU) membership in 1997–98 and debates on

---

euro crisis-related interpellations. The first of these was signed by the Left Alliance (VK 6/2010 vp), while the other four were put forward by The Finns Party (VK 2/2011 vp, VK 4/2012 vp, VK 5/2012 vp, VK 3/2013 vp).

euro crisis and Finland's participation in the bail-out measures in 2010–13, the Eduskunta and its Grand Committee have demanded further information and reports from the government or even changes to government's negotiating position. The dominant role of the government is not surprising when considering that all cabinets formed during Finnish EU membership have been surplus majority coalitions, enjoying strong majorities in the parliament. It is thus more realistic to argue that instead of genuinely directing national EU policy, the Eduskunta sets constraints or the parameters for government's European policy (Raunio 2007a).

Inside the Eduskunta, European integration has further shifted the balance of power towards the committees that have a key role in scrutinizing EU matters. This applies particularly to the Grand Committee which has become one of the most prestigious committees. European issues have also increased the workload of most committees, which essentially means that MPs must be more selective in deciding which matters receive parliamentary attention. The analysis also shows how the agenda of Eduskunta is increasingly influenced by EU, a finding which applies also to government as examined in the next section.

The cabinet and the bureaucracy[8]

Considering the central role of national governments in global and regional governance, it is not surprising that long before the term 'Europeanization' became fashionable, scholars were analysing the impact of integration on domestic executives. At the heart of this research tradition is the question of how involvement in the EU policy process alters the balance of power both among national institutions and within the executive branch itself. A key argument in this literature is that EU governance empowers the executive vis-à-vis the parliament, and inside the executive branch the civil servants vis-à-vis the ministers. In the cabinet the main beneficiar-

---

8   Here the terms 'government' and 'cabinet' are used when referring to the actual government (the team of ministers lead by the PM) and the 'executive branch' when referring to the whole government apparatus (cabinet, ministries, and civil servants).

ies are arguably the PM and other portfolios with a strong European dimension such as finance minister. These findings apply, by and large, both to studies of domestic institutions and of individual policy sectors (Featherstone & Radaelli 2003; Graziano & Vink 2007; Goetz & Meyer-Sahling 2008; Ladrech 2010; Bulmer & Lequesne 2013)

Regarding national coordination of EU policy, previous research indicates both gradual convergence and diversity between the structures and objectives of national coordination mechanisms, delegation of policy formulation from the government down to individual ministries and prime ministerial empowerment (*e.g.* Kassim *et al.* 2000; Gärtner *et al.* 2011; Kassim 2013). Research on Finnish EU coordination system has produced similar findings (Lampinen *et al.* 1998; Kinnunen 2003; Laffan 2006; Hyvärinen 2009; Johansson & Raunio 2010; Hämynen 2011). The Finnish EU coordination system has remained basically unchanged since Finland joined the Union in 1995. As indicated in the previous section, it was strongly influenced by the Danish model that appealed particularly because of its emphasis on broad societal consensus and parliamentary scrutiny. Indeed, the publicly stated priority of the Finnish EU coordination system is to manufacture national unanimity or at least broad elite consensus, which can arguably be translated into additional influence during EU level bargaining.

Overall, the Finnish EU coordination system is formalized, with individual officials working according to established vertical and horizontal forms of interaction within a clearly defined administrative structure. At the lowest level of the coordination system are 37 sections (in 2014), each chaired by an official from the responsible ministry. If an agreement is reached, the section procedure provides a sufficient basis for determining Finland's position. Above sections is another bureaucratic coordination body, the Committee for EU Affairs, but it principally deals with matters of administrative nature and only exceptionally discusses individual EU issues.

The ministerial EU committee, officially titled the Cabinet Committee on European Union Affairs, defines the national position in politically, financially or legally significant EU matters. The Cabinet EU Committee is chaired by the PM and is open to all ministers, which makes it well-suited for building compromises between governing parties. Unlike full plenary sessions of the government where issues are pre-cooked and substantial discussions are rare, the Cabinet EU Committee is designed as a venue for actually debating EU matters. Despite being formally only a preparatory body, the ministerial EU Committee in practice approves Finnish positions ahead of Council and European Council meetings. The EU Secretariat, originally located in the foreign ministry, was transferred to the prime minister's office (PMO) in 2000 reflecting the fact that EU policy is led by the government and the PM.[9] The principal duties of the EU Secretariat include ensuring the smooth functioning of the national coordination system, supplying timely instructions to the Finnish Permanent Representation together with competent ministries, and acting as a secretariat to the Cabinet EU Committee and to the Committee for EU Affairs.

The previous section showed how the agenda of the Eduskunta is increasingly influenced by European integration. Turning now to intra-cabinet EU coordination, the analysis focuses on two inter-linked questions: which European issues are debated by the government and who – bureaucrats or political parties – determines which EU matters are on the cabinet agenda (Hyvärinen & Raunio 2014a, b). The analysis is based on two sets of data. The first consists of all protocols (agendas) of Cabinet EU Committee meetings from 1995 to 2012 (N = 696). These public, concise documents provide information about the length of each meeting, the names of ministers and civil servants present, the discussed agenda points and the decision reached or, more precisely, whether the proposed national position was approved or amended (and how). This dataset is used to study the distribution of issues by policy sector in order to establish which EU matters are debated by the government. The second dataset comprises seven semi-structured interviews, carried out in April–May 2013, with key civil servants who either currently work or have worked in the EU Secretariat.

Cabinet EU Committee protocols demonstrate that the number of meetings, on average 39 meetings per year, has not varied significantly, notwithstanding a moderate increase since the beginning of the euro crisis (43 to 45 meetings per year in 2009–2012). It is established practice that the committee meets on a weekly basis on Friday mornings. Written procedure may be utilized if the minis-

9   Official name since 2013 is the Government EU Affairs Department.

terial EU committee does not convene either due to lack of issues requiring political debate or to an official journey of the PM or during holiday seasons. Protocols of written procedures are regrettably only available from 2005 onwards, showing large yearly variation from only ten written procedures in 2007 to 40 written procedures in 2011. The duration of Cabinet EU Committee meetings, 72 minutes on average, has remained relatively stable.

Regarding the distribution of issues in the Cabinet EU Committee, the agendas are divided into three categories of matters: (a) individual EU matters and European Council meetings, (b) Council meetings and informal ministerial meetings, and (c) cases pending before the CJEU.[10] Group (a) consists largely of so-called 'general affairs' including negotiations on EU enlargement, preparation of the multi-annual budgetary frameworks, and institutional issues such as Treaty reforms (36,5 per cent of issues in group (a)). EU external affairs are also commonly debated by ministers (12,4 per cent) as are economic and financial issues, especially in recent years (14,2 per cent). Other EU policy sectors are discussed clearly less often as individual agenda points. European Council meetings figure prominently in Cabinet EU Committee protocols (8,3 per cent of issues in group (a)), especially since 2009 reflecting the increased frequency of European Council meetings. Hence, the European Council agenda significantly influences the agenda of the ministerial EU Committee. This empowers the PM, charged with presenting the European Council agenda and the tentative national positions to fellow ministers, and the EU Secretariat whose task it is to prepare the background document.

Another important group of issues coordinated by ministers are Council meetings and informal ministerial meetings at the EU level (group (b)). It is established practice that every Council meeting is coordinated in the Cabinet EU Committee. This allows ministers and their advisors as well as line ministry officials to be informed about EU matters across the board and to demand modifications to the tentative national positions where necessary. The quantitative data reveals that general affairs and foreign affairs are once again dominant, accounting for 29,1 per cent of issues in group (b). Ecofin

10   The categorization by issues is based on Council configurations
      (http://www.consilium.europa.eu/policies/council-configurations?lang=en).

Council/Eurogroup and the Agriculture and Fisheries Council also form an important part of all Council meetings coordinated in the ministerial EU Committee (12,8 per cent both). Other Council configurations each account for less than 10 per cent of issues in group (b). The third group of issues discussed in the ministerial EU Committee is cases pending before the CJEU with a particular link to Finland. In 2009 it was decided, apparently by high-level officials at the EU Secretariat, that only the most important cases, *e.g.* those with large potential financial implications, should be coordinated by ministers. The decision has translated into a significant drop of CJEU cases in ministerial committee protocols. Yet, even earlier the Cabinet EU Committee tended to rubberstamp the proposed course of action, and substantial discussions on court cases were rare.

With the exception of Council and European Council meetings that are by default coordinated by ministers, usually only high politics issues – topical and often horizontal EU matters of particular political or financial importance – make their way to the EU Cabinet Committee agenda. Here the EU Secretariat and especially its high-ranking officials perform a key filtering or gatekeeping role in intra-government EU coordination. The interests of the governing parties do not seem to play any significant part in agenda formulation. One interviewee commented that 'it might not notably affect the agenda of the Cabinet EU Committee if we had different ruling coalition', whereas another interviewee was even more straightforward in saying that 'the agenda does not reflect the priorities of the governing parties.' Reflecting changes in EU governance, the focus has shifted increasingly to European Council and euro zone summits. The fact that Cabinet EU Committee meetings now revolve more around European Councils and major EU matters means that in other EU issues individual ministers and ministries have more freedom in formulating national positions.

Even if the Cabinet EU Committee is the principal forum for formulating Finnish EU policy within the government it is not the only organ charged with this task. The government plenary session officially approves all government communications to the parliament in EU matters that fall within the competence of the Eduskunta (Section 96 of the constitution), such as (normally) the Commission's legislative proposals. For example, in 2012 altogether 82 such government communications were approved, usually without debate. The three other ministerial committees also occasionally deal with EU issues. The Cabinet Finance Committee as well as the Cabinet Committee on Economic Policy sometimes discuss EU economic and monetary policy. The Cabinet Committee on Foreign and Security Policy regularly debates issues with relevance to EU foreign and security policy. EU matters are probably also discussed by coalition party leaders but understandably there is no data about these informal meetings. Finally, long-term Finnish EU policy is outlined in the government programme, in the government EU report issued mid-term (PMO 2013), and in annual document 'Finland's key EU policy goals'. These documents present, however, the Finnish objectives very generally, giving considerable leeway for politicians and bureaucrats to later define the best course of action.

As in the Eduskunta, EU membership has substantially increased the workload of the cabinet, and this has reinforced the delegation of issues to civil servants and also the need for the cabinet to be more selective when planning its agenda. The analysis thus indicates that while Council and European Council meetings are always coordinated – at least formally – in the ministerial EU committee, key civil servants in the PMO are clearly well-positioned to influence which other European matters receive attention by the government. Direct influence or instructions by either the governing parties or by the PM are rare. This lack of explicit partisan influence may be the product of the relatively consensual nature of Finnish governance and the logic of managing multi-party coalitions, and certainly one could expect direct interventions by parties or the PM to be more frequent in member states with more ideologically cohesive governments and clearer alternation in power such as Sweden, France, the UK or Spain. However, at the same time the findings offer strong support for the thesis about the empowerment of prime ministers, with particularly the stronger role of the European Council reinforcing the domestic leadership of the PM (Johansson & Tallberg 2010).

Governmental EU coordination or debate mainly revolves around important and horizontal EU matters such as Treaty reforms or European Council meetings or topical highly salient issues like the euro crisis. Individual laws or legislative packages are discussed by ministers only when they have far-reaching political or financial consequences, like the EU climate and energy package approved in 2008. The increasing significance of the European Council and of salient matters such as the euro crisis in shaping the agenda of the ministerial EU committee also imply that individual ministers have more freedom of manoeuvre in their own jurisdictions. On a more positive note, and in line with developments in the Eduskunta and its Grand Committee, the euro crisis has clearly politicized and livened up debates in the ministerial EU committee. European integration and euro area decision-making in particular have clearly strengthened the position of the finance minister, a cross-national development already underway even without any direct effects of EU governance.

Overall, it appears that the agendas of EU institutions, more precisely those of the Council and of the European Council, largely shape the ministerial EU committee agenda, with basically all issues routinely 'downloaded' from the European level. Governments in other member states may be more selective, preferring to focus on a smaller number of salient matters (Kassim *et al.* 2000). Formally governmental EU coordination thus works as planned – national positions are coordinated at the highest political level in a ministerial committee, at latest before the final decision is taken in Brussels. In reality, only more salient, topical and often horizontal European issues are actually debated by the government, an important finding which implies that while bureaucratic domestic EU coordination may function effectively, achieving political control or accountability of such coordination can nonetheless present quite a challenge for the cabinet.[11]

11 As in domestic policy, we must be very careful about drawing any conclusions about the level of political guidance or control as there is hardly any empirical data on the accountability of civil servants in Finnish EU policy. The only real exception is the Nordic study on political coordination in EU matters, according to which in 1998 Finnish civil servants received fewer guidelines or instructions from government than their colleagues in the other Nordic countries (Jacobsson *et al.* 2004; Lægreid *et al.* 2004: 355–361).

The government and the president: dual leadership in foreign policy

This section analyses how national leadership and coordination of EU and foreign policies have operated in Finland, with the government responsible for EU matters while the president co-directs foreign policy together with the government (Raunio 2011, 2012). Examining the government's proposal for the new constitution (HE 1/1998), plenary debates in the Eduskunta, opinions of parliamentary committees and external experts heard by them, and the statements of political parties, it is obvious that the dual leadership in external relations resulted more from party-political compromise than from any rational analysis of the weaknesses and strengths of alternative leadership systems (Saraviita 2000: 8–45; Jyränki 2006: 162–164; Raunio 2008a: 154–159).

European policy belongs almost exclusively to the jurisdiction of the government. The government decides Finland's positions and who represents the country in the Council and the European Council. The jurisdiction of the government covers all EU matters, but in EU's Common Foreign and Security Policy the government must act in 'close cooperation' with the president. The preparation of CFSP matters does not substantially differ from the overall processing of EU issues. Foreign ministry is the main body responsible for policy formulation, but national positions are always coordinated with PMO (Tiilikainen 2003; Raunio 2008b). Treaty amendments fall more clearly under the competence of the president. The government and specifically PMO together with the foreign ministry are responsible for domestic preparations for IGCs. The president has the formal right to appoint the national delegation to the IGC, but the government is Finland's main negotiator in the IGC. Once the IGC has finalised the new Treaty, the president authorizes the government to sign the text, and after the Eduskunta has approved the Treaty, the president decides on its ratification in a presidential session of the government and confirms the law implementing the Treaty in Finland.

Turning to foreign policy, the Constitutional Law Committee of the Eduskunta (PeVM 10/1998: 26; see also HE 1/1998: 146) stipulated before the constitution entered into force the following rules for foreign policy formulation and decision-making: 'The president must make all significant foreign policy decisions and actions together with the government and on the basis of the government's preparatory work. The actual forms of cooperation will depend on the significance of the issues. In broad-ranging matters discussions between president and the entire government are required. In more urgent matters it may, however, be sufficient for the president to consult the Cabinet Committee on Foreign and Security Policy or an individual minister, primarily the PM, foreign minister, or the minister responsible for preparing the issue.' In practice co-leadership is executed through the Cabinet Committee on Foreign and Security Policy and essentially weekly dialogue between the president and the PM and/or the foreign minister (Tiilikainen 2003; Oikeusministeriö 2002; UaVM 13/2006; Raunio 2008a, b).

Without any doubt the biggest challenge has been drawing a clear line between EU policy and foreign policy matters. The strong links between EU policy and foreign affairs make such cat-egorizations inherently difficult, as national foreign and security policies are increasingly influenced by European level coordina-tion processes and policy choices. A good example is relations with Russia – always a salient issue for Finland. The EU has its own multi-faceted policy towards Russia, and hence Finland's bilateral relations with Russia are strongly linked to and influenced by EU's policies vis-à-vis Russia. While the effectiveness of CFSP can be questioned, it is plausible to argue that the linkage between the two levels – national foreign policies and EU's external relations – will become stronger in the future (Tiilikainen 2006; UaVM 13/2006: 9; Venice Commission 2008: 17; Raunio 2008a, b).[12]

Hence it is completely logical that the president has tried to legit-imize her role in EU affairs and particularly CFSP matters through the strong linkage between European and foreign policies. In order

---

12   According to the Venice Commission (2008: 14) this was foreseen by the draft-ers of constitution: 'In defining the area of governmental primacy by reference to an entity, the EU, whose competence is continually shifting/expanding, the framers of the Finnish Constitution have deliberately provided for a growing area of primary governmental competence in foreign policy. The growth of common positions and strategies in the EU common foreign and security policy (CFSP), *e.g.* as regards what has traditionally been a crucially important part of Finnish foreign policy, its relationship with Russia, means that issues previously regarded as purely bilateral will now be regarded, depending on the circum-stances, as partially, largely, or wholly, within the Government's primacy.'

for the president to genuinely lead foreign policy, she must also be actively involved in EU policy. To quote President Tarja Halonen (the president from 2000 to 2012): 'It is not possible to discuss foreign and security policy without considering the influence of the Union. EU penetrates everything'.[13] This in turn produces tensions and conflicts between the president and the government. The president has attempted to influence national integration policies, particularly in CFSP matters, while the government defends its turf and has adopted organisational and procedural practices that explicitly marginalize the president, especially during the preparatory stage of the policy process.

Perhaps the best example is from autumn 2005 when the government introduced the Act on Military Crisis Management and certain associated Acts (HE 110/2005). According to the proposed law the president – as the commander-in-chief of the defence forces (Section 128) – would have decided on Finland's participation in EU-led crisis management operations. However, the Constitutional Law Committee (PeVL 54/2005) disagreed, stating that the government should take the decision regarding both participation and the deployment of national units for the operations. The committee emphasized the strong interdependence between the preparatory work carried out in the EU institutions and the national decision on participation. It would be illogical if the government was responsible for the earlier stages of the policy process and the president for the decision on whether to participate, as the latter is obviously influenced by the former. But the committee was not unanimous, and importantly, the majority of the experts heard by the committee – mainly professors of law with long-standing expertise on constitutional questions – saw that the president should decide on Finland's participation. (Niskanen 2006, 2009: 141–145.)

Relations with Russia provide another good example. Constitutionally bilateral relations with foreign states fall under the co-leadership of Section 93, but as explained above, Finnish-Russian relations are increasingly influenced by the EU, not least because trade policy is in the competence of the Union. As a result, presidential activism in relations with Russia has not always been welcomed by the government. The president and the PM have had several

---

13   A. Astikainen, 'Presidentti ei voi olla reservissä', *Helsingin Sanomat* 24.12.2003.

behind-the-scenes disputes about who is the leading actor towards Russia. Furthermore, during Finland's EU presidency in the latter half of 2006 there were disagreements between the government and the president about who should chair some of the meetings between EU and third countries. The PM emerged victorious as it was interpreted that during the EU presidency the Finnish representative was in the meetings primarily representing the Union, not Finland. However, outside EU presidencies the situation is more complicated, with the government and the president having different views about who appoints and leads Finnish delegations (Meres-Wuori 2008: 112–113). Following the Lisbon Treaty the government appoints delegations to summits between the EU and third countries.[14]

But the problem that really symbolized these jurisdictional conflicts was the policy of 'two plates' – dual representation in the European Council. The Constitutional Law Committee decided prior to EU membership that the PM should represent Finland in the European Council (PeVM 10/1994: 4). However, according to President Ahtisaari (1994–2000) the president should have the right to decide on his participation in the European Council. In May 1995 PM Paavo Lipponen announced a statement, formulated jointly with the president's office, according to which the PM will always attend the European Council and the president as she chooses. The Constitutional Law Committee (PeVM 10/1998: 26) adopted in 1998 again a position according to which the PM should represent Finland in the European Council. This would facilitate parliamentary control and would also be logical as the government's competence covers all EU matters. In significant CFSP matters the government should act in close cooperation with the president. The Constitutional Law Committee, the Grand Committee (the EU committee), and the Foreign Affairs Committee subsequently restated this position several times.

Until the Lisbon Treaty entered into force (see below), President Halonen participated in the majority of European Council meetings (Niskanen 2009: 175–186). When the president attended the

---

14 In May 2010 the government appointed, against the views the president, the Finnish delegation to the EU-LAC (Latin America and Caribbean) summit. 'Hallitus otti loputkin EU-asioista itselleen', *Helsingin Sanomat* 8.5.2010.

European Council, the foreign minister had to leave the meeting room – despite the fact that agenda items had been prepared by PMO (perhaps together with the foreign ministry) and belonged to the competence of the government. The question was very important in terms of parliamentary accountability. As discussed in the second section of this chapter, in EU affairs the Eduskunta enjoys very strong information rights. The PM must inform both beforehand and afterwards the Grand Committee of European Council meetings, with the Foreign Affairs Committee enjoying similar rights in CFSP matters. The government also informs the Eduskunta and particularly the Foreign Affairs Committee about foreign affairs, a policy area which under the old constitution was practically beyond parliamentary influence. Foreign Affairs Committee has meanwhile on several occasions complained that the president has not been willing to share relevant information with it.[15] Moreover, dual representation arguably made it more difficult for foreign observers to understand who leads Finnish EU policy (UaVM 13/2006: 10; Jyränki 2007: 303; Nousiainen 2008: 55; Venice Commission 2008: 15). It is probable that not all of the politicians in the European Council, or the media covering the meetings, knew the wording of the Finnish constitution.

The Lisbon Treaty formalized the position of the European Council as one of the EU institutions, and this provided an 'external' solution to the policy of two plates. After the Lisbon Treaty entered into force, each country is represented in the European Council by either its prime minister or the head of state. The government and the Eduskunta agreed that the PM would be representing Finland. According to the government's new bill for amending the constitution (HE 60/2010), the PM would represent Finland in the European Council and in other EU meetings where the political leaders of the

---

15   See for example P. Salolainen, 'Tieto ulkopolitiikasta ei kulje eduskuntaan', *Helsingin Sanomat* 18.1.2010. The current president Sauli Niinistö (2012–) vowed in his election campaign to improve dialogue with the Foreign Affairs Committee, and there are signs that the situation has indeed improved. See T. Uusivaara, 'Salolainen: Presidentin ja eduskunnan välinen tiedonkulku parantunut', *Yle Uutiset* 26.6.2012. It also appears that the overall exchange of information between the government and president functions better under Niinistö than particularly during the final years of Halonen's presidency which were plagued by jurisdictional conflicts between the two executives. See K. Huhta, 'Niinistö haluaa lisää tietoa Venäjästä', *Helsingin Sanomat* 23.3.2013.

member states are represented (such as informal meetings between the leaders of member states and summits between the EU and third countries). However, to the extent that this is possible within the EU framework, the government could in exceptional circumstances decide that also the president represents Finland in EU meetings. The presence of both the PM and the president would, so the argument goes, indicate that the issue is of particular salience to Finland and would also strengthen Finland's bargaining position. Hence according to a constitutional amendment (Section 66) from 2012 'The Prime Minister represents Finland on the European Council. Unless the Government exceptionally decides otherwise, the Prime Minister also represents Finland in other activities of the European Union requiring the participation of the highest level of State.'

The Finnish case has also wider relevance in terms of foreign policy leadership. Regimes with dual executives, such as many semi-presidential systems, are prone to intra-executive conflict, particularly when constitutions leave room for interpretation. This is certainly the case in Finland as the constitution does not contain rules about solving conflicts between the president and the PM.[16] Hence disagreements can produce policy deadlock and will favour the status quo. Indeed, even the first sentence of Section 93 is open to different interpretations, depending on whether one emphasizes the beginning ('directed by the President') or the end ('in co-operation with the Government') of the sentence (Nousiainen 2008: 47). According to PMO the president's views should be in line with those of the government, while the president's office emphasizes that the positions of the government must not contradict the president's views.

As the president has hardly any administrative machinery of her own, she is very dependent on preparatory work carried out by the government. The president is kept informed and can try to shape national positions, but the balance of power clearly favours the government. Not surprisingly, the president's office has felt that

16 According to a constitutional amendment from 2012 (Section 58) the position of the Eduskunta is decisive in cases of disagreements between the president and the government. Only a small share of foreign policy matters, basically those issues necessitating formal decision-making, would be decided under that procedure.

the government has occasionally forgotten to inform or consult the president, particularly in foreign policy matters on the agenda of EU institutions. This in turn fuels intra-executive competition and rivalry, with the president making active use of her remaining powers. Both executives meet foreign leaders and hold speeches both home and abroad, and can thus further their own objectives (Jyränki 2000: 207; Niskanen 2009: 249–267; Hallberg *et al.* 2009: 320–371). But while the president has multiple avenues to influence Finland's foreign and European policies, it is apparent that her position is increasingly marginalized.

This section has indicated that there can be a rather poor 'fit' between domestic dual leadership in external relations and EU governance. The biggest challenge is posed by jurisdictional disputes and the competition for authority. In several semi-presidential EU member states both the government and the president are involved in national foreign and/or European policy, particularly in France, Lithuania, Poland, and Romania. In these countries the standard constitutional solution is that of government presiding over EU affairs, with the president either alone or together with the government directing foreign policy. The main difficulty lies in drawing a clear line between EU and foreign policies. National foreign policies are increasingly influenced by and linked to EU, and hence the foreign policy powers of the presidents are circumscribed by the on-going development of CFSP. As a result, presidents arguably have a legitimate justification for becoming more strongly involved in European affairs. This in turn produces jurisdictional conflicts, as the government (supported by the parliament) will defend its turf against presidential encroachments. It hence appears that in semi-presidential systems domestic strains will be the more or less inevitable outcome when the formal rules vest the direction of foreign and/or EU policy conjointly in the president and the government. (Raunio 2011, 2012)

At the same it must be emphasized that despite tensions and occasional public conflicts, overall foreign policy co-leadership has functioned rather smoothly. Co-leadership is based on institutionalised consultation procedures, and hence potential conflicts can be identified and normally resolved before they cause problems in the actual implementation of foreign policy. It is also probable that the constitutional amendments from 2012, and particularly the fact that the PM alone represents Finland in the European Council, have clarified the rules of dual leadership. But these amendments also push the president further to the background, with the government and the PM clearly the stronger of the two executives in foreign policy leadership.

Concluding discussion

Considering that individual countries face broadly similar challenges in adjusting to European integration and internationalization, it is not surprising that the findings of this chapter are in line with research on other EU member states. However, it can be argued that the effect of internationalization has been particularly profound in Finland. After all, the post-Cold War context and impending EU membership contributed to fundamental constitutional change which strengthened parliamentary features and reduced substantially the powers of the president. European integration was thus a major engine of domestic constitutional reform.

Inside the cabinet regional and global integration have empowered the PM and the finance minister. The prime minister represents Finland in the European Council and other summits and national EU policy is coordinated from PMO, while recently the financial and euro crises have increased the visibility and importance of finance ministers. Examining the executive branch as a whole, the political dynamics of the EU's policy process has definitely reinforced bureaucratization, with extensive delegation to civil servants that are responsible for formulating national positions and representing them in the working groups of the Commission and the Council. Finnish civil servants have become part of European and in some cases global networks or policy communities. This presents a major challenge for national parliaments, particularly in terms of informational asymmetries. Eduskunta deserves credit for its systematic EU scrutiny model, with Brussels-bound ministers appearing in the Grand Committee before and after Council and European Council meetings. The regular appearance of ministers in the EAC has probably also resulted in improved coordination within the cabinet and forces the ministers to be more informed of the issues processed in their ministries. Nonetheless, it is clear that even with such systematic and comprehensive scrutiny the Eduskunta is 'one step behind' of the government, but at least it can set constraints for government's European policy.

But perhaps the most important finding concerns the agenda of Finnish politics, which is increasingly influenced and even determined by European and global policy processes. Finland has joined regional and global integration in order to gain both economic and security benefits (*e.g.* Väyrynen 1991; Arter 1995; Jenssen *et al.* 1998; Raunio & Tiilikainen 2003). While participation in international governance enables Finland to influence European and global decisions, it also means that domestic politics is strongly penetrated by decisions taken outside of national borders. It is of course difficult to exactly measure how much EU and global agreements constrain national policy-making, but particularly European integration sets growing limits to domestic legislation.[17] European and global commitments have also increased the workload of national institutions. The government and the Eduskunta are substantially burdened by such externally initiated policy processes, and the agendas of both institutions are increasingly dominated by the agendas of EU institutions. It is safe to predict that the interdependence between national, European and global levels will increase, and such strengthening of 'multi-level governance' implies that the developments outlined in this chapter will only become stronger in the future.

---

17   Between 1995 and 2009 12 per cent of laws approved by the Eduskunta contained an explicit reference to the EU (Wiberg & Raunio 2012). Overall, the share of domestic legislation influenced by European integration has increased (Brouard *et al.* 2012), but perhaps even more significant is the interconnectedness of domestic, European and global politics. Not only does an increasing share of matters formally decided at the national level have a European or global dimension, but also debates on EU laws or global processes can be dominated by domestic concerns. Hence national policy-making in Finland and other democratic countries is subject to stronger external political and legal constraints (Bergman & Strøm 2011).

References

Ahlbäck Öberg, S. & Jungar, A.-C. (2009). The Influence of National Parliaments over Domestic European Union Policies. *Scandinavian Political Studies* Vol. 32, 4: 359–381.

Arter, D. (1995). The EU Referendum in Finland on 16 October 1994: A Vote for the West, not for Maastricht. *Journal of Common Market Studies* Vol. 33, 3: 361–387.

Auel, K. & Raunio, T. (2014). Debating the State of the Union? Comparing Parliamentary Debates on EU Issues in Finland, France, Germany and the United Kingdom. *Journal of Legislative Studies* Vol. 20, 1: 13–28.

Bergman, T. & Strøm, K. (eds.) (2011). *The Madisonian Turn: Political Parties and Parliamentary Democracy in Nordic Europe.* Ann Arbor, The University of Michigan Press.

Brouard, S., Costa, O. & König, T. (eds.) (2012). *The Europeanization of Domestic Legislatures: The Empirical Implications of the Delors' Myth in Nine Countries.* New York, Springer.

Bulmer, S. & Lequesne, C. (eds.) (2013). *The Member States of the European Union.* 2nd ed. Oxford, Oxford University Press.

Eduskunta (2005). *EU-menettelyjen kehittäminen: EU-menettelyjen tarkistustoimikunnan mietintö.* Helsinki, Eduskunnan kanslian julkaisu 2/2005.

Eduskunta (2010). *EU-asioiden käsittelyn kehittäminen Eduskunnassa: EU-asioiden käsittelyn kehittämistyöryhmän mietintö.* Helsinki,

Eduskunnan kanslian julkaisu 1/2010.

Featherstone, K. & Radaelli, C.M. (eds.) (2003). *The Politics of Europeanization.* Oxford, Oxford University Press.

Goetz, K.H. & Meyer-Sahling, J.-H. (2008). The Europeanisation of national political systems: Parliaments and executives. *Living Reviews in European Governance* Vol. 3, 2: (http://europeangovernance.livingreviews.org/Articles/lreg-2008-2/).

Graziano, P. & Vink, M.P. (eds.) (2007). *Europeanization: New Research Agendas.* Basingstoke, Palgrave Macmillan.

Gärtner, L., Hörner, J. & Obholzer, L. (2011). National Coordination of EU Policy: A Comparative Study of the Twelve "New" Member States. *Journal of Contemporary European Research* Vol. 7, 1: 77–100.

Hallberg, P., Martikainen, T., Nousiainen, J. & Tiikkainen, P. (2009). *Presidentin valta: hallitsijanvallan ja parlamentarismin välinen jännite Suomessa 1919–2009.* Helsinki, WSOY.

Hefftler, C., Neuhold, C., Rozenberg, O., & Smith, J. (eds.) (2015). *The Palgrave Handbook of National Parliaments and the European Union.* Basingstoke, Palgrave Macmillan.

Hyvärinen, A. (2009). *Suomen mahdollisuudet vaikuttaa valmisteilla olevaan EU-lainsäädäntöön.* Helsinki, Oikeuspoliittisen tutkimuslaitoksen tutkimuksia 241.

Hyvärinen, A. & Raunio, T. (2014a). Mistä EU-asioista hallitus keskustelee ja kenen aloitteesta? Suomen hallituksen Eurooppa-politiikan koordinaatio vuosina 1995–2012. *Politiikka* Vol. 56, 2: 87–100.

— (2014b). Who Decides What EU Issues Ministers Talk About? Explaining Governmental EU Policy Co-Ordination in Finland. *Journal of Common Market Studies* Vol. 52, 5: 1019–1034.

Hämynen, L. (2011). *Suomen vaikuttaminen Euroopan unionin lainvalmisteluun ja direktiivien kansallinen täytäntöönpano.* Helsinki, Oikeuspoliittisen tutkimuslaitoksen tutkimustiedonantoja 108.

Jacobsson, B., Lægreid, P. & Pedersen, O. K. (2004). *Europeanization and Transnational States: Comparing Nordic Central Governments.* London, Routledge.

Jenssen, A.T., Pesonen, P. & Gilljam, M. (eds.) (1998). *To Join or Not to Join: Three Nordic Referendums on Membership in the European Union.* Oslo, Scandinavian University Press.

Johansson, K. M. & Raunio, T. (2010). Organizing the Core Executive for European Union Affairs: Comparing Finland and Sweden. *Public Administration* Vol. 88, 3: 649–664.

Johansson, K. M. & Tallberg, J. (2010). Explaining Chief Executive Empowerment: EU Summitry and Domestic Institutional Change. *West European Politics* Vol. 33, 2: 208–236.

Jyränki, A. (2000). *Uusi perustuslakimme.* Turku, Iura Nova.

— (2006). Kansanedustuslaitos ja valtiosääntö 1906–2005. In

Eduskunnan muuttuva asema. Suomen eduskunta 100 vuotta, osa 2. Helsinki, Edita: 9–177.

— (2007). Presidential Elements in Government: Finland: Foreign Affairs as the Last Stronghold of the Presidency. *European Constitutional Law Review* Vol. 3, 2: 285–306.

Jääskinen, N. (2000). Eduskunta: Aktiivinen sopeutuja. In T. Raunio & M. Wiberg (eds.), EU *ja Suomi: Unionijäsenyyden vaikutukset suomalaiseen yhteiskuntaan.* Helsinki, Edita: 114–134.

Karlas, J. (2012). National Parliamentary Control of EU Affairs: Institutional Design after Enlargement. *West European Politics* Vol. 35, 5: 1095–1113.

Kassim, H. (2013). Europeanization and Member State Institutions. In S. Bulmer & C. Lequesne (eds.), *The Member States of the European Union.* 2nd edition. Oxford, Oxford University Press: 279–312.

Kassim, H., Peters, B.G. & Wright, V. (eds.) (2000). *The National Co-ordination of EU Policy: The Domestic Level.* Oxford, Oxford University Press.

Kinnunen, J. (2003). Managing Europe From Home: The Europeanisation of the Finnish Core Executive. Dublin, Organising for EU Enlargement Project, OEUE Phase 1, Occasional Paper 3.1, 09.03.

Koivula, T. & Sipilä, J. (2011). Missing in action? EU crisis management and the link to domestic political debate. *Cooperation and Conflict* Vol. 46, 4: 521–542.

Ladrech, R. (2010). *Europeanization and National Politics*. Basingstoke, Palgrave Macmillan.

Lægreid, P., Steinthorsson, R.S. & Thorhallsson, B. (2004). Europeanization of Central Government Administration in the Nordic States. *Journal of Common Market Studies* Vol. 42, 2: 347–369.

Laffan, B. (2006). Managing Europe from Home in Dublin, Athens and Helsinki: A Comparative Analysis. *West European Politics* Vol. 29, 4: 687–708.

Lampinen, R., Rehn, O. & Uusikylä, P. (eds.) (1998). EU-*asioiden valmistelu Suomessa*. Helsinki, Eduskunnan kanslian julkaisu 7/1998.

Mattila, M. & Raunio, T. (2005). Kuka edustaa EU:n vastustajia? Euroopan parlamentin vaalit 2004. *Politiikka* Vol. 47, 1: 28–41.
— (2012). Drifting further apart: National parties and their electorates on the EU dimension. *West European Politics* Vol. 35, 3: 589–606.

Maurer, A. & Wessels, W. (eds.) (2001). *National Parliaments on their Ways to Europe: Losers or Latecomers?* Baden-Baden, Nomos.

Meres-Wuori, O. (2008). *Suomen ulko- ja turvallisuuspoliittisesta pää-töksentekojärjestelmästä*. Helsinki, Ulkoasiainministeriön julkaisuja 8/2008.

Moravcsik, A. (1994). Why the European Union Strengthens the State: Domestic Politics and International Cooperation. Harvard, Centre for European Studies Working Paper no. 52.

Niskanen, M. (2006). Onko sotilaal-linen kriisinhallintalaki ulkopolitiikan johtamista vai EU-asia? *Lakimies* Vol. 104, 2: 244–256.
— (2009). *Tasavallan presidentin ulko- ja turvallisuuspoliittinen päätösvalta Suomen valtiosäännössä*. Rovaniemi, Acta Universitatis Lapponiensis 170, Lapland University Press.

Nousiainen, J. (2008). Kolmenlaista parlamentarismia. In *Suomen ja kansanvallan haasteet. Suomen eduskunta 100 vuotta, osa 12*. Helsinki, Edita: 34–57.

Oikeusministeriö (2002). Selvitys perustuslakiuudistuksen toimeenpanosta. Perustuslain seurantatyöryhmän mietintö. Helsinki, *Oikeusministeriön työryhmämietintöjä* 2002:7.

Raunio, T. (2005). Holding Governments Accountable in European Affairs: Explaining Cross-National Variation. *Journal of Legislative Studies* Vol. 11, 3–4: 319–342.
— (2007a). Euroopan unionin vaikutus eduskunnan työhön. In J. Kallenautio, T. Tiilikainen, T. Raunio, R. Paasilinna, I. Seppinen (eds.) *Kansainvälinen eduskunta. Suomen eduskunta 100 vuotta, osa 11*. Helsinki, Edita: 215–261.
— (2007b). Open List, Open Mandate? Links between MEPs and Parties in Finland. *Perspectives on European Politics and Society* Vol. 8, 2: 131–146.
— (2008a). Parlamentaarinen vastuu ulkopolitiikkaan – selvitys Suomen ulkopoliittisen päätöksentekojärjestelmän toimivuudesta. Perustuslaki 2008 –työryhmän muistio. Helsinki, *Oikeusministeriön työryhmämietintöjä* 2008:8: 152–179.

— (2008b). Parlamentaarinen vastuu ulkopolitiikkaan: Suomen ulkopolitiikan johtajuus uuden perustuslain aikana. *Politiikka* Vol. 50, 4: 250–265.

— (2009). National Parliaments and European Integration: What We Know and Agenda for Future Research. *Journal of Legislative Studies* Vol. 15, 4: 317–334.

— (2011). Semi-presidentialism and the Dual Executive in EU Affairs: What Can We Learn from the Finnish Experience? In T. Persson & M. Wiberg (eds.), *Parliamentary Government in the Nordic Countries at a Crossroads: Coping with Challenges from Europeanisation and Presidentialisation*. Stockholm, Santérus Academic Press: 301–325.

— (2012). Semi-presidentialism and European integration: lessons from Finland for constitutional design. *Journal of European Public Policy* Vol. 19, 4: 567–584.

— (2015). The Finnish Eduskunta and EU: the strengths and weaknesses of a mandating system. In C. Hefftler, C. Neuhold, O. Rozenberg & J. Smith (eds.), *The Palgrave Handbook of National Parliaments and the European Union*. Basingstoke, Palgrave Macmillan: 406–424.

Raunio, T. & Hix, S. (2000). Backbenchers Learn to Fight Back: European Integration and Parliamentary Government. *West European Politics* Vol. 23, 4: 142–168.

Raunio, T. & Tiilikainen, T. (2003). *Finland in the European Union*. London, Frank Cass.

Raunio, T. & Wiberg, M. (2010). How to Measure the Europeanisation of a National Legislature? *Scandinavian Political Studies* Vol. 33, 1: 74–92.

Ruostetsaari, I. (2003). Euroeliitissä vai politiikan sivuraiteella? Europarlamentaarikon asema suomalaisessa valtarakenteessa. *Politiikka* Vol. 45, 3: 194–211.

Saraviita, I. (2000). *Perustuslaki 2000: Kommentaariteos uudesta valtiosäännöstä Suomelle*. Helsinki, Kauppakaari.

Tiilikainen, T. (2003). Suomen ulkopoliittinen johtamisjärjestelmä uuden perustuslain mukaan. *Politiikka* Vol. 45, 3: 212–222.

— (2006). Ulko- ja turvallisuuspolitiikka: Suomen linjan täydellinen muodonmuutos. In T. Raunio & J. Saari (eds.), *Eurooppalaistuminen: Suomen sopeutuminen Euroopan integraatioon*. Helsinki, Gaudeamus: 206–233.

Venice Commission (2008). Opinion on the Constitution of Finland. Opinion No. 420/2007, Strasbourg, 7 April 2008.

Väyrynen, R. (1993). Finland and the European Community: Changing Elite Bargains. *Cooperation and Conflict* Vol. 28, 1: 31–46.

Wiberg, M. & Raunio, T. (2012). The Minor Impact of EU Legislation in Finland. In S. Brouard, O. Costa & T. König (eds.), *The Europeanization of Domestic Legislatures: The Empirical Implications of the Delors' Myth in Nine Countries*. New York, Springer: 59–73.

Winzen, T. (2013). European integration and national parliamentary oversight institutions. *European Union Politics* Vol. 14, 2: 297–323.

Vertical and Horizontal Mobility of the Finnish Political Elite

ILKKA RUOSTETSAARI

The shift from societal conflict to consensus took place very rapidly in Finland since the late 1960s (see the introductory chapter by Karvonen *et al.*). Especially the Finnish elites have been characterized by close cooperation (Arter 1999) and interconnectedness, even to such an extent that the national elite structure has been termed as a power elite (Ruostetsaari 1993). This chapter assesses whether the interconnectedness between various elite groups has changed in Finland in terms of vertical (recruitment) and horizontal (mobility between the elites) circulation in the context of the substantial social changes that have occurred since the early 1990s. The analysis focuses especially on political elite as it is the only elite group that is mainly recruited through elections (Bachrach 1967).

Mobility in terms of renewal, replacement, circulation, or interconnection plays an important role in classical elite theories. Elite replacement occurs in two ways, by a gradual process of 'infiltration', which was described by Gaetano Mosca (1939) and called by Vilfredo Pareto (1963) the 'circulation of elites', or by a violent revolution involving the total replacement of one group of elites by another. According to Pareto, the most obvious and most common hindrance of free circulation is the aristocratic principle; in other words, the descendants of elite members are pushed into elite positions irrespective of their talent, while more talented individuals are excluded from the elites. If this process is taken to the extreme, the elite will be closed and begins to degenerate. Hence, relatively free circulation – both upwards and downwards – in social hierarchy is a precondition for a healthy and strong society. Likewise, according to Mosca recruitment to the ruling class takes on an aristocratic tendency when new members are recruited from the descendants of the existing ruling class, which will cause the society to degenerate due to a loss of contact with the needs and interests of the rest of the society. In contrast, a democratic tendency is more prominent where the ruling class is renewed by the inclusion of some members from the lower class through a process of very gradual infiltration (Parry 1969: 39, 45–50, 60–63). Hence, countries that are characterized by high social mobility are generally seen as more open than those where social mobility is low. From the point of view of justice and the functioning of democracy, the equality of opportunity interrelated with social mobility is viewed in liberal democracies as an important social goal (Härkönen 2010: 52, 65–66).

Yet, C. Wright Mills referred to horizontal circulation or interlocking between elites as a source of cohesion among the power elite. According to his theory, elite cohesion is determined by the intensiveness of the connections between institutional hierarchies. If several mutual connections and joint interests exist between institutions, the elite members of these institutions will have a tendency to form a coherent group. 'Institutional closeness' is most extensive when individuals frequently move between leading positions at the linked institutions. For example, Mills referred to directors of big U.S. firms who had held important public offices but returned after their resignation from government to work in the business sector. The ease of changing roles indicates the extent of cohesion among the power elite; *i.e.*, as roles are changed more and the institutional closeness grows, the power elite will become increasingly cohesive (Mills 1956: 10–11, 19, 287–288). In other words, as the convergence and overlap between various elites grow stronger, we may perceive the beginnings of a monolithic elite. In contrast, if mobility between the various elite categories is relatively weak, and if the separation generated by specialization and expertise is clear and solid, we may lean towards a pluralist interpretation of elite configuration (Dogan 2003: 5).

According to the classical formulation, the essential criterion for the existence of an elite is not the accumulation of power in the hands of a small group of people who take care of day-to-day decision-making; rather this group must constitute a cohesive and self-conscious group. These characteristics are found in almost all elite definitions, and theories of elites and empirical research on such groups have typically described a closed elite in terms of 'three Cs' (Meisel 1958: 361) – group consciousness, coherence, and conspiracy, the last term referring to a common will to act rather than to secret machinations (Parry 1969: 31–32). The framework of this chapter combines the approaches of elite theorists, and incorporates vertical and horizontal elite circulation into one schema that can be outlined by cross-tabulating the variables of openness and coherence as shown in Figure 1 (modified from Scott 1991: 119).

		DEGREE OF COHERENCE	
		high	low
DEGREE OF OPENNESS IN RECRUITMENT	low	Exclusive	Segmented
	high	Inclusive	Fragmented

Figure 1. Types of elite structures

The first dimension in the typology is the openness of the elite structure, which may vary from low, *i.e.*, elites being recruited from a single social stratum, to high, *i.e.*, where elites come from multiple strata. In the latter case, the proportion of members recruited from any one stratum (*e.g.* the upper class) is about the same as that of this class in the general population. The degree of openness also implies the vertical circulation of elites, which is vital for their renewal from the general citizenry. The second dimension, the degree of coherence, refers to horizontal circulation, combining variables of cohesion and unanimity. The elite structure is highly coherent if its members are closely intertwined in terms of mobility, interaction and unanimity. An elite structure may be termed exclusive if it is recruited from one social stratum and if it is highly coherent. 'Fragmentary elite structure' describes a situation in which elites are recruited from many different social strata and show little or no coherence (Ruostetsaari 1993: 332; see also Higley & Moore 1981; 2001).

Elite theorists have agreed that democratic regimes are subject to regular, systematic elite competition, ascent (Schumpeter), mobility (Weber), and circulation (Pareto) (Pakulski & Körösényi 2012: 16). The importance of competition between elites as a

necessary condition for democracy has been accentuated by democratic elitism (see Etzioni-Halevy 1993; Higley 2007; Engelstad
2010). However, critics of democratic elitism have stressed that
it does not exclusively meet the classical criteria for democracy as
control from the citizenry applies only to the political elite, not
other elite groups (Bachrach 1967). In fact, rival elites may be internally oligarchic since they are closed from citizens' involvement.
We argue that the degree of democracy ultimately depends both
on the openness of the elites (active vertical circulation) as stressed
by Pareto and Mosca, and on the unconnectedness of the elites
(low horizontal circulation), as depicted by Mills and democratic
elitism, more than on elite competition per se. Hence, autonomy
between elites is seen here as an important precondition for
democracy (Etzioni-Halevy 1993: 99–101). In short, in terms of the
elite typology (Figure 1), the exclusive elite structure is inadequate,
whereas the fragmentary elite structure offers best model for the
criteria of classical democracy (see Ruostetsaari 2006). However,
very intense vertical elite mobility due to an excessive turnover
among elite members does not contribute to a democracy because
it may destabilize the decision-making process and decrease the
level of experience held by leaders and the attractiveness of the
offices (Pakulski & Körösényi 2012: 153).

The aim of the chapter is to examine the extent to which mobility of the political elite compared to other elite groups has changed
in Finland in terms of vertical and horizontal circulation in the
context of the substantial social changes that have occurred since
the early 1990s. We assess changes, firstly, in the openness of the
Finnish elite structure by analysing vertical social mobility (recruitment to the elites). The variables associated with the openness of
the elite structure include gender, region of birth, level of education and social stratum. In other words, an open elite structure is
characterized by a broad recruitment basis, *i.e.*, the elite includes
women and men, has been recruited from several social strata, and
represents different geographical regions and educational levels.
Secondly, we focus on the coherence of the elite structure, by analysing changes in horizontal social mobility (exit from the elites
and circulation within the elites), in interaction networks within
elites as well as attitudinal unanimity among the elites.

Substantial societal changes since the early 1990s

In the 1990s, Finland plunged into the deepest recession in the country's history. Gross national product (GNP) decreased by more than ten per cent between 1991 and 1993, and the value of the national currency fell almost 40 per cent, moreover, unemployment climbed to 18 per cent, and 130 000 jobs, a quarter of all industrial employment, were lost. Moreover, the nature of unemployment changed. Traditionally, unemployment hit employees of factories and logging sites, but for the first time in Finnish history, educated people and the middle class also lost their permanent earnings and employment. Furthermore, a bank crisis also took place and many businesses went bankrupt. Social services were cut, and the welfare state began to disintegrate as a result of the cuts in government expenditures. The recession brought misery to many and also facili-tated a redistribution of wealth, *i.e.*, some got rich at the expense of others' emergencies. On the basis of national economic indicators, Finnish economy collapsed more drastically in the early 1990s than any other developed market economy after the Second World War (Kuisma & Keskisarja 2012: 389, 398).

In addition to the recession, other megatrends that occurred in Finnish society in the 1990s included the collapse of the Soviet Union, and hence, of the bilateral trade between Finland and its east-ern neighbour. Finland joined the European Union (EU) in 1995. The political elite adopted the euro as the national currency in 2002 despite the fact that the majority of the population never supported Finland's membership in the euro zone (Karttunen 2009). The monetary markets were liberalized, and elements of neo-liberalism such as deregulation, competition, and privatization were launched in the public sector.

Even though Finnish society did not fully recover from the recession in the next decade (Kiander 2001: 62–65), the slump was followed by rapid economic growth based mainly on governmental investments in research and development and the expansion of the electronics industry, especially Nokia Ltd. Finland's economic boom was halted by the international financial crisis in 2008. As Finnish economy is heavily dependent on exports, GNP decreased by eight per cent in 2009 compared to 2008. Although this reces-sion was only about half as severe as the 1990s recession, GNP still decreased in Finland more than in other euro area countries and in those EU member states that had joined the Union prior to 2004.[1] However, the recession emanating from 2008 has so far lasted longer than the recession of the early 1990s.

The social changes that have taken place since the early 1990s have significantly affected the lives of Finns and have increased societal inequalities. Even though income disparities in Finland remain low based on international standards, they have grown more than those of any Organization for Economic Cooperation and Development (OECD) member country since the 1990s. Finnish social inequalities, such as low access to education, poverty, and health disparities are also passed down family lines. Exceptionally broad differences in mortality and life expectancy between socio-economic groups plague Finland when compared with many other European states (Tarkiainen *et al.* 2011: 3657a). The great recession was especially difficult for young people who had recently completed comprehensive school and were seeking employment. Experiences of uncertainty, injustice, unemployment, short-term jobs, and bankruptcies became 'an experience of the generation' for them (*e.g.*, Virtanen 2001).

In short, Finnish society has been severely shaken by these major social changes. Despite deep displeasure among the population regarding the consequences of the great recession, the international financial crisis, and the euro crisis (specifically Finland's involvement in the bail-outs targeted to over-indebted EU member states), no street riots or major protest movements have emerged. This lack of citizen action may result from the state-centered tradition of the Finnish civil society dating back to Russian rule in the 19th century (see Konttinen 1991: 92, 120; Alapuro 1990: 214–249), although in the first decades of independence Finland was a deeply politicized country, divided into various political camps, including the nationalist far-right Lapua movement of the early 1930s (see the introductory chapter of this volume).

Recent studies show that the shadow of the recession and the neo-liberal economic policies have significantly reduced social mobility (*e.g.*, Jokinen & Saaristo 2002). However, they do not suggest a decided freezing of Finnish society, even when some evidence of decreased social mobility was detected (Härkönen 2010: 59). As the

---

1   M. Pohjola, 'Taantuma ei ollut ennätyksellisen syvä', *Helsingin Sanomat* 1.9.2010.

unemployment rate tripled during the recession of the 1990s, it can be supposed that this development has decreased social mobility. The recession generated 'downward' mobility as it is easier to accept lower status jobs under strong unemployment rate (Sirniö 2010: 70–71). As the societal changes since the early 1990s have focused most profoundly on people of the lowest socio-economic positions and caused dissatisfaction among them vis-à-vis political decision-makers, we first hypothesize that

> recruitment to the political elite (which is the sole elite group whose membership depends mainly on electoral support), has changed more than recruitment to other elites and the recruitment pattern of the political elite has become more closed for the lowest socio-economic strata.

Moreover, several scandals have loomed large in the media during the period under study, and all of these scandals have focused on the elites in politics, administration, and business and their activities since the 1970s. The number of scandals involving the elite has grown from four in the 1970s, ten in the 1980s, to 21 in the 1990s, and finally to 37 in the new century. To a growing extent, these scandals have led to the resignation of elite members from their positions (Kantola & Vesa 2011: 43; see also Uimonen 2009). In particular, the political elite was shaken by the campaign funding scandal of 2008, which is the most serious political scandal in Finland to date as measured by publicity surrounding the events (Kantola 2011a: 165). The scandal undermined the legitimacy of the major political parties and affected the results of the general election in 2011, with the electoral support of the populist The Finns Party increasing from 4.1 per cent in 2007 to 19.1 per cent.

These scandals may have disrupted cohesion and mutual trust among the elites, especially between the political elite and other elite groups. Now, the elites are being watched much more closely than they were in the 1970s, when the ascendancy of decision-makers in politics and the economy was more stable and accepted publicly and in the mass media. Moreover, the moral standards that have been applied to the elites have tightened. As a result of this, an elite member who has been hit by a scandal can no longer be sure of exoneration by the 'old boys'. In fact, an elite may manifest its autonomy by revealing damaging information about other elites, or by publicly criticizing and vilifying them (Etzioni-Halevy 1993: 100). Therefore, scandals may pave the way for newcomers, especially when they bring down well-established power wielders (Kantola *et al.* 2011: 88). Indeed, the exposed scandals have been seen to erode the ascendancy of the elites and augment democracy (Kantola, 2011b: 31; Kantola & Vesa 2011: 51).

Moreover, 'gentlemen's agreements', dating back to the period before deregulation, the great recession, and the bank crisis, lost their relevance, which ultimately caused the disintegration of interaction networks, especially among the business elite but also between the elites of business, administration, and politics (Kiander & Vartia 1998: 73). This 'new era' characterized by liberalized financial markets, increased competition, European integration, and globalization necessitated new modes of operation. As such networks and 'rules of the game' derived from the time of regulated economy were no longer operational in their typical forms. For instance, the new Stock Exchange Act introduced the concept of insider regulations, which imposed new conditions on the interplay between the business elite and other elites (Ruostetsaari 2003: 39). In short, the retention of elite positions may have become more difficult due to decreased societal stability and increased scandals implicating the elites. Hence, we hypothesize, secondly, that

> the coherence of the political elite has decreased most; exit and circulation from the political elite has increased more than from other elites and the interaction and attitudinal unanimity of the political elite with other elites have decreased most.

Method and data

This study is methodologically based on positional approach (see Hoffman-Lange 1987: 31). The first step was to outline the Finnish elite structure in 1991 by analysing the power structures and the roles of institutions and organizations in various societal sectors based on information from previous studies and official documents (Ruostetsaari 1993). Secondly, the elite members were identified based on the highest ranking positions that individuals have held in a wide array of institutional fields. The elite structure in 2001

(Ruostetsaari 2006) and 2011 were constructed identically by analysing changes in society and organizational structures. The figures in Table 1 refer to the numbers of elite positions included in the elite groups, not the number of individuals holding them (on the positions included in the elite structure, see Appendix 1). For instance, an MP chairing a parliamentary committee and chairing an important non-governmental organization (NGO) is included twice in the elite structure, the elites of politics and organizations. The combination of various elite groups was *a priori* entitled as power elite.

A precondition for the research framework was that the questionnaire that was to be presented to the elites must be as similar as possible in all surveys. The first postal survey was conducted among elites in November–December 1991 (response rate 66.9 per cent), the second in September–October 2001 (53.5 per cent) and the third one in September–October 2011 (postal survey and Internet inquiry, 34.3 per cent). The response rates of the various elite groups were as follows: political elite 60, 52 and 25 per cent; administrative elite 62, 62 and 47 per cent; business elite 55, 46 and 21 per cent; organisational elite 70, 55 and 35 per cent; mass media elite 67, 44 and 31 per cent; scientific elite 64, 61 and 34 per cent; and cultural elite 63, 53 and 35 per cent.

The decrease in response rate reflects the general trend in postal survey studies. As the respondents were guaranteed anonymity, the loss of respondents within various elite groups cannot be specified.[2] Even if the response rate was clearly lower in 2011 than in previous surveys, the rate of response decreased quite uniformly in all elite groups since the first survey. The lower response rates among politics and business elites when compared with other elites in 2011 may result from the campaign funding scandal (see above), as the focal point of the scandal were the close ties between business and

---

2   However, the respondents were asked their occupation but only on the basis of their elective offices. The response rate of the members of the political elite who function in political party organizations increased from 1991 to 2001 but decreased afterwards. The response rate of business elite members working in co-operatives increased until 2001 while that of elite members functioning in private business in 2011 was lower than in 1991 and 2001. Similarly, within the organizational elite the response rate of the elite members from NGOs was the lowest in 2011.

Table 1. Compositions of the Finnish elites in 1991–2011

Elites and Sub-elites	Number of Positions		
	1991	2001	2011
The government	18	20	22
Parliament	46	59	59
Party organizations	61	59	60
Political state secretaries	1	1	13
Local councils and boards	18	18	20
Regional councils	*	20	19
MEPs and commissioner	*	17	14
POLITICS TOTAL	144	194	207
Ministries	78	90	79
Governmental bureaus	37	30	39
Judiciary	18	23	27
Defence forces	20	16	22
Church	20	22	24
Regional state administration	22	21	21
Municipalities	18	18	20
Regional councils' administration	*	19	19
EU civil servants	*	29	39
ADMINISTRATION TOTAL	213	268	290
State-owned firms and public utilities	46	48	51
Cooperatives	40	33	25
Private business	98	137	158
Property	15	15	16
BUSINESS TOTAL	199	233	250
Wage-earner organizations	54	69	64
Business organizations	50	69	78
Civic organisations	54	71	79
Organizations in local and provincial administration	46	*	*
ORGANISATIONS TOTAL	204	209	221
Daily press	41	45	42
Other papers	29	29	30
TV, radio	50	61	79
MASS MEDIA TOTAL	120	135	151

Universities	22	21	31
Governmental research institutes	19	18	28
Private research institutes	16	14	15
Foundations	14	14	16
Associations	15	9	16
Academy of Finland	41	53	51
SCIENCE TOTAL	127	129	157
Art administration	13	16	16
Fields of art	63	63	63
Influential personalities	27	27	26
Honorary art professors and academicians	11	11	28
CULTURE TOTAL	114	117	133
ELITES TOTAL	1121	1285	1409
*= organisations were not included in the elite			

political decision-makers, especially MPs. Overall, the whole data from 1991 to 2011 is not substantially and systematically biased to such an extent that it would invalidate a comparative analysis.

Recruitment to the elites

Recruitment of women

Taking all elite groups together the representation of women increased from 12 per cent in 1991 to 19 per cent in 2001 and 26 per cent in 2011. However, compared to the proportion of women in the general population (about 51 per cent since 1991), the under-representation of females in the elite groups is still large (SVT 2012). Differences between various elite groups were significant. Specifically, female representation was largest in the political elite with 35 per cent in 1991, 37 per cent in 2001, and 43 per cent in 2011, followed, respectively, by the elites of the mass media (11, 27 and 33 per cent), culture (12, 19 and 26 per cent), organizations (12, 15 and 25 per cent), science (8, 16 and 23 per cent), administration (5, 14 and 22 per cent) and business (3, 4 and 6 per cent). Female involvement increased least in the political elite. This can be explained by the fact that the proportion of female MPs in Finland and other Nordic countries has been among the highest in Europe and the world since the early 20th century (*e.g.* Christmas-Best & Kjær 2007: 86).

Regional recruitment

Finnish elites were regionally located in southern Finland, where four-fifths of the elite lived, which can be explained by the fact that the headquarters of most organizations included in the elite struc-ture were located in the south, specifically in Helsinki. The propor-tion of Finnish elites located in southern Finland has decreased marginally since the early 1990s, from 83 per cent in 1991, 82 per cent in 2001, to 81 per cent in 2011. However, these figures were markedly higher than those among the general population; 58 per cent in 1991, 60 per cent in 2001, and 62 per cent in 2011 (SVT 2012). The electoral system with its multiple constituencies (see the chapter by Bengtsson) probably explains why the share of the elite living in southern Finland has been the lowest (73, 72 and 74 per cent) and those of living in northern Finland the highest (12, 13 and 11 per cent) among the political elite. The proportion of elite living in central Finland increased slightly (9, 10 and 12 per cent), which was markedly lower than that of the general population (23, 22 and 21 per cent). The percentage of elite living in northern Finland was notably low (7, 6 and 5 per cent) which was also lower than that of the general population (19, 18 and 18 per cent).

In terms of the regional recruitment, southern Finland was clearly over-represented; more than three-fifths of the elite spent their youth (ages 10 to 18) in the south. However, regional recruit-ment pattern has broadened since the early 1990s. The share of elite living in southern Finland in their youth was 65 per cent in 1991, 67 per cent in 2001, and 60 per cent in 2011. At the same time, the proportion of those recruited from central Finland (21, 18 and 24 per cent) and northern Finland (14, 15 and 16 per cent) increased modestly. The proportion of the elite recruited from southern Finland was the lowest among the political elite until the early 2000s but in 2011 it was third lowest after the elites of administra-tion and organizations (59, 61 and 62 per cent). Recruitment from northern Finland was highest among the political elite until the early 2000s but since then it has decreased significantly and was in 2011 lower than among all other elites (18, 22 and 10 per cent).

Education

Members of the Finnish elite were much better educated than the population at large. While 87 per cent of elite had taken the matriculation examination in 1991, this share had grown to 90 per cent a decade later and to 92 per cent in 2011. In 1991 the lowest matriculation exam rate was in the organizational elite (78 per cent), but it was lowest in the political elite in 2001 (77 per cent) and in 2011 (81 per cent). The mean age of elite members was 51 in 1991, 54 in 2001, and 55 in 2011. In the general Finnish population of those aged between 50 and 54, 39 per cent had only completed basic education (*i.e.* comprehensive school) in 1999 as compared to 28 per cent in 2009 (SVT 2001: 482; 2011: 381). In contrast, among elite members this share was 6 per cent in 1991, and 2 per cent both in 2001 and 2011.

The share of elite holding a university degree increased from 82 per cent in 1991 to 87 per cent in 2001 and to 88 per cent in 2011. The number was the lowest in the media elite (68 per cent) followed by the political elite (81 per cent) in 1991, in the political elite in 2001 (68 per cent), and in the cultural elite (76 per cent) followed by the elites of business (78 per cent) and politics (79 per cent) in 2011. Moreover, 8 per cent of the elite in 1991, and 7 per cent in both 2001 and 2011 had completed a degree in polytechnics. Of the overall population aged 50–54, the share with the highest level of education (university or polytechnic degree) was 26 per cent in 1999 and 30 per cent in 2009 (SVT 2001: 482; 2011: 381). The educational differences between the elites and the population are still prominent though they have diminished slightly since the early 1990s.

Social stratification

While the representation of the descendants of fathers who held leading positions increased slightly (18 per cent in 1991 and 2001, 20 per cent in 2011), the share of the middle class, *i.e.*, elite members whose fathers were upper or lower functionaries, entrepre-

neurs, or private practitioners, decreased (50, 47 and 43 per cent).
However, the representation of the lower classes increased among
the elites. In other words, the proportion of descendants of blue-
collar workers increased since the early 1990s (14, 15 and 18 per
cent) while that of farmers was virtually the same (18, 19 and 18 per
cent). Including the descendants of fathers functioning as leaders,
entrepreneurs, and private practitioners in the upper class, we may
deduce that the representation of this stratum was particularly
stable from the early 1990s onwards (31, 30 and 31 per cent). If we
include descendants of blue-collar workers and farmers in the
lower class, the Finnish elite structure opened up to the lower class
(32, 34 and 36 per cent). Even if the present study was not based on
a random sample, we can argue that the increase in the terms of the
recruitment of the lower class (4 per cent) in a relatively short
period of two decades was significant (Table 2).

Table 2. Social background of elite members' fathers in 1991–2011 (per cent)

	1991	2001	2011
Leading position	18	18	20
Upper functionary	20	21	18
Lower functionary	17	14	14
Blue-collar	14	15	18
Entrepreneur or private practitioner	13	12	11
Farmer	18	19	18
Other	–	–	2
Total	100	100	100
N	678	590	423

However, regarding social stratification within the elites, interesting and unexpected differences are observed. The number of the
lower class within elite groups was greatest in the political elite
until 2001 (42 and 41 per cent in 1991 and 2001; this excludes the
organizational elite in 1991). Yet, it was highest in the business elite
in 2011. The marked increase in the representation of the lower
class in the business elite (26, 35 and 45 per cent) resulted from the
fact that this elite group included farmers' descendants (from 19
per cent in 1991 to 34 per cent in 2011), while the representation of
blue-collar workers' descendants remained marginal (7, 12 and 11
per cent). However, elitism in the recruitment to the business elite

concurrently increased; the share of descendants whose fathers functioned in leading positions increased (19, 24 and 26 per cent), while that of upper and lower functionaries decreased markedly (37, 32 and 17 per cent).

Following the business elite, representation of the lower class was highest among the organizational elite (39 per cent) in 2011, followed by elites in politics (37 per cent), administration (36 per cent), science (32 per cent), the media (27 per cent), and culture (25 per cent). In fact, after the early 1990s, the lower class was least represented in the cultural elite, due to the marginal representation of farmers' descendants within this group. This does not mean that the cultural elite group has been closed to farmers' descendants; instead, this might be explained by the notion that a cultural career appeared to be a precarious option for social and economic advancement in agrarian families. In fact, the upper class, descendants of fathers functioning in leading positions, entrepreneurs, or private practitioners, has been represented in the highest numbers in the cultural elite since the early 2000s (48 per cent in 2001, 39 per cent in 2011), and it was second highest in the cultural elite 1991 (37 per cent) after the business elite (38 per cent).

Compared to the general population, the upper stratum was overrepresented, while the blue-collar workers were underrepresented in the elites. Based on the Erikson-Goldthorpe (1992) classification system, the share of the highest class, upper functionaries (or upper professions) among men aged between 25 and 63 men was 11 per cent in 1990 and 12 per cent in 2000. The number of lower functionaries (or lower professions) was 20 per cent and 23 per cent in 1990 and 2000, respectively, while that of office workers was 1 per cent and 2 per cent, moreover, that of customer service employees was 3 per cent and 4 per cent. The proportion of private entrepreneurs was 10 per cent in 1990 and 2000 and that of farmers was 8 per cent and 6 per cent, respectively. The blue-collar workers comprised as many as 47 per cent (1990) and 45 per cent (2000) of the general population. In an international comparison, the share of blue-collar workers was closest to that of Germany (47 per cent) but larger than that of Sweden (36 per cent), Italy (35 per cent) and Great Britain (34 per cent), which has traditionally been characterized as a class society (Erola 2010: 31–38; but see the introductory chapter by Karvonen *et al.*). Hence, we may conclude that descendants of fathers who functioned as leaders, upper functionaries, and farmers were overrepresented, while the descendants of blue-collar workers in particular but also of lower functionaries to a lesser extent were underrepresented in the elites compared to the overall population.

Elite coherence

Circulation among the elites

The starting point for the assessment of turnover in the elites is the mean age of elite members, which was 51 in 1991, 54 in 2001, and 55 in 2011. The general retirement age in Finland was 65 until 2005, but for most civil servants it was 63 years. Since 2005 the general retirement age has been 63–68 years. Even today chief executive officers in big businesses generally retire at the age of 60. MPs have no retirement age. Hence, most elite members cannot hold their elite positions as long as two decades under ordinary circumstances.

However, 48 persons held their original elite positions throughout the study period (1991–2011). For instance, if a person was member of the political elite in 1991 and still held the position in the same elite group in 2001 and 2011, she maintained her *original* elite position throughout the period. Considering that some individuals moved from one elite group to another, the number of individuals who retained an elite position within some elite group was 68. The retention of elite positions was most common in the elites of politics and administration, where position is based on elections or appointments (Table 3). Since the total number of elite positions was more than one thousand from 1991 to 2011, the retention of elite positions was quite limited.

Circulation among elites is analysed in Tables 4 and 5, both of which are based on the composition of the elites in 1991–2011 (Table 1), not on the surveys. 'Exit' in the tables indicates the number of elite members who left the elite for one reason or another (such as lost their leading position in their own organization, moved to a lower position, retired, or died). The percentages in the tables are calculated based on all elite positions, not on the number of elite members. For instance, we can see in Table 4 that in 1991–2001 25 per cent of the political elite retained their position

Table 3. Retention of the elite positions 1991–2011 by persons

Elite Group	Position in Original Elite Group	Position in Any Elite Group
Politics	12	18
Administration	11	15
Business	7	9
Organizations	2	6
Mass Media	2	3
Science	9	12
Culture	5	5
Total	48	68

Table 4. Circulation between the elites in 1991–2001 by positions (per cent)

Original Elite Group	Pol.	Adm.	Bus.	Org.	Med.	Sci.	Cul.	Exit	N–91
Politics	25	3	3	6	–	–	–	63	144
Administration	1	26	3	2	–	1	–	66	213
Business	1	3	19	7	–	4	–	66	199
Organizations	1	5	6	15	–	1	1	72	294
Mass Media	1	–	1	1	26	–	1	71	120
Science	–	2	1	5	–	22	–	70	127
Culture	–	–	1	1	–	–	18	80	114

Table 5. Circulation between the elites in 2001–2011 by positions (per cent)

Original Elite Group	Pol.	Adm.	Bus.	Org.	Med.	Sci.	Cul.	Exit	N–91
Politics	21	3	6	7	1	1	1	62	194
Administration	1	23	–	1	–	2	–	72	268
Business	1	1	18	3	–	4	1	72	233
Organizations	2	4	4	10	–	4	–	76	209
Mass Media	–	–	–	1	19	–	1	79	135
Science	–	5	1	1	–	28	–	66	129
Culture	–	–	1	–	–	–	13	86	117

in that elite group, while 3 per cent gained an elite position in the administrative elite, 3 per cent in the business elite, and 6 per cent in the organizational elite, while 63 per cent left the elite.

Comparing the periods of 1991–2001 and 2001–2011, the retention of elite positions decreased. Exit from the elites markedly increased in all sectors excluding politics (63 per cent in 1991–2001, 62 per cent in 2001–2011) and science (70 and 66 per cent). Seemingly, leading politicians managed to retain their posts in elections, and the scientific elite is composed mainly of professors with permanent positions. In fact, positions in the political elite were most secure, while exit was clearly most common in the cultural elite (80 per cent in 1991–2001, 86 per cent in 2001–2011). However, exits increased the most among the mass media elite (71 and 79 per cent).

Secondly, maintenance of the *original* elite position decreased in all groups with exception of the scientific elite. In the latter group, it increased significantly (from 22 per cent in 1991–2001 to 28 per cent in 2001–2011). The decrease was greatest in the mass media elite (26 and 19 per cent) and smallest in the business elite (19 and 18 per cent). Thirdly, circulation among the elites was minor; in fact only a few elite members changed their elite group. During the period 1991–2001, circulation was most common in the business elite, where 15 per cent moved to another elite group or gained a new elite position in another elite group along with their original position. This can be explained by the fact that some business leaders (7 per cent) moved to interest groups that belong to the organizational elite. Business elite was followed by the elites of organizations (14 per cent), politics (12 per cent), science (8 per cent), administration (7 per cent), the mass media (4 per cent), and culture (2 per cent). Comparing the period 2001–2011 with the previous period, circulation decreased in all elite groups with the exception of the political elite (in which circulation increased 7 per cent) and the organizational elite, where it remained the same.

In fact, the circulation that occurred between the political elite and other elite groups may be considered a notable phenomenon. As many as 11 per cent in 1991–2001 and 17 per cent in 2001–2011 of holders of political elite positions gained a new position in another elite group or changed their elite group in 2001–2011. Mainly, they moved to the elite groups of business and organizations. In contrast, circulation from the elites of culture and the mass media to other elite groups was minimal after the early 1990s. This finding about the rather active circulation between the political elite and other elite groups is important in the sense that low circulation of individuals between societal sectors or vertical segmentation has been identified as a problem in Finland. In order to break down rigid bureaucratic barricades and augment coordination between the administrative branches, the government launched intersectoral policy programs in the 2000s (Tiihonen 2009), but they failed to attain the role originally planned, as integrative instruments of strategic planning (National Audit Office of Finland 2010).

Interaction networks among the elites

We begin by examining the structure of interaction networks prevailing among various elite groups. Unfortunately, it was impossible to analyse direct contacts between elite members for two reasons. First, due to lack of space we could not list all the elite members, over one thousand names, in the questionnaire and to inquire about the respondent's contacts with these individuals. Second, and more importantly, the respondents were guaranteed anonymity. Hence, we focus on elite members' contacts with the 42 institutions included in the elite structure. The holders of top leading positions at these institutions were included in the elite structure. The respondents were presented with a structured question: 'The following is a list of instances and institutions with which you may have had contact in connection with your job, positions of trust, leisure pursuits, etc. Please state for each the 'frequency of your contacts' and the 'nature of your contacts'.'

Next we consider the positions occupied by different organizations or institutions in the interaction network of the elite (Table 6). This was done by using an index created on the basis of responses to the question of frequency of interaction. The three response alternatives, 'at least once or twice a month', 'a few times a year', and 'less often or not at all' were scored on a 0–100 scale, the mean being treated as 'frequency' and reflecting those respondents who scored above 0 being treated as 'intensity'. This index, which can be called density, is a combined variable which takes into account both the frequency of interaction and its intensity.[3]

3   To calculate the intensity of the interaction, different coefficients, *i.e.* weights, were assigned to the frequency of contacts. The coefficient for the option 'at least once or twice a month' was designated 100, for the option 'a few times a

At the beginning of the 1990s, the most central institution in the
power elite network, covering all elite groups, was the mass media,
whose position in the interaction network can be characterized by
index value 75. In 2011 mass media maintained its most central
position despite dropping to the second, lower circle in the network
(index value 68 in 2001 and 67 in 2011). At the same time the third
circle in the interaction network (index 50–59) was occupied by
three institutions: the government (52), private firms (50), and
banks (51). Of these, the government dropped to the fourth circle
in 2001 (48) but rejoined the third circle in 2011 (53). Private firms
maintained their position in 2001 (51) but dropped clearly to the
fourth circle in 2011 (41). The role of banks weakened significantly:
while it was included in the third circle in 1991 (51), it dropped
to the fourth in 2001 (49) and to the fifth in 20011 (30). In 1991
the fourth circle of intensity was composed of two institutions,
central government agencies (42) and universities (including the
universities of applied sciences) (48). Since that time the central
government agencies dropped to the lower circle (39 in 2001 and 33
in 2011). By contrast, the density of universities increased in 2001
(52) and 2011 (50).

Overall, the density of three-fifths of institutions in the interaction network has decreased since the early 1990s. The few modest

---

year' 50, and 'less often or not at all' 0. Based on this approach, the same level
of interaction (frequency) can be achieved in several ways, *e.g.* a few who have
many contacts as well as many who have few contacts. The concept of intensity
separates these cases. This means that the weight of frequent contacts (at least
once a month) in the intensity of interaction is twice as high as in relatively
infrequent interactions (a few times a year). The frequency of interaction in the
last option is so low that it carries no weight at all in the intensity measure. The
intensity of interaction between the power elite and institution A was obtained
by multiplying by 100 the portion of those who have had contact with A at least
once or twice a month and by adding to this figure the percentage, multiplied
by 50, of those who have had contact with A a few times a year followed by
dividing this sum by the total number of contacts, *i.e.* the percentages of both
those with a few monthly contacts and those with few contacts. The maximum
intensity value is 100, which is obtained if all members of the power elite have
had interaction with A at least once or twice a month. The index describing the
density of interaction was obtained by multiplying the total number of contacts
by intensity divided by 100. The latter division by 100 is done simply in order
to obtain a comparable figure. The maximum value for this index is thus also
100; the higher the score, the more frequent the interaction of the power elite
with institution A (see Petersson 1989: 36–37).

Table 6. The density of interaction network between the power elite and various institutions in 1991–2011 by index

Institution	Year		
	1991	2001	2011
The mass media	75	68	67
The government	52	48	53
University/of applied sciences	48	52	50
Private firm	50	51	41
Municipality and federation of municipalities	34	38	36
Other research institute	36	37	34
Central government agency	42	39	33
Entrepreneur or business organization	36	33	33
Political party: national organization	33	30	32
Employers' organization	34	37	31
Ministry of Education and Culture	34	32	31
Other association	30	36	31
Bank	51	49	30
Ministry of Finance	34	28	30
Parliamentary group	29	29	30
Wage-earner organization	36	33	29
Ministry of Employment and the Economy	28	26	29
State regional administration	*	26	29
Cultural organization	34	30	27
Parliamentary committee	26	25	27
State-owned firm or public utility	35	30	25
Prime Minister's Office	22	23	23
Ministry of Social Affairs and Health	20	21	22
Political party: regional organization	23	21	22
Regional Council	20	25	22
Ministry of Transport and Communications	20	23	21
Political party: local organization	25	23	21
Armed forces	23	23	20
Ministry for Foreign Affairs	29	25	20
Cooperative firm	23	19	19
Ministry of Agriculture and Forestry	16	18	18
Ministry of the Interior	22	23	18
Agricultural producers' organization	20	20	17
Church	19	17	17
Ministry of Defence	19	16	16
Ministry of Justice	13	16	16
Ministry of the Environment	24	18	16
Judiciary (courts, police)	12	13	15
Environmental protection organization	16	13	13
The President of the Republic	10	15	12
Women's organization	11	11	11
Consumer organization	9	10	8
N=	696	609	431

exceptions were the judiciary (+3), Ministry of Justice (+3), the president (+2), Ministry of Agriculture and Forestry (+2), Ministry of Social Affairs and Health (+2), regional councils (+2), municipalities and their federations (+2), universities (+2), government (+1), parliamentary groups (+1), and parliamentary committees (+1). The density of interaction decreased most with banks (−21), state-owned firms and public utilities (−10), Ministry for Foreign Affairs (−9), central government agencies (−9), private firms (−9), Ministry of the Environment (−8), mass media (−8), wage-earner organizations (−7), and cultural associations (−7).

All in all, the interaction networks of Finnish elites have dispersed since the early 1990s and the number of institutions with which they interact very intensively has decreased. In other words, the interaction network links elites to each other more loosely. Furthermore, the number of institutions included in the inner core of the interaction network was reduced and partially changed after the early 1990s. Within the circle of elites there were only slight deviations from this general trend. However, the density of contacts of the mass media elite and also to a lesser extent of the scientific elite with various institutions increased more than those of other elites. This indicates the centrality of the mass media as a hub of communication network among the elites.

Turning to the interaction network of the *political elite*, the most central institutions in terms of density in 2011 were national organizations of political parties (87), the government (83), local organizations of political parties (83), parliamentary groups (82), mass media (82), regional organizations of political parties (81), and municipalities (72). The density of interaction decreased since 1991 for three-fourths of institutions, excluding the government (+9), regional councils (+14), municipalities (+9), church (+7), entrepreneur or business organizations (+2), universities (+2), the president (+1), and mass media (+1). The density decreased most in the cases of the Ministry of the Environment (−25), central government agencies (−23), cooperative firms (−22), banks (−21), and the Ministry for Foreign Affairs (−20).

To summarize, political institutions maintained their positions in the power elite interaction network in 1991–2011. In fact, the density of political institutions, excluding local party organizations and the president increased in the interactions network since the early 2000s.

Attitudinal unanimity among the elites

The attitudes of the elites on ten potential social conflict dimensions are assessed in Table 7. Linearly the attitudes have changed only in terms of rich/poor and men/women; the first dimension was evaluated strong more frequently while the second one was seen strong more infrequently. The elites of culture and business differed most from the other elites; while the former perceived all conflicts on average stronger than other elites the latter perceived them weaker.

Table 7. The proportion of elite members who perceived social conflict dimensions very or fairly strong in 1991–2011 (per cent)

Conflict Dimension	1991	2001	2011
Growing centers/peripheral regions	52	90	75
Rich/poor	49	62	73
Native Finns/immigrants	61	73	68
Politicians/the people	73	62	73
Employed/unemployed	58	62	50
Industrial firms/nature protection	86	40	51
Employers/employees	64	30	56
Socialists/bourgeoisie	18	11	24
Men/women	21	12	11
Finnish speaking/Swedish speaking	14	12	19
N=	689	619	434

The coherence of the elite structure was analysed utilizing the means of standard deviation of the conflict dimensions (Table 8), which decreased from 0.723 in 1991 to 0.626 in 2001, reflecting increasing attitudinal unanimity within the elites. By contrast, since then the mean of standard deviation increased slightly to 0.647 in 2011. The attitudinal difference of the political elite – as well as all other elites excluding the organizational elite – from the power elite (all elite groups together) decreased until 2001 but then increased in 2011 even if did not return to the level of 1991.

Table 8. Attitudes among elite groups on the conflict dimensions
measured by the mean of standard deviation in 1991–2011

Elite Group	1991	2001	2011
Political	0.750	0.635	0.676
Administrative	0.736	0.587	0.599
Business	0.692	0.579	0.609
Organizational	0.695	0.662	0.623
Mass media	0.651	0.606	0.625
Scientific	0.756	0.633	0.685
Cultural	0.717	0.648	0.741
Power Elite	0.723	0.626	0.647

Neo-liberal endorsement of the regime

The attitudinal difference between the elites was also assessed by a sum variable composed of four attitudinal statements: 'Science and technology are able to solve in the future most current problems', 'Democracy is functioning in Finland so well that the talk about citizens' weak possibilities to influence are groundless', 'The ownership is centralized alarmingly in our country' (reversed scale), and 'A great deal of public services should be privatized in our country in order to intensify service production'. As these statements measure, on one hand, trust in the regime and its ability to solve social problems, and, on the other hand, support for the doctrine of New Public Management highlighting deregulation and privatization, which spread also to Finland in the early 1990s, the sum variable can be named as neoliberal support of the regime (Table 9). The components of the sum variable correlate fairly well with each other, *i.e.* they measure the same issue (Cronbach alfa 0.51 in 1991, 0.67 in 2001, and 0.59 in 2011), which means that leaving out any of components would deteriorate the sum variable. The higher the value of the sum variable, the higher the endorsement of the neo-liberal regime.

Neo-liberal endorsement of the regime decreased in terms of the mean in 1991–2001 but then increased even if it did not reach in 2011 the level of the early 1990s. However, there were significant differences between various elites; endorsement was lowest among the political elite in 1991, while since then it has been clearly lowest among the cultural elite and second lowest among the political

Table 9. Neo-liberal endorsement among the elites in terms of mean (M) and standard deviation (ST)

	1991			2001			2011		
Elite Group	M	ST	N	M	ST	N	M	ST	N
Political	2,58	0,78	86	2,68	0,80	87	2,66	0,75	47
Administrative	3,03	0,65	128	2,82	0,74	168	2,85	0,63	135
Business	3,33	0,63	109	3,43	0,69	93	3,28	0,66	47
Cultural	2,84	0,78	142	2,87	0,81	112	2,83	0,76	73
Mass Media	2,75	0,66	80	2,51	0,70	59	3,03	0,78	46
Scientific	3,03	0,68	81	2,88	0,83	77	2,99	0,62	51
Cultural	2,67	0,72	72	2,40	0,74	60	2,54	0,79	46
Power Elite	2,91	0,74	698	2,83	0,81	616	2,86	0,72	434

Note: Responses were scaled from 1 to 5 with 1 meaning totally agree and 5 meaning totally disagree.

elite. In terms of standard deviation, the coherence of the power elite decreased until 2001 but was in 2011 even higher than in 1991. The attitudinal difference of the political elite from the power elite decreased in terms of both the mean and the standard deviation until 2001, but increased to some extent in 2011.

Conclusion

The goal of the chapter was to analyse whether social mobility on the elite level had changed in Finland in the context of major social changes. There were interesting differences between political elite and other elite groups. Female representation was higher in the political elite since the early 1990s than in any other elite group. However, female involvement increased least in this elite group from 1991 onwards. The proportion of the elite recruited from southern Finland was the lowest among the political elite until the early 2000s, but in 2011 it was third lowest after the elites of administration and organizations. On the other hand, recruitment from northern Finland was highest among the political elite until the early 2000s, but since then it has decreased significantly and was in 2011 lower than among all other elites. Hence, the recruitment pattern of the political elite has moved to closer other elites since the early 2000s.

In 1991 the lowest matriculation exam rate was in the organizational elite followed by the political elite while it was lowest in the political elite in 2001–2011. The share of elite holding a university degree was the lowest in the media elite in 1991 followed by the political elite. In 2001 the proportion was lowest in the political elite, while in 2011 it was the smallest in the cultural elite followed by the elites of business and politics. All in all, the educational level of the political elite increased since the early 1990 which was also the case in most other elites, but the political elite moved closer to other elites in terms of education. Regarding social stratification the political elite has changed most. If we include the descendants of blue-collar workers and farmers in the lower class, the proportion of the lower class within the elite groups was greatest in the political elite until 2001. By contrast, in 2011 it was highest in the business elite followed by elites of organizations and politics. Recruitment from the lower class decreased in 1991–2011 most in the elites of organizations (–6 per cent) and politics (–5), while it increased in the elites of business (+19), administration (+7), science (+5), culture (+3), and mass media (+1).

These findings support our first hypothesis. Concerning socio-economic background, the political elite changed more than other elites and it moved closer to the other elite groups since the early 1990s. This means that the political elite has become more closed for the lower class: the qualifications necessary for recruitment to the political elite have become more similar than those in the other elites. However, recruitment into the Finnish power elite, all elite groups together, opened up to the lower classes, especially to the descendants of blue-collar workers and farmers, from the early 1990s onwards.

Turning to elite coherence, the retention of elite positions was most common in the elites of politics and administration, where positions are based on elections or appointment. In fact, the retention of positions increased among the political elite, while exit from it decreased since the early 1990s. However, the maintenance of the original elite position decreased in all elite groups with exception of the scientific elite. The maintenance of the original position was the third most common in the political elite after the elites of administration and science. Mobility or circulation between the

elites was minor, but it was the third most frequent in the political elite after the elites of business and organizations. Circulation
between the political elite and other elite groups is noteworthy, as
11 per cent in 1991–2001 and 17 per cent in 2001–2011 of holders
of political elite positions gained a new position in another elite
group or changed their elite group in 2001–2011. In short, in line
with the second hypothesis, the circulation between the political
elite and other elites increased, but unlike we expected, exit from
the political elite did not increase when we compare the political
elite with other elites.

The interaction networks of Finnish elites have dispersed since
the early 1990s; that is, the interaction network links elites to each
other more loosely. However, the density of political institutions
among the interaction networks of the power elite increased in
the early 2000s. Hence, in terms of interaction networks of the
political elite our findings do not support the hypothesis. The
attitudinal difference of the political elite, as well as other elites
excluding the organizational elite, from the power elite decreased
in terms of social conflicts until 2001 but increased in 2011 even
if did not return to the level of 1991. Moreover, concerning neo-
liberal endorsement of the regime, the attitudinal difference of
the political elite from the power elite decreased until 2001, but
increased again by 2011. These results offer partial support for the
hypothesis, but only dealing for the period 2001–2011. Overall, our
findings are thus mainly contradictory with the second hypothesis.

In the introduction to this chapter, we argued that the state of
democracy ultimately depends on the openness of the elite groups
(active vertical circulation) as well as the unconnectedness of the
elites (low horizontal circulation). In terms of the typology of elite
structures (Figure 1), the exclusive elite structure is least compat-
ible with the criteria of classical democracy, while the fragmentary
elite structure is the best fit for the criteria of classical democracy.
Examining all elites together, Finland has moved on the dimension
of openness of recruitment slightly in the direction of an inclusive
elite structure, but on the dimension of coherence the country
has moved in the direction of a fragmented elite structure. These
results, the opening up of the elite structure and decreasing elite
coherence, are positive developments in Finnish society since the
early 1990s (Ruostetsaari 2013; 2015).

It seems evident that the important social changes in Finland since the early 1990s have exerted most effect on the political elite. However, in the case of the political elite the development has not been as positive as the general trend. The Finnish political elite has moved closer to other elites in terms of recruitment and coherence: the openness of the political elite has decreased in relation to people with lower socio-economic positions, while horizontal circulation and interaction has increased between the political elite and other elites. This development indicates that the political elite intertwines more with other elites. The interweaving of elites is incompatible with the basic theorem of democratic elitism, which holds that autonomy and rivalry between elites will balance power and hinder any elite group from gaining a dominant position (*e.g.* Etzioni-Halevy 1993). By contrast, it supports previous interpretations of the existence of a Finnish power elite (Ruostetsaari 1992; 2003). Despite increased openness and decreased coherence among Finnish elite groups, the changes observed in the elite structure since the early 1990s are not dramatic. The Finnish elites are still interconnected, with the exception of the cultural elite, for example in terms of the self-consciousness of the elite members; therefore, we can legitimately speak of the existence of a power elite in Finland, even if it is in decline (Ruostetsaari 2015).

However, we may assess horizontal mobility of the political elite not only from the perspective of democratic elitism, but also more generally in light of societal mobility. The increased horizontal mobility of the political elite and its growing interweaving with other elites may have also positive effects as they can break down rigid barricades between societal sectors. As the political elite is the sole elite group whose ascendancy depends mainly on electoral support, this, in turn, may spread citizens' involvement from politics to other societal sectors, provided that the political elite is responsive to the citizenry.

References

Alapuro, R. (1990). Valta ja valtio – miksi vallasta tuli ongelma 1900-luvun vaihteessa? In P. Haapala (ed.), *Talous, valta ja valtio*. Tampere, Vastapaino: 237–254.

Arter, D. (1999). *Scandinavian Politics Today*. Manchester, Manchester University Press.

Bachrach, P. (1967). *The Theory of Democratic Elitism. A Critique*. Boston, Little, Brown.

Christmas-Best, V. & Kjær, U. (2007). Why so Few and Why so Slow? Women as Parliamentary Representatives in Europe from a Longitudinal Perspective. In M. Cotta & H. Best (eds.), *Democratic Representation in Europe. Diversity, Change, and Convergence*. Oxford, Oxford University Press: 77–101.

Dogan, M. (2003). Introduction: Diversity of Elite Configurations and Clusters of Power. In M. Dogan (ed.), *Elite Configurations at the Apex of Power*. Leiden/Boston: Brill: 1–15.

Engelstad, F. (2010). Democratic Elitism – Conflict and Consensus. In H. Best & J. Higley (eds.), *Democratic Elitism: New Theoretical and Comparative Perspectives*. Leiden and Boston, Brill: 61–77.

Erikson, R. & Goldthorpe, J. H. (1992). *The Constant Flux: A Study of Class Mobility in Industrial Societies*. Oxford, Clarendon Press.

Erola, J. (2010). Luokkarakenne ja luokkiin samastuminen Suomessa. In J. Erola (ed.), *Luokaton Suomi? Yhteiskuntaluokat 2000-luvun Suomessa*. Helsinki, Gaudeamus: 27–44.

Etzioni-Halevy, E. (1993). *The Elite Connection. Problems and Potential of Western Democracy*. Cambridge, Polity Press.

Higley, J. (2007). Democracy and Elites. In F. Engelstad & T. Gulbrandsen (eds.), *Comparative Studies of Social and Political Elites*. Amsterdam, Elsevier: 249–263.

Higley, J. & Moore, G. (1981). Elite Integration in the United States and Australia. *American Political Science Review* Vol. 75, 3: 581–597.

— (2001). Political Elite Studies at the Year 2000: Introduction. *International Review of Sociology* Vol. 11, 2: 175–180.

Hoffman-Lange, U. (1987). Surveying National Elites in the Federal Republic of Germany. In G. Moyser & M. Wagstaffe (eds.), *Research Methods for Elite Studies*. London, Allen & Unwin: 27–47.

Härkönen, J. (2010). Sosiaalinen periytyvyys ja sosiaalinen liikkuvuus. In J. Erola (ed.), *Luokaton Suomi? Yhteiskuntaluokat 2000-luvun Suomessa*. Helsinki, Gaudeamus: 51–66.

Jokinen, K. & Saaristo, K. (2002), *Suomalainen yhteiskunta*. Helsinki, WSOY.

Kantola, A. (2011a). Tyhjää vai täyttä julkista elämää? In A. Kantola (ed.), *Hetken hallitsijat*. Helsinki, Gaudeamus: 164–179.

— (2011b). Modernin julkisuuden teoria ja käytännöt. In A. Kantola (ed.), *Hetken hallitsijat*. Helsinki, Gaudeamus: 17–41.

Kantola, A. & Vesa, J. (2011). Skandaalit ja julkinen elämä

Suomessa. In A. Kantola (ed.), *Hetken hallitsijat*. Helsinki, Gaudeamus: 42–64.

Kantola A & Vesa, J. & Hakala, S. (2011). Notkean myrskyn silmässä: vaalirahaskandaali. In A. Kantola (ed.), *Hetken hallitsijat*. Helsinki, Gaudeamus: 65–88.

Karttunen, M. (2009). *Evidence of Partisan Emphasis on* EMU *during 1994–199: Comparing Finnish Parties*. Acta Politica 38. Department of Political Science. Helsinki, University of Helsinki.

Kiander, J. (2001). *Laman opetukset. Suomen 1990-luvun kriisin syyt ja seuraukset*. Julkaisuja 27:5. Helsinki, Valtion taloudellinen tutkimuskeskus.

Kiander, J. & Vartia, P. (2001). *Suuri lama. Suomen 1990-luvun kriisi ja talouspoliittinen keskustelu*. Helsinki, Taloustieto.

Konttinen, E. (1991). *Perinteisestä moderniin. Professioiden yhteiskunnallinen synty Suomessa*. Tampere, Vastapaino.

Kuisma, M. & Keskisarja, T. (2012). *Erehtymättömät. Tarina suuresta pankkisodasta ja liikepankeista Suomen kohtaloissa*. Helsinki, WSOY.

Mills, C. W. (1956). *The Power Elite*. New York, Oxford University Press.

Mosca, G. (1939). *The Ruling Class*. New York & London, McGraw-Hill.

National Audit Office of Finland (2010). Politiikkaohjelmat ohjauskeinona. Valtiontalouden tuloksellisuustarkastuskertomukset 212. Helsinki, National Audit Office of Finland

Pakulski, J. & Körösényi, A. (2012). *Toward Leader Democracy*. London, Anthem Press.

Pareto, V. (1963). *The Mind and Society: A Treatise on General Sociology*. New York, Dover.

Parry, G. (1969), *Political Elites*. London, Allen & Unwin.

Petersson, O. (1989). *Maktens nätverk. En undersökning av regeringskansliets kontakter*. Helsingborg, Carlssons.

Ruostetsaari, I. (1993). The Anatomy of the Finnish Power Elite. *Scandinavian Political Studies* Vol. 16, 4: 305–337.
— (2003). *Valta muutoksessa*. Helsinki, WSOY.
— (2006). Social Upheaval and Transformation of Elite Structures: The Case of Finland. *Political Studies* Vol. 54, 1: 23–42.
— (2013). Opening the Inner Circle of Power: Circulation in the Finnish Elites in the Context of Major Societal Changes 1991–2011. *Comparative Sociology* Vol. 12, 2: 255–288.
— (2015). *Elite Recruitment and Coherence of the Inner Core of Power in Finland. Changing Patterns during the Economic Crises of 1991–2011*. Lanham, Lexington Books

Scott, J. (1991). *Who Rules Britain?* Cambridge, Polity Press.

Sirniö, O. (2010). *Sosiaalinen liikkuvuus Suomessa 1985–2005*. Sosiologian pro gradu -tutkielma. Helsinki, Helsingin yliopisto.

SVT (2001). *Official Statistics of Finland*. Helsinki, Statistics Finland.

SVT (2011). *Official Statistics of Finland*. Helsinki, Statistics Finland.

SVT (2012). *Official Statistics of Finland.* Helsinki, Statistics Finland.

Tarkiainen, L., Martikainen, P., Laaksonen, M. & Valkonen, T. (2011). Disparity in life expetancy between income quintiles, 1988–2007, *Suomen Lääkärilehti* Vol. 66, 48: 3651–3657a.

Tiihonen, S. (2006). *Ministeriön johtaminen.* Tampere, Tampere University Press.

Uimonen, R. (2009). *Median mahti.* Helsinki, WSOY.

Virtanen, M. (2001). *Fennomanian perilliset. Poliittiset traditiot ja sukupolvien dynamiikka.* Helsinki, SKS.

Appendix 1:

The Positions Included in the Elite Structure in 1991–2011

The political elite

The government: cabinet ministers and political state secretaries, incumbent and former presidents of the republic.

Parliament: the speakers, chairmen of the parliamentary groups and parliamentary committees, deputy chairmen of the parliamentary committees in 1991, all members of the grand committee (so-called EU committee) and secretary generals of the parliamentary groups in 2001–2011.

Political party organizations: chairmen, deputy chairmen and party secretaries of the political parties represented in the parliament, chairmen of the youth-, student-, and women organizations.

Local councils and boards: chairmen of the councils (*i.e.* the highest elective officials) in the biggest cities in 1991, chairmen of the boards in the biggest cities in 2001–2011.

Regional councils: chairmen of the boards (*i.e.* elective officials) in 2001–2011.

MEPs and a commissioner: members of the European Parliament and members of the European Commission.

The administrative elite

Ministries: permanent secretaries, permanent state under-secretaries and director generals (*i.e.* heads of the departments) of the ministries.

Governmental bureaus: director generals

Judiciary: the chancellor of justice of the council of state, the parliamentary ombudsman, the presidents of the supreme courts, the supreme administrative courts, the special courts and the courts of appeal. The presidents of the administrative courts in 2001–2011.

Defence forces: commander of the defence forces, commanders of the branches, heads of major departments of the main headquarters, the commanders of military counties (in 1991 and 2011), the commanders of military defence areas (2001).

Church: bishops and cathedral deans of the Evangelical Church, bishops of the Orthodox Church.

Regional state administration: county governors (1991–2001), heads of the county administrative boards (1991), chief directors of the centres for the employment and the economy (2001), regional state administrative agencies (2011), centres for economic development, transport and the environment (2011).

Municipalities: city managers of the biggest cities.

Regional councils' administration: chief directors (2001–2011)

EU civil servants: Finns working at least as department heads in the EU and members of the Committee of Regions (2001–2011).

The business elite

CEO, chairman of the board, chairman of the supervisory board of state-owned firms, cooperative firms and the biggest private firms by turnover, the most well-off private citizens measured by property tax (1991–2001) and combined earned income and capital income (2011)

The organizational elite

Wage-earner organizations: all chairmen of the central organizations, chairman, the first deputy chairman and the highest hired employee of the biggest (by the number of members) unions.

Business organizations: CEO, chairman and the first deputy chairman of the employer and business organizations.

Civic organizations: chairman and the highest hired employee of the well-established civic associations.

Organizations in local and provincial administration: chairman of the board and the highest hired employee of regional planning authorities/provincial federations (1991).

The mass media elite

Editors-in-chief of the biggest newspapers and the periodical press by circulation, managing editors of the Finnish News Agency, managers and managing editors of the biggest TV and radio channels.

The scientific elite

Universities: rector and chancellor, chairman of the board
recruited outside the university (2011).

Governmental research institutes: chief director, chairman of
the board (2011).

Private research institutes: chief director and the chairman of
the board.

Foundations: chairman and the highest hired employee of the
big foundations for funding scientific research

Associations: chairman and the highest hired employee of associations functioning in the field of research.

Academy of Finland: Director general, members of the board,
academicians of science, research professors (1991) and academy professors (2001–2011).

The cultural elite

Art administration: Secretary general and members the
Central Art Council

Fields of art: chairman and the highest hired employees of the
associations functioning in various fields of art

Influential personalities: publicly recognized and awarded individuals functioning in various fields of art and culture.

Honorary art professors and academicians: art professors,
academicians of art (2011).

Subtle Power – Analysing Power in the Real-Life Context of Talvivaara Mine

MAIJA MATTILA

As is evident throughout this volume, power is a complex concept that sets challenges to its empirical analysis. Often this difficulty is overcome through taking an institution under study and concentrating on one or at best a few aspects of its functions. This approach yields information of power use that Barnett and Duvall (2005) would call either compulsory or institutional power. The former refers to direct control and the latter to indirect control of one actor over another. In their typology, however, Barnett and Duvall (2005: 12) suggest additionally two further expressions or forms of power: structural power and productive power. In examining the latter two forms, interest is in the production of actors' social capacities and in the actors' perceived interests and self-understandings. The difference between the two is that the structural form includes direct structural relations, whereas productive power encompasses more general and scattered social processes. This is how the productive power is described by the authors:

> Productive power, by contrast, is the constitution of all social subjects with various social powers through systems of knowledge and discursive practices of broad and general social scope. Conceptually, the move is away from structures, per se, to systems of signification and meaning (which are structured, but not themselves structures), and to networks of social forces perpetually shaping one another. (Barnett & Duvall 2005: 20.)

This chapter proceeds in tow with this understanding of structural and productive power. Thus, in search of power in Finland the gaze

is turned to sets of political actors and to the ways they construct
their own positions *vis-à-vis* other actors. To this end, a case study
was conducted. It allowed including institutional actors, such as
ministers, members of parliament and authorities, but also actors
without any institutional setting, such as civic actors, into the
analysis. In this way, it was possible to analyse different actors'
mutual relations and meaning-making and trace power relations
in a real-life context. The chapter, thus, provides a cross-section
of Finnish political landscape. Moreover, the case could have been
any political issue involving the different levels of actors, as long as
it involved more or less active citizens in addition to institutional
actors. For the activism and due to the exceptional political activity, the case was chosen to be politics involving Talvivaara mine in
eastern Finland.

Talvivaara was a mine in Sotkamo municipality, Kainuu province, in eastern Finland. It was opened in 2007, and went bankrupt
in November 2014. Since spring 2013 the state of Finland was
the single biggest owner of the mine with its portion of about 16
percent of the stock-enlisted shares, and other shares were largely
owned by private households. The state ownership was organized
through a limited liability company Solidium, fully owned by the
state. After the bankruptcy, the state bought the mining operations, and shares, still owned by previous owners, practically lost
their value. The mine continued functioning under the new state-
owned company, Terrafame. Hence, actors on many levels and both
locally and nationally have been involved. Thirdly, as the mine is
situated in a rather remote and sparsely populated eastern Finland
with many challenges regarding unemployment and low public
revenue figures, its significance to the public has been greater than
it would have been in some other case. For these reasons, power
was studied in the context of this particular case.

In search of structural and productive power, these questions
will be answered in this chapter: What roles did different actors
play in the case? What institutional powers did they possess, what
were the limits to their power use? How did the actors perceive
their own roles and the others' roles? How did they talk about their
own actions? As power here is understood as something diffuse in
social processes, it is acknowledged that it does not reside only in
predetermined institutional processes, but it can rather be detected

anywhere. Hence, the power of institutions, such as the parliament of Finland, is not taken for granted, but instead approached open-mindedly asking, what exactly is its role. The same question is asked regarding ministers, public authorities and civic actors.

The data consists of interviews of these actors, observation of citizen assemblies and demonstrations, media data and official reports both by the company and public institutions or actors from 2012 and 2013. A popular understanding of representative democracy, here referred to as the standard account of representation, is used as a theoretical tool in putting the actors' accounts into place. That is, the ways actors perceived themselves and others were compared to the way different actors' roles are pictured in the representative democracy context. According to this account, institutions fulfil their representative roles when they are duly authorized and accountable; the people authorize the parliament in elections, the parliament selects the cabinet, and the cabinet exercises its executive powers through authorities. In turn, authorities are accountable to the cabinet, cabinet to the parliament and the parliament to the people. (Curtin 2007: 524–525; Lupia 2006: 34, 36; Müller *et al.* 2006: 3; Saalfeld 2000: 354; Strøm 2006: 65.) As a follow-up question to the research questions listed above, it was studied how the data supported picturing the Finnish political system like this.

The chapter will proceed first with the presentation of the case, accompanied with a presentation of the representative system in Finland and an overview of the activism in section two. After that, the empirical analysis proceeds in three phases. First, section three will take a closer look at the civic actors' roles. The motivations for activism and the ways activists perceived politicians are presented. The section is designed to give an account of the activists' perspectives to the case, their self-understandings, and their understandings of other actors' roles and power. Secondly, section four discusses MPs' roles. This part concentrates on assessing linkages between MPs' territorial backgrounds, ideologies, and political parties. Their relation to civic activism is also touched upon. Thirdly, section five turns to the executive, understood as consisting of cabinet ministers and authorities. This section is based on ministers' understanding of their possibilities to use power and compares the perspectives of municipal authorities to state authorities. Finally, the conclusion summarizes these analyses and draws an overview of the political power use in Finland in this given case.

Case background

Short history of the Talvivaara mine

The Talvivaara mine was opened in 2007 and it produced mainly nickel, but also zinc, copper, and cobalt as by-products (Talvivaara Mining Company 2013: 5). Additionally, uranium has been found in small levels. The mine area is situated in Sotkamo municipality, Kainuu province in eastern Finland. Emigration and high unemployment figures are characteristic to the region, as well as large areas of untouched wilderness and clean nature, both of the features being in line with many other rural areas in eastern and northern Finland. This is the reason to the fact that the Talvivaara mine carried an immense promise to the worsening economy of the region and was hence initially warmly welcomed.

The hopeful atmosphere at the beginning was among others reflected in a speech given by the minister of the environment at the time Paula Lehtomäki (Centre Party) at the laying of the mine's foundation stone in August 2007. Having Kainuu as her home region, she stated that the Talvivaara mine was 'switching on a new light for us, the Kainuu people'. She emphasized that Talvivaara had wide-ranging and long-running effects not only to the Kainuu region but to the whole of eastern Finland. Nonetheless, she additionally addressed people that had had doubts and prejudice by highlighting the strict environmental permit process and future follow-up in terms of environmental issues. (Lehtomäki 2007) Indeed, at the time, critical voices were sparse but existing. They consisted mainly of those that had had to move away from the area or whose earlier calm and nature-centered environment changed rapidly due to the mine construction.[1]

From spring 2013 until the bankruptcy in autumn 2014 the State of Finland was the single biggest owner of the Talvivaara shares, owning roughly 16 percent of the mine. Otherwise the company

1   S. Oinaala, 'Miljardin tonnin monttu', *Helsingin Sanomat* 28.10.2007.

was largely owned by private households, the biggest of them being the founder and CEO Pekka Perä – as of August 2014, the 50 largest owners owned only about one-third of all the shares. The fact that Talvivaara was largely owned by private households throughout its history further strengthened its image as the Saviour of Kainuu.

Nevertheless, soon after the opening of the mine people in the surrounding area started to make environmental observations, concerning mainly dark dust, odorous emissions and changes in water bodies (Talvivaara Mining Company 2013: 62). In 2011, authorities gave recommendations for water usage concerning two nearby lakes, in principle restricting usage of lake water in sauna. Later, the recommendation was extended to cover three more lakes and two rivers, ranging to use of fish, as well (Talvivaara Mining Company 2013: 40).[2] Following this, the publicity of the mine changed from positive to negative, it concerning almost solely environmental problems.

In addition to these regular observations, major incidents have taken place as well. The most severe of them was a massive wastewater leakage from a broken gypsum pond to the surrounding nature in November 2012. The company was forced, according to its own words, to run massive amounts of metal-containing and acid waters to water bodies outside the mine area. (Talvivaara Mining Company 2013: 36) The incident was significant particularly from the viewpoint of political action, both by politicians and civic actors, which seriously took off during and after the leakage. It forced *inter alia* ministers, MPs and local councillors to take a stance in the issue, as well as marked a boost for the newly formed Stop Talvivaara movement aiming at the shut-off of the mine. Simultaneously, the media publicity ballooned and the massive coverage continued during the weeks to come. The attention was quite exceptional, and only the very top news having wide effects receive coverage of that scale.

While resulting in extremely negative publicity, the environmental challenges affected the company's finances as well. The company's consolidated financial statements show that the loss in 2013 amounted to EUR 812.5 million, compared to the loss of EUR 103.9 million in 2012 and 5.2 million in 2011. The poor result was for both 2012 and 2013 explained with the water balance situation,

---

2   In 2014 some of the restrictions were removed.

and for 2013 a major factor to the massive loss was write-downs on inventory and property, plant and equipment due to company reorganization proceedings. (Talvivaara Mining Company 2014: 2; Talvivaara Mining Company 2013: 6) In 2013 the company had tried to solve the difficult situation by organizing a rights issue in April. As a result of the issue Talvivaara raised EUR 250.8 million, after which CEO Perä assured that the funds raised would secure functioning of the mine for years to come.[3] In the issue, State of Finland invested tens of millions of public money to the company and thus became the single largest owner of the company. However, in November 2013 the company filed for corporate reorganization and a year later went bankrupt.

Talvivaara in the Context of the Representative System

The case relates to the political system in many ways. First, the fact that public money is at stake makes the company matters public matters. This includes, for example, questions of how to handle environmental issues, whether or not Finland should invest into the company, and the future of the company as a whole. This aspect involves foremost the minister responsible for ownership steering, who until October 2013 was Heidi Hautala of the Greens, and later Pekka Haavisto of the same party. The state ownership was organized through a limited liability company Solidium, which is the model of how state ownership in general is organized in Finland. Following from this, it is Solidium that owns the shares, but on the other hand, Solidium is fully owned by the state.

Secondly, as mining is invasive industry in terms of its surroundings to begin with, and as this particular mine has had severe environmental issues, the mine directly affects people's living environment. These negative effects are accompanied by effects that can be deemed positive, such as a boost to the regional economy and increase in the number of jobs. From both sides and for many citizens, whether or not the mine exists is not an irrelevant question. The environmental issues generated civic activism and they also involved closely the minister of the environment, Ville Niinistö,

3   J. Aaltonen, 'Mielenosoittajat yrittivät estää Talvivaaran annin', *Helsingin Sanomat* 9.3.2013.

of the Greens. The civic activism built partly around the symbol of Stop Talvivaara, which to some degree joined people opposing the mine.

Finally, as all other private enterprises, the case involved public administration in the form of issuing permits and monitoring. The work of the authorities is framed by laws, statutes, ministerial guidelines etc., which are outcomes of political processes, such as legislation in the parliament. The municipal level is responsible for issuing building permits, which in this case was the task of the municipal council of Sotkamo. Municipalities in the area are also responsible for the environmental protection of their residents. Major actors in this respect were the joint municipal authorities of Ylä-Savon SOTE and Kainuun SOTE, meaning that the municipalities in the area have formed these authorities and delegated some of their powers to them, such as health care issues and environmental protection. In addition to these municipal power representatives, also state authorities were involved as permit providers and supervisors. The environmental permits to Talvivaara were licensed by the regional state administrative agency of northern Finland (the 'AVI') and the competent supervising authority is the Kainuu Centre for the Economic Development, Transport and the Environment (the 'Kainuu ELY'), working under the Ministry of the Environment. The issuing of permits in Finland includes an environmental impact assessment process that entails *e.g.* public hearings.

These aspects create a network of institutions and actors that each have their own perspectives, roles, and tasks in relation to the case. From a democratic perspective, one way to picture the actors involved is the delegation and accountability chain, here called the standard account of representation (see Urbinati & Warren 2008: 389; Pollak *et al.* 2009: 1), pictured in Figure 1 below.

While Figure 1 presents how democracy is realized through different institutional arrangements, it is quite restricted in terms of civic activism, as people are foremost seen as an electorate. The people's democratic power is delegated in elections in which the parliament and the municipal councils are authorized. The parliament further authorizes the cabinet and makes legislation. Regional state bureaus ELY and AVI that regulate businesses, such as mining, function within the limits of existing legislation and under the administrative branches of respective ministries. This is a chain through

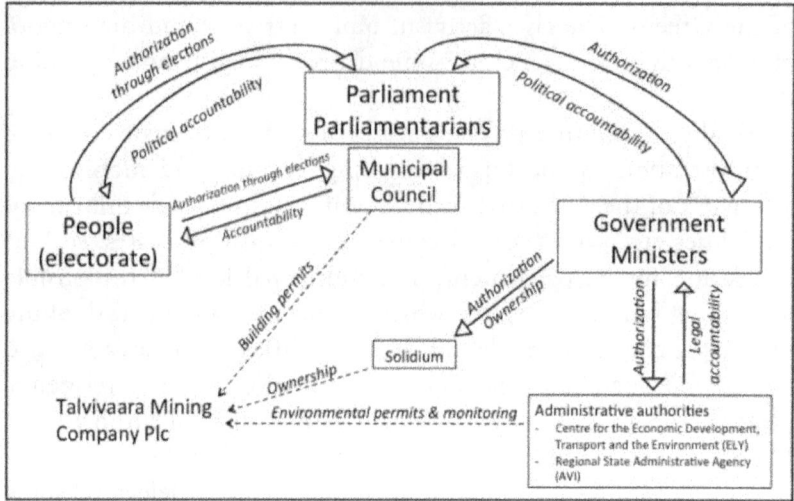

Figure 1. Standard account of representation

which, in a minimalistic view, democracy can be seen realized as long as elections are in place, there is a competent and accountable cabinet and state bureaus follow the law. (See Christiano 1996: 209–210; Manin *et al.* 1999: 10; *cf.* Laycock 2004: xi.)

The chain of accountability goes the other way round: state bureaus are legally bound, the cabinet is politically accountable to the parliament, and the parliament and the municipal council are politically accountable to the people in the next election. The chain is similar but not identical regarding the ownership of the Talvivaara company through Solidium. It is in principle a private company that is led like companies usually are. The minister responsible for ownership steering in the cabinet has leverage over Solidium, but no direct decision-making power. Thus, the chain of accountability is not continuous or totally consistent. (On the connection between delegation/authorization and accountability, see Pitkin 1972.)

In this chapter, the roles of different actors are analysed *vis-à-vis* each other and Figure 1. It is examined whether the actors 'comply' with the figure or whether the power relations are organized by the actors in a way that differs from this understanding. The three levels of actors, civic actors, members of parliament and the executive, and the self-understandings of their roles are analysed based on a variety of theoretical approaches.

While Figure 1 lies at the heart of the common understanding of representative government, another understanding rather highlights representation as something that necessarily entails construction and interpretation of the represented entity (Hayward 2009: 121; Pettit 2009: 76; Saward 2010: 109). Hence, through re-presenting issues and groups of people, political actors politicize issues, question their nature as given and expose them to political decision-making. This politicizing includes questions of who has the right to represent whom and how the interests of the represented are defined (on representation as claims-making, see Saward 2006, 2010).

In the same vein, then, constituency is not taken for granted. Rather, it is asked how the portrayals of different constituencies serve as a tool in yielding political leverage or even power. As stated in the introduction, emphasis is on the productive power – on the ways meaning and signification are produced and experienced in social processes and practices, as well as on the production of social identities. (Barnett & Duvall 2005: 20–21) This calls for taking a step away from the rationale that representation is based foremost on territorial constituencies, which is how political institutions in the western world have been built, and instead asking what role does the territory play for different actors.

The analysis is based on 29 interviews consisting of interviews with the former minister responsible for ownership steering, 14 MPs from either the Oulu or North Savo constituencies[4], 11 civic actors and three public officials. The interviews were carried out between December 2012 and December 2013 in Helsinki, Tampere, Sotkamo, Iisalmi and Kajaani in Finland. Additionally, three self-organized citizen assemblies[5] and three demonstrations[6]

---

4   Talvivaara mine is located in the area of constituency of Oulu, but the border between Oulu and constituency of North Savo goes very close to the mine. Thus, also all the MPs from Iisalmi municipality on the North Savo side of the border were interviewed. This way, then, all MPs that came from the nearby area to the mine were interviewed for the study.

5   The assemblies took place in Iisalmi on 8 December 2012, in Helsinki on 7 March 2013, and in Tampere on 10 September 2013.

6   The demonstrations took place in Helsinki on 14 November 2012 (this demonstration was only observed through the media) and on 8 March 2013, and in Tampere on 12 September 2013.

were observed. In addition to the interviews and observation, the data includes media material and official reports by the Talvivaara Mining Company Plc and public administration. Based on this material, analysis of the role of the minister of the environment was also included, although he was not interviewed.

Overview of activism

As a grace note, the Talvivaara case sheds light on Finnish environmental activism, which is here shortly introduced. In general, the Finnish way of exercising civic rights is characteristically non-radical and conciliatory, and often setting up movements has led to establishing formal registered associations, or existing associations have functioned in the background of emerging movements. From this follows that movements that have not formed associations have remained relatively small and weak. (Siisiäinen & Kankainen 2009: 97; see also Luhtakallio 2012)

In general, the post-Second World War Finnish civic activism can be divided into four different phases. The first, in the 1960s and 1970s, was characterized by paying attention to industrial effluents, as opposed to more traditional environmental conservation. The second wave, some ten years after the first, conceptualized environmental issues as distinctively political and social issues. It took advantage of wide-ranging and well-organized publicity as a resource, but followed the traditional Finnish way of acting by forming a registered association (see Alapuro 2005; Siisiäinen & Kankainen 2009: 94).

The symbol of the new radical thinking was the Koijärvi movement that for the first time in a radical manner used civil disobedience as a way to act.[7] According to the movement founders, prior to the events in Koijärvi they had alternative targets of action, Koijärvi being one of them. Hence, environmental activists had waited for a suitable case to emerge to take action on. The movement paved

7   The Koijärvi movement gathered together scattered environmental activists
    to protect the Koijärvi lake and its avifauna against landowners' plans to drain
    the lake in 1979. Members of the movement built a dam to stop the draining
    and chained themselves to worksite vehicles in order to prevent the police from
    removing them from the area. (Metsämäki & Nisula 2006: 243–44)

the way for other similar protests in a frame of direct, yet non-violent civic action, and consequently a wave of local protests took place. The Green League party was founded in the aftermath of the Koijärvi events, and the first two Greens' MPs were elected to the parliament in the 1983 elections. (Rasimus 2006: 75–76)

Further, the third wave of environmental protest formed around issues concerning use and protection of forests, claiming that interest groups representing the forest industry and economy had too long had too much influence on how forests were used. The fourth wave, finally, combined environmental protection and issues relating to global justice, equality, political power use and income distribution. In the same vein, politicization of private lives in the form of vegetarianism and veganism occurred. (Rasimus 2006: 77–78)

The Talvivaara activism does not directly resemble any of the above-mentioned phases or forms of protest. Unlike in the case of Koijärvi, resistance in the Talvivaara issue rose largely from local discontent and worry for the region's environment and people's livelihoods. For this part, the activism is similar to that of the 1980s when local inhabitants in Central Finland rose against forest industry to make it diminish its effluents to natural waters. There, too, the actors were foremost those who felt the impacts most concretely. (See Ylönen 1998)

While the Stop Talvivaara movement has received support nationwide, the core of activists has been local/regional and self-organized. Additionally, many nearby inhabitants have been active on their own, without identifying with the Stop Talvivaara movement, *e.g.* by filing complaints on authorities' actions to the judicial system. There has neither occurred downright civil disobedience, and the activists have actively reported on their observations around the mine area to the authorities.

Neither have there been signs of questions concerning global justice, and to some activists even mining in Finland in general is something they have not concerned themselves with (although many have). Rather, the activism can be described as local and regional resistance that has got support from existing environmental associations and activist groups, both locally and nationally. Some individuals have been active also in relation to other mining projects in Finland, but by far not all. Being active in mining issues in general, moreover, is distinctively a regional issue, as mining in large scale affects mostly northern and eastern Finland. Thus, the complex nature of the mining issue suggests that labelling the activism as an environmental movement would be too straightforward. Further, the activism in its entirety cannot be called a 'movement' to begin with, as some actors have related themselves only very loosely to the Stop Talvivaara movement.

Indeed, to isolate environmental politics from other political issues would make it difficult to understand the Talvivaara activism (and potentially other activism as well). The activism has been in dialogue with formal political institutions, seeking to correct the authorities' actions and to influence other political actors. It has not, for the most part, criticized the western lifestyle as such (although some of the activists have) or been used to build participants' subjectivities. Instead, it has involved many material and interest-related questions, both on local and national level, as well as posed a question of power relations between a private business and the public. For these reasons the activism was analysed in the context of different political fora, such as the parliament and authoritative instances, as those fora are supposed to embody territorial interests through representation.

In the following, the chapter will move to the empirical part in which each set of actors will be taken in turn: first the civic activists, then MPs, and finally the executive. For the civic actors, the motivations for activism as well as the perceived role of politicians are examined. This is to determine the role the activists themselves assumed in the context of political system. Their answers to interview questions and the passages below reflect what can be legitimately said about becoming and being an activist, as much as they are accounts of how the interviewees felt. As such, the statements can be taken both to inform about the political civic activist culture in Finland, and to simultaneously constitute that very culture. As an underlying perspective, this applies to the analyses of MPs' and the executive's roles as well.

A closer look at activism

Motivations for activism

The civic activism, both in Stop Talvivaara and otherwise, largely arose from experiences of local inhabitants or of those who had their summerhouses close to the mine area. Many of the 11 interviewed civic activists told that they had no previous experience from activism, but that they had rather activated themselves in the process. This was due to sense of injustice in what was happening in the surroundings of the mine. It was stated that a small group of nearby inhabitants had realized that 'things were not going right' (Civic actor 5) and that amongst other things blastings in the mine construction site were not carried out according to the rules and regulations. The way the nearby inhabitants had acted was rather authority-oriented, as they *inter alia* had made remarks to the authorities and in general contacted the authorities whenever they had noticed problems in their surroundings. It was pointed out that the environmental permit conditions for the mine had not been right to begin with and that compliance with the permit terms had not been pressed for properly by the authorities (Civic actor 11).

Hence, the sense of injustice was backed by referring to the law and the ways authorities had acted; the administrative system was described as something that had failed the citizens as they had to take initiative on their own. They did not do it willingly, but rather because they were forced to a corner. The following passages exemplify the argumentation based on this kind of sense of injustice:

> Saying something and doing another doesn't fit into my sense of justice to the degree that ... And then that it was just next to us what was happening, so I thought I had to do something. That we won't accept this. (Civic actor 5)

> [T]his mine is incomprehensible in that it has been given a permit under these kinds of conditions, and in that it is not strictly demanded that it has to realize the so-called closed circulation. What they were saying all along was that 'yeah we have a closed circulation, we are the only mine that has that', but that only means that the metal factory won't use clean water but that the water they use is recycled. But everything that comes to the waste water, it's not clean, it has terrible amounts of sulphate and

manganese and all those fancy elements that I don't even remember.
(Civic actor 11)

Overall, in looking at the arguments about the critics' motivations,
arguments about things not going the way they should have gone
rose above other arguments. Either it was argued that problems
were to be foreseen based on mine plans and on the initial environment impact assessment program (Civic actor 10 & Civic actor 4),
or the activism of some had started after actual impacts, such as
odours and alleged water contamination (Civic actor 6).

Further, the criticism towards the mine and the authorities was
accompanied with the acknowledgement that there truly was a
need to have jobs in the region, while at the same time it was argued
that it could not happen at any cause:

> It's very clear to me that this world and this country need to be devel-
> oped and we need to go forward and do things. That we cannot brake,
> but it has to happen in accordance with laws and statutes and such, so
> that operations are socially acceptable. (Civic actor 5)

Additionally, it was *inter alia* explained that the mine itself was not
objected to, but the major effects on nature that it caused (Civic
actor 10). Thus, the argumentation appealed to common sense,
the interviewees avoiding attaching themselves to the image of
traditional nature conservationists. The 'common sense approach'
was coupled with stressing many of the speakers' commonness as
opposed to some faceless authorities, power, or even something
that looked like a conspiracy:

> ... there is some big shot that has given the impression of the Stop
> Talvivaara movement that we are nearly criminals. We are perfectly nor-
> mal citizens from all walks of life, but it somehow feels that we would not
> be, although we operate within law, and we are from side to side from
> different occupations. [---] My own personal view is that, during this
> process, I have lost the belief that in Finland the people would have the
> power. It's not true, it's with those who govern the money, they have the
> power. (Civic actor 7)

> I don't know under whose protection this is. (Civic actor 6)
> … the project has all along had the blessing of politicians and decision-makers, that it will be done. So I don't know whether it's the uranium behind all this or is it only about getting employment to Kainuu. (Civic actor 11)

Through this rhetorical division between the common people and the faceless authorities, interestingly, the interviewees assumed a role of speaking for the people. In many cases this was not explicit, and some even stated that they did not represent anybody but themselves (Civic actor 9). Nevertheless, making the division and thus claiming themselves to be representatives of the people seemed necessary for the interviewees to politicize the issue and thus make room for themselves to act politically.

While for many this did not seem as a conscious strategic choice, for an interviewee who, unlike many others, had a long history in activism, highlighted the wide support the Stop Talvivaara movement had across Finland (Civic actor 1). Whether or not the movement had the support described by the interviewee, he deemed it beneficial for his cause to assure that it was widely supported. Another thing that he deemed important to note was the struggle between local people and the mining industry, and he very strongly stated that he through the movement represented the Savo (a region south from Talvivaara, next to Kainuu) people. Conceptualizing the situation as a struggle between the people and the mining industry enabled politicizing of the issue. This further strengthens the interpretation that claiming to represent a larger entity plays a role in politicizing issues.

Conceived role of politicians

As said above, the 'commonness' of the activists was built in relation to rulers such as authorities and political decision-makers. When the civic actors' self-understandings were this way rhetorically constructed, 'the other' was left rather undefined. Nonetheless, in continuing analysing the data and putting under loop the ways politicians were conceived, the data showed that municipal councillors and MPs were perceived quite differently by the activists, as opposed to how cabinet ministers and authorities were perceived.

That is, it was acknowledged that 'ordinary' councillors and MPs did not and could not have influence on the matter, at least not right now, but that ministers and authorities should. This perspective was evident in what some of the interviewees explained to be expecting from MPs. While their actions (or non-acting) were criticized, what was mostly wanted from them was outspoken support. They were not expected to contact the ministers of their own party or to do anything themselves, but simply to *say* something. The criticism towards high-level politicians showed in interviews as follows:

> Politicians come to visit and appear in the papers that tell that this or that minister observed the mine with a helmet on. They are on their high horses saying that this is terrible, reassuring that this will get better. But nothing changes. It's all just big circus and theatre. (Civic actor 5)
> [---] [W]e have had ministers to visit, I mean, from the highest level of politics. [---] But when they go back to their postings, it's somehow a big wheel that turns and nothing else seems to have importance except for economic necessity. (Civic actor 4)

In the same vein, nonetheless, it was perceived that the role of politicians was somewhat restricted:

> On the other hand, I accept that things happen slowly [in politics], but I wish that this would affect their talking, comments and doings... So that sometimes, after a while, there would be changes in legislation or in actions or in general instructions, that years from now one could notice that it made a difference to have a discussion on this issue. (Civic actor 5)
> But, of course, Talvivaara is such a big actor and as the state is strongly involved, it is difficult for a basic MP to ... (Civic actor 4)

In some passages, politicians were excused for not acting:

> But we cannot really require that politicians would understand what is going on if our media is not capable of maintaining the discussion. (Civic actor 1)

> I think this depends on general awakening of the people. Politicians will awaken as a result of that. (Civic actor 4)

These passages show a combination of disappointment, low expectations and the role of general atmosphere and actions of the media in defining the doings or non-doings of politicians. Indeed, this account resembled that of what Pitkin (1972: 63–64) associates with some features in proportional representation, namely that a representative organ, such as a municipal council or a parliament, is supposed to deliberate rather than govern, which is the job of the executive. As the tasks of deliberation and governing are distinguished, it is viewed that the parliamentary organs are supposed to provide the multitude of perspectives that are represented in the society, but the executive is expected to make the actual decisions and to act. In this governing task, it is less relevant whether different views are being represented, or rather that the executive is supposed to represent the good of the whole.

Having the standard account of representation in mind, it seems that the activists did not act it out in the sense that MPs would have been the foremost targets of their actions. They had, quite rightly, identified the executive and the authorities as power holders. This raises questions about the role of the MPs. Is their role to promote the interests of their background region and if so, how are the interests defined and how do they relate to the MPs' wider role? I will examine these questions in the following through the analysis of the MPs' interviews.

Constructing representation – MPs' perspectives

Holding on to one's views

The interviews with MPs were guided by loosely combining ideas from different ways of analysing representation, but avoiding clinging to any one of them. In short, the term 'representation' both in scholarly and every-day discussions evoke normative aspirations for the representatives to represent the people as accurately as possible in order representation to be democratic – this idea is also included in the standard account of representation. This might refer to descriptive similarity in terms of demographical variables, or similar opinions between representatives and the represented (see *e.g.* Miller & Stokes 1963; Marsh & Wessels 1997; Holmberg

2000). Here these accounts of representation are contrasted to the more flexible understanding in which representation is thought to re-interpret and even create the constituency, and thus the gaze is turned towards the processes of doing that.

First, as in all issues, it is evident also in the Talvivaara case that there is no one will of the people for the representatives to follow. This is one main argument in the newer representation theories which highlight that the will of the represented cannot be taken for granted and thus that there is no way of evaluating whether representation is good or bad by conducting measurements based on such an assumption. What could be expected from MPs, though, was that they would have made an attempt to convince the interviewer of the fact that they tried to comply with whatever the people wanted.

This was not the case, nevertheless. As the MPs were asked how they balanced between the different demands of the people in their respective constituencies in the Talvivaara issue, many of them replied that they did not balance at all. Instead, it was held that they needed to be consistent in their political actions and, additionally, in many occasions, it became apparent that the view each had taken was based on a set of values or ideological commitments. A few passages from the interviews are in order to clarify this point:

> I do not balance with these kinds of issues. People need to make their own decisions regarding whether they vote for me or not, but I think that these issues are not to be balanced with. (MP 11)

> I do not balance at all but instead I form my own picture of the issue, so that I can feel being on sound basis. The emissions need to be restricted, and that is the only way mining can continue in Talvivaara and the only way we can save the mining business important to us in Finland. (MP 7) I cannot begin to swing, to change my views. I have to hold on to the same view, this is my fourth term in the office and I have held on to the same view and won support to it [---]. (MP 3)

The interviewed MPs were very well aware of the different, even polarized, views of the people in the area and some of them found themselves balancing between the need for jobs and environmental issues. However, this usually seemed to be an inner struggle that involved rethinking one's own values and goals rather than a struggle *vis-à-vis* people's opinions. But, in addition to the explicit answers to the question, another interpretation can be drawn from the answers: stressing their immovability in the issue was also a way to talk to their own supporters. Perhaps, then, in the Finnish political culture it is more valued to be principled than to follow the popular moods.

Moreover, particularly the last passage reflected thinking based on the so-called responsible party government model, according to which responsiveness and thus democracy is thought to realize in the foreseeable actions of parties as power holders. In that thinking, parties and electoral candidates as the representatives of their parties give their opinions to a certain issue prior to the election and then, in the name of democracy, they are expected to follow the pre-electoral views when in office. (Dalton 1985: 270; Marsh & Norris 1997: 153–154) The two former passages reflected more of a Burkean understanding of representatives as holders of a free mandate rather than ambassadors of their constituencies.

This discussion twines around the mandate/independence controversy (Pitkin 1972). While many normative accounts and certainly the popular understanding of democratic representation depart from the requirement of instructed mandate, it has also been argued that it is the very gap between representatives and the represented that enable democratic politics. In this account, it is rather the open contestation of different perspectives that create democratic politics than closeness between representatives and the represented in terms of opinions. (Ankersmit 2002: 36; Näsström 2006: 334) Thus, deeming the above-presented MPs' self-understandings as undemocratic would be too bold. What seems to be necessary to do, nevertheless, is to assess whether Figure 1 promptly describes our political system, particularly in what comes to MPs' position in it. In the following, the territorial aspect of MPs' work is examined.

Geography, ideology, and the party

As presented in the theory section, territoriality is the criterion for democratic representation that has been institutionalized in most of the world's electoral systems. The institutions based on

MAIJA MATTILA

this rationale imply that the representatives ought to have a special link and a sense of representation in relation to their territorial constituencies. It is thought that representation transmits people's feelings and opinions to the system, thus realizing democracy. In the following, the question of whether or not there is a special linkage is addressed.

As the activists called for public criticism from the MPs, this appeared to be the task of the MPs from their own perspective as well. In an issue like this, an issue that did not involve legislation, MPs made frequent references to their speeches and writings to assure the interviewer of them having been active. In a sense, the case served MPs in furthering their political goals in general. While their geographical background did play a role as many highlighted interests of eastern and northern Finland, the interests of the region were looked through ideological and value-based lenses:

> [W]hat I have called for is a national mining know-how programme and I, if you may, lobby, or influence the minister Gustafsson [former Minister of Education and Science], and now the current minister Kiuru, I lobby for strengthening of mining know-how at the University of Oulu. [---] I believe that mines do have a future in Finland, but this cannot go the way it has gone, from one mistake to another. (MP 13; MP of the Social Democratic Party)

> We were at first, and still are, very glad that Kajaani and Kainuu region, for years having suffered from unemployment and emigration and factories being shut down, that we got work and the whole mining industry in Finland, and I continue to think like that, it is good to have jobs. We just need to refine it. [---] The worst thing would be others changing their minds more than me [about mining industry, towards negative stands] and that starting to have an effect on permit processes and economic investments [---]. (MP 15; MP of the National Coalition Party)

In this way, hence, while the views of what was good for the Kainuu region were quite similar with different MPs from different parties, that is, having jobs but not at any expense, the way different aspects were highlighted varied according to different political stances. Thus, each interviewed MP did stress that they had the best of their region in sight, but what that actually meant alternated. From this perspective, then, seeing MPs just as ambassadors of their own regions, which is to a certain degree supposed by the electoral system, seems inaccurate. More accurate would be to conclude that a territorial perspective is spoken out, and it can be used to benefit the speaker's political ends.

Further, the electoral system and territorial constituencies also imply that the MPs might have a special role within their parties concerning the issues of their own constituencies. In the interviews, nonetheless, it became evident that the distribution of work within the parliamentary groups followed more the lines of committee postings than the constituency-related backgrounds of the MPs. Fellow MPs from the same party were trusted to handle the issue for example in the environment committee, regardless of their geographical background. Many MPs additionally deemed not to have a special advisory role within the parliamentary group. However, while the issue did not affect MPs' work done within the parliament, the MPs of the constituencies of Oulu or North Savo had been more or less active in contacting the company and making public statements regarding the issue.

As the idea of territorial representation did not fully follow the standard account of representation, a potentially problematic element in highlighting locality related to civic activism. Namely, as locality of actors is often seen as a source of legitimacy, it can also be used to de-legitimize civic activism. The following passages reflect how legitimacy and locality went hand in hand in the MPs' interviews:

[---] [I]t is a bit like opposing the Vuotos reservoir, the activists probably come from elsewhere and the movement is activated from the outside. (MP 2)

It is usually with these movements that they are more like from Bulevardi [a street in Helsinki] than local. This is the case with the Sami issue and with many others, as the activist group does not necessarily live or never even visited the locality. (MP 15)

It is easy in the Esplanadi park [in Helsinki] to clap hands together and say that the Talvivaara mine has to be shut down, and afterwards go to Kappeli [a restaurant in Helsinki] for a punch. These things are not that simple. (MP 9)

Many of these and other MPs did, nevertheless, acknowledge the role of civic activism and the principle that allowing peaceful civic activism was important to democracy. Despite of that, it is rather interesting how locality and legitimacy were linked, when, after all, nearly all the MPs did see wider implications of the Talvivaara case to mining industry in Finland in general. Clinging to the demand of locality of civic actors delegitimized the activism without having to even to begin answering to their criticism.

The executive's alternating perspectives

We have now dealt with citizen activism and the role of the MPs. If the MPs seemed to have been sidelined from the issue, let us look at whether it was the executive where the power lay. From the executive side, former minister responsible for ownership steering and regional state and municipal authorities were interviewed for the study. Each of them will be taken in turn.

According to the former minister responsible for ownership steering Heidi Hautala the possibilities of the minister to intervene in the case were limited. This was mainly due to the fact the state ownership was organized through Solidium that was not directly accountable to the minister. Hautala explained Solidium to be a paradox in itself: it was supposed to be detached from politics, while at the same time it was fully owned by Finland and, as such, could not be detached from political agenda. Thus, Solidium has informed the minister responsible for ownership steering about decisions that might have public relevance, such as laying off staff, but it is merely a matter of informing and collaboration, and less a matter of minister taking over some decisions. (Interview with Heidi Hautala, 10 December 2013.)

Either the minister did have as little power as Hautala described, or the tricky organization of state ownerships were used as an excuse for some of the decisions that the minister took. Namely, apparently the question of whether Solidium should invest into the company in the share issue of 2013 was discussed with the minister. Through the decision to increase Solidium's ownership in the company, the minister had indirect leverage and the investment allowed Talvivaara to carry on its operations.

The power of the minister of the environment also seemed like nothing but clear-cut. The green minister Ville Niinistö took publically a more active role than his predecessor Paula Lehtomäki of the Centre Party in the Talvivaara issue. This was at least partly evident due to the fact that the major wastewater leakage occurred during Niinistö's term of office. As a reaction to the more critical voice of the new minister three shareholders of the company made a request to the Chancellor of Justice to determine whether the minister had acted against his official duties in giving the statements he had given and instructing the regional state authorities regarding Talvivaara. The minister was found not to have influenced the authorities inappropriately (Resolution OKV/681/1/2012). The complaint, however, reflected the minister's problematic position. It was referred to by the minister himself later, when he explicated that he could not interfere with the authorities' decisions.[8] His power was restricted to giving general authoritative instructions for the future, and not much was to be done by him while the situation was on in terms of restricting operations of the company. Nonetheless, it was mentioned by an interviewee that the ministries have the right to lay down regulations, and through that means it would have been possible to restrict the company. (Authority 3) Again, the question is how much a minister *could have had* power, had s/he decided to use it to the maximum.

Moving on to the authorities, the regional state officials framed their work as administration defined by the law. Particularly one of the interviewees spoke of the Talvivaara case on an impersonal level and using passive modes. The perspective was that a number of events had taken place in Talvivaara, events that had occurred surprisingly and thus caused a special need for monitoring. The amount of work was highlighted and explained that the authorities had readily intervened in reported problems. This was backed with a report compiled by the Ministry of the Environment, hence stressing that these were not just the interviewee's own words but that it had been noted by others, as well.

This account can be seen against the backdrop of the fact that the regional state authority Kainuu ELY particularly had received

---

8　'Ville Niinistö ja tapaus Talvivaara', *Ylen aamu-tv*. Finnish Broadcasting Company YLE, 14.11.2012.

criticism from different directions, not least in public, for not reacting timely to problems and for allowing the company to continue
contaminating the nature (*e.g.* Pietikäinen & Hassi 2012).[9] In the
interviewee's speech, the reactions of local people to the situation
were referred to as 'negative experiences of the neighbourhood/
surrounds' (*ympäristö* in Finnish), which had led to the above-
mentioned activeness of the authorities. Indeed, the impetus coming from the people was called *demand*, in economic terms. Later,
it was emphasized that the authorities were for parties involved,
who play a role in activating the authorities, and not for publicity,
which ought not be allowed to have an effect on what the authorities decided. When explicitly asked about the Stop Talvivaara
movement, the reply was that it was excellent to have such kind
of citizen monitoring and that monitoring in general happened
in collaboration with the surrounding civil society. However, the
interviewee doubted the measurements carried out by the movement and reserved for activists the role of *informateur* rather than
actor:

> Well, let's say that civic movements are perhaps not supposed to carry
> out measurements but an observation that there is a disturbance or
> that something is not in order is very much enough for a supervisor.
> (Authority 1)

As the role of the actor was in the interviewee's speech reserved for
the authorities, they nevertheless were said to be bound by laws and
ministerial guidelines. What gave them extra discretion, nonetheless, was a 'surprising, unforeseen and unexpected' event (words of
the interviewee), which was exactly how the water balance issue in
the mine was characterized by the interviewee. At the same time,
it was concretely referred to the much-criticized decision by the
Kainuu ELY that allowed the company to release wastewater to the
environment. As the situation was characterized surprising, as a
result, it was this very characterization that gave the authorities in
the first place the right to make the decision.

---

9   See also T. Mainio, 'Talvivaaran YVA-selvitys laadittiin virheellisin tiedoin',
     Helsingin Sanomat 28.3.2012; T. Mainio, 'Luottamus virkamiehiin koetuksella',
     Helsingin Sanomat 26.10.2012.

In the same vein, it was estimated that the Talvivaara case was a hotter topic in southern Finland than in the nearby area. This was suspected to be because of 'modern-day interest of the media' and the opportunity to discuss issues in the social media. The media got indirectly criticized for having increased the administrative work as they had been, among others, those who had asked for administrative information that the authority was obligated to provide. These requests for information, again, had come from other parts of Finland rather than from the surrounding area, according to the official. For this part, the interviewee used same kind of argumentation that the MPs who appealed to locality as a basis for actors' legitimacy.

From the interviewee's administrative perspective, as the role of the citizens did not go through the media, they had a role to play in the administrative process itself:

> Well, citizens have levels, ways and possibilities to influence pretty much a lot in different phases. (Authority 1)

The different phases of citizen influence were further listed, including public hearings regarding permit to search for ore, mining permit and environmental impact assessment process. All the permits, such as the environmental permit, or decisions regarding changes in permits, were subject to appeal, and this was also mentioned as a point of influence for the citizens. Moreover, according to the interviewee, making notifications of observations was possible for the people.

Further, another official of the Kainuu ELY took the Stop Talvivaara movement to be one of the centre's 'customer groups' whose notifications had been handled in the same way than other notifications. (Authority 2) From this perspective, then, citizens were understood sporadically, and whether they had organized themselves collectively or not was irrelevant.

The sphere of politics was constituted as something outside the centre and actions of politicians as oriented towards publicity and general issues. Talvivaara was also mentioned to be a politically delicious issue and the attention paid to it after the 'accident', referring to the wastewater leakage in November 2012, was 'political'. (Authority 2) It was also mentioned that the fact that politicians were interested in the issue had activated citizens and that it seemed that nearly every Finn had an opinion of the case. As to the pressure posed by the situation, nevertheless, it was stated that the role of a civil servant was protected in the sense that the own responsibility was clearly defined. (Authority 2) In answering a question about whether the minister of the environment had interfered too much in ELY's actions, the interviewee replied that 'politicians are politicians and everyone has issues that are particularly close to themselves'. (Authority 2) The reply was continued by saying that they as authorities were mainly in contact with the officials of the ministry, but that the fact that the minister of the environment was from the Green party clearly did have a role to play.

All in all, the perspective of the regional state authorities followed quite rigidly the standard account of representation: their job was to follow the law, to take responsibility of the tasks assigned to them in the law and to follow the ministerial instructions in doing that. Moreover, the role of citizens was also defined in the law, the role being mainly in different phases of permit procedures and as informateurs. Citizens were to be taken individually, not as groups, but each notification having the same weight. Politics was taken to be a realm outside the centre, with the exception of the minister of the environment. The events in Talvivaara were described in an impersonal manner in a way that gave an impression that, from the official perspective, it was in a sense irrelevant of *who* had caused the events to happen in the first place. Here the administrative language collided with the language of the activists who were asking 'who is to blaim, who is to take responsibility?' As in their interviews and in the publicity also the Kainuu ELY had been targeted, for the officials in the centre it seemed impossible to comprehend the accusation, as they were only fulfilling the task ascribed to them.

A very different view of the chain of events was given by a municipal official. He criticized the permit conditions for being too vague and the Kainuu ELY for not executing its supervising duties to the full. He took a very different stand on the mine and stated that

[I]f we take a purely environmental perspective, I think personally that the functions should be shut down in a controlled manner. (Authority 3)

Unlike the government officials of the Kainuu ELY, a personal stand was taken to begin with. However, the other of the officials interviewed from the Kainuu ELY did take a stand in the following way:

> If we think what is best from the environmental perspective, first of all, it is a question of very wide-ranging operations and, as it has been made clear also in the publicity, it cannot just be stopped, it takes years before it can be safely shut down and if we go there, it is not insignificant who takes care of the operations in the end. It requires very, you know, strong know-how that the local people here have, because they are used to working with it. Whatever happens, it is not allowed to pose any kind of risk to the environment. (Authority 2)

Like the official of the joint municipal authority, the regional state official claimed to be speaking from the environmental perspective. The difference was, apart from the fact that the two interviewees winded up in opposite conclusions, that the state official presented the argument in a passive mode (*'it cannot just be stopped'*), whereas the municipal official used active mode (*'I think personally...'*). Yet, at the same time, the government official *did* take a personal stand in advocating the local know-how. Another difference between the two was in how they viewed civic activism. The two state officials stressed that the citizens as individuals had a role to play and that the civic activists were received the same way as other 'customers', whereas the joint municipal authority official stated that he appreciated the activism as such:

> And I have to say that I appreciate this civic activism, it is a vital part of environmental protection that issues are raised by the Stop Talvivaara, or by these activists, things that even the authorities would not have noticed themselves. (Authority 3)

The source of legitimacy of these actors explains the different perspectives. Namely, in the context of the standard account of representation, the legitimacy of the ELY Centre officials, according to their own views, derived from the chain of delegation and authority. That is, their understanding of their own position followed the lines presented in Figure 1. Their jurisdiction came from the law and politically they were headed by the ministry. Politics was outside the centre. There was, nonetheless, a deviation to the figure: citizens had a role to play other than that of an electorate. They were *informateurs* and participants in different administrative procedures. If this position is described as a 'top-down' position, the position adopted by the joint municipal authority official reminded more of a position 'from below'. The chain of delegation was shorter, albeit the joint municipal authority formed an extra organization on top of municipalities. However, it was closer to the parliamentary functions of a regime. The role of the municipal actor did, indeed, remind more that of parliaments than that of the executive. The authority was mainly involved in the case through statements, not as a decision-maker.

In summary of the executive's role, it seems that the role of the ministers' was anything but straight forward, and that the political system itself had sought to dismantle the political control in organizing state ownership through Solidium. At the same time, the independent position of the state authorities based on the rule of law restricted actions of ministers. The actual power to suspend or even to call off the mining operations lay with the state authorities that, however, could not let any public discussion intervene their decision-making.

Conclusion

According to the analysis, the Talvivaara case engaged a number of different political actors whose activities had different targets, objectives, possibilities and limits. Table 1 presents a summary of the actors with the possibilities and limits of their actions. As is shown in the table, jurisdiction and thus the power to restrict the company resided with the government authorities of the Kainuu ELY Centre. Their power was bound by the law, which simultaneously tied the hands of political actors such as MPs and ministers. Although this follows the principle of the rule of law, the downside is that it made power seem impersonal. As shown in the analysis, the target of civic actors' activities, the authorities, was quite right – it truly was the party the exercised the power in the case. But, at the same time, it was the party of all possible targets that could not let the activity to influence its decisions. The way the government officials understood their job, that is, as neutral supervisors, clashed with the activists' view that the authorities were not performing their duties properly. While criticism was targeted directly to the Kainuu ELY, both by activists and the municipal official, the administrative position of the ELY authorities either prevented or spared them from assuming any political responsibility for their decisions.

Table 1. Actors and the possibilities and limits of their actions in the Talvivaara case.

Actor	Possibilities	Limits
Minister Responsible for Ownership Steering	• Giving authoritative guidelines for ownership	• No direct power in the decision-making of Solidium
Minister of the Environment	• Giving authoritative guidelines for nature protection • Giving statutes	• No jurisdiction in regional state authority decisions
Members of Parliament	• Influence over public opinion • Furthering of own political goals	• No direct nor formal power
Civic actors	• Activity not bound by any formal rules	• No direct nor formal power
Regional State Authority of Kainuu ELY	• Jurisdiction over the mine	• Capacities restricted by the law and ministerial guidelines
Municipal Authority	• Making statements	• No jurisdiction over the mine

For the civic actors, experienced injustice functioned as a motivation for many to become active in the first place. Thus, the activism did not arise from simple political disagreement, but rather from the experience that the political and administrative system did not work in the way that it should have worked. Perhaps this is also the reason for the fact that the activity relied quite heavily on technical information and on the outspoken aim to inform people about what was really going on. Again, it was perceived that the authorities were not doing their job properly. This criticism was not targeted solely at administrative authorities, but also to political actions. This became apparent particularly in passages that referred to invisible forces behind the mining policies. However, the criticism was foremost targeted at the political actors within the executive, and less at parliamentary actors – MPs were excused for not doing more.

It looks, then, that MPs were almost altogether sidelined. They were not assumed any other role than that of speaking out their views – *speaking* was the activity that was required from them. This was in line with the way the MPs themselves understood their roles. To them, their main task was committee work and legislation. The distribution of work among MPs within one party followed more the lines of committee postings than those of residence. That is, nearly no one of the interviewed MPs took themselves to be playing a decisive role in their parliamentary groups relating to Talvivaara because they came from nearby areas of Talvivaara. Instead, those who were members in relevant parliamentary committees, such as the Environment Committee, were assumed a role. This did not mean that all the interviewees would not have stated something on the issue both publicly and in the interview – many did and had done this to a great extent. But within their parliamentary groups or parties they did not see themselves having a special role based on their residence.

As the *de facto* legitimacy of MPs comes from their territorial voting districts (constituencies), the geographical aspect was not totally absent from the speech of the MPs. To the contrary, many of them stressed the perspective of eastern and/or northern Finland. This was however done through ideological lenses and the interests of the region were emphasized according to one's ideological views. Furthermore, it became clear that balancing between people's views did not form a challenge for most of the MPs, as they thought that holding on to their political views and own values was their foremost task.

It appears, then, that the holder of actual political power was somewhat hard to find. Activism could then at best raise issues to the publicity and notify observations to the authorities. While the political and administrative system is geared to avoid arbitrariness of power holders through basing the system on the rule of law, it does not bend, according to this study, very flexibly to situations that deviate from business-as-usual. Political actors, even the most powerful, faced limitations from different directions. First, juridical system set framework for actors in political institutions such as the parliament and the cabinet. Those institutions have specific tasks defined in constitution and law: parliamentary work builds around legislation, and ministerial work is specifically monitored by the Chancellor of Justice. Because the Talvivaara issue did not fit plainly to the predetermined assignments, reacting (or pro-acting) to it did not have a clear slot in the political agenda. Politicians were left to define themselves whether to act, including giving statements, or not, and this decision was always a matter of politics. MPs could talk freely, but they remained fairly powerless, while cabinet members needed to be careful with what they said, not only from political but also from juridical perspective.

Second, while there are limitations deriving from the way public institutions are set up and different tasks assigned to actors within them, the Talvivaara case makes apparent the tension in terms of public/private relations. This tension is present in all state ownerships, as they are organized through Solidium. This arrangement, while brought on by the state itself, created disparity between public expectations towards to the state ownership in relation to *e.g.* jobs, the environment, and regional issues, and the actual possibilities of state actors to use power. As a result, economy has been separated from what is understood as political, and, at the same time, the realm of politics has been shrunken to institutionally defined roles. This diminished the power of both MPs and the executive. Moreover, it was difficult for the politicians to step in when difficulties occurred, although many of those difficulties, such as environmental problems, could not be confined to the economical realm.

This problem was further emphasized by the fact that Talvivaara was a stock-enlisted company, which particularly restricted what even Solidium as an owner could do. This and the organization of the state ownership induced a situation where the problems of Talvivaara were handled partially using private business *modus operandi*, not political. As the state's role was manifold to begin with, it being simultaneously owner, supervisor, and a representative of people's interests, it needed to assume different perspectives that were not always easily combined. The owner holds inside information that *e.g.* prevents it from withdrawing from ownership. Moreover, demands about environmental issues are hard to place in public, as the state has people's money at stake. This in turn drives state actors to influence the company as an owner behind the scenes, which is contrary to the idea of open and transparent governance. Hence, multiple lines of influence crossed on different levels, touching also the borders of public and private, making the border itself vague. What this study suggests through analysing the problematic embedded in the Talvivaara issue is that the use of power is subtle and it takes place in processes that are sometimes hard to trace. This is probably the case in other regimes as well, and Finland makes no exception to the rule.

References

Alapuro, R. (2005). Associations and Contention in France and Finland: Constructing the Society and Describing the Society. *Scandinavian Political Studies* Vol. 28, 4: 377–399.

Ankersmit, F. (2002). Representational Democracy. An Aesthetic Approach to Conflict and Compromise. *Common Knowledge* Vol. 8, 1: 24–46.

Barnett, M. & Duvall, R. (2005). Power in global govern-ance. In M. Barnett & R. Duvall (eds.), *Power in Global Governance*. Cambridge Studies in International Relations. Cambridge, Cambridge University Press: 1–32.

Christiano, T. (1996). *The Rule of the Many. Fundamental Issues in Democratic Theory*. Colorado/Oxford, Westview Press.

Curtin, D. (2007). Holding (Quasi-) Autonomous EU Administrative Actors to Public Account. *European Law Journal* Vol. 13, 4: 523–541.

Dalton, R. (1985). Political Parties and Political Representation. Party Supporters and Party Elites in Nine Nations. *Comparative Political Studies* Vol. 18, 3: 267–299.

Hayward, C.R. (2009). Making interest: on representation and democratic legitimacy. In I. Shapiro, S.C. Stokes, E.J. Wood & A.S. Kirshner (eds.), *Political Representation*. Cambridge, Cambridge University Press: 111–135.

Holmberg, S. (2000). Issue Agreement. In P. Esaiasson & K. Heidar (eds.), *Beyond Westminster and Congress. The Nordic Experience*. Columbus, Ohio State University Press: 155–170.

Laycock, D. (2004). Introduction. In D. Laycock (ed.), *Representa-tion and Democratic Theory*. Vancouver, UBC Press: iix–xxii.

Lehtomäki, P. (2007). Speech on 22 August 2007 at http://valtioneu-vosto.fi/ajankohtaista/puheet/puhe/fi.jsp?oid=202899, read 08 October 2013.

Luhtakallio, E. (2012). *Practicing Democracy. Local Activism and Politics in France and Finland*. Houndmills, Palgrave Macmillan.

Lupia, A. (2006). Delegation and its perils. In K. Strøm, W. C. Müller & T. Bergman (eds.), *Delegation and Accountability in Parliamentary Democracies*. Paperback ed. Oxford/New York, Oxford University Press: 33–54.

Manin, B., Przeworski A. & Stokes S. (1999). Introduction. In A. Przeworski, S. Stokes & B. Manin (eds.), *Democracy, Accountability, and Representation.* Cambridge, Cambridge University Press: 1–26.

Marsh, M. & Norris, P. (1997). Political representation in the European Parliament. *European Journal of Political Research* Vol. 32, 2: 153–164.

Marsh, M. & Wessels, B. (1997). Territorial Representation. *European Journal of Political Research* Vol. 32, 2: 227–241.

Metsämäki, M. & Nisula, P. (2006). *Aktivistit. Suomalaisten kansalaisliikkeiden tarina.* Helsinki, Edita Prima Oy.

Miller, W. E. & Stokes, D. E. (1963). Constituency Influence in Congress. *The American Political Science Review* Vol. 57, 1: 45–56.

Müller, W. C., Bergman T. & Strøm K. (2006). Parliamentary Democracy: Promise and Problems. In K. Strøm, W. C. Müller & T. Bergman (eds.), *Delegation and Accountability in Parliamentary Democracies.* Paperback edition. Oxford/New York, Oxford University Press: 3–32.

Näsström, S., (2006). Representative Democracy as Tautology: Ankersmit and Lefort on Representation, 334. *European Journal of Political Theory* Vol. 5, 3: 321–342.

Pettit, P. (2009). Varieties of public representation. In I. Shapiro, S.C. Stokes, E.J. Wood & A.S. Kirshner (eds.), *Political Representation.* Cambridge,

Cambridge University Press: 61–89.

Pietikäinen, S. & Hassi, S. (2012). *Question for written answer E-004384/2012 to the Commission.* European Parliament.

Pitkin, H. (1972). *The Concept of Representation.* Berkeley, University of California Press.

Pollak, J, Bátora, J, Mokre, M, Sigalas, E. & Slominski, P. (2009). On Political Representation. Myths and Challenges. RECON *Online Working Paper* no. 3.

Rasimus, A. (2006). *Uudet liikkeet – Radikaali kansalaisaktivismi 1990-luvun Suomessa.* Tampere, Tampere University Press.

Resolution OKV/681/1/2012. *Resolution to the complaint "Ympäristöministerin menettely Talvivaaraa koskevien lausuntojen ja kannanottojen (lausumien) esittämisessä syksyn 2011 ja kevään 2012 aikana",* Office of the Chancellor of Justice, 21 February 2013.

Saalfeld, T. (2000). Members of Parliament and Governments in Western Europe: Agency Relations and Problems of Oversight. *European Journal of Political Research* Vol. 37, 3: 353–376.

Saward, M. (2006). The Representative Claim. *Contemporary Political Theory* Vol. 5: 297–318.
— (2010). *The Representative Claim.* Oxford, Oxford University Press.

Siisiäinen, M. & Kankainen, T. (2009). Järjestötoiminnan kehitys ja tulevaisuudennäkymät Suomessa. In *Suomalaiset osal-*

listujina. Katsaus suomalaisen kansalaisvaikuttamisen tilaan ja tulevaisuuteen. Oikeusministeriön julkaisuja 2009:5. Helsinki, Oikeusministeriö (Ministry of Justice): 90–137.

Strøm, K. (2006). Parliamentary Democracy and Delegation. In K. Strøm, W. C. Müller & T. Bergman (eds.), *Delegation and Accountability in Parliamentary Democracies.* Paperback edition. Oxford/New York: Oxford University Press: 55–106.

Talvivaara Mining Company Plc (2013). *A Controlled Revival, Annual Report 2012.*

Talvivaara Mining Company Plc (2014). *2013/Financial Statements.*

Urbinati, N. & Warren, M.E. (2008). The Concept of Representation in Contemporary Democratic Theory. *Annual Review of Political Science* Vol. 11, 1: 387–412.

Ylönen, M. (1998). Liikkeen ja valtasuhteiden muodostuminen ympäristökonfliktissa. In K. Ilmonen & M. Siisiäinen (eds.), *Uudet ja vanhat liikkeet.* Tampere, Vastapaino: 245–280.

Gender Equality Achieved?
Women in Finnish Politics

MARI K. NIEMI

When it comes to gender equality, Nordic countries have an outstanding reputation. Social activism, large numbers of female MPs and the wide-scale participation of women in the workforce, form the basis of the often referred to 'Nordic equality model' (Liljeström 2009: 232). The most gender-balanced parliaments have typically been in the Nordic countries and these nations have also been among the most approving of women's leadership roles (Norris & Inglehart 2001: 127, 131–132).

However, even in generally progressive Nordic countries like Finland, women's breakthrough to top positions in politics is a fairly recent phenomenon. Leadership has traditionally been viewed as a masculine activity and political leadership is no exception. Only as recently as in the early 21st century first women occupied the most prestigious and powerful positions in Finnish politics: those of president and prime minister. At the end of 2015, only one of eight Eduskunta parties had a female chair; Christian Democrats' Sari Essayah led the smallest party of Eduskunta.

In this chapter, the focus is on political leadership. More precisely, it is on women's journey to the leadership of the three largest and the most influential political parties: the Social Democratic Party of Finland (SDP, established in 1899), the Centre Party (CP established in 1906) and the National Coalition Party (NCP established in 1918). By 2015, the Centre has had two women leaders while the SDP has had one. National Coalition is yet to have a female leader. Women's candidacies within these parties and the election of the first women leaders will be discussed in the context of women's wider representation and leadership in Finnish politics. The following questions will be examined: How does the case of Finland resonate with previous studies on women's leadership in politics? How did the first women leaders achieve leadership positions in the three parties? When it comes to allocating leadership positions in Finland, has gender equality already been achieved?

Contextual and theoretical background, data and methods

In general, women's progress to leadership positions in politics has been slow. Worldwide, in the 1960s, three women became national leaders. These were followed by six in the 1970s and seven in the 1980s. A more dramatic change took place in the 1990s when 26 women obtained positions of top executive leadership. The number of new women leaders nearly quadrupled between the 1980s and 1990s and the pattern was repeated in the 2000s (Jalalzai & Krook 2010: 7).

Norwegian Labour Party's Gro Harlem Brundtland was the first Nordic woman to become both a leader of a large political party and the prime minister in 1981. Like her contemporary, Margaret Thatcher, the Conservative leader in the United Kingdom, Brundtland has become an early example of a powerful European female prime minister. In Iceland, a female politician, Vigdís Finnbogadóttir, was elected president in 1980, but the position is more symbolic than powerful. These female leaders of the 1980s remained exemplary exceptions, as women's wider breakthrough to the most influential political positions did not materialise in the Nordic region before the 21st century.

In the Nordic context, the pace of Finnish women's breakthrough to leading positions was average, with Norway being the forerunner. In Finland, the first female candidate participated in a large party's leadership election in 1987, but it was not until 2002 before the first woman, Centre Party's Anneli Jäätteenmäki, was elected as party leader. She became prime minister in 2003. Iceland had its first female prime minister in 2009 when the Social Democratic Alliance's Jóhanna Sigurðardóttir took office. Denmark had its first female top political executive in 2011 when Helle

Thorning-Schmidt, leader of the Social Democrats since 2005, became prime minister. Unlike other Nordic countries, Sweden has not had a female prime minister yet. The Swedish Social Democrats elected its first female leader, Mona Sahlin, in 2007, but the party remained in opposition under her rule. Another major political party of Sweden, the Moderates, chose their first woman leader Anna Kinberg Batra in 2015.

The recent volume edited by Drude Dahlerup and Monique Leyenaar, *Breaking Male Dominance in Old Democracies* (2013a), offers useful tools for analysing the level and depth of male dominance in politics (Tables 1–2). Table 1 identifies the dimensions of male dominance in politics. It can also be used as an analytical instrument for scrutinising why so few women have reached top positions in politics. All measures identified in it have been, and to some extent still are, present in Finnish politics.

Women's under-representation in politics and vertical and horizontal sex segregation were clearly evident in Finnish politics until the 1980s. They impacted on women's possibilities to rise to parties' leadership positions (Figures 1–2, Table 3). The tradition of allocating not only the most valued cabinet portfo-

Table 1. Model identifying dimensions of male dominance in politics

1. Representation: Women's numerical under-representation in elected assemblies
2. Politics as a workplace: Male-coded norms and practices in elected assemblies
3. Vertical sex segregation: Unequal gender distribution of positions in political hierarchies
4. Horizontal sex segregation: Limited access of women to a range of portfolios and committees
5. Discourses and framing: Gendered perceptions of politicians
6. Public policy: Policies biased in favour of men. No concern for gender equality

Source: Dahlerup & Leyenaar 2013b: 8.

Table 2. Degree of male dominance based on numerical representation

Degree	Per centage of women elected
Male monopoly	< 10
Small minority of women	10–25
Large minority of women	25–40
Gender balance	40–60

Source: Dahlerup & Leyenaar 2013b: 10.

lios but also the lesser leadership positions within the Eduskunta
and party organisations mainly to male parliamentarians meant
that there were fewer women than men with eminent experience to choose from when recruiting party leaders. For example,
in SDP, only one of the 37 parliamentary group chairs so far
has been a woman (Tarja Filatov, 2007–2010) and only two of
the party's 22 party secretaries have been women (Ulpu Iivari,
1987–1991; Maarit Feldt-Ranta, 2005–2008). (Niemi 2014a;
Niemi 2014b: 49–57.)

The lack of women in leadership positions, such as party chairs
and prime ministers, has conditioned the previous research done
in the field, and this study at hand is not an exception. There are
more studies focusing on the details of individual women's political careers than comparative and quantitative works on the topic
(Jalalzai & Krook 2011: 8). However, in their article on gender
and party leadership, O'Neill and Stewart (2009) compared the

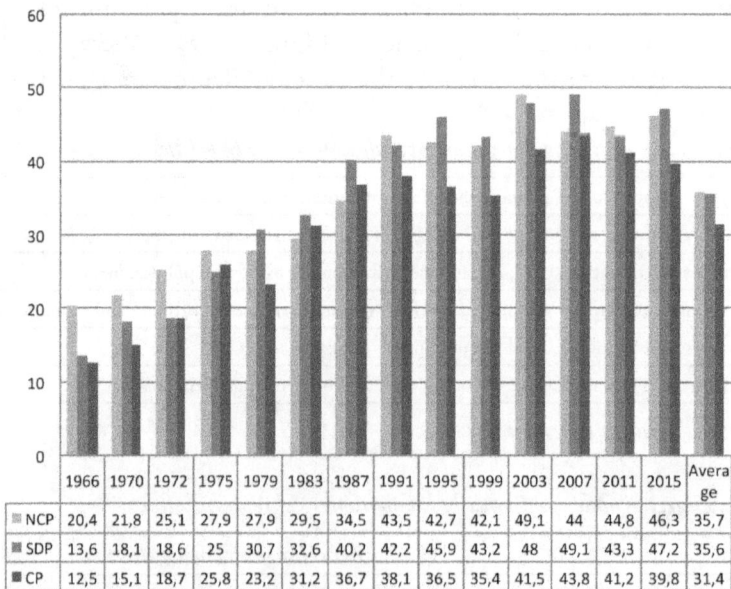

	1966	1970	1972	1975	1979	1983	1987	1991	1995	1999	2003	2007	2011	2015	Average
NCP	20,4	21,8	25,1	27,9	27,9	29,5	34,5	43,5	42,7	42,1	49,1	44	44,8	46,3	35,7
SDP	13,6	18,1	18,6	25	30,7	32,6	40,2	42,2	45,9	43,2	48	49,1	43,3	47,2	35,6
CP	12,5	15,1	18,7	25,8	23,2	31,2	36,7	38,1	36,5	35,4	41,5	43,8	41,2	39,8	31,4

Figure 1: Women's share of candidates in general elections in NCP, SDP and CP,
1966–2015 (%)

Source: Statistics Finland, General Election Statistics 1966-2015.
www.tilastokeskus.fi. Figure by: Samuli Maxenius & Annu Perälä.

Men Women

16 16 16   16
            15
        13 13   14 14   14 14
                                    12
                            11   11
                        10   10 10   10
                                9 9   8 8   9   9
                            7 7   8   9   9
                                                            5
        3   3   3   4
    1   1   2   2   2   3
1968 1970 1972 1972 1975 1976 1977 1979 1982 1983 1987 1991 1995 1999 2003 2003 2007 2010 2011 2015
          (2)   (2)

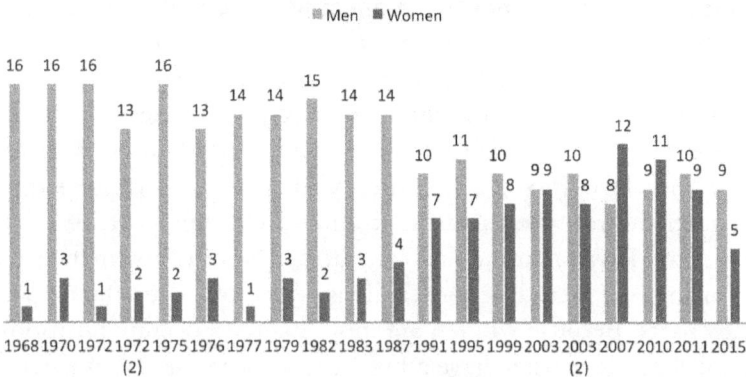

Figure 2: Male and female cabinet ministers in Finland's appointed cabinets, 1968–2015

Source: Statistics Finland: General Election Statistics 1966–2015. www.tilastokeskus.fi. Figure by: Samuli Maxenius & Annu Perälä.

experiences of male and female party leaders at the provincial and federal levels in Canada between 1980 and 2005. Canada provides a good case study given the relatively large number of women (21) included in their data of 135 party leaders. According to their research, the major parties are less likely to elect women as their leaders, while parties on the ideological left are more likely than other parties to select women (see also Bashevkin 2010; Shea & Harris 2006; Kittilson 2006: 49). In Canada, the leadership races won by women were as competitive, or even more competitive, than those won by men. Interestingly, none of the women won their leadership by acclamation, although a sizeable proportion of the men did. Moreover, the mandate secured by women leaders was less overwhelming. Stewart and O'Neill argue that the absence of consensus around the selection of female leaders, particularly in major parties, explains why men were found to enjoy longer tenures as leaders. In addition, parties led by men gained greater electoral success than those led by women.

There is also another explanation for women's shorter terms as leaders. According to several studies on women's leadership in both politics and business, women have been more likely elected to lead parties or business organisations that have lost their support or market share and reputation than in organisations that are success-

ful and prosperous. In politics, women have been elected to symbolise change and have been seen as an opportunity to gain positive
publicity for the party (O'Brien 2015; Trimble & Arscott 2003: 10,
71, 76–77; Bashevkin 2010: 72; O'Neill & Stewart 2009; Ryan *et
al.* 2010: 57, 61–62; see also Thompson 2000: 257; Haslam & Ryan
2008). Therefore, it is not only the well-known glass ceilings that
women encounter when aspiring to climb to leading positions.

Ryan and Haslam argue that after being recruited, women leaders continue to face different challenges compared to their male
counterparts. Because women are more likely to occupy positions
that are precarious, they have a higher risk for failure. Women are
either appointed to lead organisations that are in crisis or they
are not given the resources and support needed to succeed. As a
consequence, women leaders often find themselves on a glass cliff,
a slippery position that is extremely difficult to maintain (Ryan &
Haslam 2005; Haslam & Ryan 2008).

In politics, men have been the norm to which women have been
compared to. This means that women politicians have had the
pressure to prove their suitability and credibility to the masculine
world of politics. Oftentimes, that demand has been in conflict
with gender stereotypes that assume women to be more unselfish,
friendlier, more caring, more conciliatory and more empathetic
than their male counterparts, leading women to be criticised either
for being too 'soft' for politics or acting too 'rough' for their gender
(on stereotypes see Rhode & Kellerman 2007; Keohane 2010: 121,
125–126; Carli & Eagly 2007; Pittinsky *et al.* 2007; Heilman 2001;
Jensen 2008: 158, Styrkársdóttir 2013).

Gaining and losing party leadership is deeply rooted in the political and societal context, as well as in the political practices adopted
by the party in question. Different parties do not only have varying
methods of choosing their leaders; they also treat their leaders differently based on their rules, tradition and culture. Furthermore,
several contextual factors influence the evaluations made on the
candidates' abilities or the leaders' successes or failures. In the field
of leadership studies, the demand to include contextual factors in
the analysis gained ground since the 1960s and especially after the
early 1980s (Kohler & Strauss 1983; Kesner & Sebora 1994; Lowe
& Gardner 2000). Criticism concerning the lack of contextual factors in the research continued until the end of the 1990s, but since

then the situation has improved considerably (Gardner *et al.* 2010; Giambatista *et al.* 2005).

In this chapter, the primary research material consists of the 1987–2014 party leadership election results in the NCP, the CP and the SDP. During this time, 13 women have participated in the leadership elections of these parties: six in the SDP (two of them twice), four in NCP three in the CP. These figures include only those women who remained candidates until the election in the party congress. Typically, some of the candidates, both men and women, would withdraw their candidacies before the party congress if their predictable support seemed low.

The second set of data includes newspaper coverage of party leadership campaigns and leadership elections in three of the largest Finnish daily papers in 1987–2011: *Aamulehti* (AL), *Helsingin Sanomat* (HS) and *Turun Sanomat* (TS). This material includes coverage of 14 leadership campaigns and elections (SDP five, CP four, and NCP four) selected on the basis that an actual leadership succession followed the election. While election results provide concrete information on women's candidacies and success in their respective parties' elections, the newspaper material is useful in determining the duration and phases of the campaigns. It also provides valuable information on the historical and societal contexts of the elections. Furthermore, analysing the newspaper coverage makes it possible to scrutinise the gradual change of attitude around women's candidacies and to examine the arguments that support and challenge the idea of having a female leader. The research method used in the analysis is qualitative content analysis combined with historical contextualising.

Women in Finnish politics – an overview

Some of the early steps taken by women in Finnish politics were pioneering. Women in Finland were the first in Europe to obtain suffrage in 1906 together with Finnish men. In the first general elections in 1907, 19 women MPs were elected. Finland had its first woman minister in 1926 when Miina Sillanpää (SDP) became the second minister of social affairs. However, despite the promising start, it was not before 1948 when the second female minister was appointed.

In the beginning of women's journey to the top, women's organi-

sations within political parties played an important role in elevating
female candidates and pressuring parties to share high-profile positions between men and women at all levels of organisational structure (Kuusipalo 1999: 56–57; Kuusipalo 2011: 9, 69; Lähteenmäki
2000: 238; Jutila 2003: 186–191). In the 1970s, women's sections
of the Finnish parties campaigned resiliently to enhance female
representation. Subsequently, more women were elected both as
vice leaders of their parties and as cabinet ministers. During the
1970s, it became an unwritten norm to include one or two female
ministers in the cabinet (Kuusipalo 2006: 28). Still, the distribution of work in the government remained gendered — male politicians were allocated the most valued portfolios of prime minister,
finance minister and foreign minister. Until the 1990s, only one
to three women were included in cabinets, so the state of male
monopoly prevailed in the governments (Figure 2, Table 2.)

From the viewpoint of Finnish women's political activity and
representation in the parliament, the 1980s and early 1990s were
a time of rapid growth (see the chapter by Bengtsson). The rising
share of women candidates — from 26.1 per cent in the election of
1979 to 41.2 per cent in 1991 — was followed by respective growth
in the number of female MPs: from 26 per cent in 1979 to 38.5
per cent in 1991. From the perspective of voting activity, women
overtook men for the first time in the 1987 elections. Since then,
turnout among female voters has been higher than among male
voters. Overall, turnout in Finland has declined (Figure 3, table 3).

After the 1987 election, women formed a large minority in the
parliament with 31.5 per cent. Nonetheless, only 22.2 per cent of
the cabinet ministers were women. Since 1991, there has been, by
definition, a gender balance in Finnish governments, with a 40–60
per cent share between men and women. Since the 2007 elections,
representation in the Eduskunta has also become equal (Tables
2–3). However, women's leadership in the Finnish political parties
can still be described as rare and irregular. Apart from a few examples, women leaders have served only relatively short periods, most
of them in the smaller parties (Table 4).

The first Finnish female presidential candidate was Helvi Sipilä
(Liberal People's Party) in the 1982 elections. The first woman to
run for the leadership of a large political party was Vappu Taipale
(SDP) in 1987. Lacking any real chance to become elected, Sipilä's

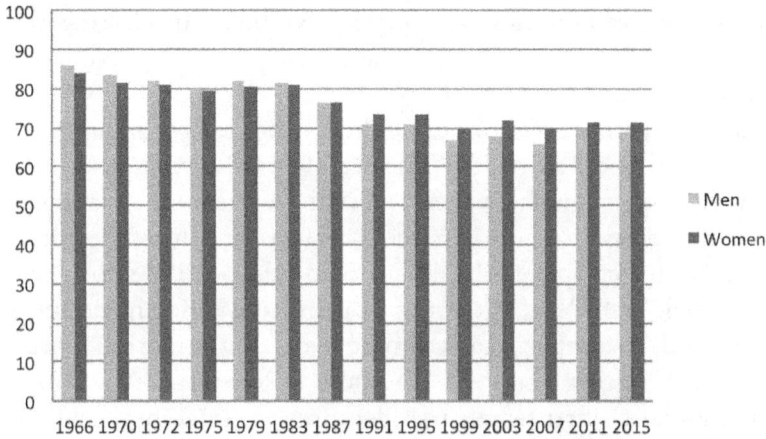

Figure 3: *Voter turnout percentage of men and women in Finland, 1966–2015*

Source: *Statistics Finland: General Election Statistics 1966-2015.*
www.tilastokeskus.fi. Figure by Samuli Maxenius & Annu Perälä.

Table 3. *Women's Share of Candidates, Votes and Elected in General Elections*
1966–2015, %

Year	Share of candidates	Vote share	Share of elected
1966	16.0	15.3	16.5
1970	17.3	19.3	21.5
1972	21.1	21.0	21.5
1975	24.2	24.9	23.0
1979	26.1	27.9	26.0
1983	29.5	29.9	31.0
1987	36.0	35.3	31.5
1991	41.2	39.2	38.5
1995	39.1	36.6	33.5
1999	37.0	38.3	37.0
2003	39.8	42.6	37.4
2007	39.9	42.1	42.0
2011	39.0	41.8	42.5
2015	39.4	51.5	41.5

Source: *Statistics Finland. www.tilastokeskus.fi.*

and Taipale's candidacies were mainly symbolic. In electing the first female president of Finland, the candidacy of Elisabeth Rehn (Swedish People's Party) in the presidential elections of 1994 was an important step. Prior to her candidacy, this long-standing parliamentarian had become the first female minister of defence in the world. Although she was not elected president, she made her way to the second round where she won 46.1 per cent of the votes. Rehn's candidacy opened the discussion on the possibility of electing a female president, gathering women from different political backgrounds to campaign for a common goal. Importantly, it paved the way for another long-term MP, Tarja Halonen (SDP), who was elected Finland's first female president in 2000. Halonen held the office for two consecutive terms until 2012.

The first woman to be elected to lead a large political party was Anneli Jäätteenmäki (CP) in 2002. She worked shortly also as Finland's first female prime minister in 2003. Other women who have been elected to lead a large party include Jutta Urpilainen (SDP, 2008–2014) and Mari Kiviniemi (CP, 2010–2012). Interestingly, women's breakthrough to political leadership in Finland took place during the same period, beginning in the late 1980s, when both the political importance and media visibility of party leaders and the prime minister grew notably.

Women's party leadership candidacies and the first breakthroughs

Finnish politics has not been an exception in the sense that women were first elected to lead small political parties and served as vice-chairs of the larger parties. Before the 21st century, Finnish women led parties that had typically less than 10 per cent of the Eduskunta seats. The Democratic Alternative was the first party to select a woman as its leader in 1986. The Greens (1987), as well as the Rural Party (1991) and the Liberal People's Party (1993) followed suit. Of the current parties represented in the Eduskunta, the NCP, the Finns Party (previously known as the True Finns) and the Swedish Peoples Party have not had a woman leader by 2015. So far, the Greens have the most gender equal leader record; half of its ten leaders have been women (Tables 4–5).

In a nutshell, all three large parties elect their leaders in the statutory party congresses held nowadays every other year. Though the leaders are elected in the party congresses for two-year terms, there are notable differences in parties' inner democracy (see the chapter by Koskimaa). In SDP, the number of representatives entitled to vote in the party congress has been smallest, even though it was increased from 350 to 500 prior to the 2014 party congress. Unlike SDP, the CP and the NCP do not have fixed amounts of delegates entitled to vote in the party congress, as the number of representatives is determined by the number of party members. During the time frame analysed, there have not been less than 700 representatives in the congresses of the NCP. However, the CP is on its own level: in the period studied, the number of votes given in its leader elections has always exceeded 2000. (Niemi 2014a: 23–25.)

The gatekeeper role of political parties has been central in terms of women's political representation and in the efforts to increase it (Kunovich & Paxton 2005: 540; see also O'Neill & Stewart 2009: 752). Interestingly, even public statements about achieving gender equality have not translated into reality within parties (see Sainsbury 2004: 73–74). SDP is an apt example of this. The party was founded in 1899 and in its famous 1903 Forssa congress' founding principles ('The Forssa Program'), it called for equality between men and women, including equal suffrage. Even though equality issues have remained at the heart of SDP's political discourse ever since, key positions within the party were allocated to male members. Hence, SDP has not stood apart from its rivals.

The role of women's organisations within the leading parties in promoting women's leadership has been substantial. Typically, they either nominated their own chairs for the positions or gave public support for another woman candidate. However, sometimes the well-intentioned efforts may have had undesirable consequences, as being seen as a specific 'women's candidate' may have contributed negatively to the female candidates' prospects. When women candidates were mostly seen as a protagonist for women's issues, they had difficulties to successfully compete with their male colleagues who were typically seen as general politicians fit to represent both male and female voters' interests. The strong presence of women's organisations may thus even have led to the marginalisation of female candidates (Kittilson 2006: 45; Kuusipalo 2011: 112; Niemi 2014b).

Table 4. Women Leaders of Political Parties Represented in the Eduskunta until 2015

Leader	Party	Years in office	Party size (seats of total 200)
Kristiina Halkola	Democratic Alternative	1986–1989	10
Heidi Hautala	The Greens of Finland	1987–1991	4
Marja-Liisa Löyttyjärvi	Democratic Alternative	1989–1990	4
Kaarina Koivistoinen	Liberal People's Party	1990–1992	0*
Tina Mäkelä	Finnish Rural Party	1991–1992	7
Tuulikki Ukkola	Liberal People's Party	1993–1995	1
Tuija Brax	The Greens of Finland	1995–1997	9
Satu Hassi	The Greens of Finland	1997–2001	9
Suvi-Anne Siimes	Left Alliance	1998–2006	22
Anneli Jäätteenmäki	Centre Party	2002–2003	48
Päivi Räsänen	Christian Democrats	2004–2015	7
Tarja Cronberg	The Greens of Finland	2005–2009	14
Jutta Urpilainen	Social Democratic Party	2008–2014	45
Anni Sinnemäki	The Greens of Finland	2009–2011	15
Mari Kiviniemi	Centre Party	2010–2012	51
Sari Essayah	Christian Democrats	2015–	5

*Party entered to parliament after the female leader had been elected in the general elections of 1991.

Seats in the parliament refer to the party's size prior to the election of a woman leader.

Source: Statistics Finland. General Election Statistics 1966-2015. www.tilastokeskus.fi.

Though SDP was not the first large Finnish political party to choose a woman leader, its women's organisation was the first to put up a female candidate to run for a party's leadership in 1987. The candidacy of Vappu Taipale was part of the SDP's women's protest against male dominance within the party. To challenge the status quo, the SDP's women's organisation nominated female candidates for all key positions, including that of the party leader. In the newspaper coverage, the women's growing activity and enthusiasm were received with astonishment and even with disapproval (TS 4.6.1987; HS 31.3.1987, HS 4.6.1987; HS 6.6.1987; AL 4.6.1987). Journalists questioned women's eagerness to contest the selections

Table 5. Women Candidates in Leadership Elections of the SDP, CP and NCP, 1987–2014

Year	Party	Candidate	Number of candidates	Share of votes I round (%)	Share of votes II round (%)
1987	SDP	Vappu Taipale	2	18.6	–
1990	CP	Eeva Kuuskoski-Vikatmaa	4	39.66	47.16
1991	SDP	Tarja Halonen	4	5.82	–
1991	NCP	Sirpa Pietikäinen	3	11.87	–
1993	NCP	Maija Perho-Santala	2	33.17	–
1993	SDP	Tarja Halonen	4	4.0	–
2002	CP	Anneli Jäätteen-mäki*	6	55.91	–
2004	NCP	Marjo Matikainen-Kallström	6	22.49	–
2005	SDP	Tuula Haatainen	3	3.14	–
2008	SDP	Jutta Urpilainen*	5	37.7	62.28
2008	SDP	Tarja Filatov	5	18	–
2008	SDP	Miapetra Kumpula-Natri	5	12.57	–
2010	CP	Mari Kiviniemi*	4	46.18	56.73
2014	SDP	Jutta Urpilainen	2	48.6	–
2014	NCP	Paula Risikko	3	30.89	41.10

Elected as a party leader.

Table 5 includes all the female candidates that have taken part of the Social Democratic Party's (SDP), the Centre Party's (CP) and the National Coalition Party's (NCP) leadership elections. Those of the candidates, both men and women, that withdrew their candidacies before the election in the party congress, are excluded from the figures. The second election round takes place if there are more than two candidates and none of the candidates receives more than half of the given votes. Table 5 includes the figures of those second rounds wherein a women candidate proceeded to the second round.

Source: Niemi 2014a: 23–25.

that already seemed clear. It was claimed that women ran just for the sake of running and that they only wanted to 'cut in', 'crush' and 'peddle' their candidates to all available leading posts (TS 4.6.1987; HS 31.3.1987, HS 4.6.1987; HS 6.6.1987; AL 4.6.1987).

Characteristically for the party culture of the time, the unanimity on Pertti Paasio, the leader-to-be at that time, had already been achieved among the party's inner circle well in advance of the party congress. Although Taipale lost the election to Paasio, women's criticism helped to break a lower glass ceiling. The party chose itself the first female party secretary in its history, Ulpu Iivari. Considering the reactions around Taipale's candidacy, it is notable that just three years later, a woman candidate was close to being elected by another party. A doctor by profession, MP and Centre Party's vice-chair Eeva Kuuskoski-Vikatmaa was an exceptionally popular politician, also beyond the Centre Party, and nearly became elected as her party's first woman leader in 1990.

In the newspapers, it was argued that Kuuskoski-Vikatmaa could improve her party's image, cooperate over parties' borderlines and be able to win over the urban voters (HS 6.4.1990; HS 7.4.1990; HS 22.4.1990; HS 15.6.1990). In the party congress, Kuuskoski-Vikatmaa won the first round of the election and made her way to the second round, which she then lost to the younger and relatively unknown Esko Aho. While many journalists admitted that Kuuskoski-Vikatmaa had actually been their personal favourite, they interpreted that choosing Aho was a wiser and safer solution. Afterwards, the idea of choosing a woman was seen as tempting but risky (TS 17.6.1990; HS 14.6.1990; TS 16.6.1990).

Although some of the first women's candidacies were welcomed with surprise, confusion and even reluctance by the press, the attitude soon changed. In several later leadership elections, journalists openly favoured female candidates. Over the course of the years studied, the presence of a woman candidate became generally interpreted as a positive sign of the party's progressive nature and female friendliness, whereas absence of one was seen to send the opposite message. Still, apart from Eeva Kuuskoski-Viktamaa's success in 1990, women candidates' support in party congress elections remained typically low, underlining the symbolic nature of their efforts (Table 5).

In some examples, the coverage of the political journalists showed such excitement around the prospect of a female candidate that it could be described as political campaigning. Furthermore, there were elections wherein the journalists' distinctive enthusiasm to see a female candidate run or be elected clearly exceeded the backing these candidates had within their parties. This was the case in 1994 when *Aamulehti* expressed multiple times the wish to see

Sirpa Pietikäinen to run for the NCP's leadership, and in 2004 when both the wider public and the media were increasingly excited about Marjo Matikainen-Kallström's candidacy, again in the NCP. However, the party organisation remained incredulous.

Even though the results of the leadership elections do not give an indication on the number of women politicians who decided not to run for leadership, they provide information on women's concrete activity in running for the top positions in their parties (Table 5). In the nearly thirty years studied, a woman candidate was elected three times: 2002, 2008 and 2010. There were altogether 15 party congresses of the SDP, NCP, or the CP in which the party leader changed. In 13 of them, there was at least one female candidate. Moreover, a female candidate – Maija Perho of the NCP – challenged the incumbent leader of her party, Pertti Salolainen, in 1993.

The CP was finally the first Finnish large political party to choose a woman leader in 2002. Anneli Jäätteenmäki was elected after serving first as a vice leader and then, more importantly, as a substitute leader of her party. Unlike several cases both preceding and following hers, her election as party chair did not create much discussion from the perspective of gender. This may best be explained by Jäätteenmäki's pathway to power. The public, as well as the Centre supporters, had already seen her occupy the position temporarily and succeed in her role, making her seem like a natural and, unlikely for a woman candidate, a safer choice.

Although there was variation between the elections, newspapers' treatment of male and female candidates typically showed deep-rooted gender stereotypes. Female candidates were oftentimes described as fresher, kinder and more upstanding than their male counterparts. Women were also generally believed to have good media and cooperation skills. Nonetheless, their mental strength and leadership abilities were often questioned (HS 10.5.1990; TS 16.6.1990; AL 4.5.1991; TS 25.4.1991; TS 25.5.1991, AL 2.6.1991; AL 11.1.2002; AL 13.1.2002; TS 30.1.2002; HS 30.1.2002; TS 11.2.2002; TS 25.2.2002; TS 12.2.2008; HS 25.2.2008; HS 5.4.2008). Typically, choosing a female leader was seen both as a strong and positive message from the parties and as a braver and riskier choice than choosing a male leader (see for example TS 4.4.1990; HS 7.4.1990; HS 14.6.1990; TS 16.6.1990, TS 17.6.1990; TS 7.6.2008; HS 7.6.2008).

The election of SDP's first female leader Jutta Urpilainen in 2008 seemed to tick all the boxes regarding the assumed gendered stereotypes in the media. The party's difficulties to renew and attract young voters had been in the headlines and, due to the electoral defeat in the 2007 elections, the incumbent leader Eero Heinäluoma resigned. By the time candidates were nominated, being a woman was widely viewed as an advantage by journalists. A 'facelift', 'rejuvenating surgery', the election of SDP leader was often described as a task that was inextricably linked to the party's public image and its efforts to look younger and fresher in order to attract young voters and educated women. The image of the leader-to-be was considered important as the leader 'provides the party its face' (HS 12.2.2008; HS 13.2.2008; HS 16.2.2008; HS 23.2.2008; HS 24.5.2008).

Among the nine candidates, Urpilainen was a second-term MP with a master of education degree. At the age 32, she was the youngest and one of the least experienced candidates (HS 5.6.2008). Her greatest strengths were 'freshness' and 'spotlessness' (HS 11.5.2008; see also HS 1.6.2008). In the end, Urpilainen won a sound victory at the party congress. After the election, her historical victory was noted but not specifically highlighted. Her age and lack of experience in both leadership and politics sparked more debate than her gender, although that discussion may have been sped up by the fact that she was a woman. Selecting such a 'fledgling' politician was interpreted both as a risk and as an opportunity for the party (HS 7.6.2008a, HS 7.6.2008b; HS 7.6.2008c; HS 7.6.2008d).

Instead of referring to the importance of gender equality, Urpilainen's selection was more often supported by utility considerations: a young female leader might improve the party's image, attract voters and bring the party back to its former glory. A young female leader also allowed the party to enjoy positive publicity and to stand as a visible symbol of change. Interestingly, when the Centre Party chose its second woman leader, Mari Kiviniemi, in 2010, the situation was relatively similar. The party was viewed as needing a new start after a long and wearing campaign funding scandal, image problems and diminishing support. It was argued that as a visible symbol of change, a young woman leader could provide the party the fresh start it desperately needed.

Discussion

In comparative terms, the Finnish case displays several similarities with other countries. In Finland, small or medium-size parties elected women leaders earlier than major political parties. Similarly, parties on the left or in the centre of the political spectrum have been more open to women's leadership than those on the right. With only a few exceptions, women's tenures as leaders have been short.

It needs to be kept in mind that the number of women who have become leaders of large political parties is still very low. Consequently, wider generalisations are not possible. However, the overall picture of women's breakthrough to the leadership in Finnish politics is, in many ways, similar to the experiences in other Western democracies. The same applies to women's rise to leadership positions in the business sector. In the media, women leaders were seen through gendered lenses, which has, due to gender stereotypes and women's novelty as leaders, given them favourable position in times when parties faced troubles. Journalists' interpretations of the candidates' strengths and weaknesses, as well as their abilities to perform convincingly and charismatically in the media, have become an essential part of discussion in party leadership contests. Candidates' skills in attracting and handling media publicity were especially underlined in connection with women candidates.

Extending more in-depth analysis to small parties' leadership elections might shed some more light to the gendered nature of leadership recruitment in Finland, but some contextual factors limit the explanatory power of those cases. Firstly, this is due to the different role and power of the small parties when compared to the largest ones. Without diminishing the importance of the leaders of smaller parties, their role in national politics is different from the leaders of the major parties from among whom prime ministers are recruited. Together with the Eduskunta elections, the leadership elections of the largest parties are the most important arena of power struggle in national politics. This difference is also likely to affect the leader selection process and the expectations placed on the leaders. It may also explain why the leadership of smaller parties has been easier to achieve for women than the equivalent role in the large parties.

Secondly, five of the thirteen women leaders of the small or mid-size parliamentary parties come from the Greens. In the Finnish party map, the Greens are a newcomer (established in 1987), and the context of its leadership elections differs notably from those of the three large parties. Of all the Finnish parliamentary parties, the Greens are the only one wherein the leadership has historically been shared equally between men and women, so the arguments and discussions around its leadership elections stem from very different grounds. Within the Greens, women leaders do not symbolise novelty or regeneration, but are an ordinary phenomenon. Thirdly, women's leadership within several smaller parties took place already in the late 1980s and during the 1990s. Since then, both the role of political parties, through the major constitutional reform, and the role of the media have changed profoundly.

Although women have taken actively part in leadership elections, the overall number of female candidates has been smaller than that of male candidates. The fact that men have outnumbered women in the leadership races has sometimes been used as an explanation of women's exiguity in the top posts. There is also some evidence that in politics women are more self-critical than similarly-experienced male politicians, for example, when it comes to deciding which positions they are suitable for or can aspire to (Lawless & Fox 2010). Other important aspects concerning candidate recruitment are the internal attitudes and support for male and female politicians within party organisations.

However, the lesser amount of women in the leadership elections is best explained by the political reality of the late 1980s and 1990s. Overall, leadership in Finnish society continued to be male-dominated (see the chapter by Murto). In politics, the idea of a woman as a serious candidate was not yet widely adopted. Apart from a few rare exceptions, women's candidacies remained symbolic by nature until the 21st century. It is likely that the apparent lack of opportunities to succeed in the election reduced women's willingness to run. There was also another, perhaps even more important reason, contributing to fewer women running than men. Until the SDP leadership election in 2008, women candidates were interpreted as each other's competitors. Female candidates were mostly believed to gain support from their female, perhaps particularly feminist fellows, within the party. Therefore, there was little ground for nominating more than one woman candidate as several women would only end up sharing already limited votes. This logic was present also in the reasoning of the women politicians themselves who sometimes withdrew their candidacies in favour of another female candidate. Furthermore, until the 1990s, party leadership selection processes tended to lack true competition and openness. In some cases, parties' inner circles reached unanimity about the leader-to-be well in advance of the party congresses. However, during the period analysed, parties slowly changed their practices concerning leadership elections. They have become more open and democratic. This transition, together with the media's appetite for female politicians, seemed to have improved women's possibilities to become elected.

Based on the media coverage of leadership elections, it is striking how rarely women candidates themselves or their supporters publicly argued for a woman's 'right' to claim leadership for equality's sake. They were careful not to openly criticise male dominance within their parties. It is of course likely that some of them did not find the state of the play problematic. However, to those who were unhappy with the status quo, it was difficult to openly and directly challenge it, as contesting male-dominance would have been a threat to party's integral unity.

References

Bashevkin, S. (2010). When do outsiders break in? Institutional circumstances of party leadership victories by women in Canada. *Commonwealth & Comparative Politics* Vol. 48, 1: 72–90.

Carli, L. L. & Eagly, A. H. (2007). Overcoming Resistance to Women Leaders. The Importance of Leadership Style. In B. Kellerman & D. L. Rhode (eds.), *Women & Leadership. The State of Play and Strategies for Change.* San Francisco, Jossey-Bass, a Wiley Imprint: 127–148.

Dahlerup, D. & Leyenaar, M. (eds.) (2013a). *Breaking Male Dominance in Old Democracies.* Oxford, Oxford University Press.

Dahlerup, D. & Leyenaar, M. (2013b). Introduction. In D. Dahlerup & M. Leyenaar (eds.), *Breaking Male Dominance in Old Democracies.* Oxford, Oxford University Press: 1–23.

Gardner, W. L., Lowe, K. B., Moss, T. W., Mahoney, K. T. & Cogliser, C. C. (2010). Scholarly leadership of the study of leadership: A review of The Leadership Quarterly's second decade, 2000–2009. *The Leadership Quarterly* Vol. 21, 6: 922–958.

Giambatista, R. C.; Rowe, W. G. & Riaz, S. (2005). Nothing succeeds like succession: A Critical review of leader succession literature since 1994. *Leadership Quarterly* Vol. 16, 6: 963–991.

Haslam, A. S. & Ryan, M. K. (2008). The Road to the glass cliff: Differences in the perceived suitability of men and women to leadership positions in succeed-

ing and failing organizations. *The Leadership Quarterly* Vol. 19, 5: 530–546.

Heilman, M. E. (2001). Description and Prescription. How Gender Stereotypes Prevent Women's Ascent Up the Organizational Ladder. *Journal of Social Issues* Vol. 57, 4: 657–674.

Jalalzai, F. & Krook, M. (2010). Beyond Hillary and Benazir. Women's Political Leadership Worldwide. *International Political Science Review* Vol. 31, 5: 5–23.

Jensen, J. S. (2008). *Women political Leaders. Breaking the Highest Glass Ceiling.* New York, Palgrave Macmillan.

Jutila, K. (2003). *Yksillä säännöillä kaksilla korteilla? Empiirinen tutkimus Suomen keskustan sisäisestä päätöksenteosta.* Doctoral Dissertation, Tampere, Tampereen yliopisto.

Keohane, N. O. (2010). *Thinking about Leadership.* Princeton, Princeton University Press.

Kesner, I. F. & Sebora, T. C. (1994). Executive Succession: Past, Present and Future. *Journal of Management* Vol. 20, 2: 327–372.

Kittilson, M. C. (2006). *Challenging Parties, Changing Parliaments. Women and Elected Office in Contemporary Western Europe. Parliaments and Legislatures.* Columbus, The Ohio State University Press.

Kohler, T. & Strauss, G. (1983). Executive Succession: Literature review and research issues. *Administration in Mental Health* Vol 11, 1:11–21.

Kunovich, S. & Paxton, P. (2005). Pathways to Power: The Role of Political Parties in Women's National Political Representation. *American Journal of Sociology* Vol. 111, 2: 505–552.

Kuusipalo, J. (1999). Finnish women in politics. In P. Lipponen & M. Setälä (eds.), *Women in Finland*. Helsinki, Otava: 55–78.

— (2006). Nainen poliitikkona ja poliitikko naisena: Politiikan sukupuolittuminen Suomessa. In A. Moring (ed.), *Sukupuolen politiikka: Naisten äänioikeuden 100 vuotta Suomessa*. Helsinki, Otava: 27–34.

— (2011). *Sukupuolittunut poliittinen edustus Suomessa*. Doctoral dissertation. Tampere, Tampereen yliopisto.

Lawless, J. L. & Fox, R. L. (2010). *It Still Takes A Candidate. Why Women Don't Run for Office*. Revised Edition. New York, Cambridge University Press.

Liljeström, M. (2009). Nordic gender equality and Finland. In S. Tiinen *et al.* (ed. committee), *Challenges for Finland and Democracy. Parliament of Finland Centennial 12*. Helsinki, Edita: 232–259.

Lowe, K. B. & Gardner, W. L. (2000). Ten years of the Leadership Quarterly: Contributions and Challenges for the Future. *Leadership Quarterly* Vol. 11, 4: 459–514.

Lähteenmäki, M. (2000). *Vuosisadan naisliike. Naiset ja sosialidemokratia 1900-luvun Suomessa*. Helsinki, Sosialidemokraattiset Naiset.

Niemi, M. K. (2014a). *Kaksi tietä huipulle. Media ja puoluejohtajuus Suomessa naisten n234*

Suomessa naisten noususta populismin aaltoon. Doctoral dissertation. Turun yliopiston julkaisuja, sarja C 385. Turku, Turun yliopisto.

— (2014b). Naisten työläs taival puolueiden johtajiksi. Naisten puoluejohtajuuden mahdollistuminen sosiaalidemokraateissa, keskustassa ja kokoomuksessa 1987–2010. *Historiallinen Aikakauskirja* Vol. 112, 1: 46–60.

Norris, P. & Inglehart, R. (2001). Cultural Obstacles to Equal Representation. *The journal of Democracy* Vol. 12, 3: 126–140.

O'Brien D. Z. (2015). Rising to the Top: Gender, Political Performance, and Party Leadership in Parliamentary Democracies. *American Journal of Political Science*. (Early version published online 10 February 2015).

O'Neill, B. A & Stewart, D. K. (2009). Gender and Political Party Leadership in Canada. *Party Politics* Vol. 15, 6: 737–757.

Pittinsky, T. L., Bacon, L. M. & Welle, B. (2007). The Great Women Theory of Leadership? Perils of Positive Stereotypes and Precarious Pedestals. In B. Kellerman & D.L. Rhode (eds.), *Women & Leadership. The State of Play and Strategies for Change*. San Francisco, Jossey-Bass, a Wiley Imprint, 93–125.

Rhode, D. L. & Kellerman, B. (2007). Women and Leadership. The State of Play. In B. Kellerman & D.L. Rhode (eds.), *Women & Leadership. The State of Play and Strategies for Change*. San Francisco, Jossey-Bass, a Wiley Imprint, 1–62.

Ryan, M. K. & Haslam, A.S. (2005). The glass cliff: Evidence that women are over-represented in precarious leadership positions. *British Journal of Management* Vol. 16, 2: 81–90.

Ryan, M. K., Haslam, A. S. & Kulich C. (2010). Politics and the Glass Cliff: Evidence that women are preferentially selected to contest hard-to-win seats. *Psychology of Women Quarterly*. Vol. 34, 1: 56–64.

Sainsbury, D. (2004). Women's Political Representation in Sweden: Discursive Politics and Institutional Presence. *Scandinavian Political Studies* Vol. 27, 1: 65–87.

Shea, D. M. & Harris, R. C. (2006). Women and Local Party Leadership. *Journal of Women, Politics and Policy* Vol. 28, 12: 61–85.

Styrkársdóttir, A. (2013). Iceland. Breaking Male Dominance by Extraordinary Means. In D. Dahlerup & M. Leyenaar (eds.), *Breaking Male Dominance in Old Democracies*. Oxford, Oxford University Press: 124–145.

Thompson, J. B. (2000). *Political Scandal. Power and visibility in the media age*. Cambridge, Polity Press.

Trimble, L. & Arscott, J. (2003). *Still Counting? Women in Politics Across Canada*. Peterborough, Broadview Press.

Evolution of Political Power in Finland

LAURI KARVONEN, HEIKKI PALOHEIMO & TAPIO RAUNIO

The chapters of this book have provided a multi-dimensional portrait of political power in Finland in recent decades. It goes without saying that when an object of study is approached from so many different angles, no single or self-evident trend will appear. But even given the variety of themes addressed in the volume, perhaps the best overall conclusion is that change is rarely once-and-for-all and definite. Rather, it is gradual and not without exceptions, and this also goes for phenomena where an overall trend is quite visible. For better or worse, political and social reality tends to be a question of 'on the one hand, and on the other'. It remains the task of social and political scientists to make sense of this sometimes bewildering reality.

A detailed summary of the findings of each individual analysis is not called for in this concluding chapter. The introductory chapter has already highlighted many of them, and for a detailed summary the reader is referred to the concluding sections of each chapter. Instead, this final chapter will reflect on themes that constitute central elements in several of the analyses. In so doing it attempts to highlight overarching trends in Finnish politics in the past four decades and assess their wider significance.

Politics in context: preconditions of change

The development of the core areas of political life in Finland – party politics and institutional relations – cannot be understood except against the background of general change in Finnish society and in Finland's international position. In both these areas, the magnitude and rapidity of change have been remarkable; the transformation itself appears rather unexpected given the previous conditions that largely determined the nature of political life in Finland.

Most importantly, Finland gradually developed from a highly conflict-prone society to a much more consensual polity. The intensity of social and political conflict dated back to the civil war immediately after Finland's independence. The revolutionary wing of the socialist movement was strong in Finland, and the nearness of Soviet-Russia also increased the fear and hostility towards socialism among the bourgeois circles. From the 1960s on, however, new ideas of conflict resolution emerged. According to this line of thought conflicts form a natural part of a pluralist society. We cannot solve conflicts once and for all, but we can manage them in various ways and thus foster social cohesion. This cultural change paved the way for a more orderly process of corporatist interest intermediation. A system of basically Scandinavian-style corporatist incomes policy was introduced in the late 1960s. In the 1970s it was institutionalized in the form of tripartite negotiations between the central labour market organizations and the government at regular intervals. This cooperation made the systematic and planned development of the Finnish welfare state possible. An intensive growth of the welfare state ensued. In 1960, the share of the total public sector expenditure of Finland's GDP was 26 per cent. In 2014 it was no less than 58 per cent.

As political parties became engaged as important participants in the effort to expand the welfare state, a more consensus-prone culture emerged also in the party system. The cleavage between socialist and bourgeois parties diminished when left-wing socialists and communists, too, committed themselves to parliamentary democracy, and right-wing parties became more tolerant towards a benevolent, relatively large welfare state. As a result, both the coalition capacity and coalition elasticity of political parties increased. The life span of cabinets increased. Up until the 1970s, minority coalitions and caretaker cabinets were common, and the average life span of cabinets was no more than one year. From the 1980s onwards, all cabinets have been majority coalitions, and in most cases they have remained in office over the whole electoral term.

One feature of consensus-seeking in Finnish politics is that since 1987 all but one of the Finnish governments have been surplus coalitions, although two of them (the cabinets led by Aho in 1994 and Stubb in 2014), as a result of internal disagreements, have ended their tenures as minimal winning coalitions. The Sipilä three-party cabinet formed after the 2015 elections between the Centre Party, the Conservatives and the Finns Party is, technically speaking, a minimal winning coalition. It too, however, is wide in ideological scope and encompassing in terms of parliamentary support (over sixty per cent of the seats in parliament). Given the stability and pragmatism of government coalitions, political parties have been willing to strengthen the parliamentary features of the political system at the expense of the powers of the president.

Equally crucial, the collapse of the Soviet Union in 1991 radically changed the context of Finnish foreign policy, indeed Finnish politics at large. It made possible the abandonment of personalized presidential leadership in foreign policy and created opportunities for an expanded co-operation with Western nations. In 1995 Finland joined the European Union (EU). This decision boosted demands to reduce the powers of the president, and to make cabinet responsible for national EU policy. In the 1990s amendments were made to the constitution that enlarged the powers of the government and parliament at the expense of the president. On a more general level, the demise of the Soviet Union marked the definite disappearance of a factor that had conditioned parliamentary politics and inter-party relations since the Second World War.

Elite-driven parliamentarization

The 1970s were the period when the role of the president as the effective executive head peaked. After the Second World War foreign policy and especially Finnish relations with the Soviet Union were at the top of the priority list of Finnish politics. The president was the uncontested leader of Finnish foreign policy. Towards the end of the long tenure of President Urho Kekkonen (1956–1981), however, tensions mounted against the strong powers of the president. The way Kekkonen used presidential prerogatives to their fullest extent gradually convinced parties and parliamentarians that a reform was necessary. Two presidential powers in particular, cabinet formation and the dissolution of parliament followed by premature parliamentary elections, gave the president basically unlimited power over political parties. Unlike his predecessors, Kekkonen did not hesitate to use these powers actively. Parties and politicians knew that they could not gain cabinet office without the acceptance of Kekkonen.

In 2000, a totally new constitution entered into force. It codified amendments made to the old constitution in the 1990s, and reduced the powers of the president even further. From 2000 onwards, the Finnish political system is essentially a parliamentary system where the president's powers are confined to foreign policy conducted jointly with the cabinet. Parliament is responsible for the selection of the prime minister and parties decide on cabinet coalitions; the president appoints the cabinet, but this is a purely formal act and does not entail real political power. The president cannot dismiss ministers, nor call for premature parliamentary elections; by the same token, he/she has no real powers over legislation. The cabinet is responsible for national EU policy.

Before 2012, the president often participated in the meetings of the European Council, the summit of the EU leaders. This created certain confusion about the role of the Finnish president in EU affairs. Presidents Martti Ahtisaari (1994–2000) and Tarja Halonen (2000–2012) had disagreements with the cabinet over the proper role of the president at these EU summits. In 2012 an amendment was made to the constitution according to which the prime minister represents Finland in the European Council. The prime minister is now the unquestioned executive leader, although the president retains a role in foreign affairs outside the European Union.

When the new constitution was drafted political elites were much more eager to reduce presidential powers than ordinary citizens. In fact, after the new constitution had entered into force, a majority of the adult population thought that the reduction of the prerogatives of the president had gone too far. They thought that the president should have more powers than provided by the new constitution. A majority of Finns wish to see a strong leadership in political life. As a result of the Ukrainian crisis and the growing tensions between Russia and the Western nations, an even larger share of Finns call for a resolute political leadership. The position of Finland as a neighbour of Russia has once again given rise to discussions about the proper balance in Finnish foreign policy: to what extent Finland should participate in foreign affairs through multilateral arenas, particularly the European Union, and to what extent it should have bilateral relations with neighbouring Russia.

Foreign policy is typically not a top issue in Finnish parliamentary elections. However, in the 2015 parliamentary election campaign foreign policy questions were more prominent than ever since 1962 (that had been an election marked by a crisis in Finnish-Soviet relations). This kind of discussion creates leeway for the president to take a more active leadership role in foreign affairs. According to the constitution, the president leads foreign policy in co-operation with the cabinet. Disagreements are more probable when president and prime minister have different partisan backgrounds. During the tenure of President Tarja Halonen (2000–2012), who had a Social Democratic background, there were tensions between her and the cabinets led by prime ministers representing the Centre Party and the Conservatives. The present incumbent Sauli Niinistö (2012–) has cohabitated with two cabinets led by his former (conservative) party plus the present Sipilä cabinet where the Conservatives are one of three roughly equal partners; similar disagreements have not occurred.

Parties – weaker and stronger

In the period covered by this volume, parties as organizations have expanded, peaked and declined. From the 1960s to the 1980s political parties, also liberal and conservative parties, increasingly adopted organizational models and working styles typical of mass parties. Figures on party membership displayed a marked increase, and the role of extra-parliamentary party grew at the expense of the parliamentary party. The staffs of extra-parliamentary parties increased and party bureaucracies prepared extensive policy programs for different sectors. This development coincided with the expansion of the Scandinavian-style welfare state.

From the 1980s onwards, the role of extra-parliamentary party organizations has declined. Membership figures have plummeted.

In 1980 there were about 600 000 members in Finnish political parties. In 2013 the total number of party members had declined to 300 000. Both the resources and power of parties in parliament increased compared to the extra-parliamentary party organizations. This development coincided with the constitutional changes that increased the powers of both parliament and cabinet at the expense of the president. The overall importance of parliamentary party groups increased in Finnish politics.

A marked change in the role of the media in the political process has taken place since the 1980s. Party newspapers and public broadcasting have lost their previously predominant position. Politicians increasingly meet their public through the media while the traditional role of extra-parliamentary parties in this intermediation has declined. In fact, media have become an important arena of policy-making. Policy proposals are to a large extent both presented and discussed in the media, and media have an important effect on the agenda of public political debate. As to the official agenda of political decision-making, the effect of the media remains more limited and indirect.

As a result of the increased coalition elasticity of political parties, a new kind of cabinet coalition became also possible. From the early years of Finnish independence to the 1980s, cabinet coalitions in Finland were closed coalitions on the left-right dimension. Parties in office were adjacent to each other on the left-right scale. Opposition parties were either to the left, to the right or both to the left and to the right of the governing coalition (some small parties in between the coalition parties could remain in opposition). When the cleavage between left-wing parties and right-wing parties lost importance, even coalitions that were open on the left-right dimension became possible. In 1987 Finland had her first coalition government (the Holkeri cabinet) based on co-operation between the Conservatives and the Social Democrats, while the Centre Party remained in opposition. This was the first majority cabinet in Finland without the participation of the Centre Party. After that four cabinets (Lipponen I and II, Katainen, and Stubb) have been open coalitions on the left-right scale. The flexible ideological postures of Finnish parties not only constitute a contrast to an earlier practice; they are also peculiar in an international comparison.

Politics and markets

The previously regulated capital markets in Finland were opened to
international competition in the 1980s. In 1999 Finland joined the
third phase of the Economic and Monetary Union (EMU). These
decisions dramatically changed the context of national economic
policy-making. Finland was one of the European nations where
devaluations of the national currency had been used frequently to
improve the international competitiveness of the export sector.
Deficits in the balance of payments had been warning bells for
politicians both in the parliamentary and corporatist arena to make
decisions that secure the international competitiveness of the economy. In the EMU regime national instruments of economic policy
making are limited compared to the years of national currency.

In the 1970s and 1980s cabinets often made it easier for the
labour market organizations to make collective wage agreements
by promising either cuts in some taxes or increases in certain
expenditures. In the present situation these kinds of carrots are
hardly available any more. In an open economy the power of economic interest groups, especially the power of labour federations,
declined compared to the earlier phase of more regulated markets.
On the other hand, the power of large enterprises may have risen.
In an open economy capital owners may make an 'investment
strike' and invest in other countries, if economic policy and the
economic situation are unfavourable to them.

Parallel with the internationalization of the economy, increasingly market-oriented practices at home have had the effect of
diminishing the role of the government and thus in fact limited
the sphere of political decision-making. While outright privatization is rarer than commonly assumed, public service is increasingly
produced outside the public sector itself. Government enterprise
increasingly functions similar to private enterprise, and government as shareholder has pursued a strictly market-oriented policy.
Citizens are often bewildered by political passiveness in contexts
where the government seemingly has superior clout thanks to its
role as the main shareholder.

The welfare state includes several projects that gradually increase
public expenditure without any new decisions. Since the 1990s
discussion on the Finnish welfare state has mainly focused on the
need to restrict the continuous rise of public expenditure. Public

expenditures have risen faster than taxes and other public revenues, and as a result public debt has increased. Still in the 1980s, Finnish public debt was low, only about 15 per cent of GDP. In the 1990s public debt rose to 60 per cent, and after a temporary reduction in the late 1990s and first years of the 21st century, it has again risen during the economic crisis that began in Europe in 2008.

The debate on the need to restrict the rise of public expenditure, to cut public expenditure and cope with the public debt, has brought to the fore the ideological gap between left-wing and right-wing parties. Left-wing parties are less eager to cut public expenditures, and to reorganize the public sector in order to reduce public debt. The prominence of the increased left-right cleavage may come to influence coalition formation between political parties. On the left-right dimension the Centre Party is in the median position. When cabinets are closed coalitions on the left-right dimension, no majority coalition can be built without the presence of the Centre Party. In the 1980s one of the motives of both Conservatives and Social Democrats in governing together had to do with sheer power. With their joint coalition, these parties could undermine the power that the Centre Party had acquired thanks to its median position. What makes predictions difficult in the mid-2010s is the fact that, largely due to the economic turmoil since 2008, a fourth major actor has entered the party-political scene in the form of the populist Finns Party. While it is imaginable that the ideologically 'connected' coalition model of the pre-1980s may reappear, the presence of vital populist party has the potential of markedly disturbing time-honoured political routines.

The bewildered citizen

In a comparative perspective, Finnish citizens display a high degree of trust in the central institutions of government a good level of knowledge about politics. Surprisingly enough, their subjective citizen competence is comparatively low; more than citizens in neighbouring West European countries, Finns frequently find politics difficult to understand. Directly and indirectly, the chapters of this book provide background for this rather unexpected fact. The extent and rapidity of change in the determinants, constitutional rules and practices of Finnish politics make it difficult for citizens to assess the division – formal as well as actual – of political power in the country. The decades of flexible, sometimes ideologically highly unorthodox surplus cabinet coalitions make the assignment of political responsibility difficult indeed. Add to this the effects of internationalization and marketization on the sphere of politics itself, and it is not difficult to comprehend the bewilderment of Finnish citizens. True, since the 1970s Finland has become dramatically more prosperous, open and tolerant than it used to be. At the same time, the forces that determine social and political power have become much more numerous, multi-layered and elusive than a generation or two ago.

Conclusion

'The powers of the State in Finland are vested in the people who are represented by the Parliament'. Thus reads one of the solemn opening paragraphs of the Finnish constitution. Like similar declarations in numerous constitutions around the world, these words are intended as a principal ideal rather than a description of reality. Still, they form a natural benchmark for a few final thoughts on the evolution of political power since about 1970.

Evidently, the idea of parliament as the supreme representative of a sovereign people has been reinforced markedly by the institutional and political changes that have taken place. The altered balance between the parliamentary and presidential spheres codified in the 2000 constitution has brought parliamentary elections and parliamentary responsibility to the fore in Finnish politics. Elections matter more than four decades ago, and electoral success is expected to manifest itself in the form of government participation. The entry into cabinet of the populist Finns Party in 2015 is a case in point.

The strengthened chain of parliamentary and electoral accountability is reinforced by the prolonged stability of Finnish parliamentarism. Cabinets have considerably better conditions to live up to electoral promises than in the 1970s. They work out ambitious political programs that are surveyed critically by the media and the public at large. Arguably, the very stability of Finnish politics is one of the keys to the social and economic development that has lifted Finland among the most prosperous nations of the world.

More than in most comparable nations, Finnish politics has always reflected the international position of the country. Much of the conflictual nature and instability of Finnish politics in earlier periods reflected, directly or indirectly, the influence of the Soviet Union. The fading of the Soviet shadow over Finland was in itself a major factor in bringing the reality of Finnish politics closer to the constitution's solemn ideal of popular sovereignty. It was, however, also a precondition for many of the institutional changes that have reinforced the parliamentary chain of accountability in Finland.

Today, many critics of the European Union argue that Finland has replaced its subservience towards the communist superpower by an equally uncritical attitude vis-à-vis Brussels. If taken literally, this view is fundamentally flawed: Finnish EU membership is the result of a solid majority of the Finns voting in favour of it, while 'Finlandization' was imposed on the country by an alien power. But it is of course quite true that the European Union is the most important external determinant of political power relations in Finland. The economic policies of the EU largely determine the playing field in which Finnish enterprises must be successful if the Finnish economy is to grow. How well Finland manages to adjust to these conditions is an issue on which a majority of Finns and their political and organizational representatives must find sufficiently common ground. Ultimately, the fundamental conditions of political power in Finland will also reflect the success and evolution of the European Union as a whole. To what extent and how the EU manages to overcome its present economic and political predicaments is perhaps *the* major key to the evolution of political power in Finland.

Contributors

GUY-ERIK ISAKSSON is professor of political science at Åbo
Akademi University
guy-erik.isaksson@abo.fi

LAURI KARVONEN is professor emeritus of political science at
Åbo Akademi University
lauri.karvonen@abo.fi

VESA KOSKIMAA is doctoral student in political science at the
University of Tampere
vesa.koskimaa@uta.fi

MAIJA MATTILA is doctoral student in political science at the
University of Tampere
maija.mattila@uta.fi

EERO MURTO is budget councillor at the Ministry of Labour and
Industry and docent of political science at the universities of
Helsinki and Turku
eero.murto@tem.fi

MARI K. NIEMI is senior researcher at the University of Turku
and visiting scholar at the University of Strathclyde
mari.k.niemi@utu.fi

HEIKKI PALOHEIMO is professor emeritus of political science at the University of Tampere and leader of the research project Political Power in Finland: An Analysis of Central Government Institutions and Actors
heikki.paloheimo@uta.fi

TAPIO RAUNIO is professor of political science at the University of Tampere
tapio.raunio@uta.fi

ILKKA RUOSTETSAARI is professor of political science at the University of Tampere
ilkka.ruostetsaari@uta.fi

ÅSA VON SCHOULTZ (née Bengtsson) is associate professor (docent) of political science at Åbo Akademi University and professor of political science at the Mid Sweden University
asa.vonschoultz@miun.se